快感

Sensual
Phrase™

Sensual Phrase

Vol. 1
Shôjo Edition

Story & Art by
Mayu Shinjo

English Adaptation/Kelly Sue DeConnick
Translation/Joe Yamazaki
Touch-up & Lettering/Rina Mapa
Cover & Graphic Design/Izumi Evers
Editor/Eric Searleman

Managing Editor/Annette Roman
Director of Production/Noboru Watanabe
Vice President of Publishing/Alvin Lu
Sr. Director of Acquisitions/Rika Inouye
VP of Sales & Marketing/Liza Coppola
Publisher/Hyoe Narita

Printed in Canada

Published by VIZ Media, LLC
P.O. Box 77064
San Francisco, CA 94107

Shôjo Edition
10 9 8 7 6 5 4 3
First printing, March 2004
Second printing, October 2004
Third printing, March 2006

www.viz.com
store.viz.com

PARENTAL ADVISORY
SENSUAL PHRASE is rated M and is recommended for mature readers. This volume contains strong language and sexual themes.

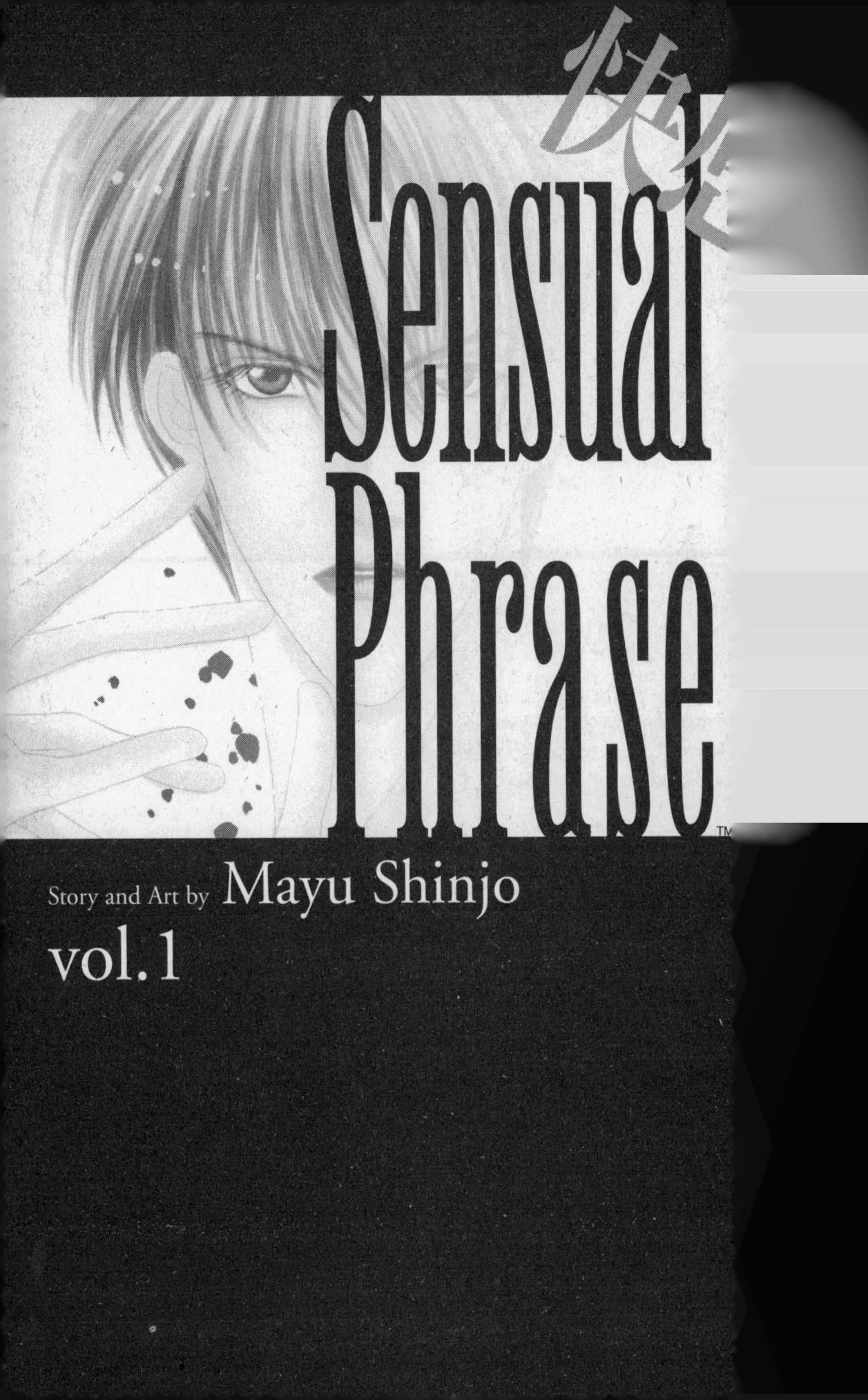

Sensual Phrase™

Story and Art by Mayu Shinjo

vol. 1

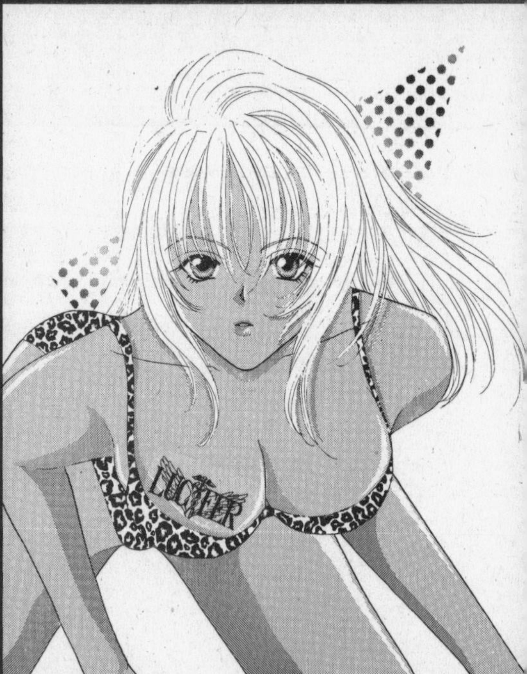
LUCIFER

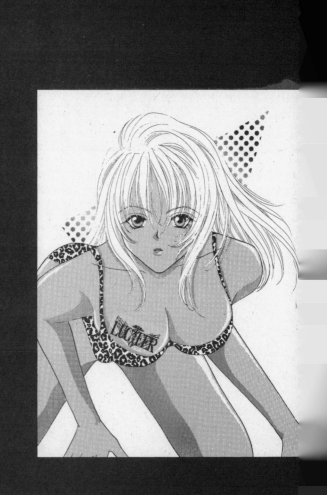

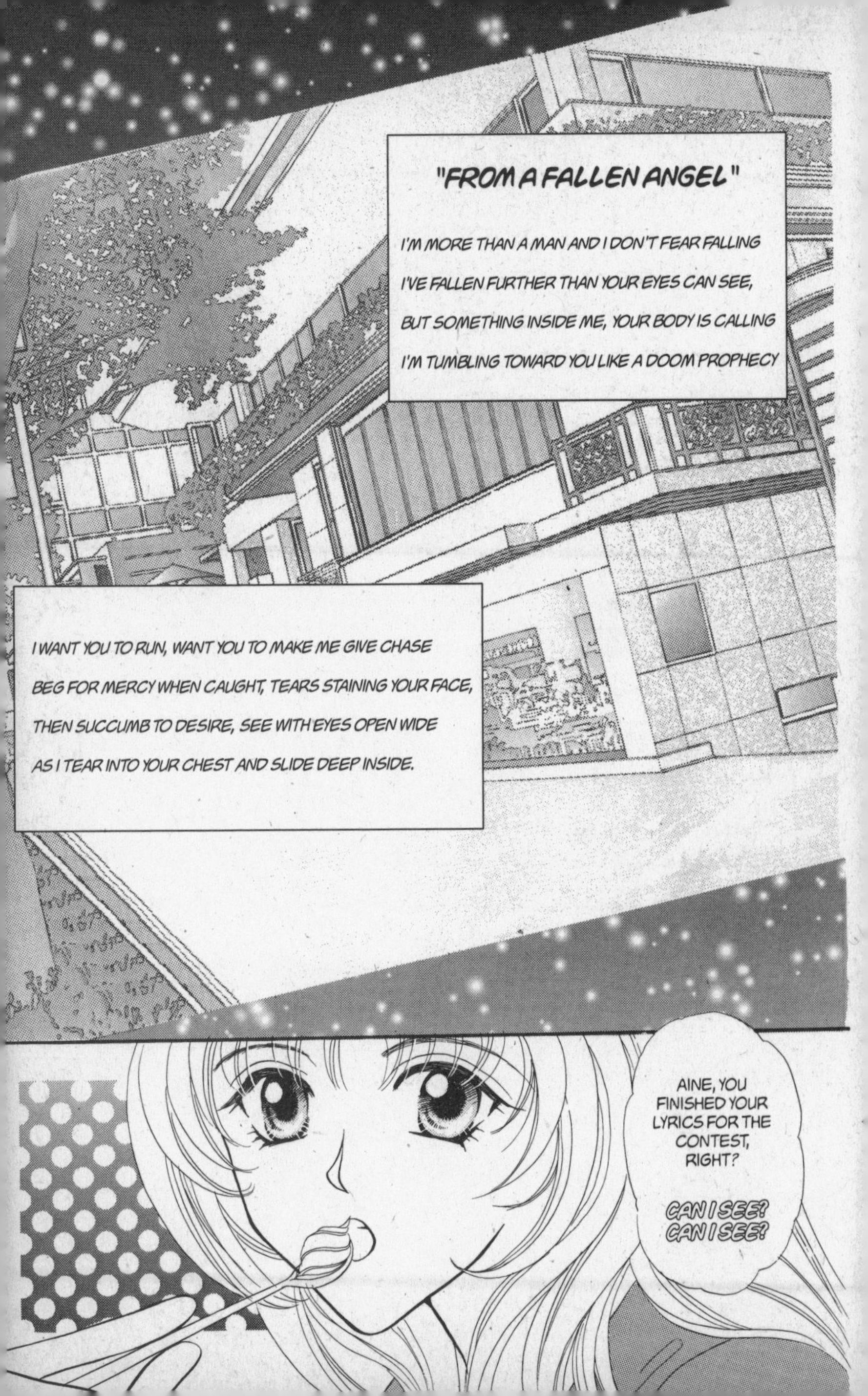
"FROM A FALLEN ANGEL"
I'M MORE THAN A MAN AND I DON'T FEAR FALLING
I'VE FALLEN FURTHER THAN YOUR EYES CAN SEE,
BUT SOMETHING INSIDE ME, YOUR BODY IS CALLING
I'M TUMBLING TOWARD YOU LIKE A DOOM PROPHECY
I WANT YOU TO RUN, WANT YOU TO MAKE ME GIVE CHASE
BEG FOR MERCY WHEN CAUGHT, TEARS STAINING YOUR FACE,
THEN SUCCUMB TO DESIRE, SEE WITH EYES OPEN WIDE
AS I TEAR INTO YOUR CHEST AND SLIDE DEEP INSIDE.
AINE, YOU FINISHED YOUR LYRICS FOR THE CONTEST, RIGHT?
CAN I SEE? CAN I SEE?

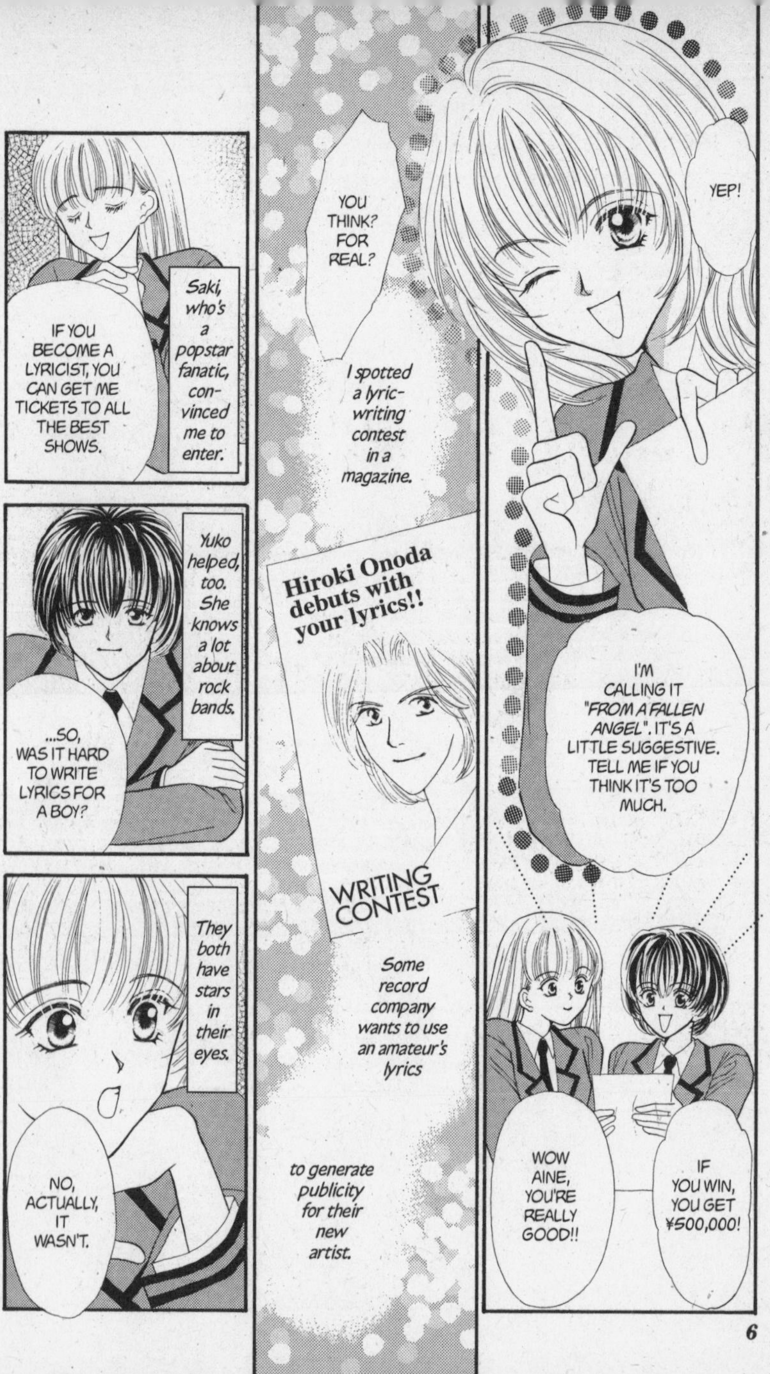
YEP!
I'M CALLING IT "FROM A FALLEN ANGEL". IT'S A LITTLE SUGGESTIVE. TELL ME IF YOU THINK IT'S TOO MUCH.
IF YOU WIN, YOU GET ¥500,000!
WOW AINE, YOU'RE REALLY GOOD!!
YOU THINK? FOR REAL?
I spotted a lyric-writing contest in a magazine.
Hiroki Onoda debuts with your lyrics!!
WRITING CONTEST
Some record company wants to use an amateur's lyrics
to generate publicity for their new artist.
Saki, who's a popstar fanatic, con-vinced me to enter.
IF YOU BECOME A LYRICIST, YOU CAN GET ME TICKETS TO ALL THE BEST SHOWS.
Yuko helped, too. She knows a lot about rock bands.
...SO, WAS IT HARD TO WRITE LYRICS FOR A BOY?
They both have stars in their eyes.
NO, ACTUALLY, IT WASN'T.

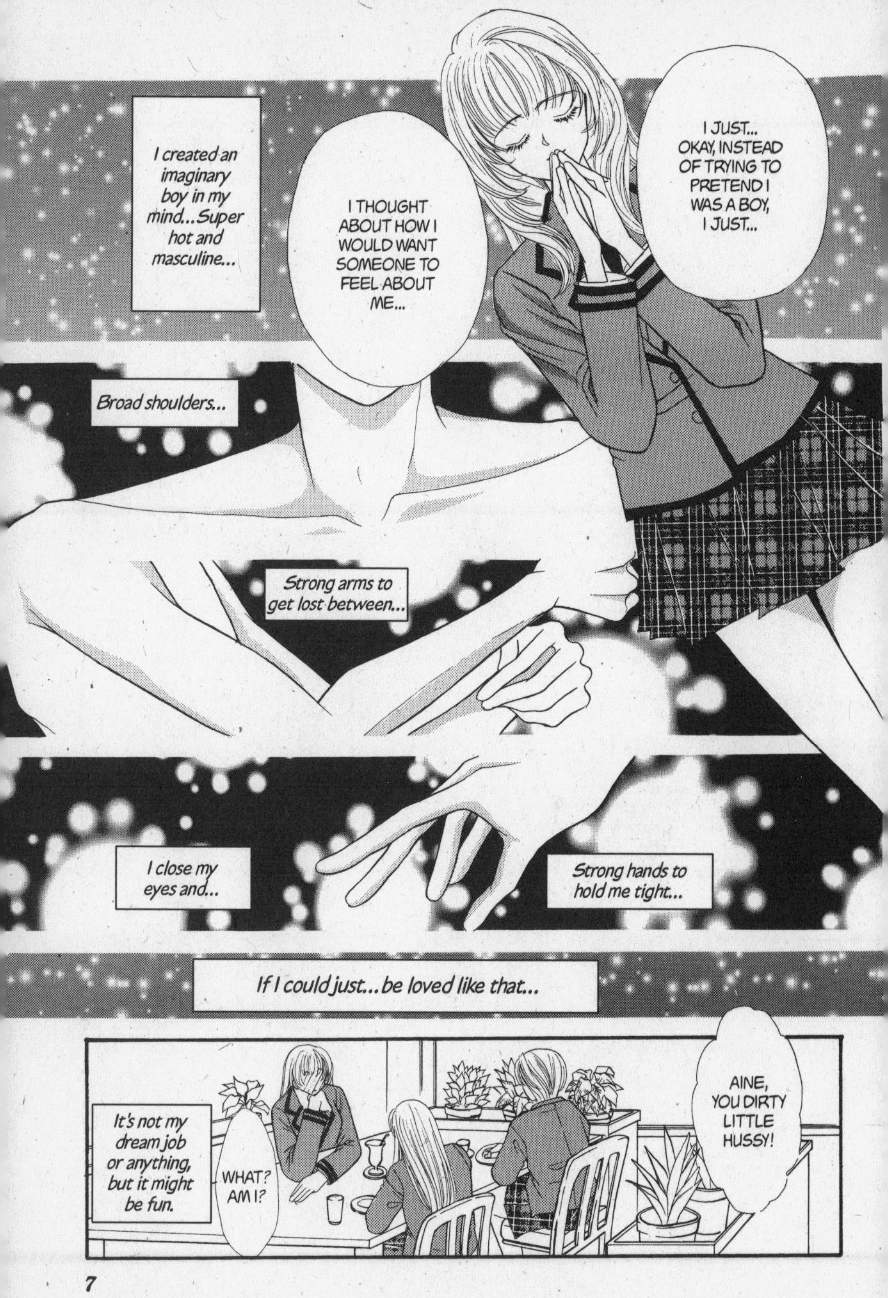
I JUST... OKAY, INSTEAD OF TRYING TO PRETEND I WAS A BOY, I JUST...
I THOUGHT ABOUT HOW I WOULD WANT SOMEONE TO FEEL ABOUT ME...
I created an imaginary boy in my mind...Super hot and masculine...
Broad shoulders...
Strong arms to get lost between...
Strong hands to hold me tight...
I close my eyes and...
If I could just...be loved like that...
AINE, YOU DIRTY LITTLE HUSSY!
WHAT? AM I?
It's not my dream job or anything, but it might be fun.

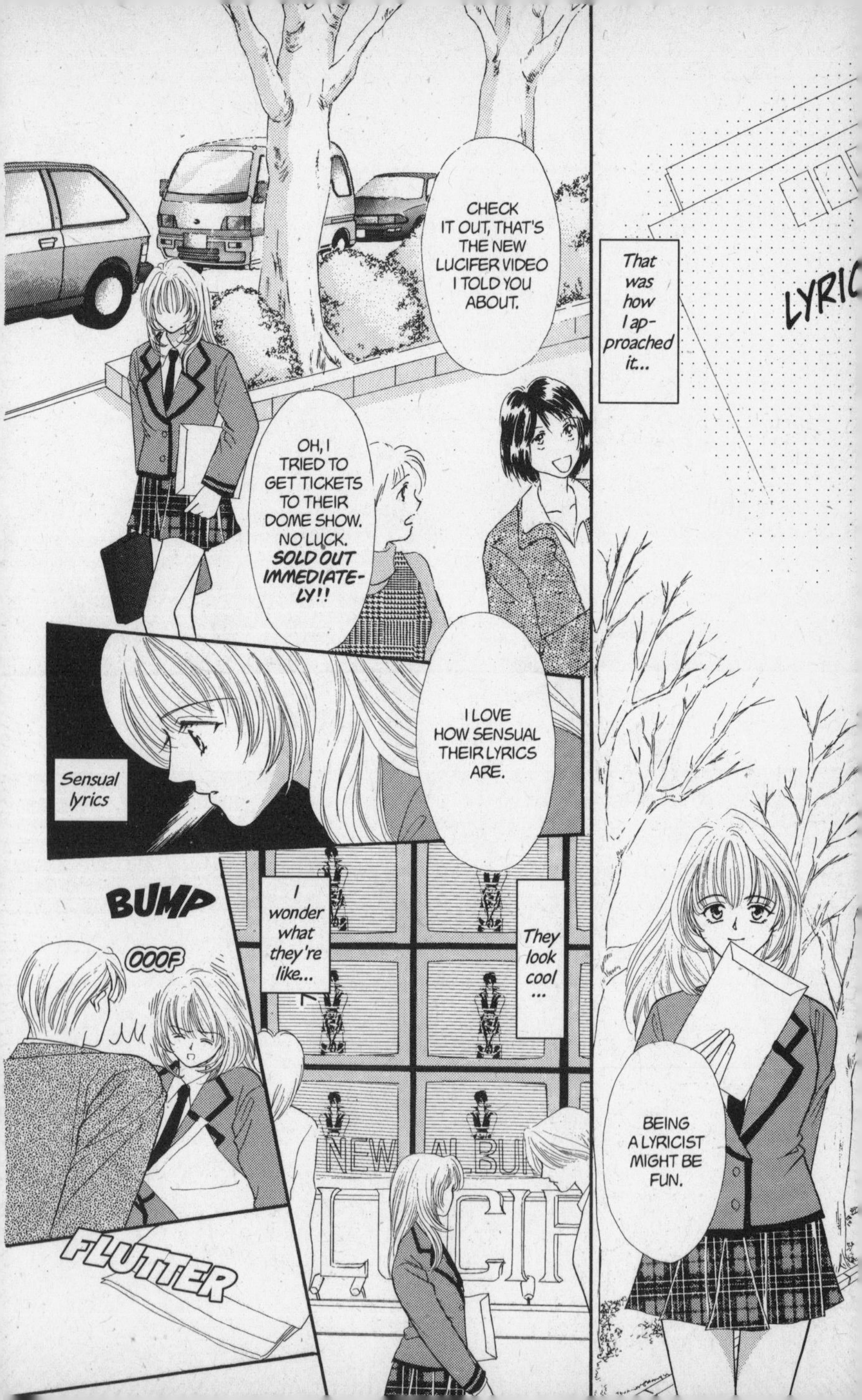
That was how I approached it...
LYRIC
BEING A LYRICIST MIGHT BE FUN.
CHECK IT OUT, THAT'S THE NEW LUCIFER VIDEO I TOLD YOU ABOUT.
OH, I TRIED TO GET TICKETS TO THEIR DOME SHOW. NO LUCK. **SOLD OUT IMMEDIATELY!!**
I LOVE HOW SENSUAL THEIR LYRICS ARE.
Sensual lyrics
They look cool...
I wonder what they're like...
BUMP
OOOF
FLUTTER

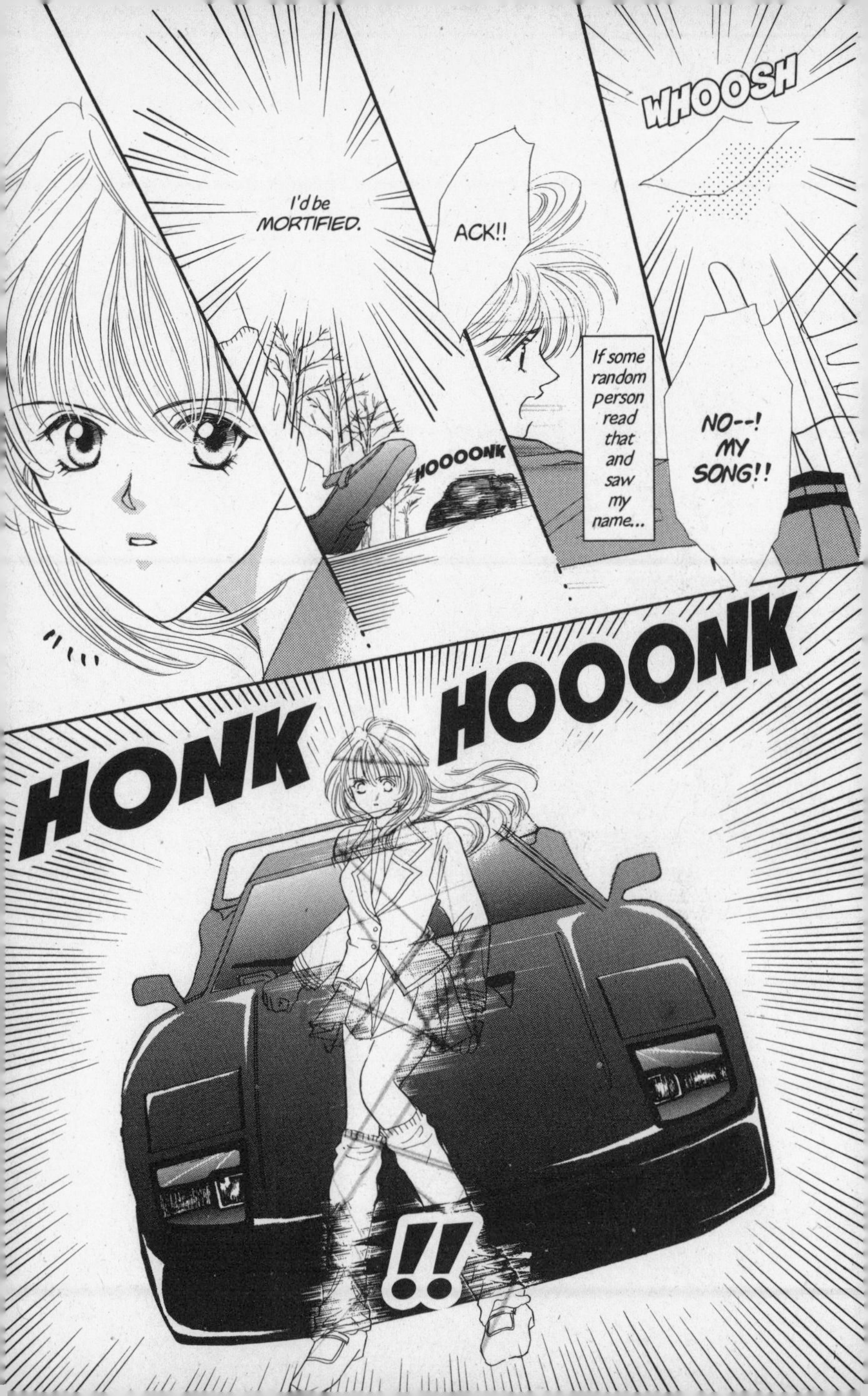
WHOOSH
NO--! MY SONG!!
If some random person read that and saw my name...
ACK!!
I'd be MORTIFIED.
HOOOONK
HOOOONK
HONK
!!

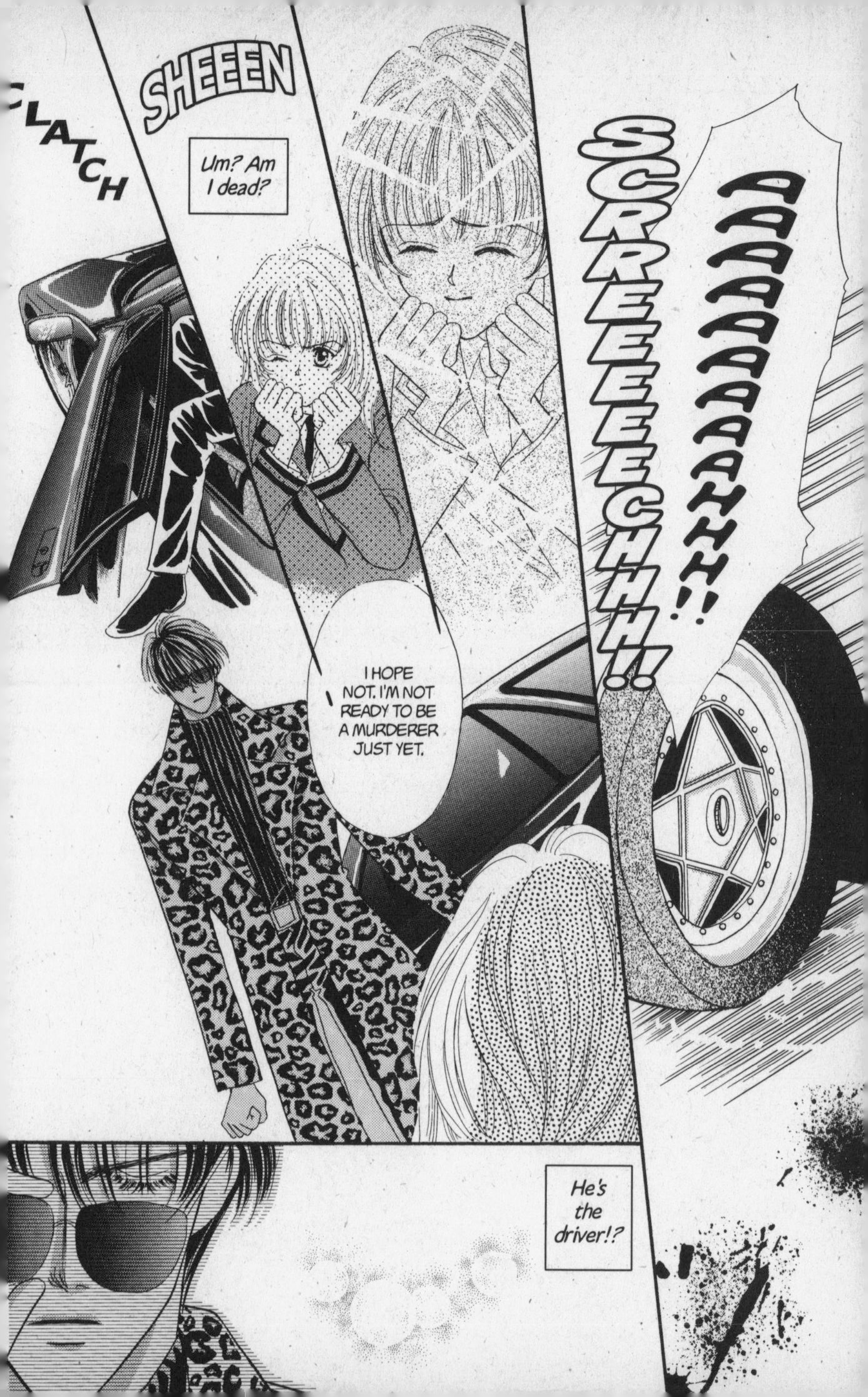
AAAAAAAAAAHH!!
SCREEEEECHHH!!
SHEEEN
Um? Am I dead?
CLATCH
I HOPE NOT. I'M NOT READY TO BE A MURDERER JUST YET.
He's the driver!?

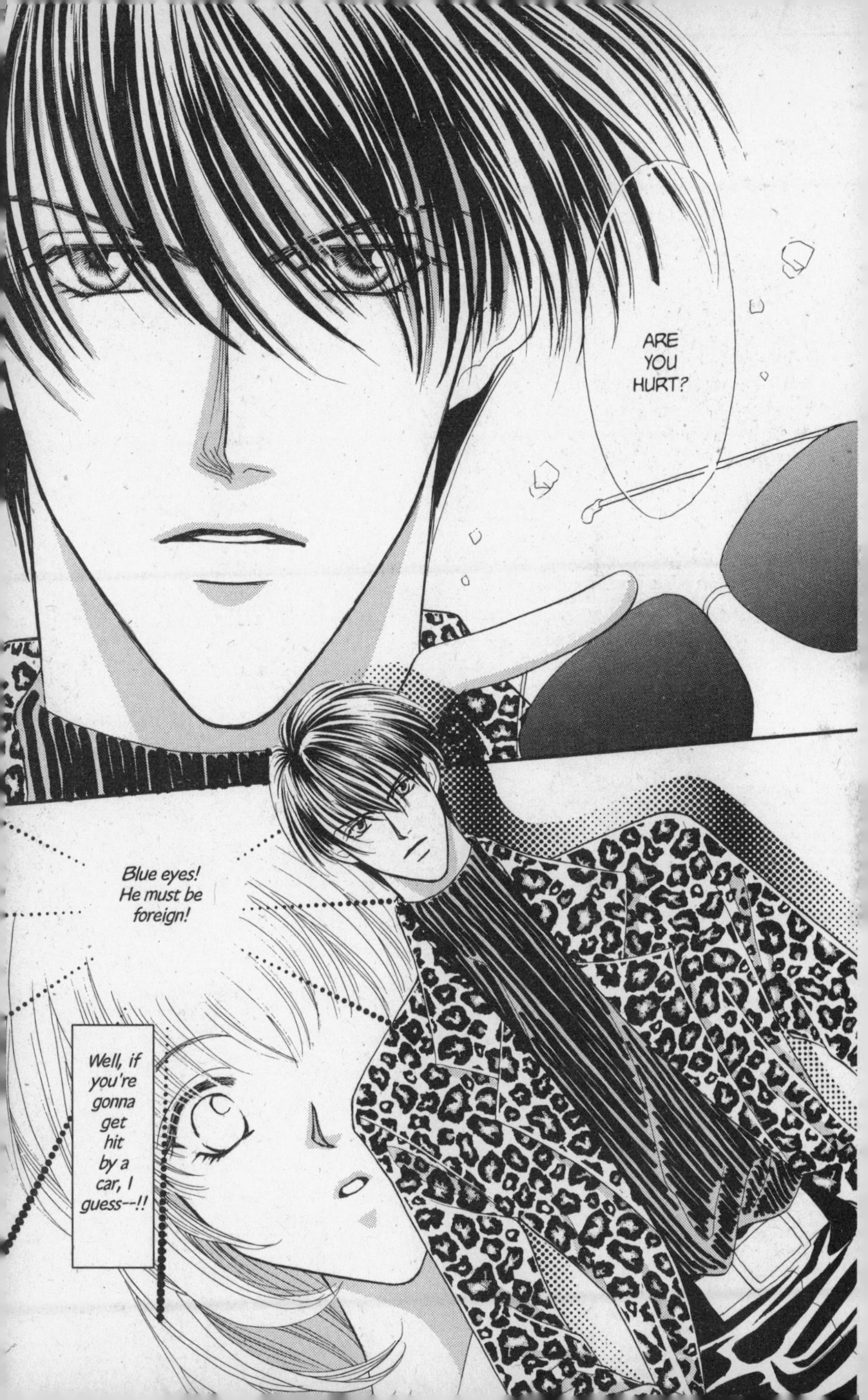
ARE YOU HURT?
Blue eyes! He must be foreign!
Well, if you're gonna get hit by a car, I guess--!!

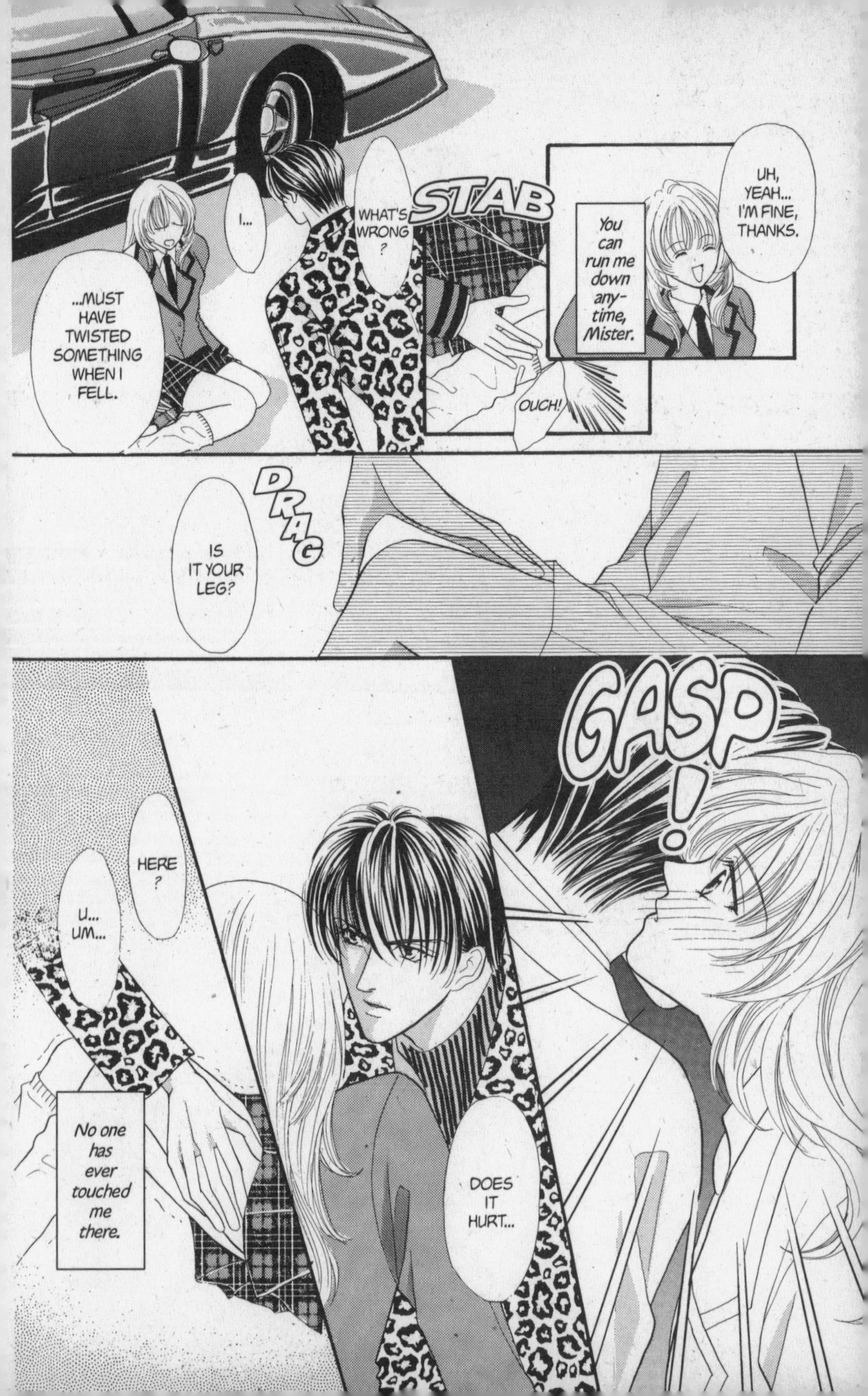
UH, YEAH... I'M FINE, THANKS.
You can run me down any-time, Mister.
STAB
OUCH!
WHAT'S WRONG?
I...
...MUST HAVE TWISTED SOMETHING WHEN I FELL.
DRAG
IS IT YOUR LEG?
GASP!
DOES IT HURT...
HERE?
U... UM...
No one has ever touched me there.

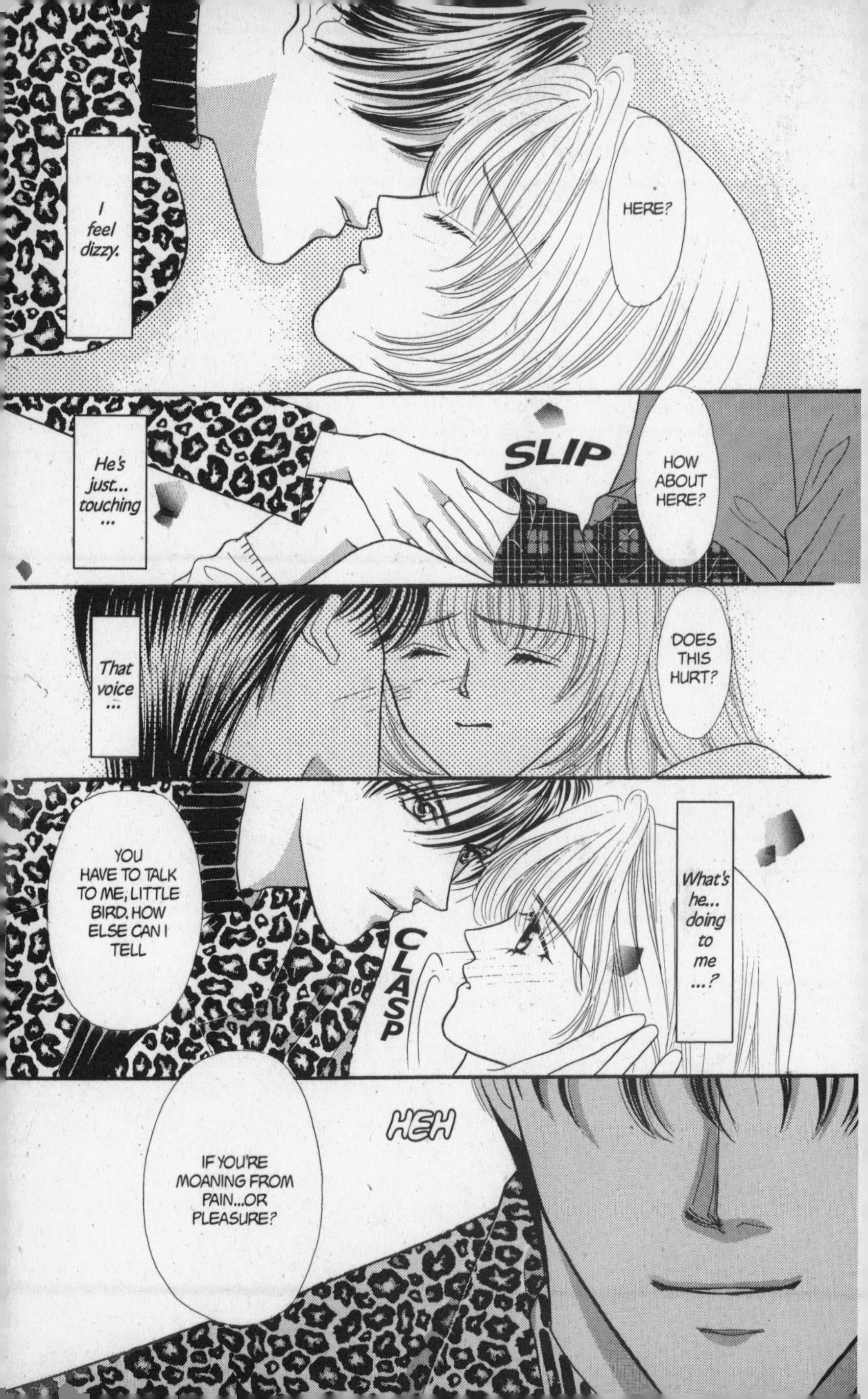
HERE?
I feel dizzy.
HOW ABOUT HERE?
SLIP
He's just... touching ...
DOES THIS HURT?
That voice ...
What's he... doing to me ...?
CLASP
YOU HAVE TO TALK TO ME, LITTLE BIRD. HOW ELSE CAN I TELL
HEH
IF YOU'RE MOANING FROM PAIN...OR PLEASURE?

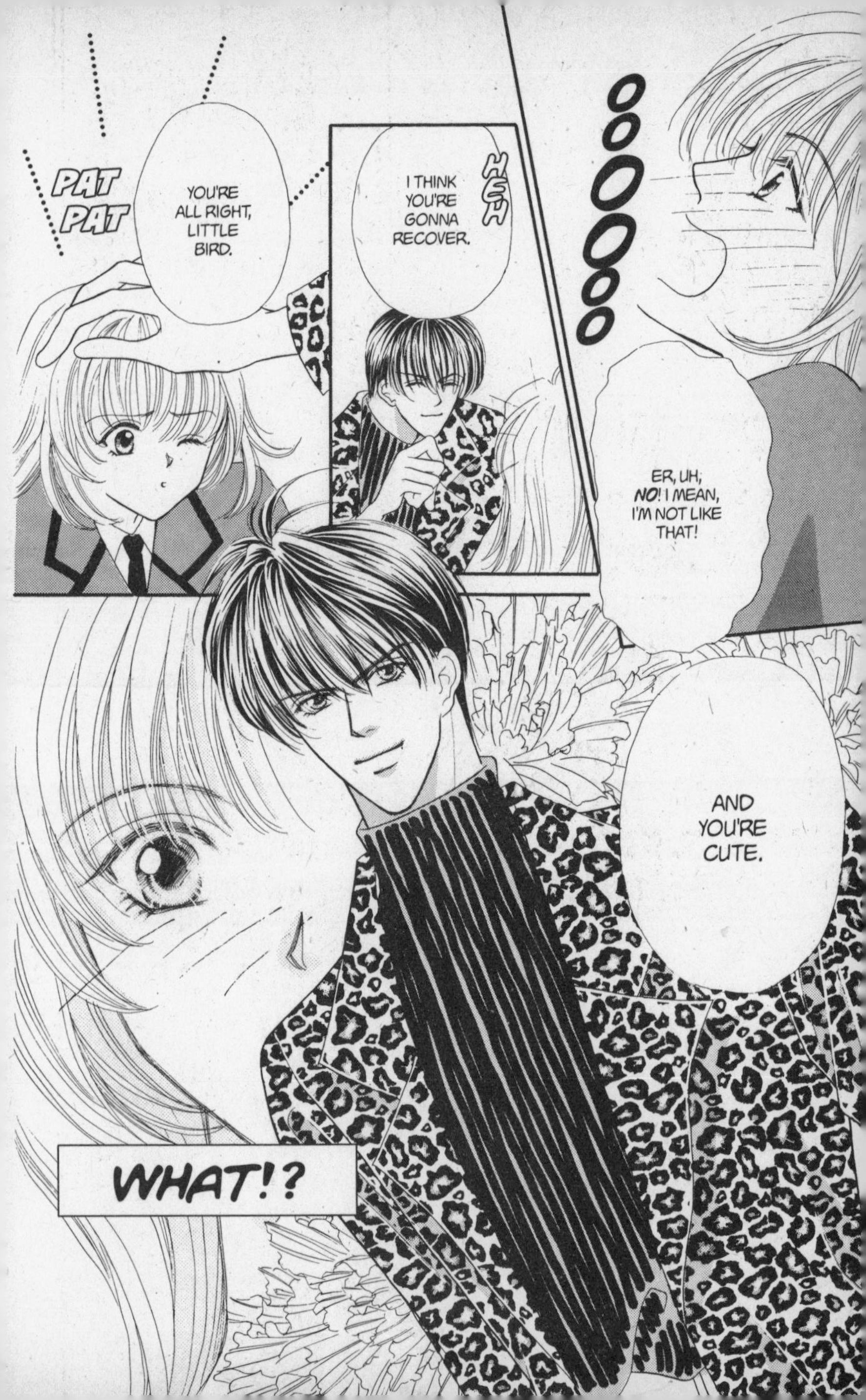
OOOOOOOO
ER, UH, NO! I MEAN, I'M NOT LIKE THAT!
HEH
I THINK YOU'RE GONNA RECOVER.
PAT PAT
YOU'RE ALL RIGHT, LITTLE BIRD.
AND YOU'RE CUTE.
WHAT!?

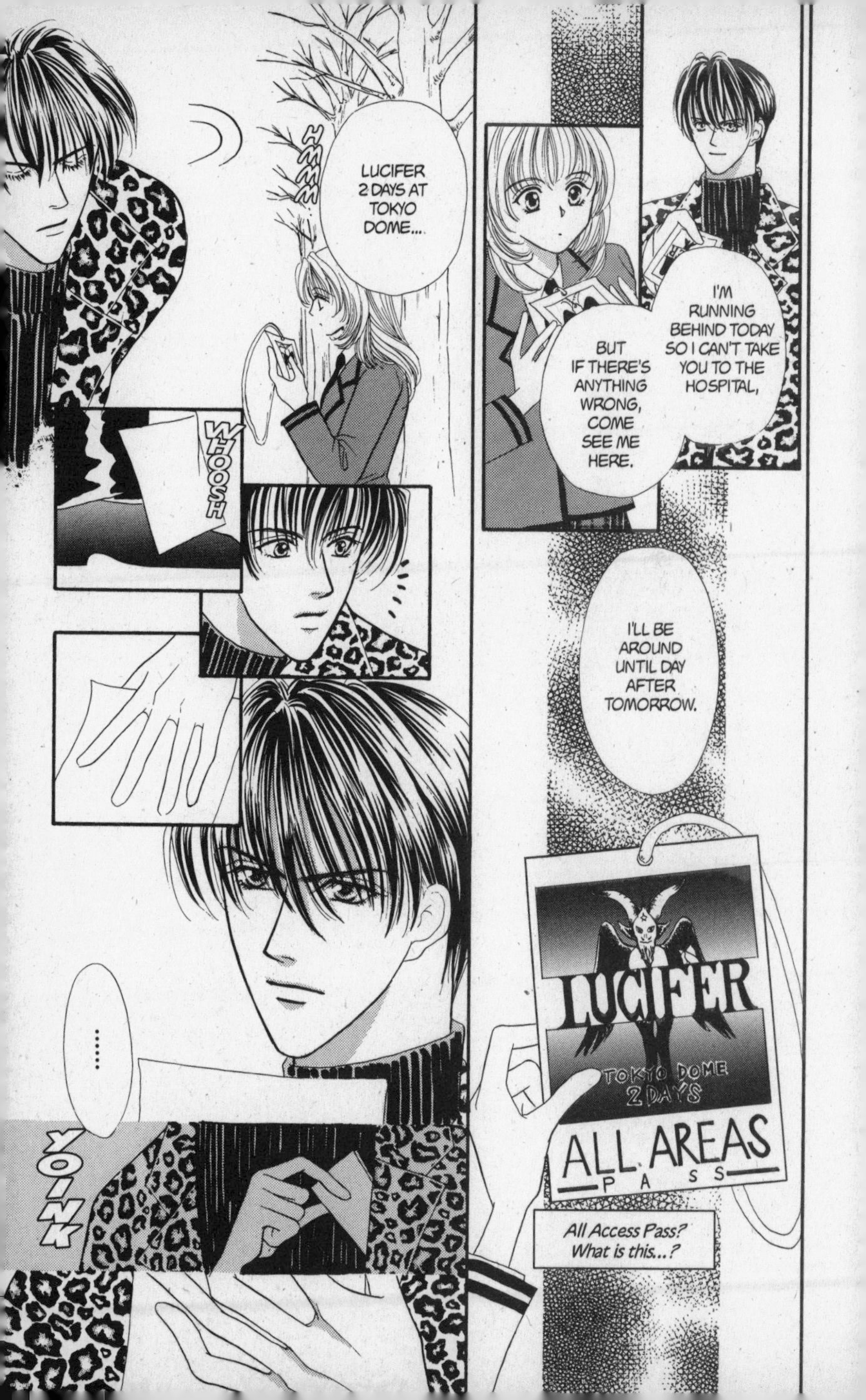
I'M RUNNING BEHIND TODAY SO I CAN'T TAKE YOU TO THE HOSPITAL,
BUT IF THERE'S ANYTHING WRONG, COME SEE ME HERE.
I'LL BE AROUND UNTIL DAY AFTER TOMORROW.
LUCIFER
TOKYO DOME 2 DAYS
ALL AREAS PASS
All Access Pass? What is this...?
HMMM
LUCIFER 2 DAYS AT TOKYO DOME...
WHOOSH
YOINK
......

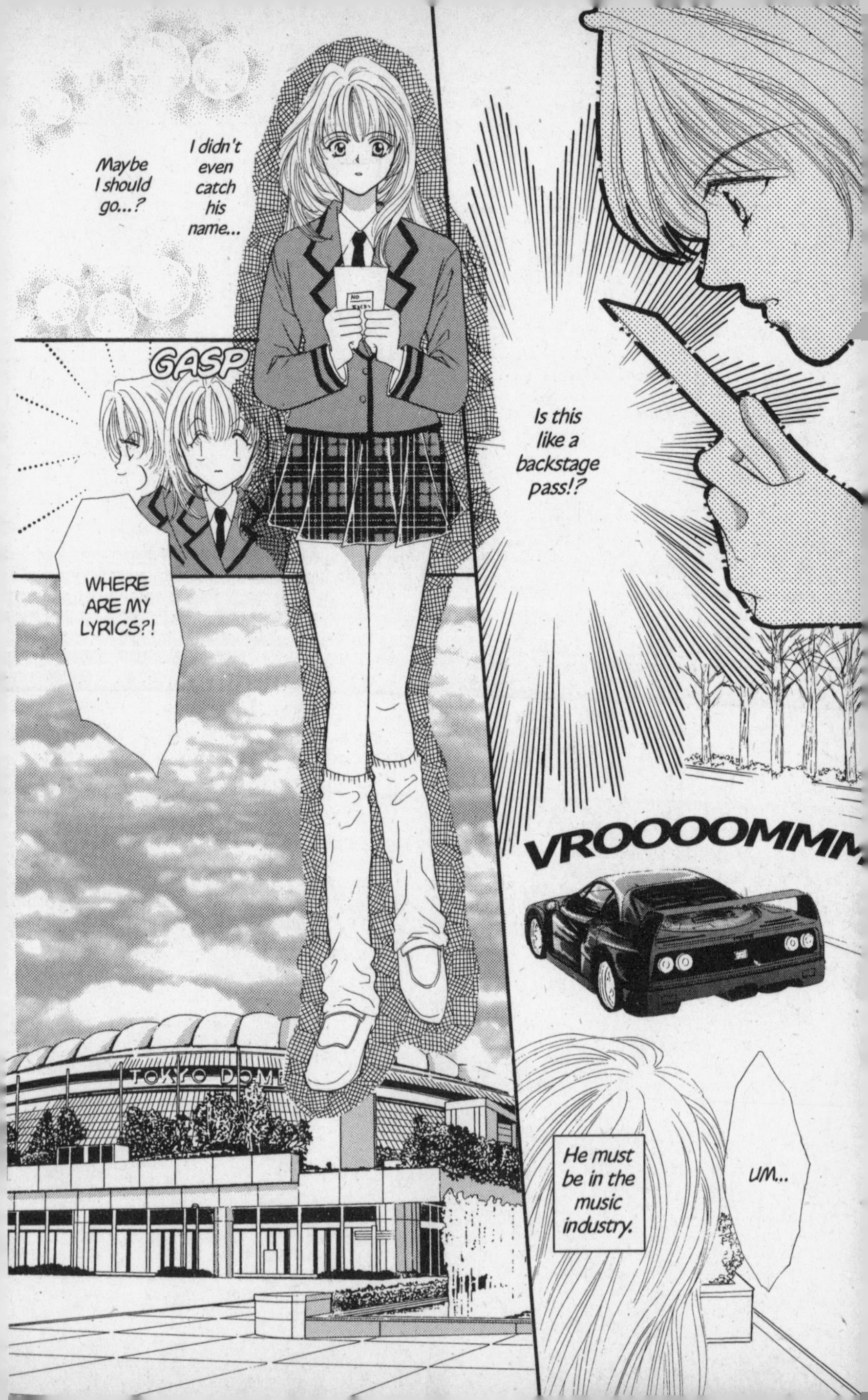
Is this like a backstage pass!?
VROOOOMMM
UM...
He must be in the music industry.
I didn't even catch his name...
Maybe I should go...?
GASP
WHERE ARE MY LYRICS?!
TOKYO DOME

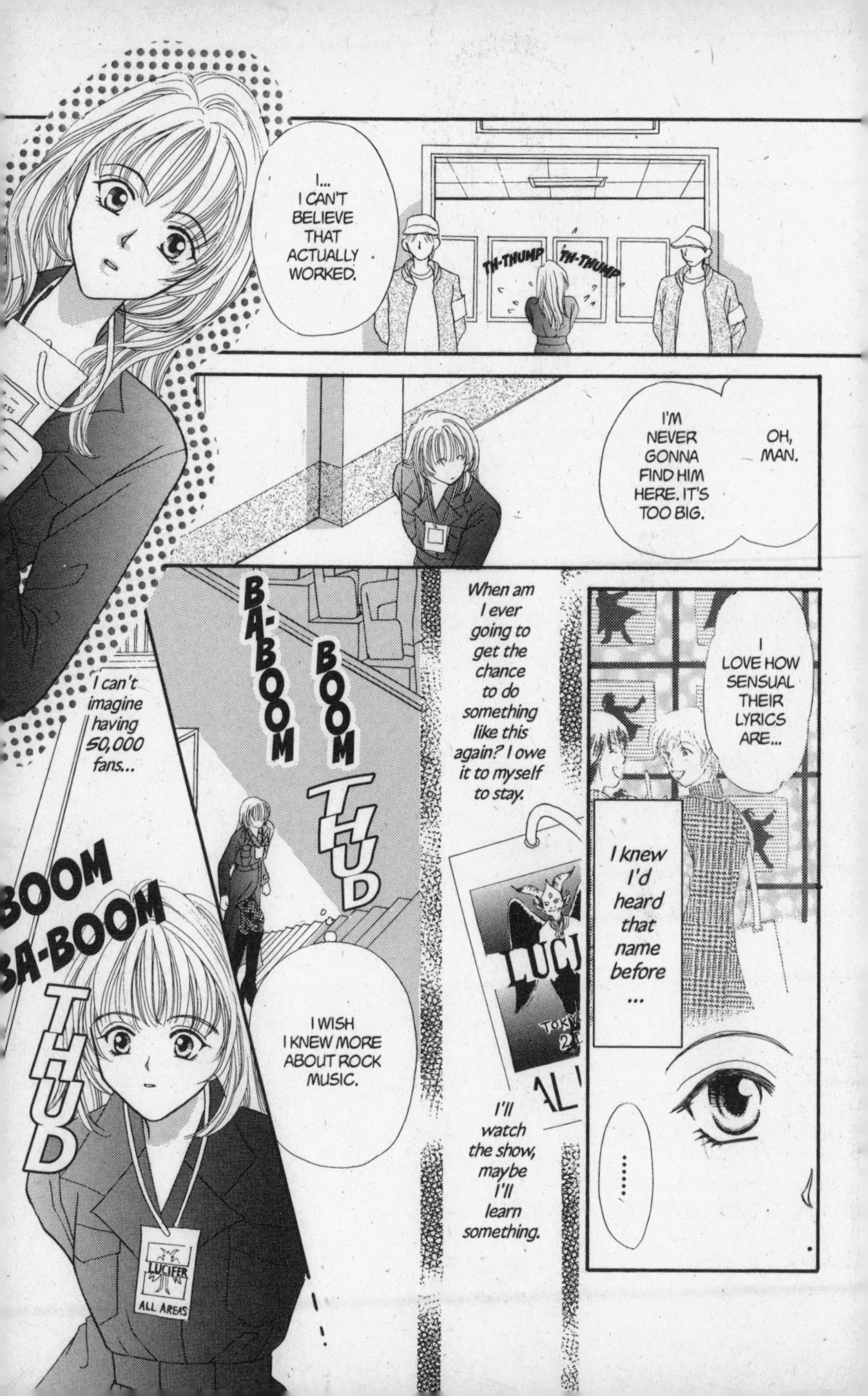
I... I CAN'T BELIEVE THAT ACTUALLY WORKED.
TH-THUMP
TH-THUMP
OH, MAN.
I'M NEVER GONNA FIND HIM HERE. IT'S TOO BIG.
I LOVE HOW SENSUAL THEIR LYRICS ARE...
I knew I'd heard that name before ...
......
When am I ever going to get the chance to do something like this again? I owe it to myself to stay.
I'll watch the show, maybe I'll learn something.
BA-BOOM
BOOM
THUD
I can't imagine having 50,000 fans...
BOOM
BA-BOOM
THUD
I WISH I KNEW MORE ABOUT ROCK MUSIC.
LUCIFER
ALL AREAS

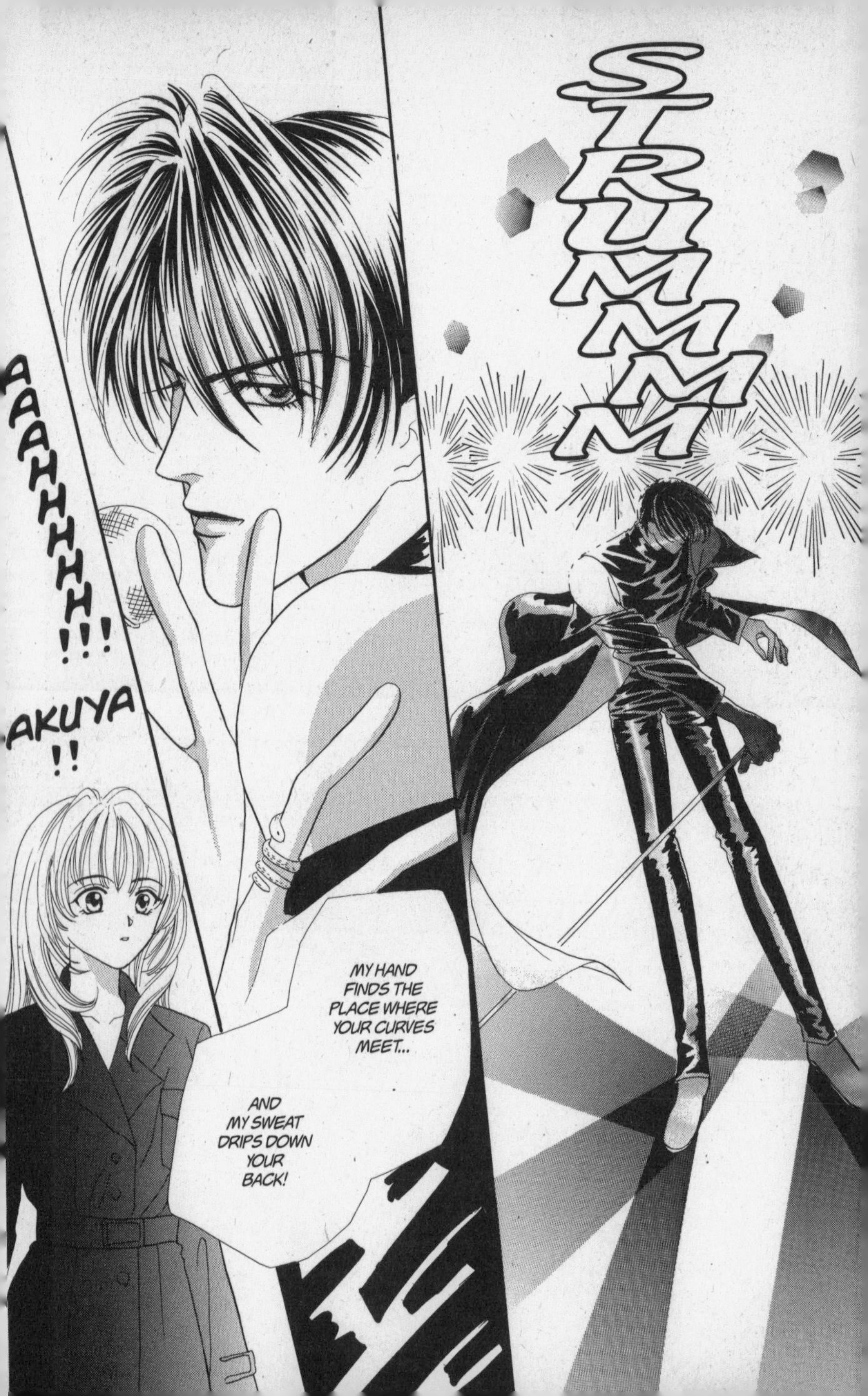
STRUMMM
MY HAND FINDS THE PLACE WHERE YOUR CURVES MEET...
AND MY SWEAT DRIPS DOWN YOUR BACK!
AAAHHHHH!!!
AKUYA!!

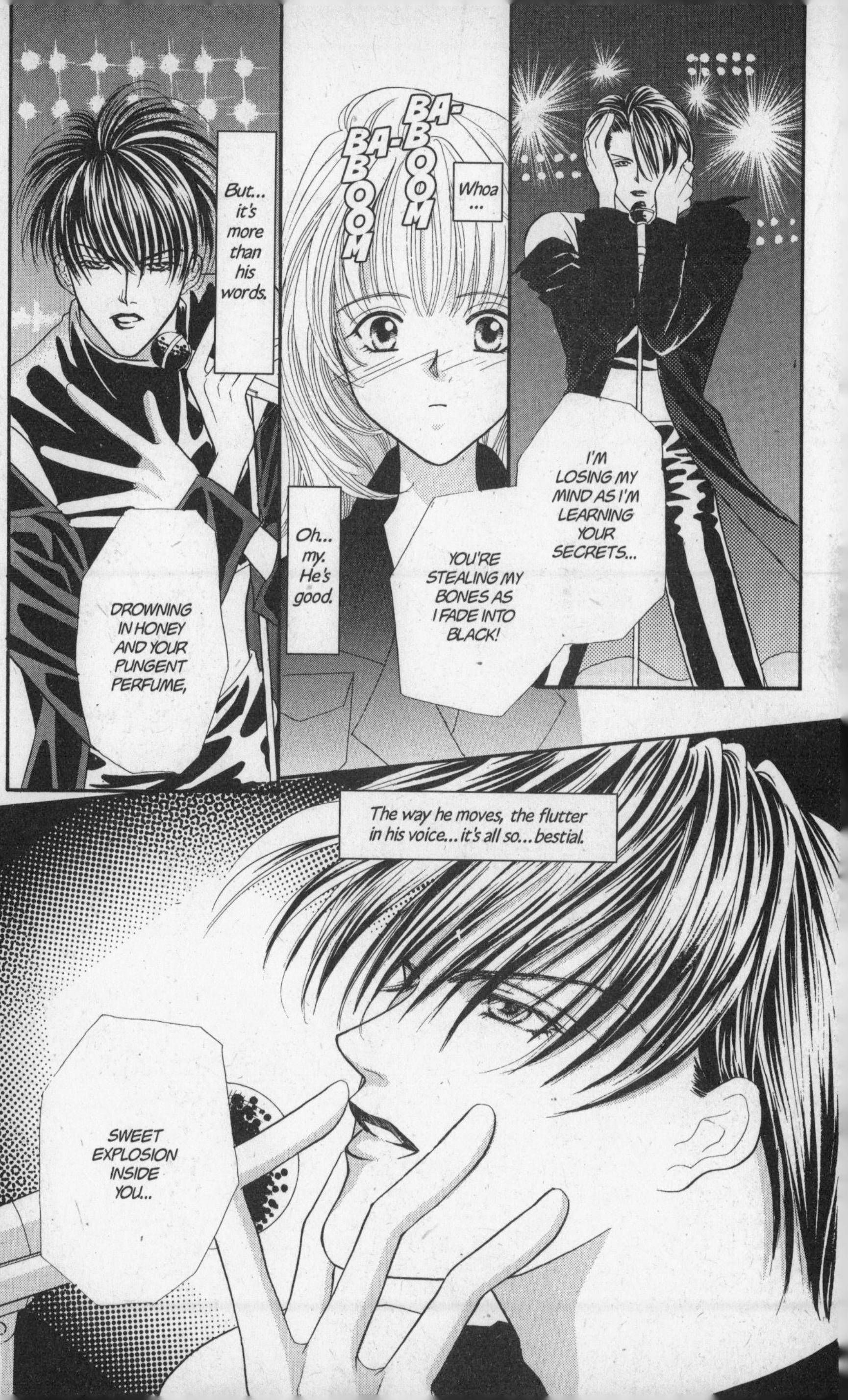
I'M LOSING MY MIND AS I'M LEARNING YOUR SECRETS...
BA-BOOM
BA-BOOM
Whoa...
YOU'RE STEALING MY BONES AS I FADE INTO BLACK!
Oh... my. He's good.
But... it's more than his words.
DROWNING IN HONEY AND YOUR PUNGENT PERFUME,
The way he moves, the flutter in his voice... it's all so... bestial.
SWEET EXPLOSION INSIDE YOU...

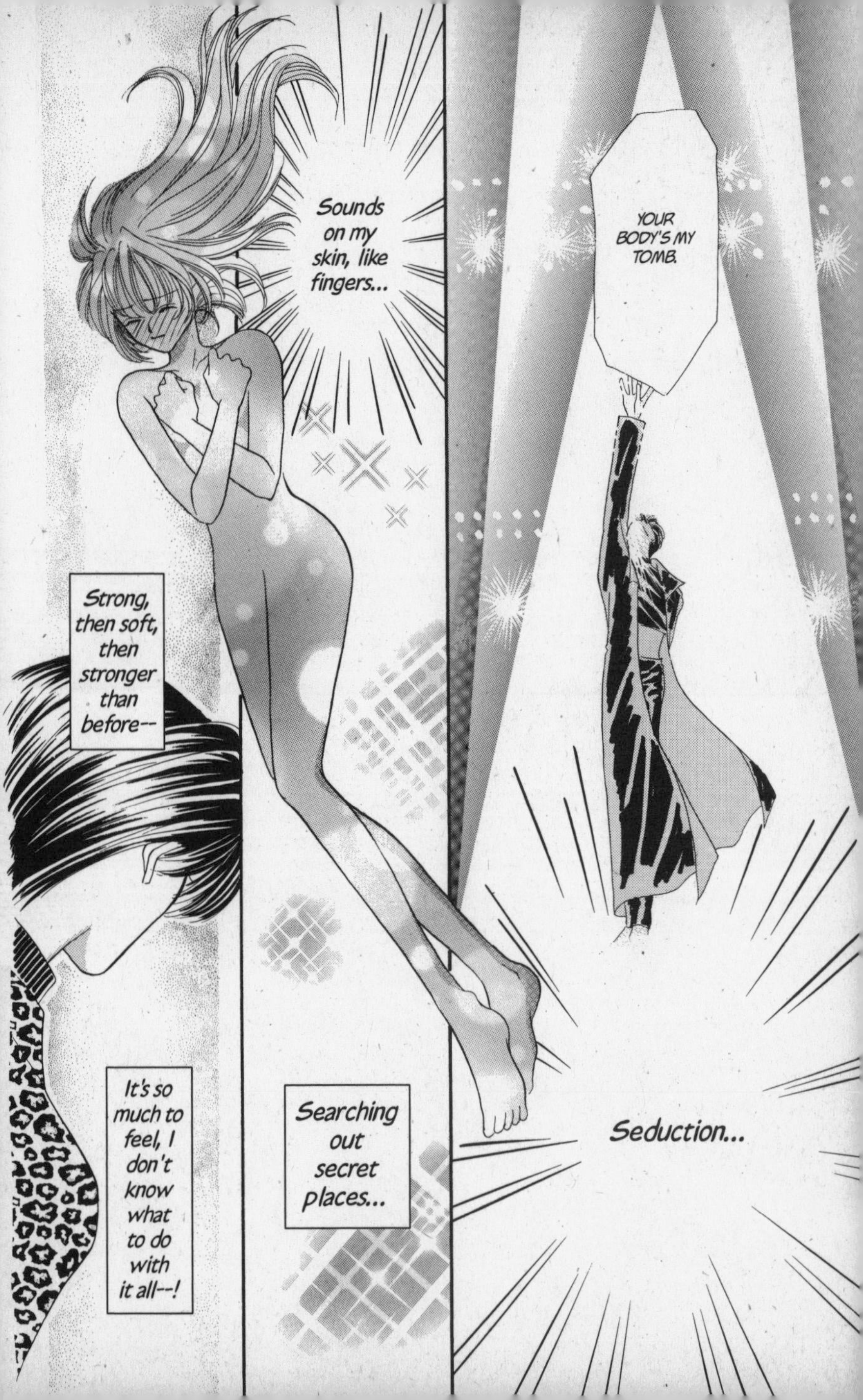
YOUR BODY'S MY TOMB.
Seduction...
Sounds on my skin, like fingers...
Searching out secret places...
Strong, then soft, then stronger than before--
It's so much to feel, I don't know what to do with it all--!

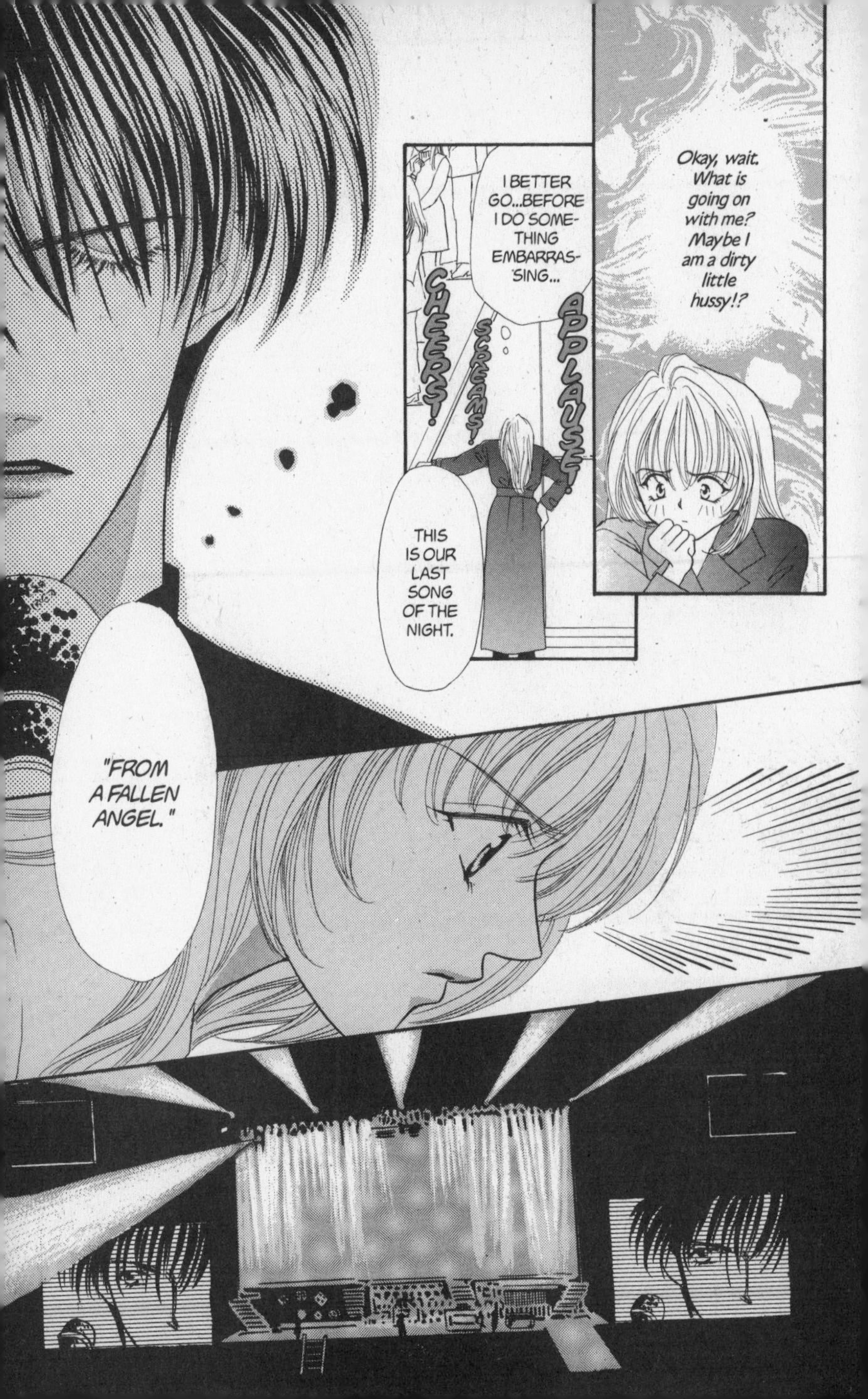
Okay, wait. What is going on with me? Maybe I am a dirty little hussy!?
I BETTER GO...BEFORE I DO SOME-THING EMBARRAS-SING...
APPLAUSE!
SCREAMS!
CHEERS!
THIS IS OUR LAST SONG OF THE NIGHT.
"FROM A FALLEN ANGEL."

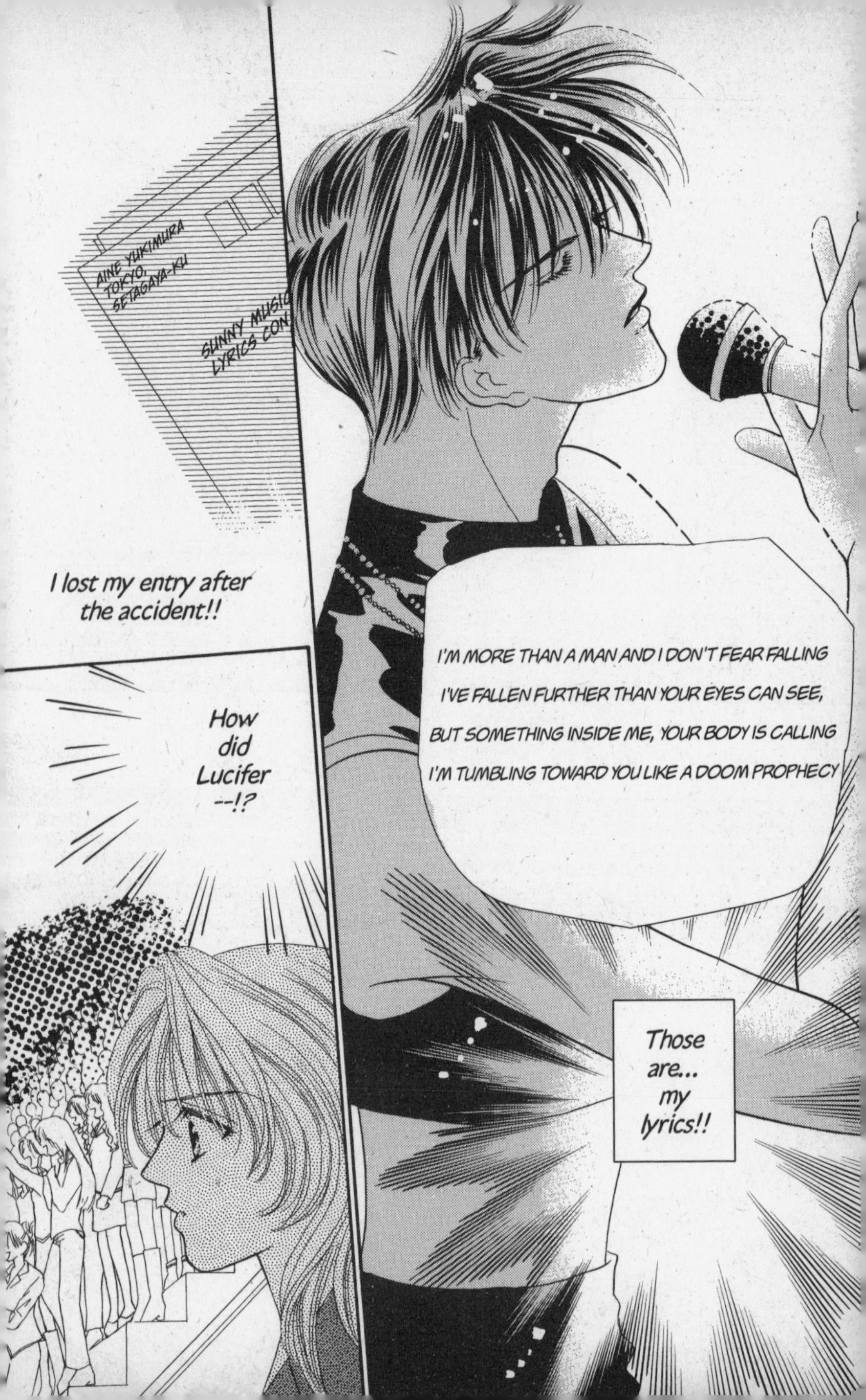
I'M MORE THAN A MAN AND I DON'T FEAR FALLING
I'VE FALLEN FURTHER THAN YOUR EYES CAN SEE,
BUT SOMETHING INSIDE ME, YOUR BODY IS CALLING
I'M TUMBLING TOWARD YOU LIKE A DOOM PROPHECY
Those are... my lyrics!!
AINE YUKIMURA
TOKYO, SETAGAYA-KU
SUNNY MUSIC
LYRICS CON
I lost my entry after the accident!!
How did Lucifer --!?

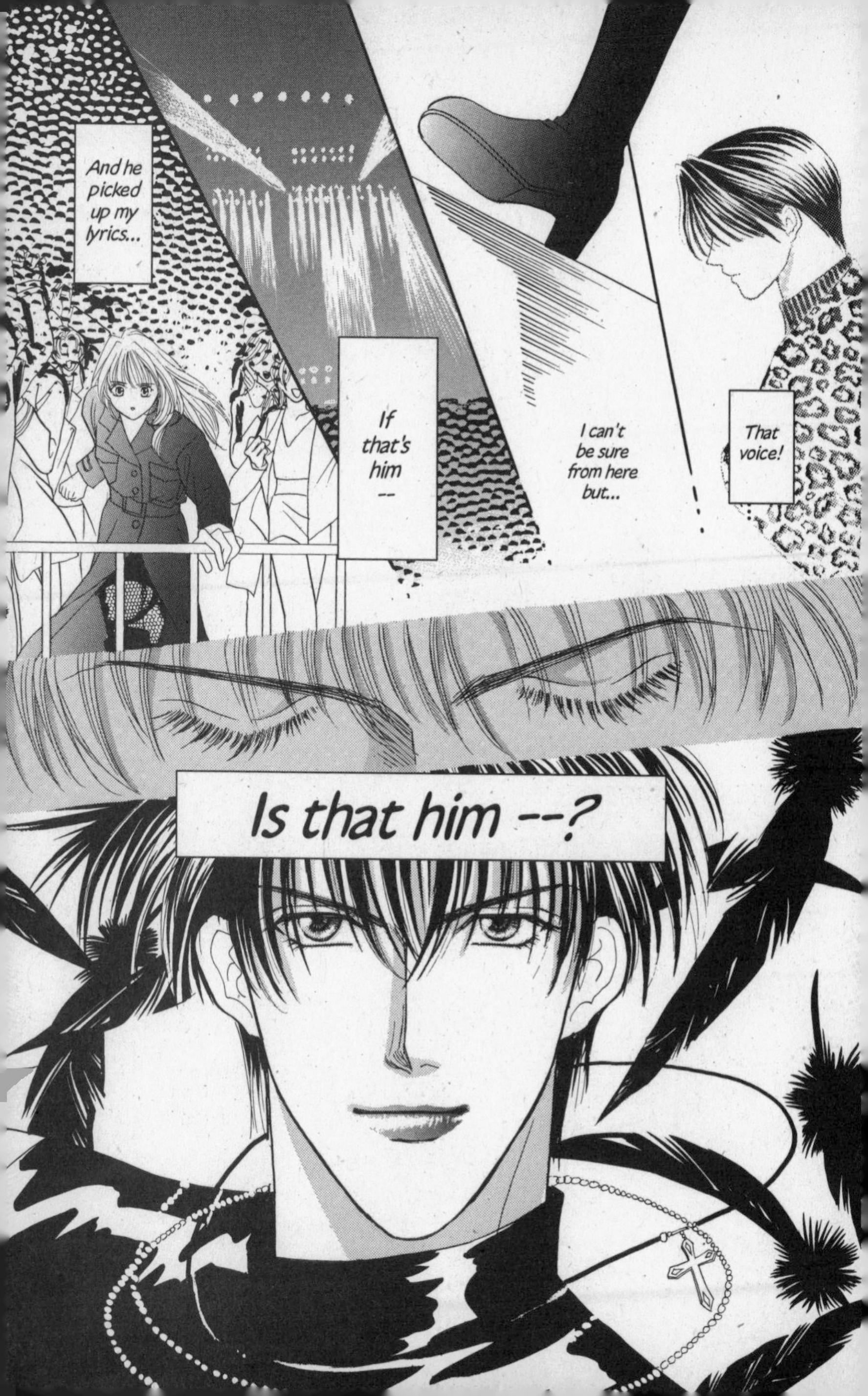
That voice!
I can't be sure from here but...
And he picked up my lyrics...
If that's him --
Is that him --?

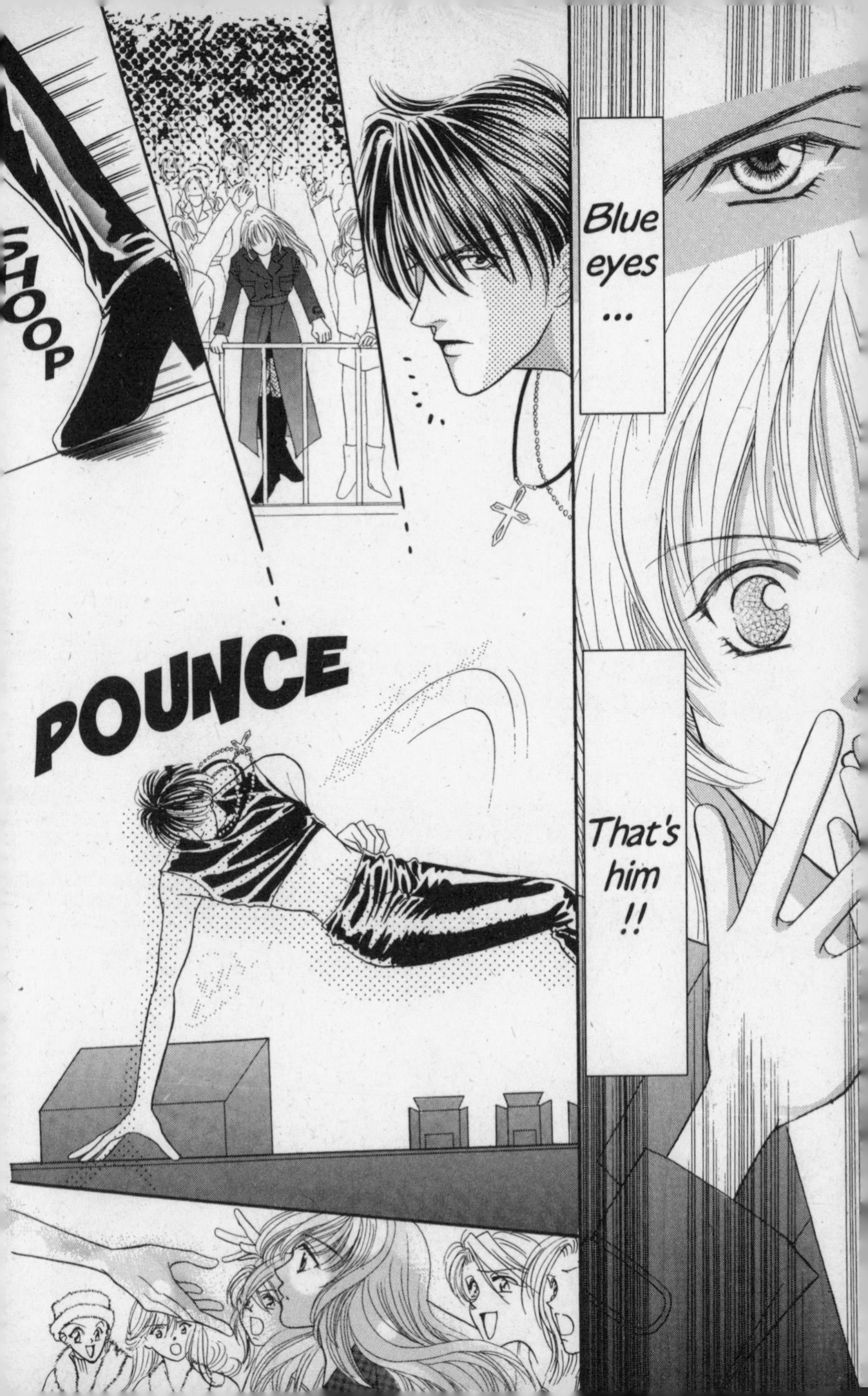
Blue eyes ...
That's him !!
SHOOP
POUNCE

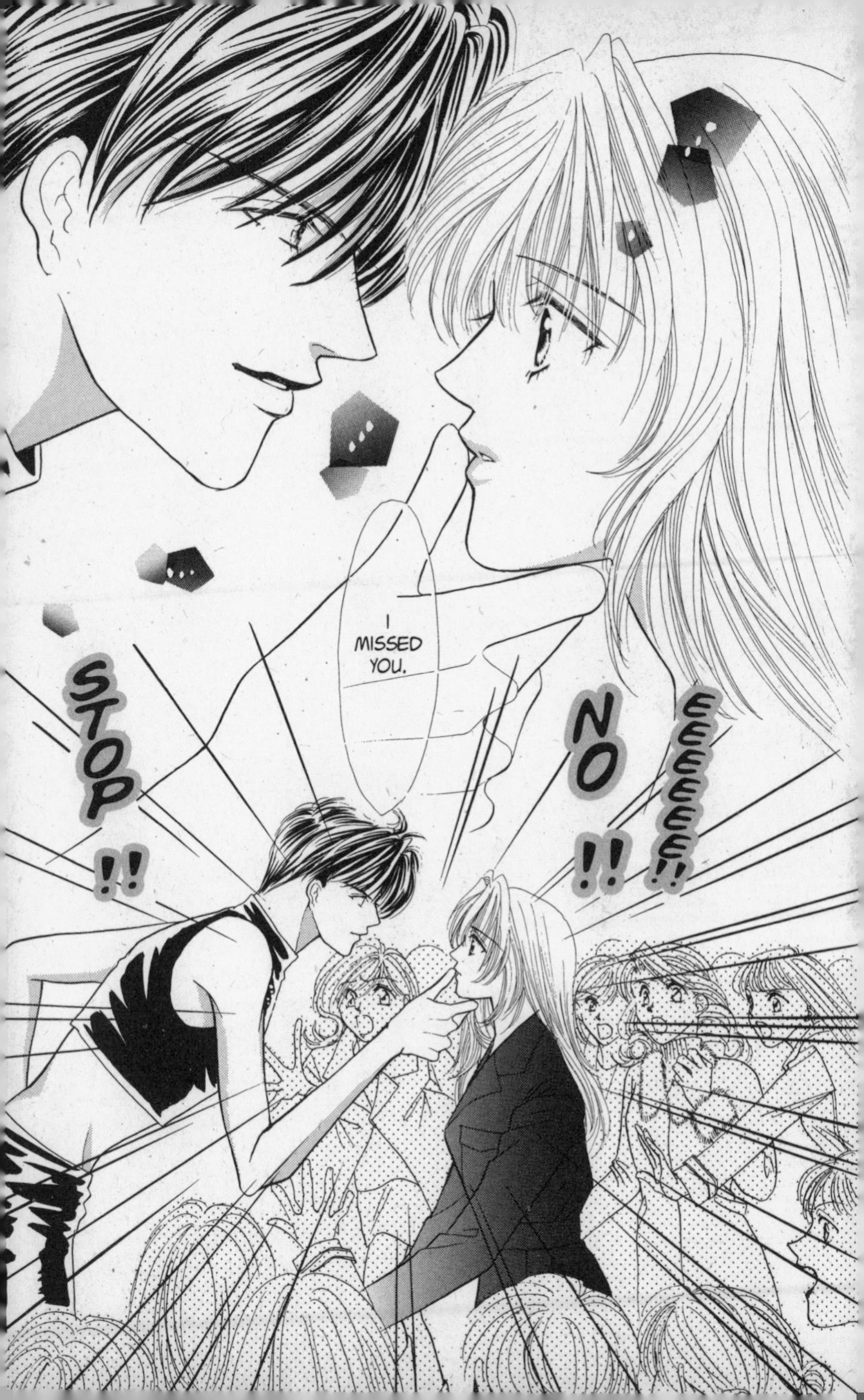
I MISSED YOU.
NO!! EEEEEE!!
STOP!!

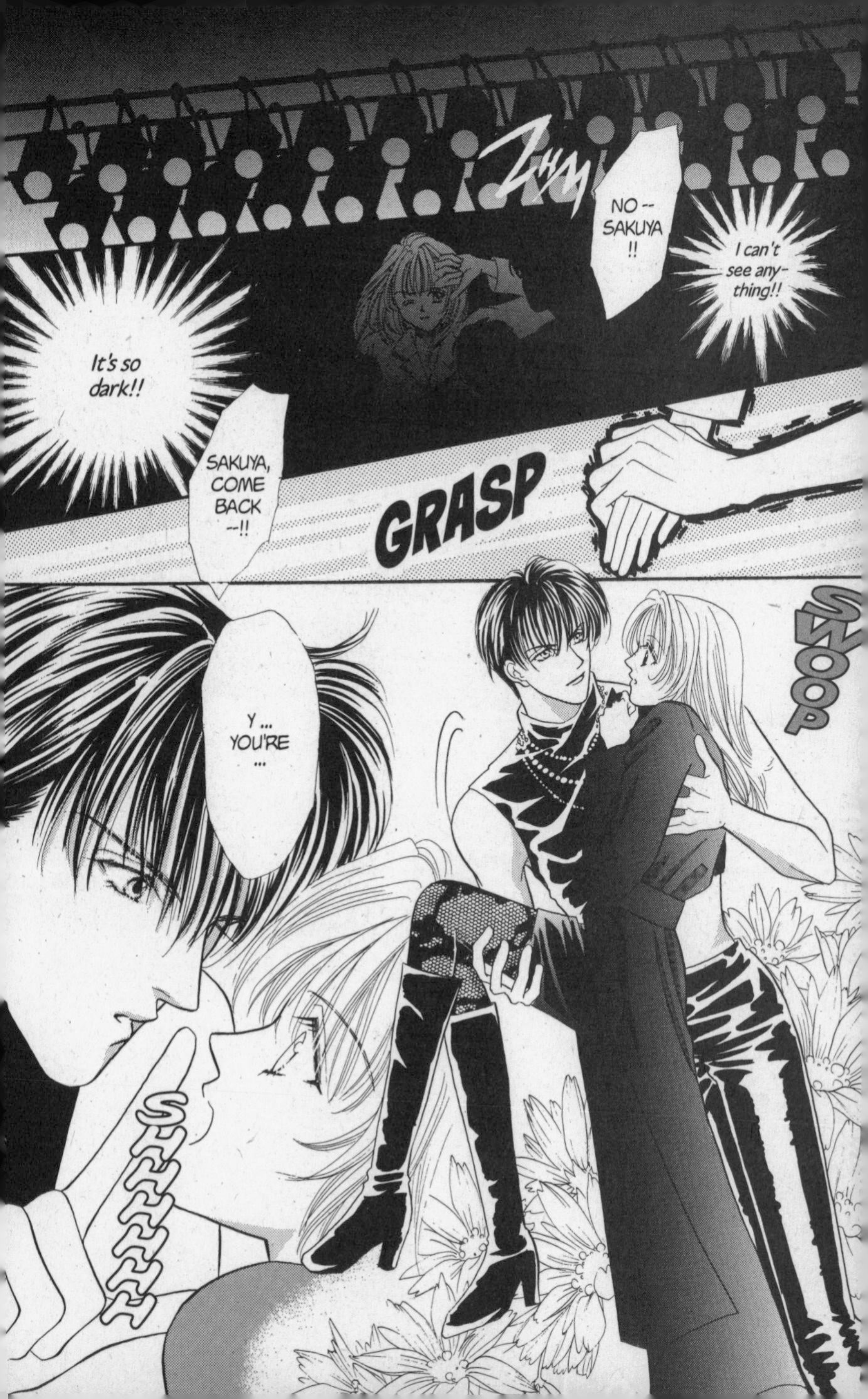

ZHM
NO -- SAKUYA !!
I can't see any- thing!!
It's so dark!!
SAKUYA, COME BACK --!!
GRASP
SWOOP
Y ... YOU'RE ...
SHHHHHHH

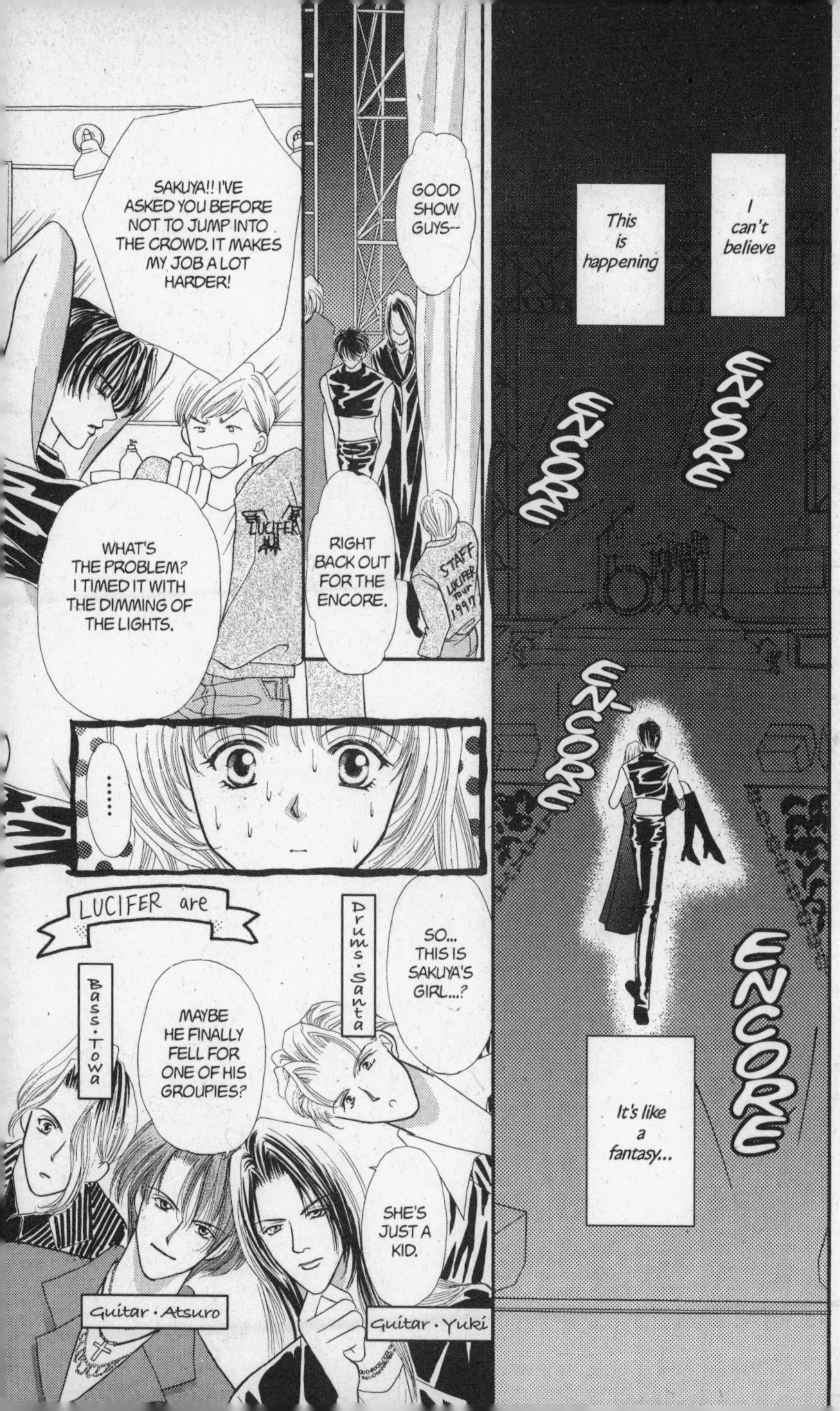
I can't believe
This is happening
ENCORE
ENCORE
ENCORE
ENCORE
It's like a fantasy...
GOOD SHOW GUYS--
RIGHT BACK OUT FOR THE ENCORE.
STAFF LUCIFER Tour 1997
SAKUYA!! I'VE ASKED YOU BEFORE NOT TO JUMP INTO THE CROWD. IT MAKES MY JOB A LOT HARDER!
LUCIFER
WHAT'S THE PROBLEM? I TIMED IT WITH THE DIMMING OF THE LIGHTS.
......
LUCIFER are
Drums・Santa
SO... THIS IS SAKUYA'S GIRL...?
Bass・Towa
MAYBE HE FINALLY FELL FOR ONE OF HIS GROUPIES?
SHE'S JUST A KID.
Guitar・Yuki
Guitar・Atsuro

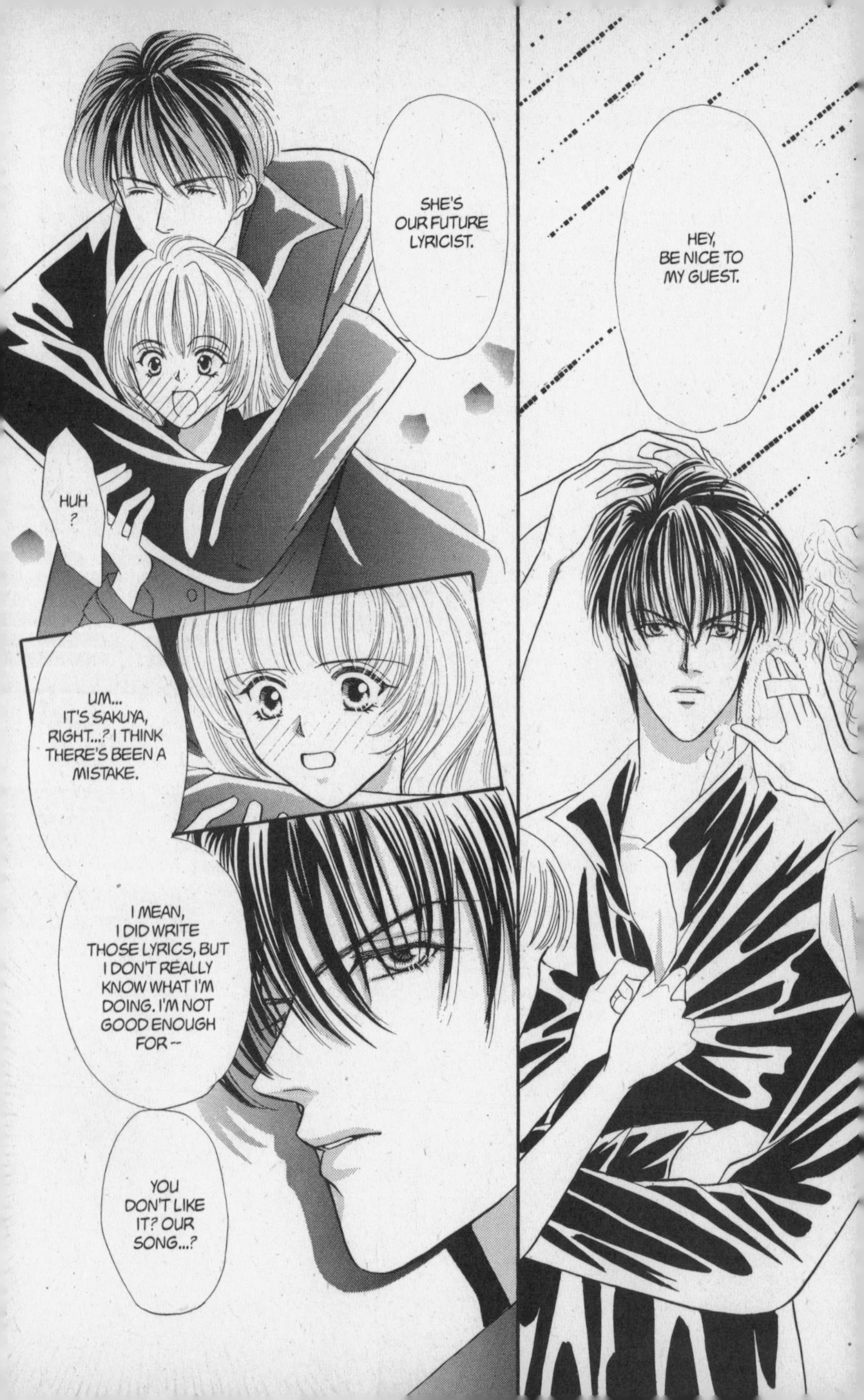
HEY, BE NICE TO MY GUEST.
SHE'S OUR FUTURE LYRICIST.
HUH ?
UM... IT'S SAKUYA, RIGHT...? I THINK THERE'S BEEN A MISTAKE.
I MEAN, I DID WRITE THOSE LYRICS, BUT I DON'T REALLY KNOW WHAT I'M DOING. I'M NOT GOOD ENOUGH FOR --
YOU DON'T LIKE IT? OUR SONG...?

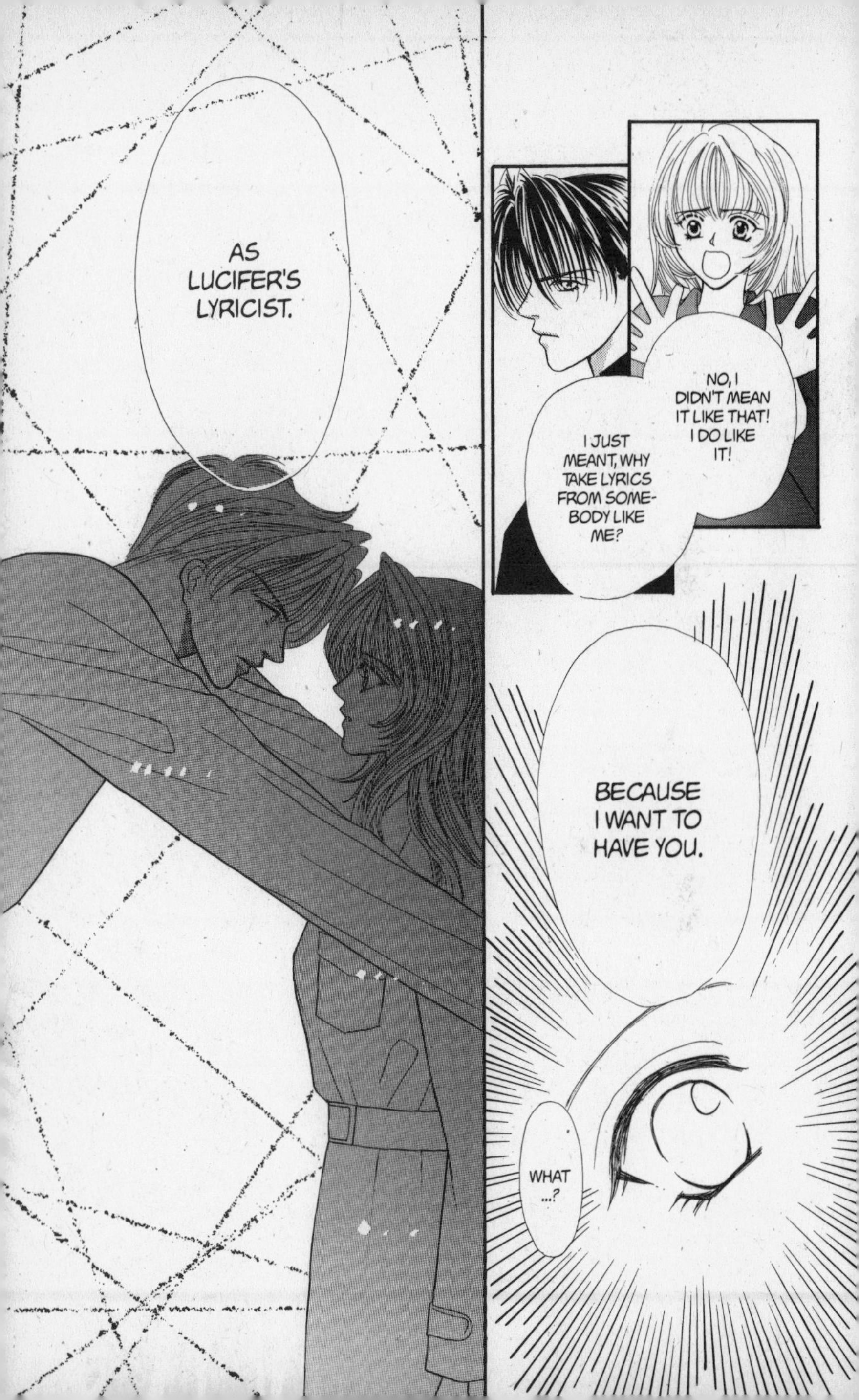
NO, I DIDN'T MEAN IT LIKE THAT! I DO LIKE IT!
I JUST MEANT, WHY TAKE LYRICS FROM SOME-BODY LIKE ME?
BECAUSE I WANT TO HAVE YOU.
WHAT ...?
AS LUCIFER'S LYRICIST.

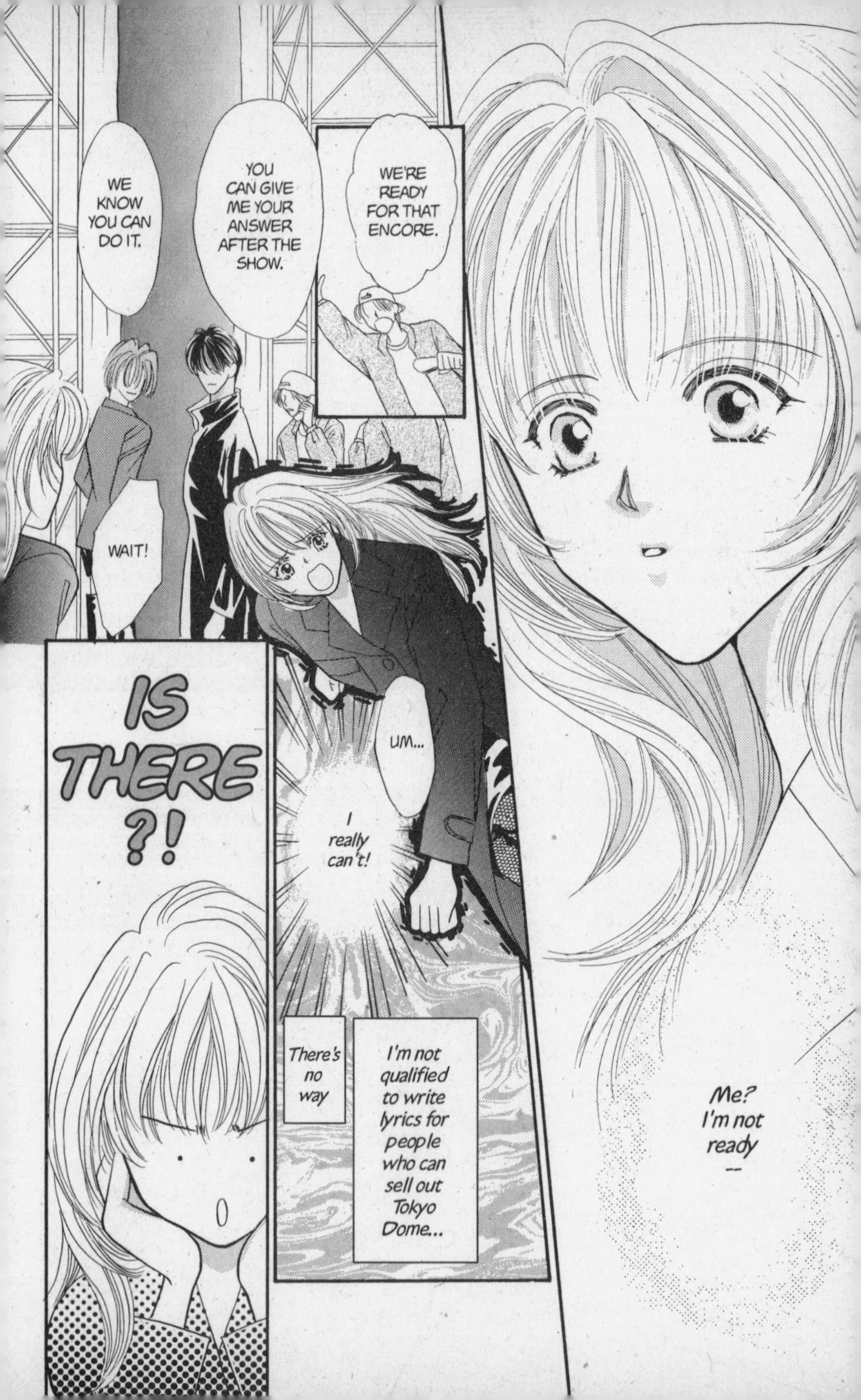
Me? I'm not ready --
WE'RE READY FOR THAT ENCORE.
YOU CAN GIVE ME YOUR ANSWER AFTER THE SHOW.
WE KNOW YOU CAN DO IT.
WAIT!
UM...
I really can't!
I'm not qualified to write lyrics for people who can sell out Tokyo Dome...
There's no way
IS THERE ?!

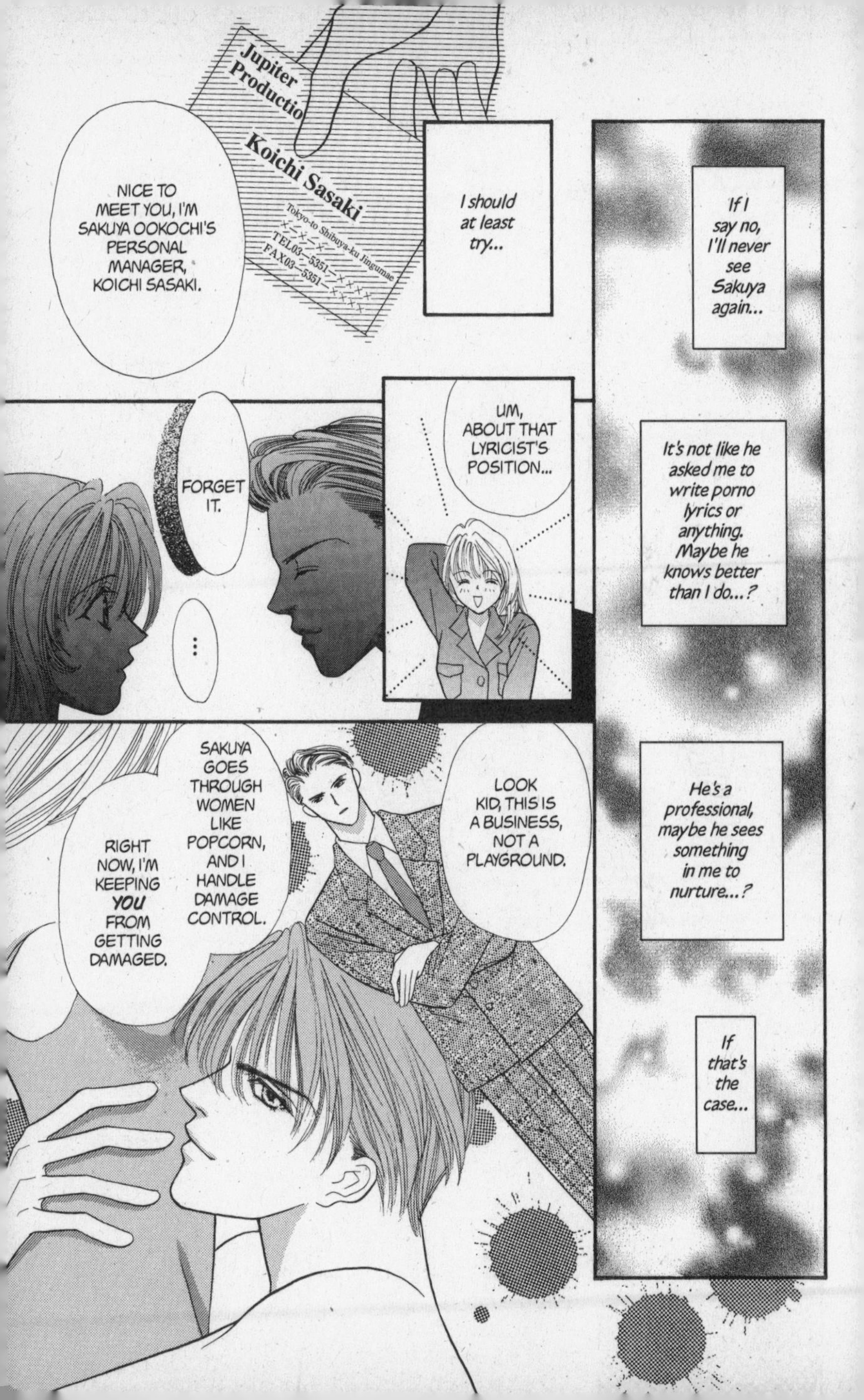
If I say no, I'll never see Sakuya again...
It's not like he asked me to write porno lyrics or anything. Maybe he knows better than I do...?
He's a professional, maybe he sees something in me to nurture...?
If that's the case...
I should at least try...
Jupiter Productio
Koichi Sasaki
Tokyo-to Shibuya-ku Jingumae
NICE TO MEET YOU, I'M SAKUYA OOKOCHI'S PERSONAL MANAGER, KOICHI SASAKI.
UM, ABOUT THAT LYRICIST'S POSITION...
FORGET IT.
...
LOOK KID, THIS IS A BUSINESS, NOT A PLAYGROUND.
SAKUYA GOES THROUGH WOMEN LIKE POPCORN, AND I HANDLE DAMAGE CONTROL.
RIGHT NOW, I'M KEEPING **YOU** FROM GETTING DAMAGED.

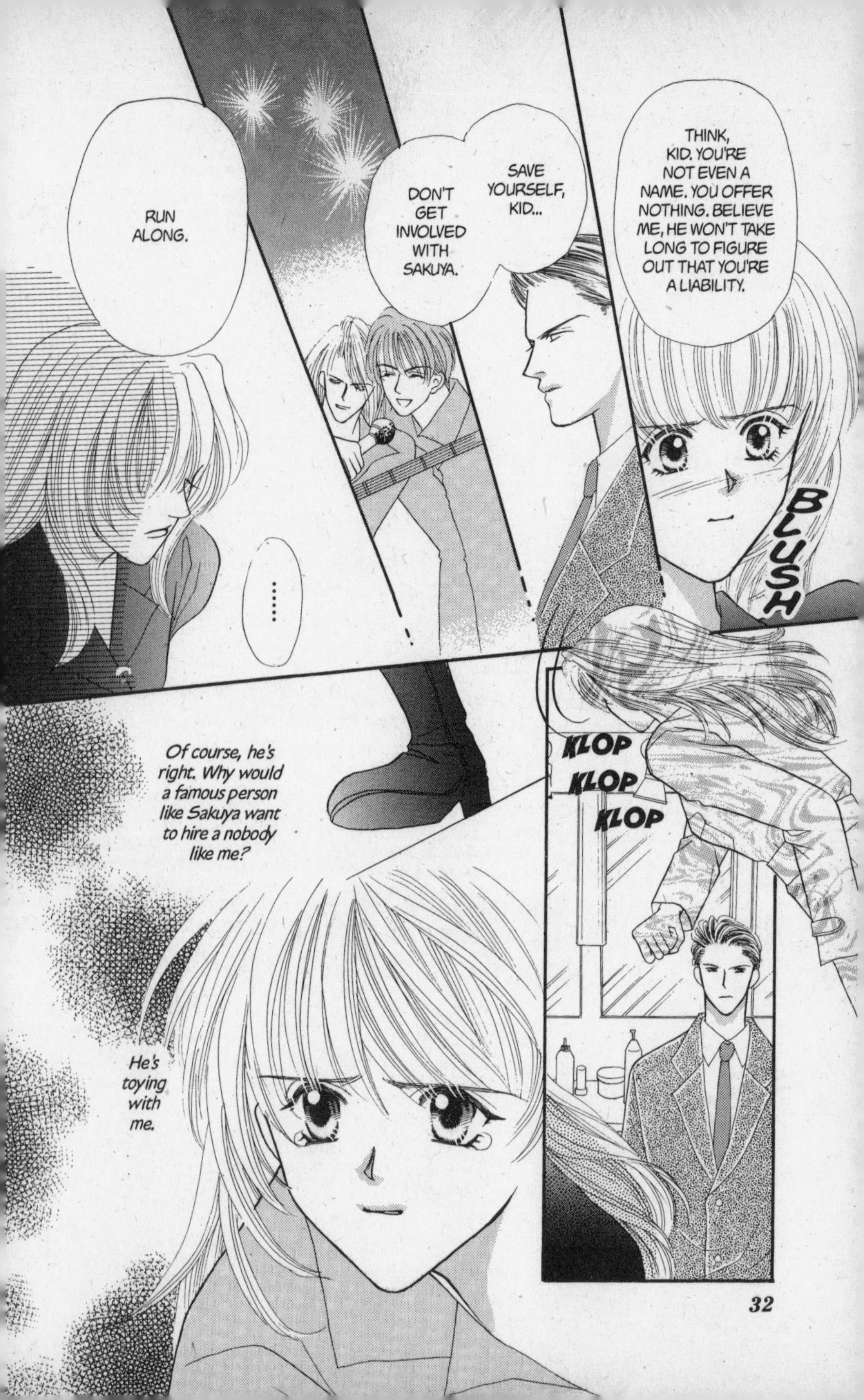

THINK, KID. YOU'RE NOT EVEN A NAME. YOU OFFER NOTHING. BELIEVE ME, HE WON'T TAKE LONG TO FIGURE OUT THAT YOU'RE A LIABILITY.
BLUSH
SAVE YOURSELF, KID...
DON'T GET INVOLVED WITH SAKUYA.
RUN ALONG.
......
KLOP
KLOP
KLOP
Of course, he's right. Why would a famous person like Sakuya want to hire a nobody like me?
He's toying with me.

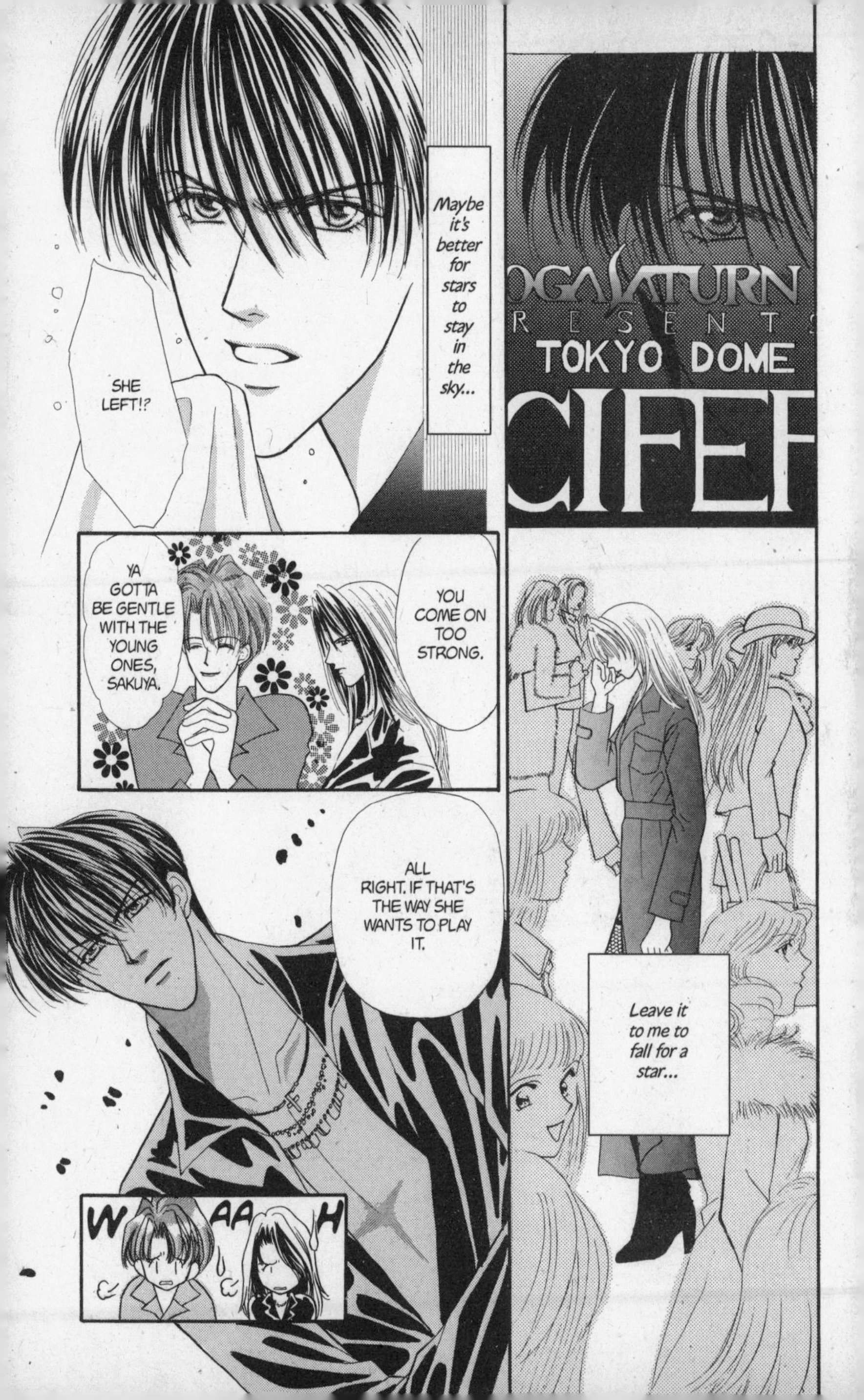
OGA SATURN
RESENTS
TOKYO DOME
CIFER
Leave it to me to fall for a star...
Maybe it's better for stars to stay in the sky...
SHE LEFT!?
YOU COME ON TOO STRONG.
YA GOTTA BE GENTLE WITH THE YOUNG ONES, SAKUYA.
ALL RIGHT. IF THAT'S THE WAY SHE WANTS TO PLAY IT.
WAAH

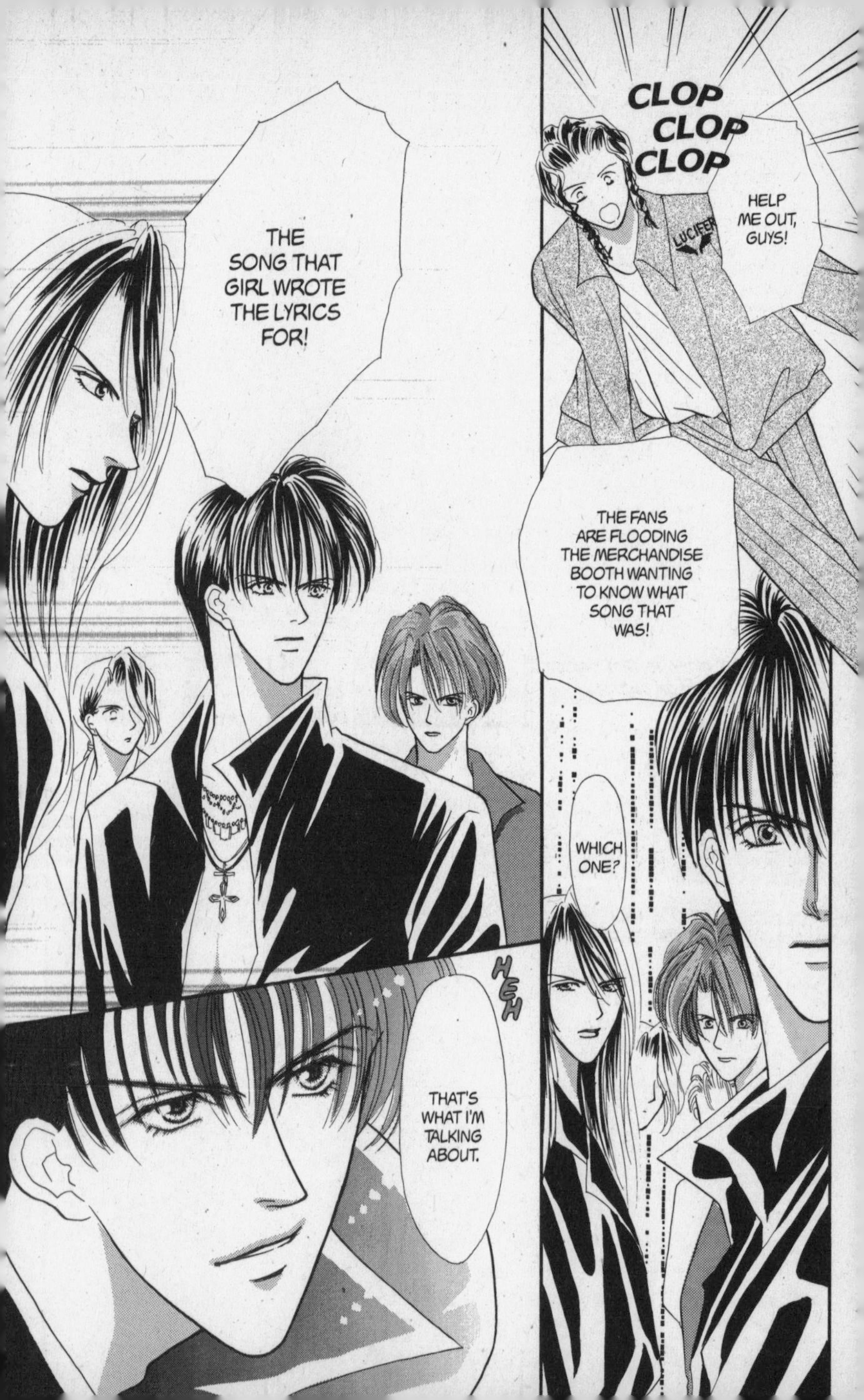
CLOP
CLOP
CLOP
HELP ME OUT, GUYS!
LUCIFER
THE FANS ARE FLOODING THE MERCHANDISE BOOTH WANTING TO KNOW WHAT SONG THAT WAS!
WHICH ONE?
THE SONG THAT GIRL WROTE THE LYRICS FOR!
HEH
THAT'S WHAT I'M TALKING ABOUT.

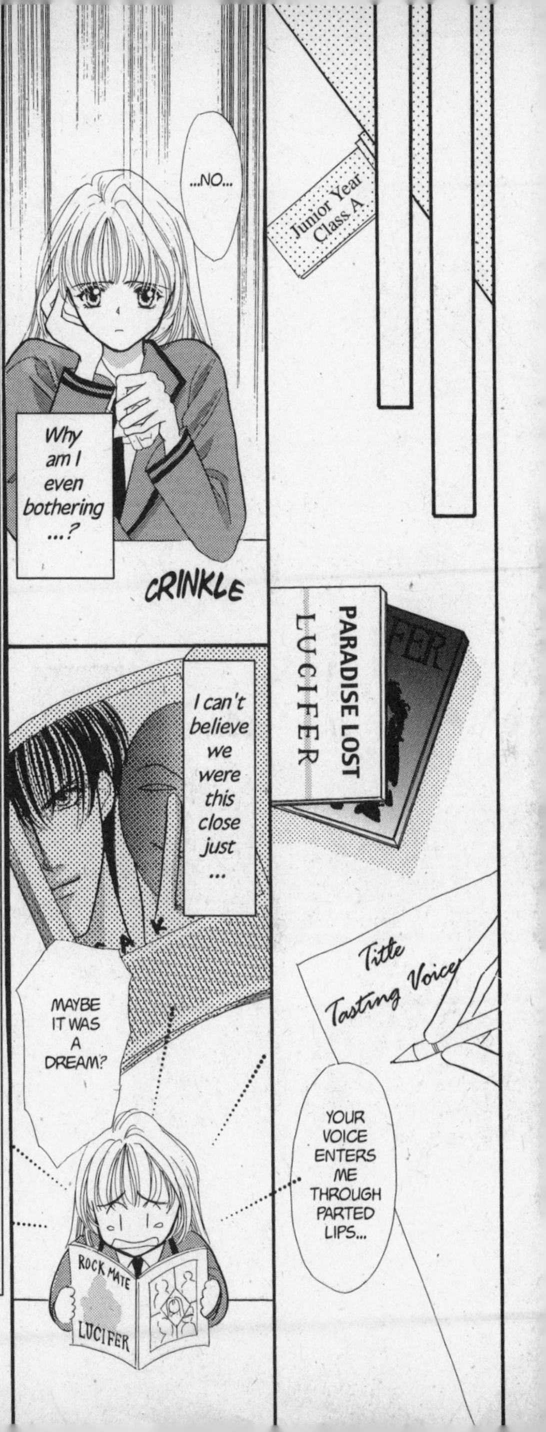
Junior Year Class A
...NO...
Why am I even bothering ...?
CRINKLE
PARADISE LOST
LUCIFER
Title
Tasting Voice
YOUR VOICE ENTERS ME THROUGH PARTED LIPS...
I can't believe we were this close just ...
MAYBE IT WAS A DREAM?
ROCK MATE
LUCIFER

Welcome Everybody!!

First off, let me introduce myself. My name is Mayu Shinjo, and I'm the artist for SENSUAL PHRASE. Thank you for reading my book!

Secondly, as you undoubtedly know by now, this manga deals with show business. What fun! I know what you're dying to ask, though. 'Who did I base my story on?' Well, a lot of people have begged me to say LUNA SEA. Everyone thinks Ryuichi Kawamura is Sakuya's model. Hyde of L'ARC-EN-CIEL comes in a close second and then, for some strange reason, Koshi Inaba from B'z (and a few random singers here and there). But Kawamura receives the most votes by far. Why is that? The truth, in all its dull glory, is that Sakuya isn't based on anyone.

I admit, Lucifer and Luna Sea sound similar but I assure you that was purely coincidental. In case you didn't know, Lucifer means Fallen Angel. Believe me, I didn't name the band to sound anything like Luna Sea.

But hey, all the singers mentioned above are incredibly handsome. Even if I wanted to use them as models, my drawing skills wouldn't allow me to.

The embarrassing truth is, I'm not too familiar with rock bands! I had to do a lot of research for this project. I called in a favor from a friend...

(To be continued)

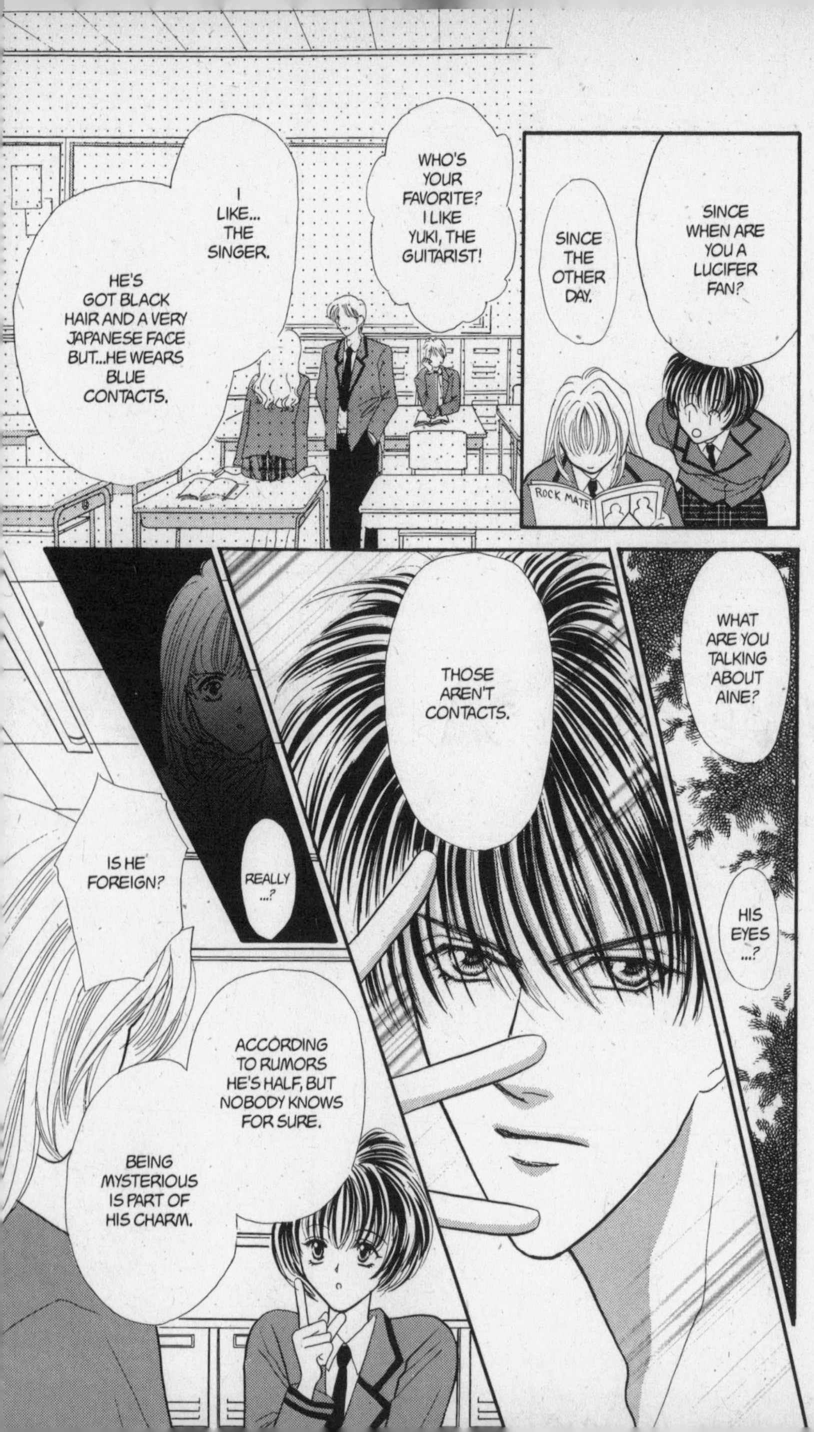
SINCE WHEN ARE YOU A LUCIFER FAN?
SINCE THE OTHER DAY.
ROCK MATE
WHO'S YOUR FAVORITE? I LIKE YUKI, THE GUITARIST!
I LIKE... THE SINGER.
HE'S GOT BLACK HAIR AND A VERY JAPANESE FACE BUT...HE WEARS BLUE CONTACTS.
WHAT ARE YOU TALKING ABOUT AINE?
HIS EYES ...?
THOSE AREN'T CONTACTS.
REALLY ...?
IS HE FOREIGN?
ACCORDING TO RUMORS HE'S HALF, BUT NOBODY KNOWS FOR SURE.
BEING MYSTERIOUS IS PART OF HIS CHARM.

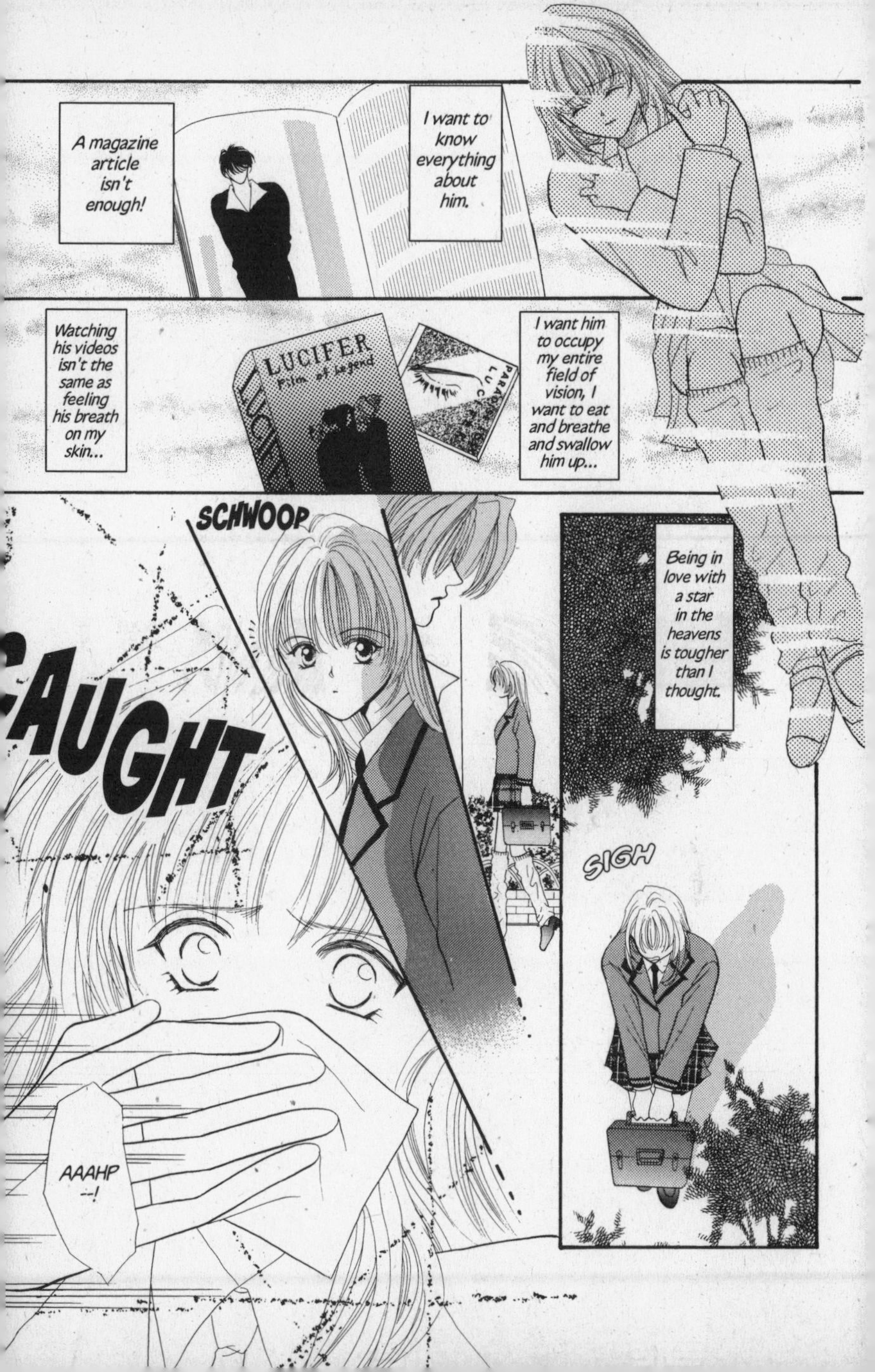
I want to know everything about him.
A magazine article isn't enough!
I want him to occupy my entire field of vision, I want to eat and breathe and swallow him up...
LUCIFER
Film of Legend
Watching his videos isn't the same as feeling his breath on my skin...
Being in love with a star in the heavens is tougher than I thought.
SIGH
SCHWOOP
CAUGHT
AAAHP --!

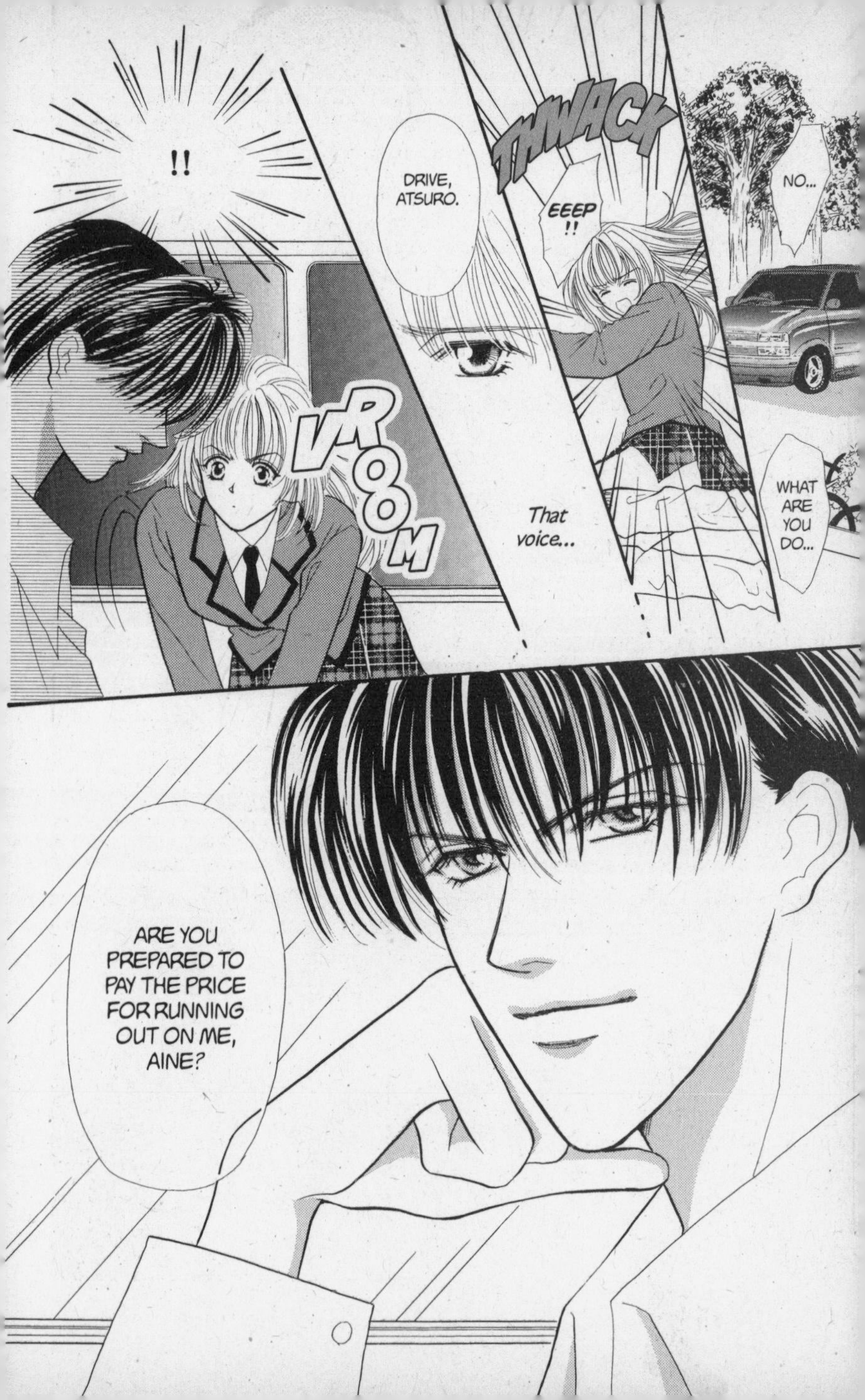
NO...
WHAT ARE YOU DO...
THWACK
EEEP !!
DRIVE, ATSURO.
That voice...
!!
VROOM
ARE YOU PREPARED TO PAY THE PRICE FOR RUNNING OUT ON ME, AINE?

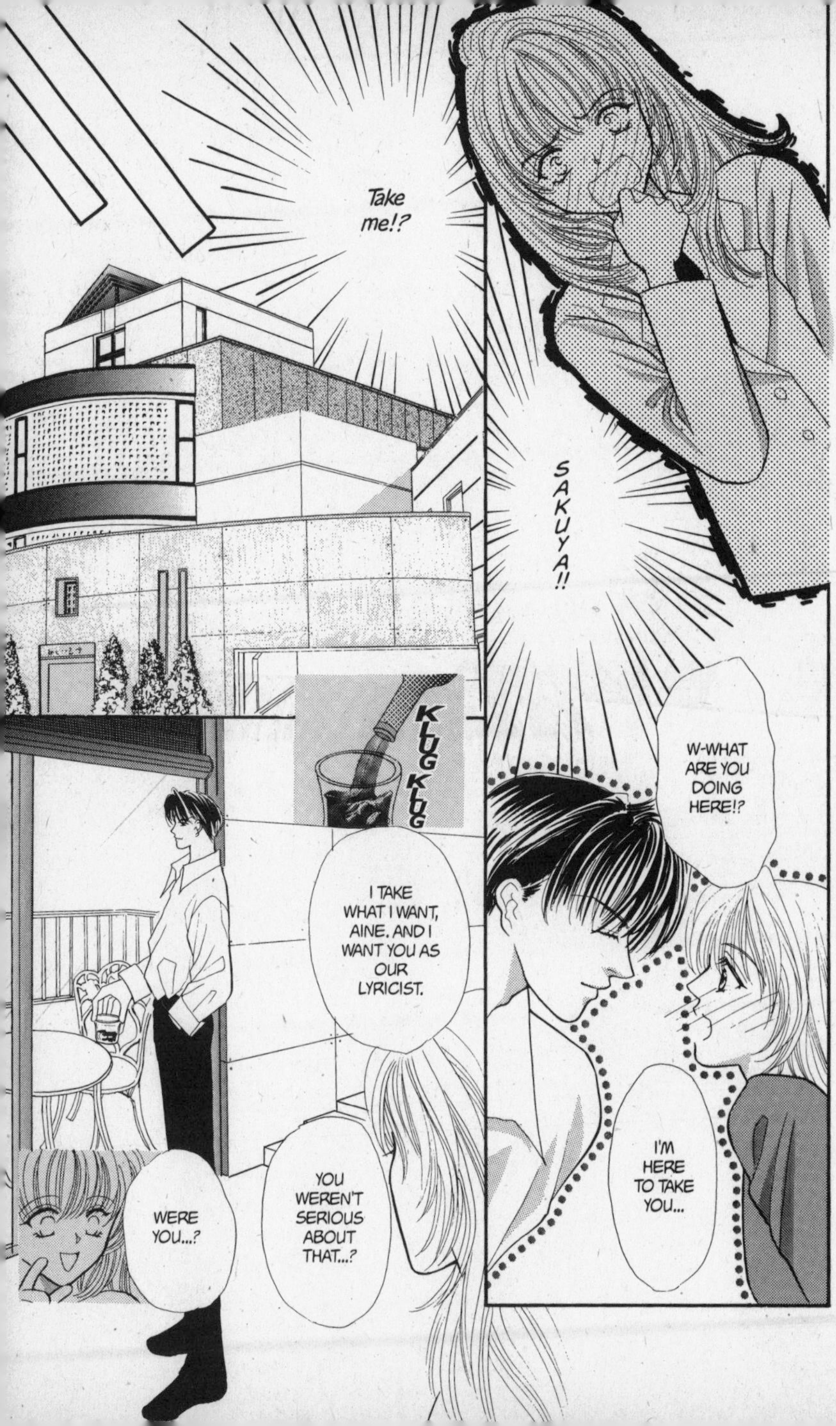
Take me!?
SAKUYA!!
W-WHAT ARE YOU DOING HERE!?
I'M HERE TO TAKE YOU...
KLUG KLUG
I TAKE WHAT I WANT, AINE. AND I WANT YOU AS OUR LYRICIST.
YOU WEREN'T SERIOUS ABOUT THAT...?
WERE YOU...?

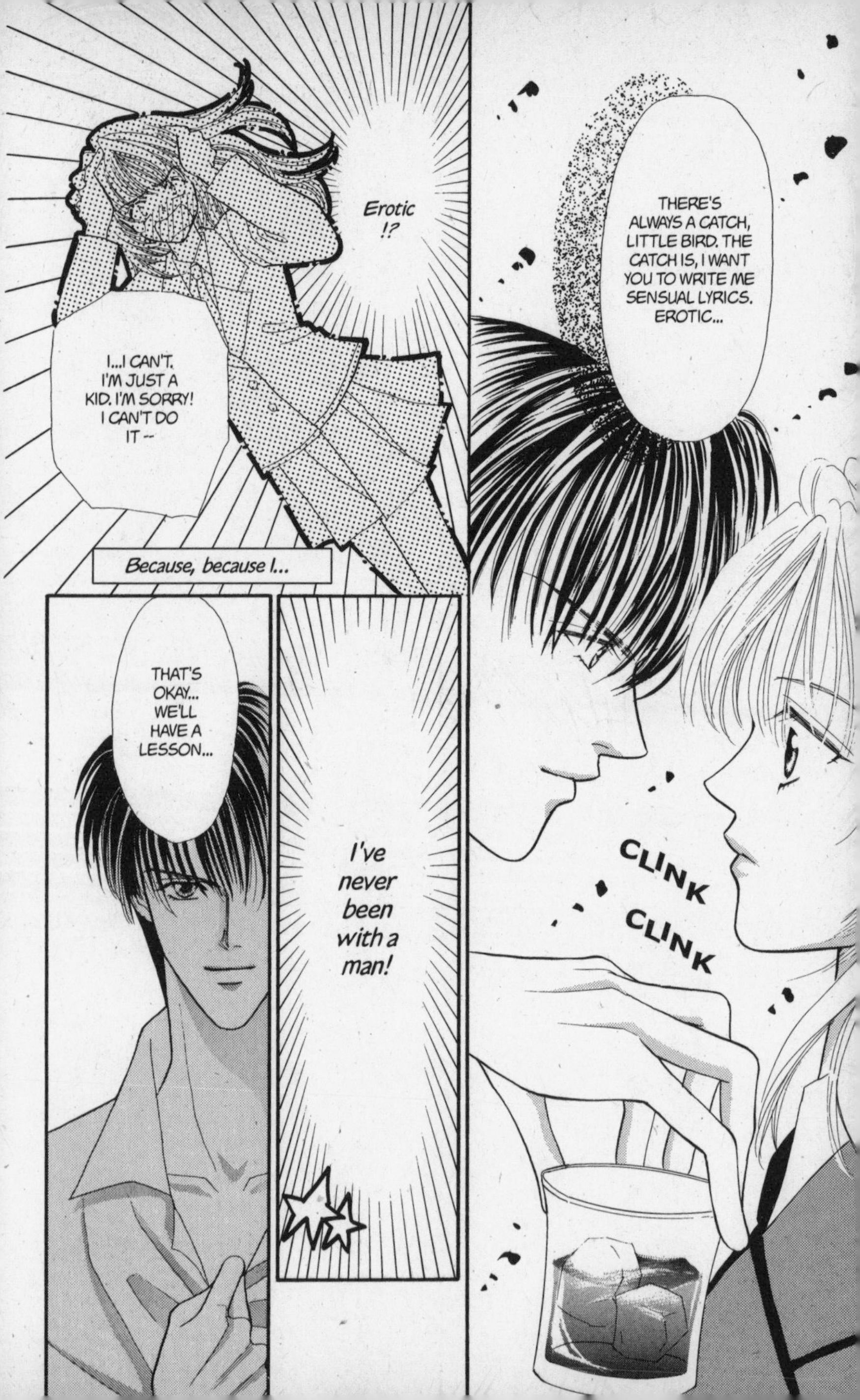
THERE'S ALWAYS A CATCH, LITTLE BIRD. THE CATCH IS, I WANT YOU TO WRITE ME SENSUAL LYRICS. EROTIC...
CLINK
CLINK
Erotic !?
I...I CAN'T. I'M JUST A KID. I'M SORRY! I CAN'T DO IT --
Because, because I...
I've never been with a man!
THAT'S OKAY... WE'LL HAVE A LESSON...

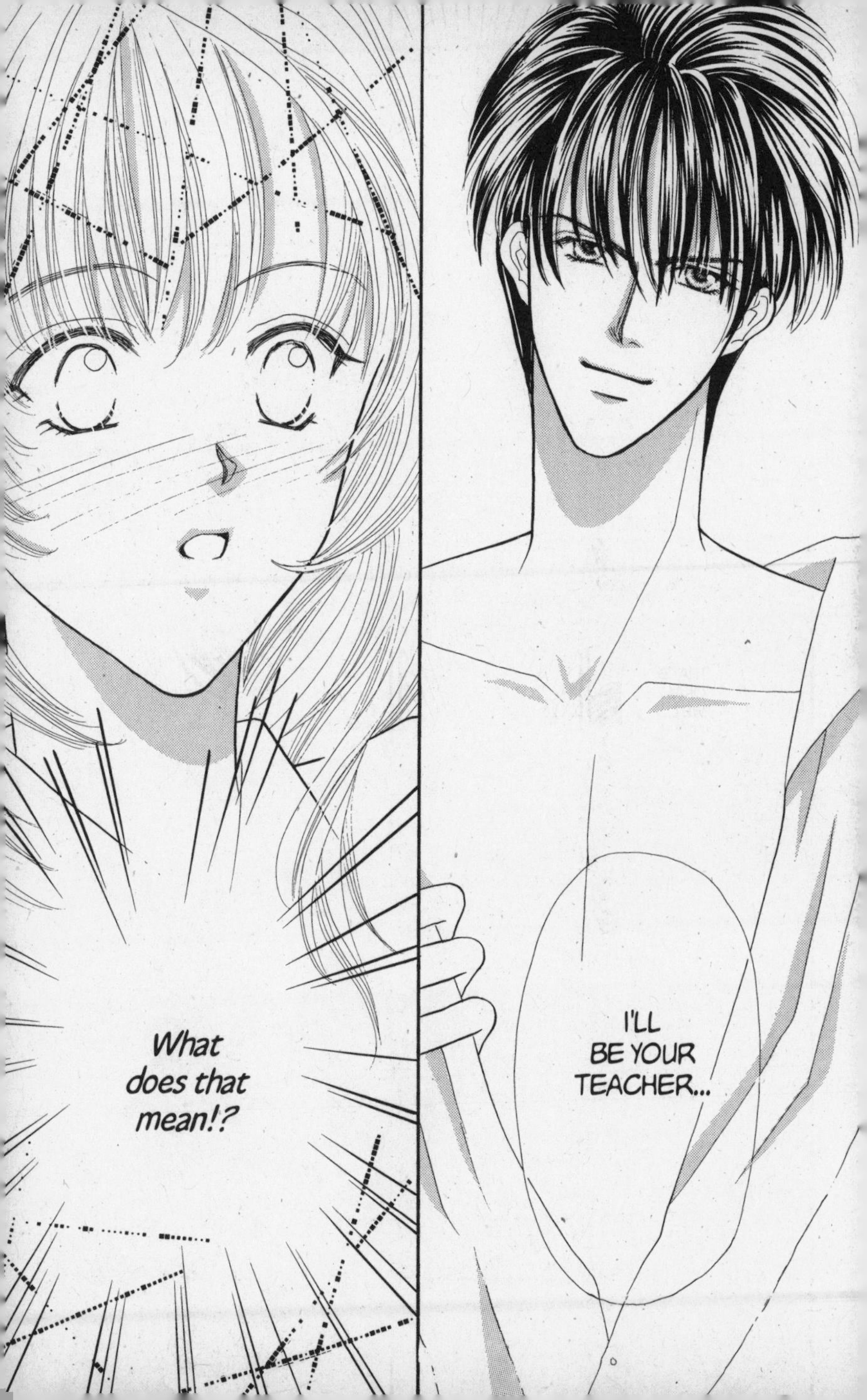
I'LL BE YOUR TEACHER...
What does that mean!?

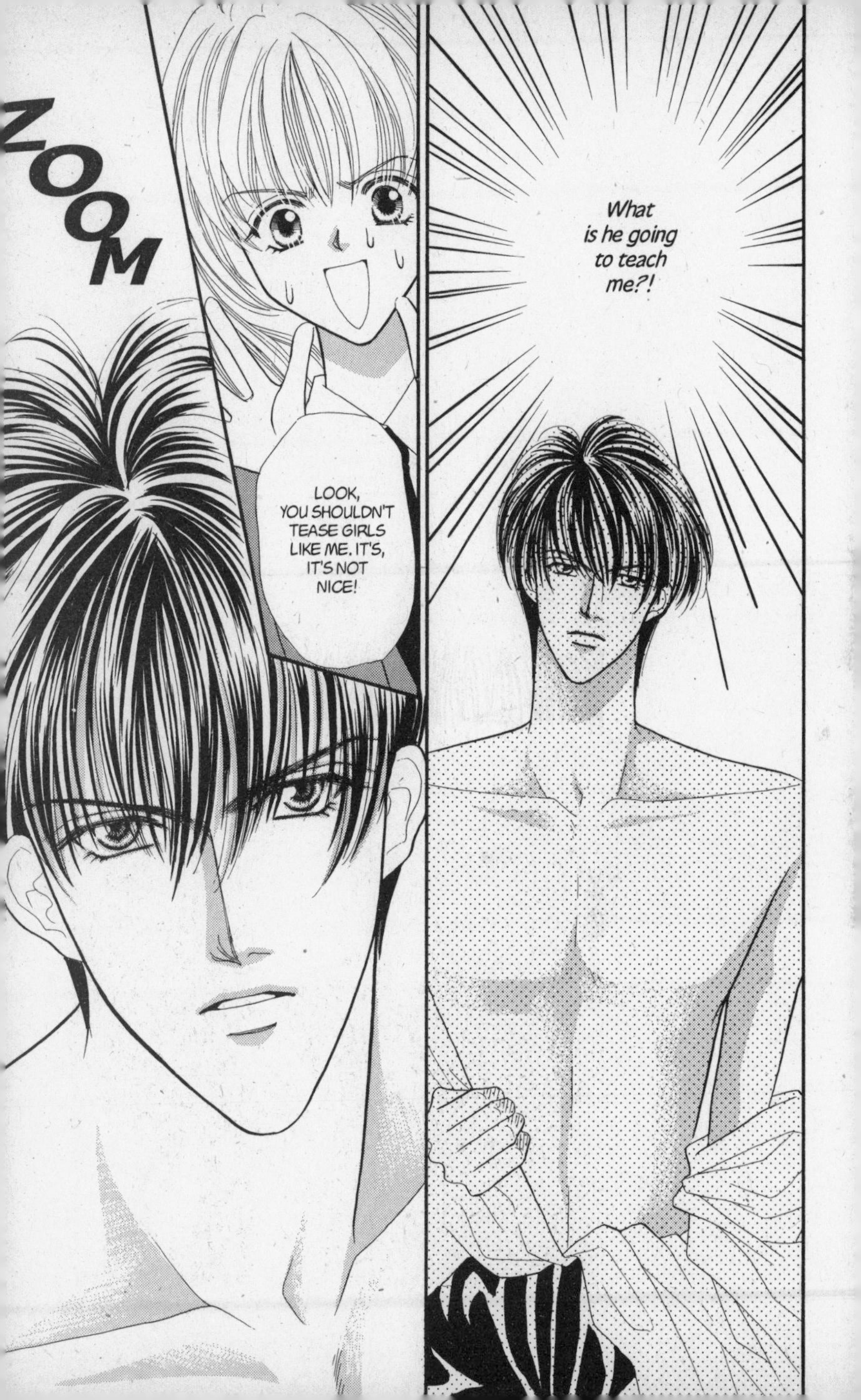
What is he going to teach me?!
ZOOM
LOOK, YOU SHOULDN'T TEASE GIRLS LIKE ME. IT'S, IT'S NOT NICE!

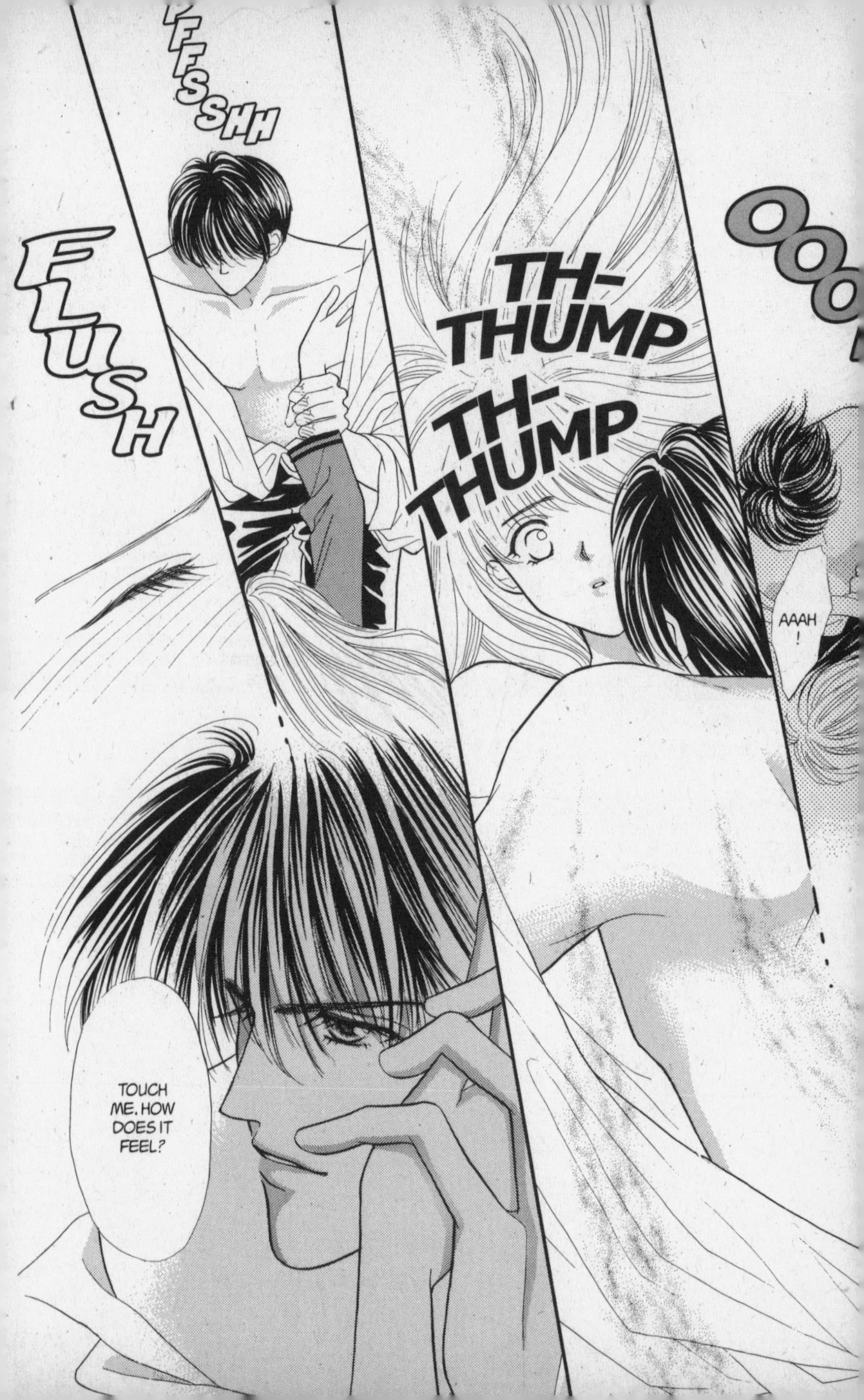
OOO
AAAH!
TH-THUMP
TH-THUMP
FFSSHH
FLUSH
TOUCH ME. HOW DOES IT FEEL?

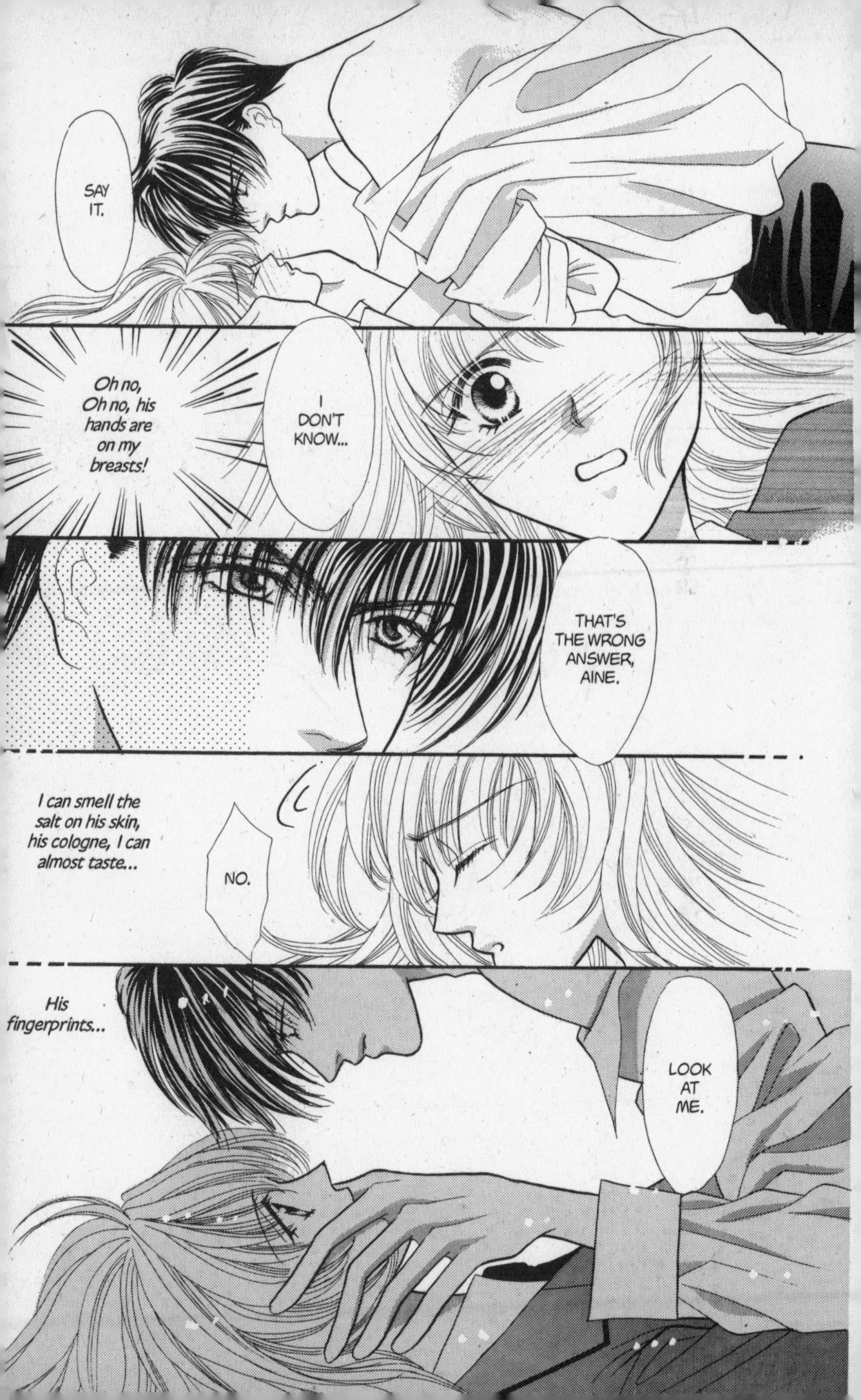
SAY IT.
I DON'T KNOW...
Oh no, Oh no, his hands are on my breasts!
THAT'S THE WRONG ANSWER, AINE.
NO.
I can smell the salt on his skin, his cologne, I can almost taste...
LOOK AT ME.
His fingerprints...

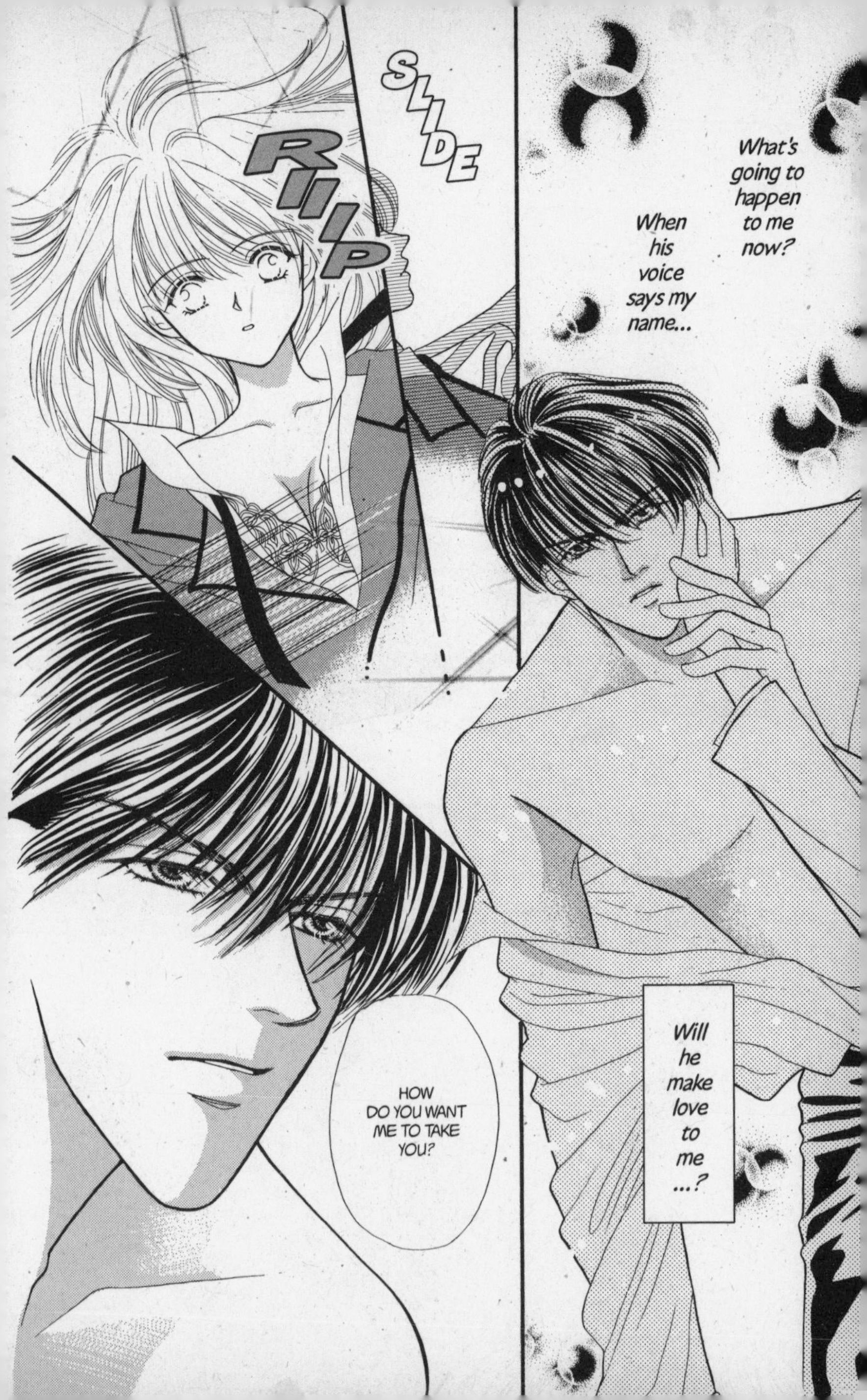
What's going to happen to me now?
When his voice says my name...
Will he make love to me ...?
SLIDE
RIIIP
HOW DO YOU WANT ME TO TAKE YOU?

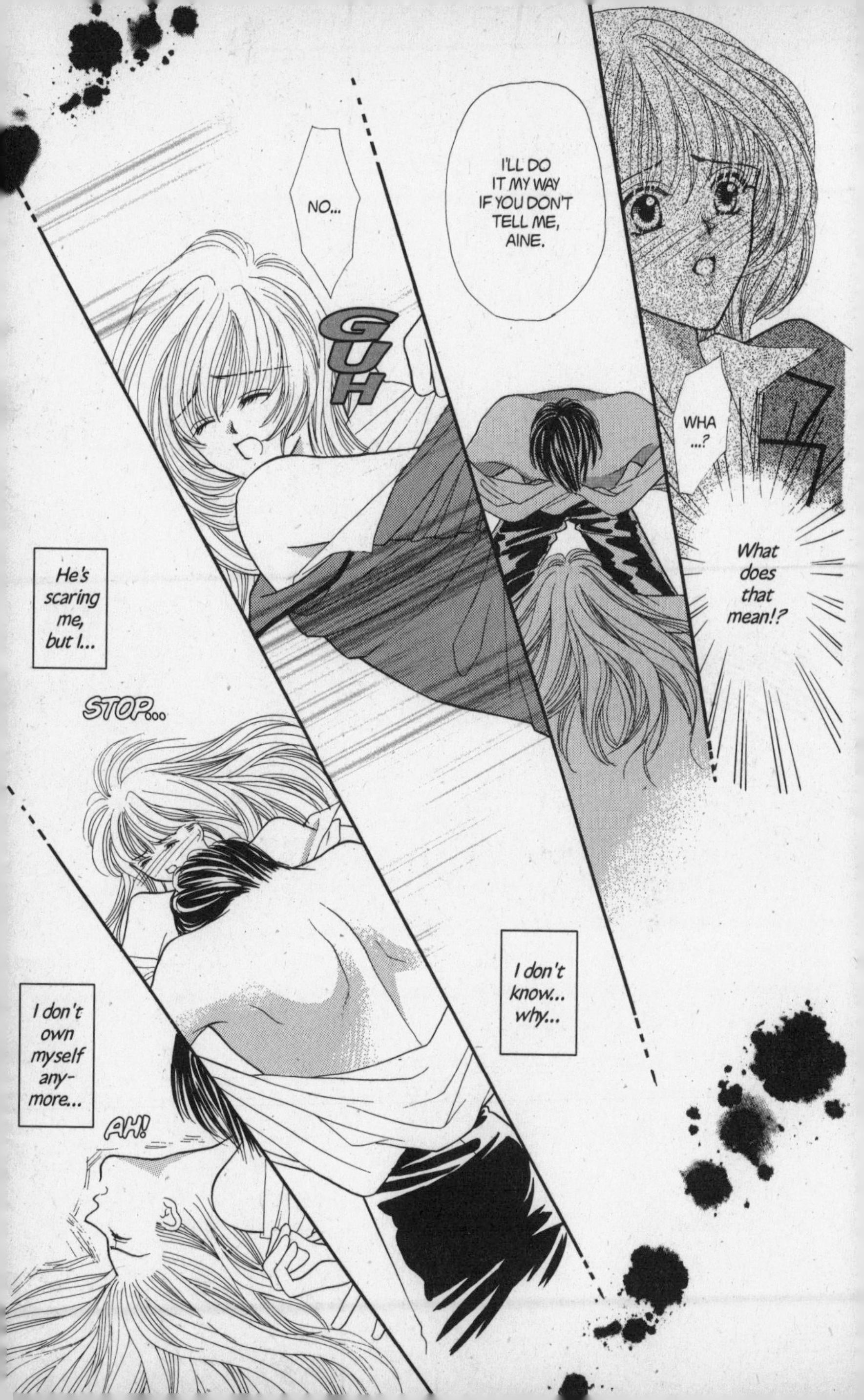
WHA ...?
What does that mean!?
I'LL DO IT MY WAY IF YOU DON'T TELL ME, AINE.
NO...
GUH
I don't know... why...
He's scaring me, but I...
STOP...
I don't own myself any-more...
AH!

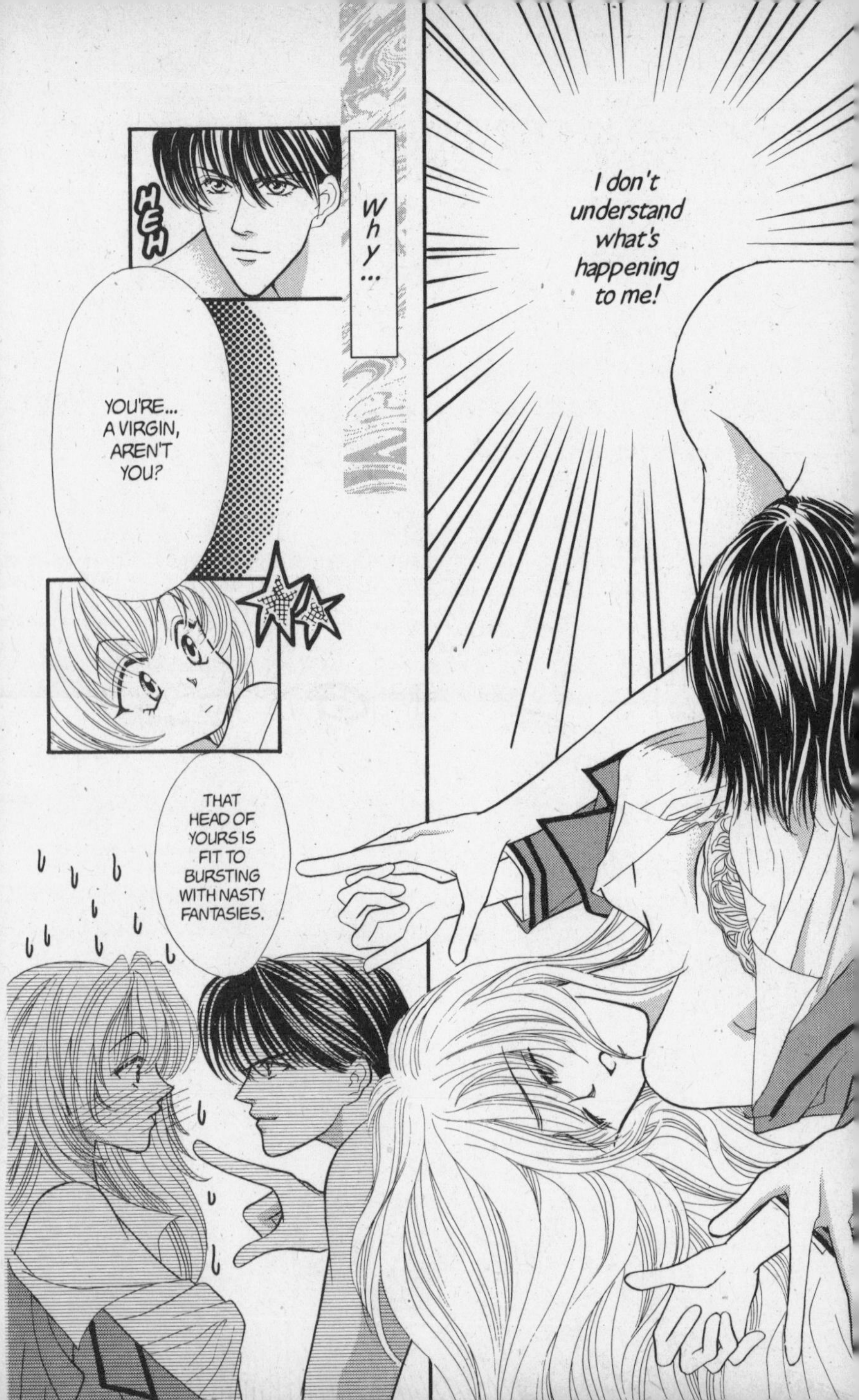
I don't understand what's happening to me!
Why...
HEH
YOU'RE... A VIRGIN, AREN'T YOU?
THAT HEAD OF YOURS IS FIT TO BURSTING WITH NASTY FANTASIES.

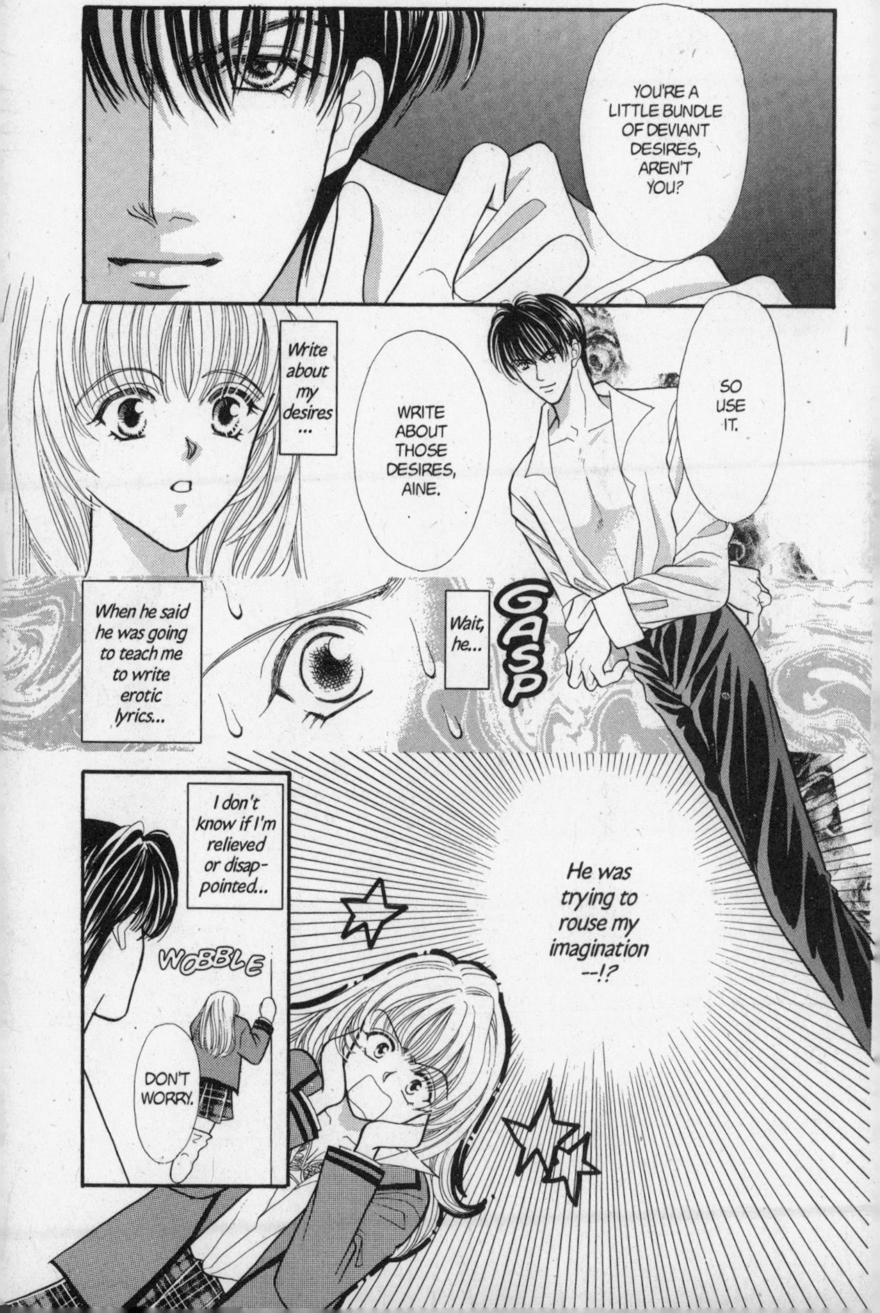
YOU'RE A LITTLE BUNDLE OF DEVIANT DESIRES, AREN'T YOU?
SO USE IT.
WRITE ABOUT THOSE DESIRES, AINE.
Write about my desires...
Wait, he...
GASP
When he said he was going to teach me to write erotic lyrics...
He was trying to rouse my imagination --!?
I don't know if I'm relieved or disap- pointed...
WOBBLE
DON'T WORRY.

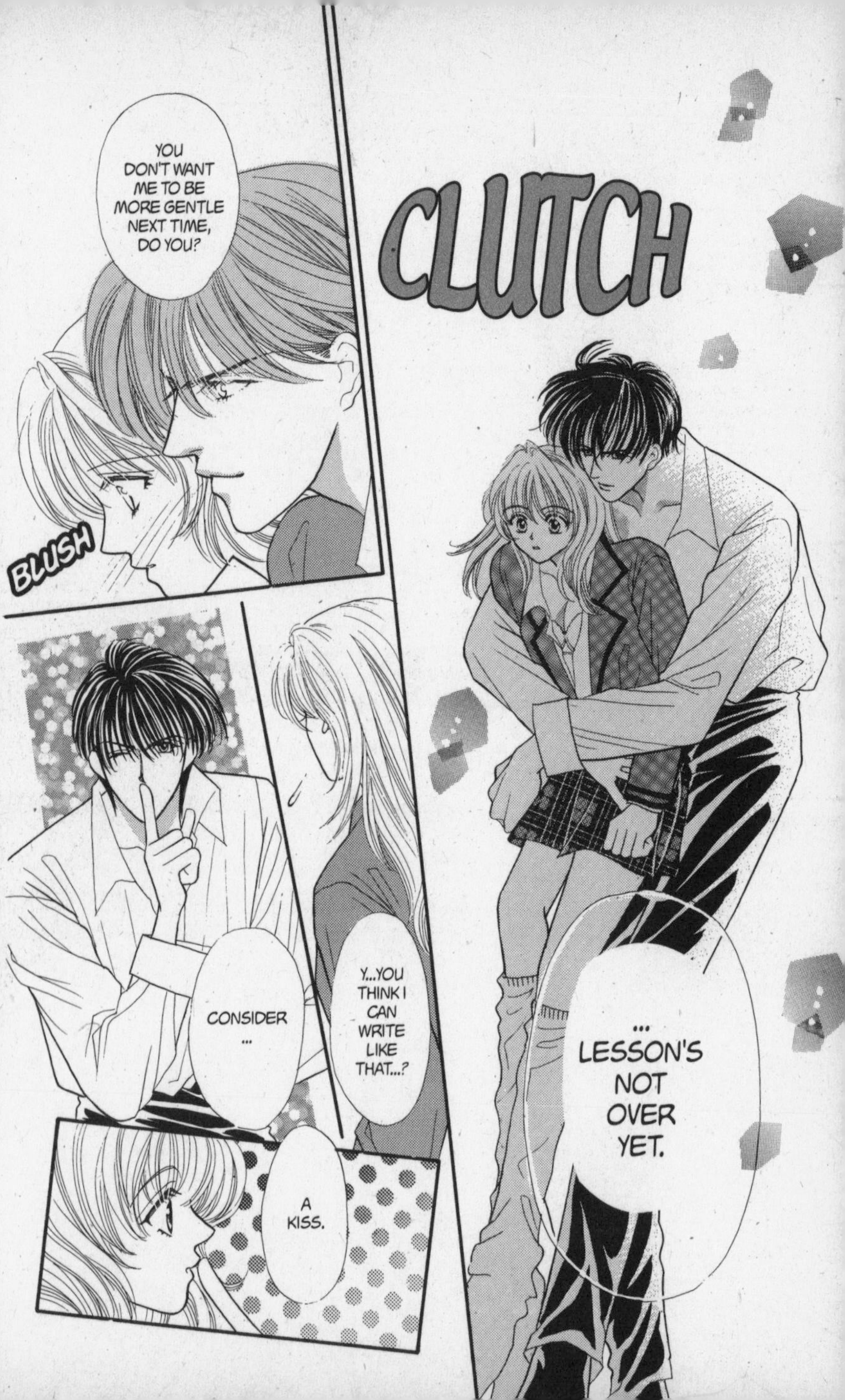
CLUTCH
... LESSON'S NOT OVER YET.
YOU DON'T WANT ME TO BE MORE GENTLE NEXT TIME, DO YOU?
BLUSH
Y...YOU THINK I CAN WRITE LIKE THAT...?
CONSIDER ...
A KISS.

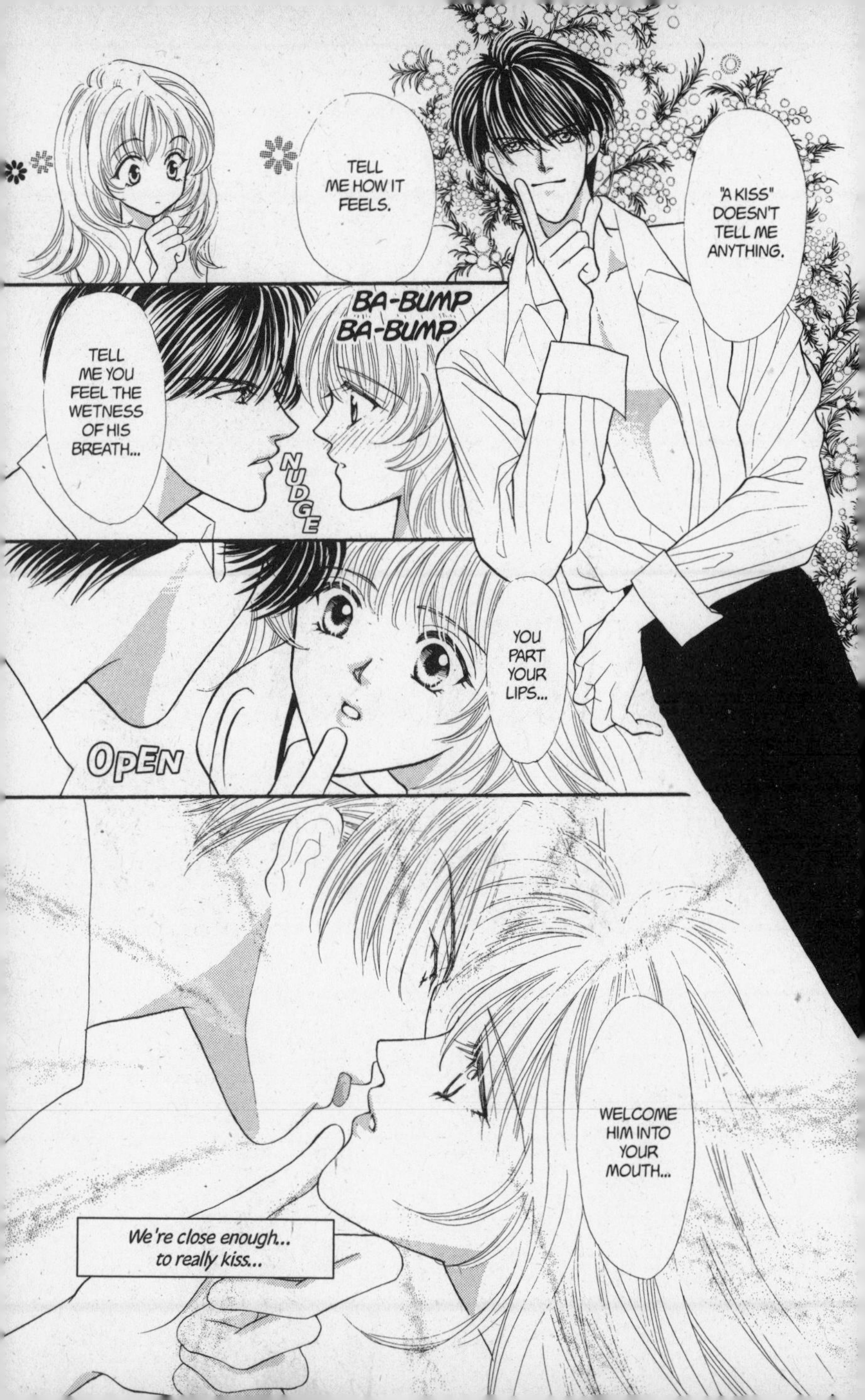
"A KISS" DOESN'T TELL ME ANYTHING.
TELL ME HOW IT FEELS.
BA-BUMP BA-BUMP
TELL ME YOU FEEL THE WETNESS OF HIS BREATH...
NUDGE
YOU PART YOUR LIPS...
OPEN
WELCOME HIM INTO YOUR MOUTH...
We're close enough... to really kiss...

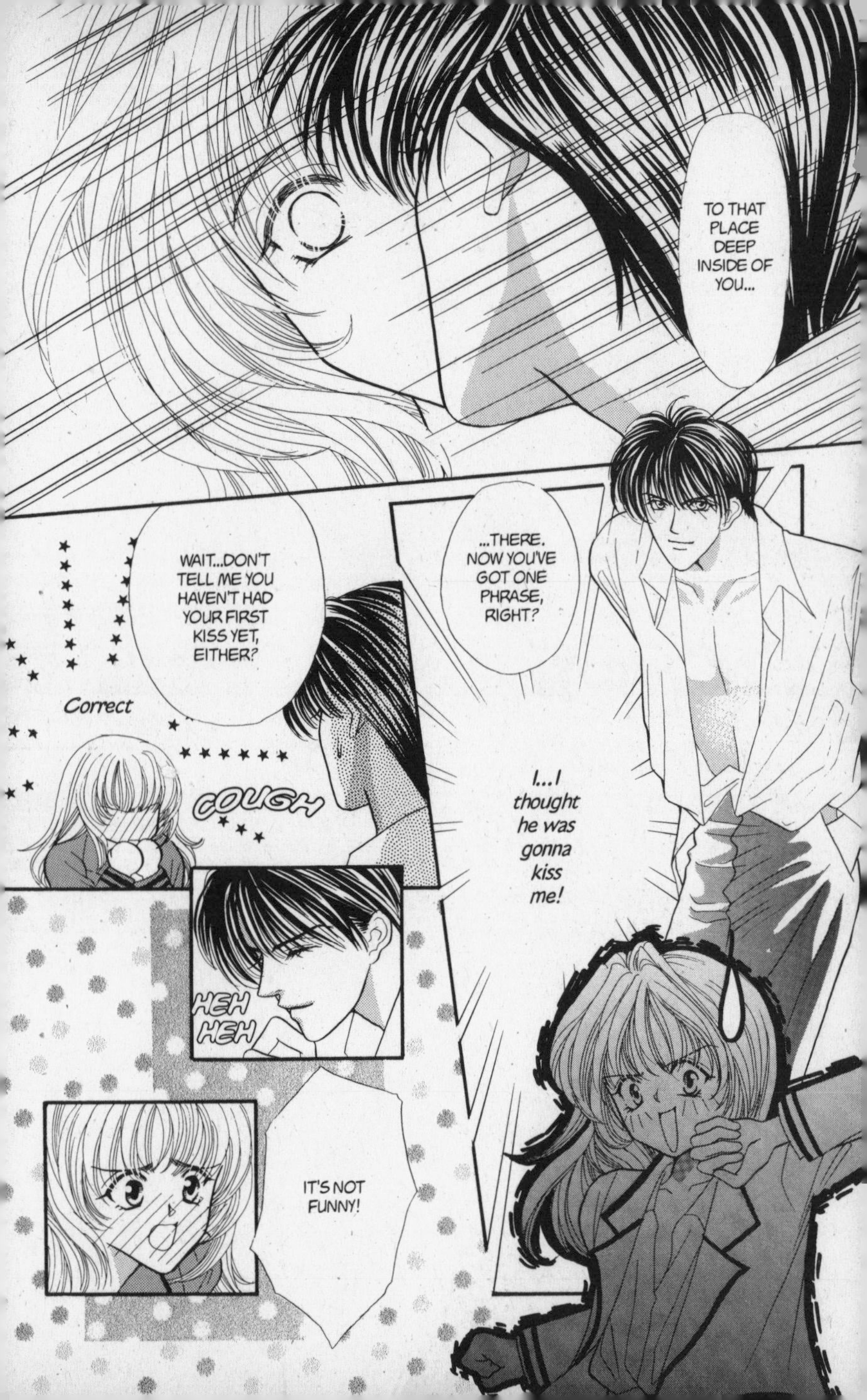
TO THAT PLACE DEEP INSIDE OF YOU...
...THERE. NOW YOU'VE GOT ONE PHRASE, RIGHT?
I...I thought he was gonna kiss me!
WAIT...DON'T TELL ME YOU HAVEN'T HAD YOUR FIRST KISS YET, EITHER?
Correct
COUGH
HEH HEH
IT'S NOT FUNNY!

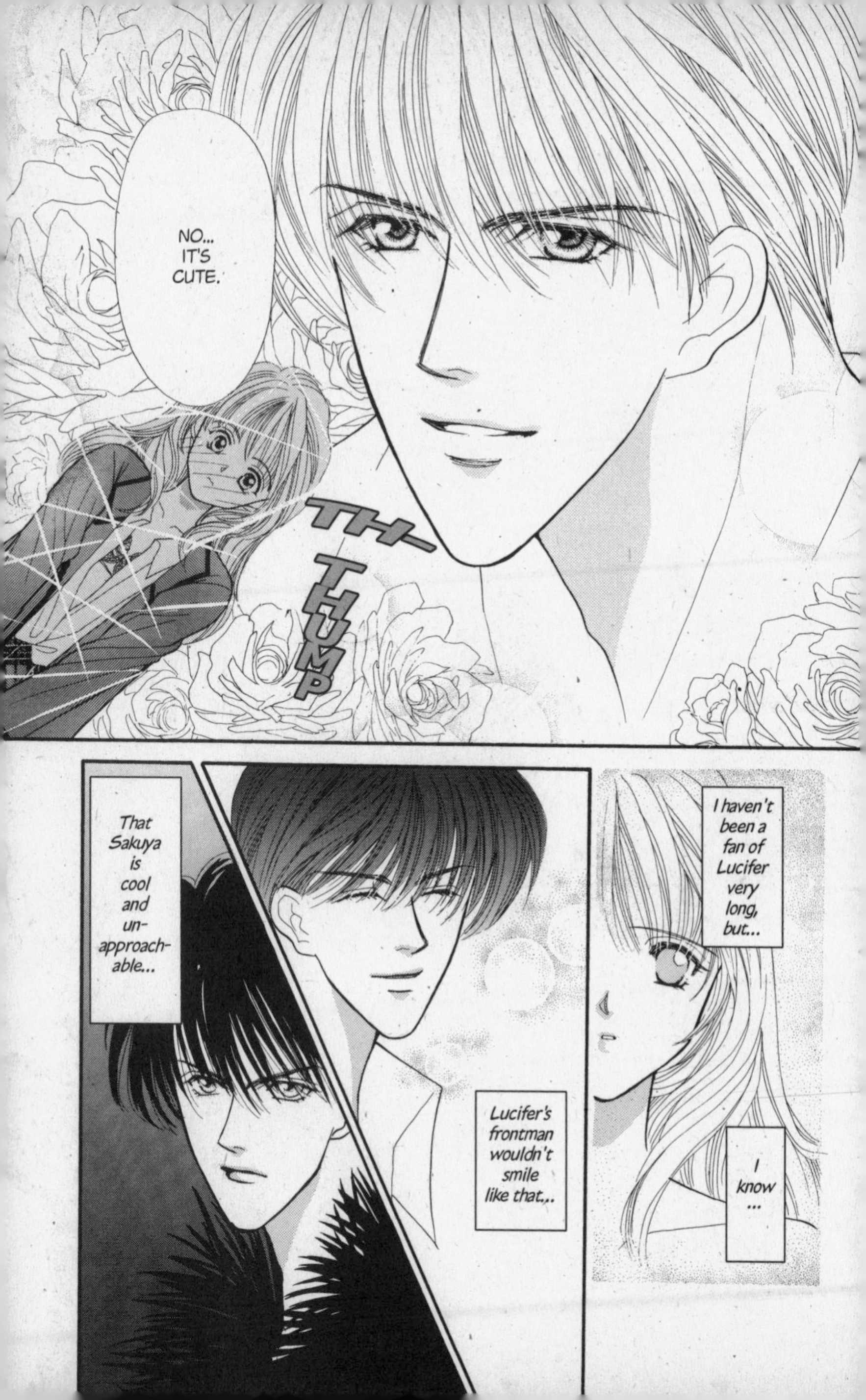
NO... IT'S CUTE.
TH-THUMP
I haven't been a fan of Lucifer very long, but...
I know ...
Lucifer's frontman wouldn't smile like that...
That Sakuya is cool and un-approach-able...

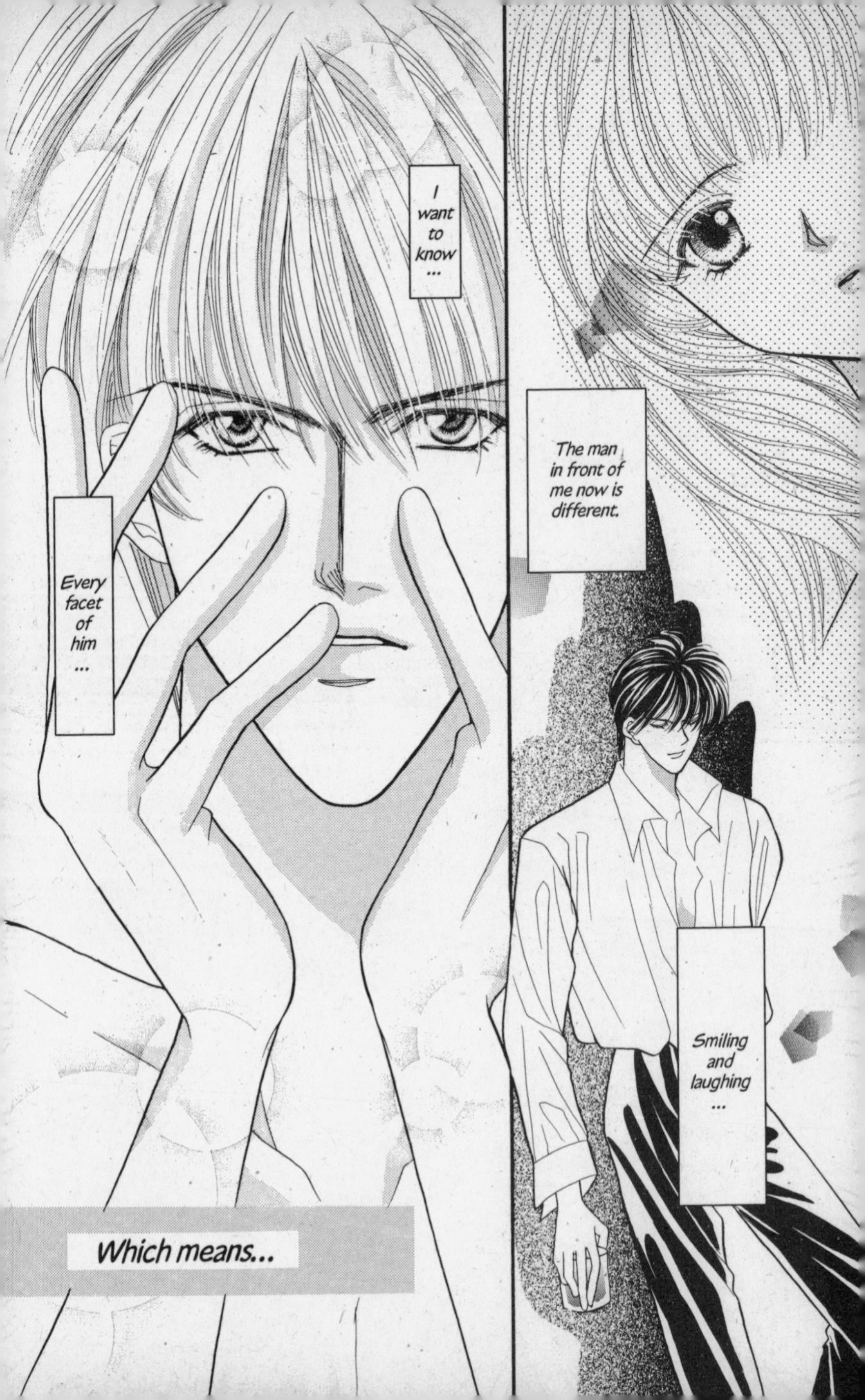
The man in front of me now is different.
Smiling and laughing...
I want to know...
Every facet of him...
Which means...

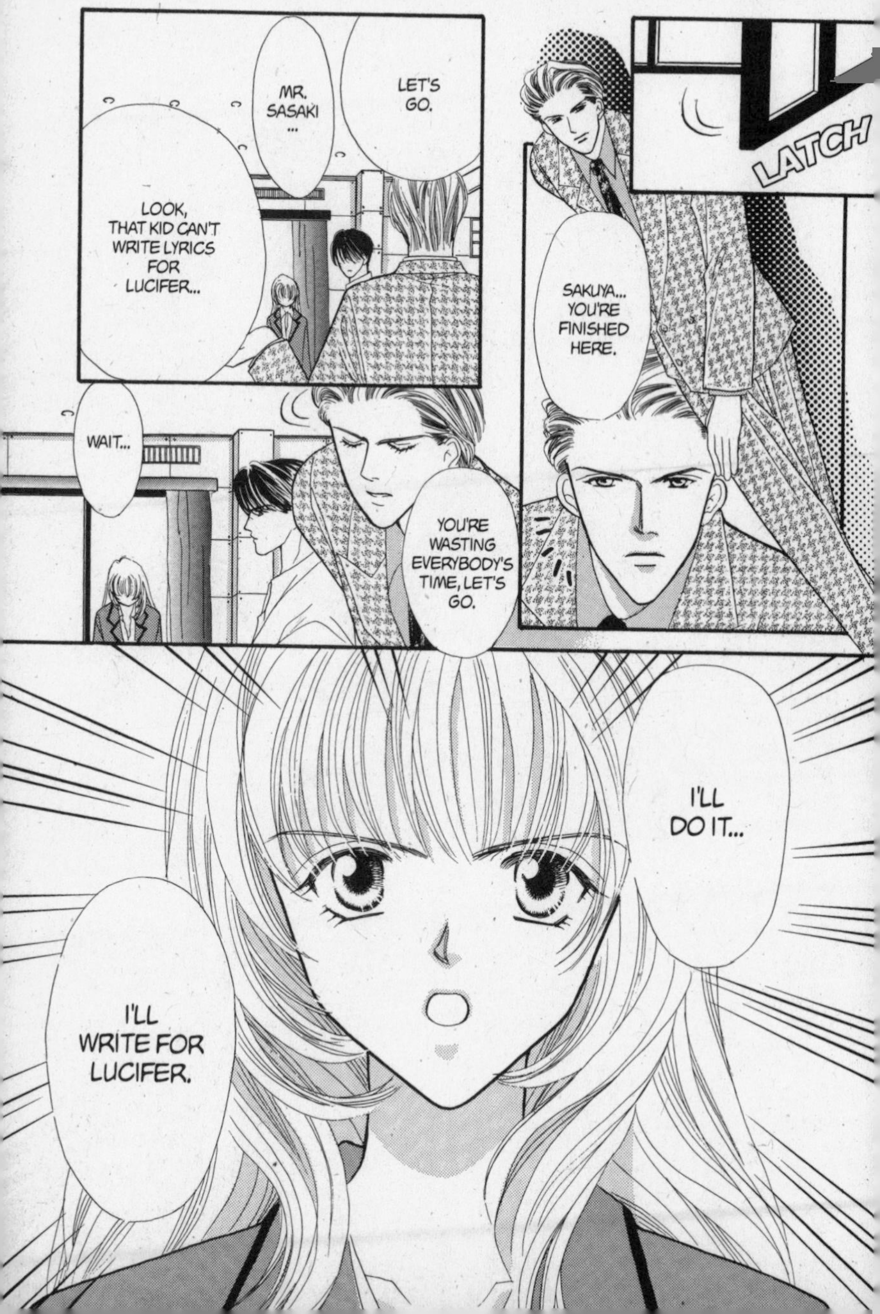
LATCH
SAKUYA... YOU'RE FINISHED HERE.
LET'S GO.
MR. SASAKI ...
LOOK, THAT KID CAN'T WRITE LYRICS FOR LUCIFER...
YOU'RE WASTING EVERYBODY'S TIME, LET'S GO.
WAIT...
I'LL DO IT...
I'LL WRITE FOR LUCIFER.

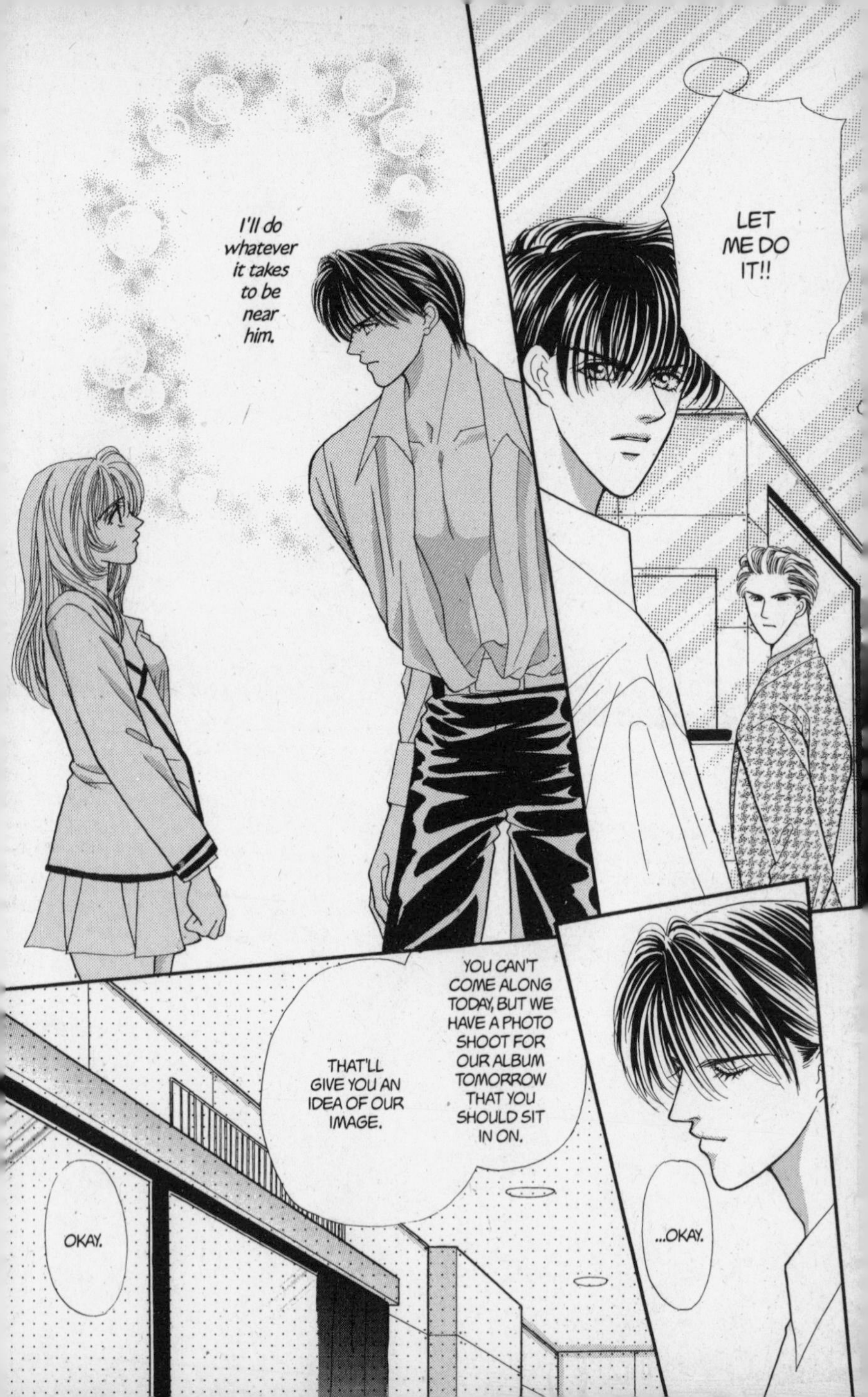
LET ME DO IT!!
I'll do whatever it takes to be near him.
...OKAY.
YOU CAN'T COME ALONG TODAY, BUT WE HAVE A PHOTO SHOOT FOR OUR ALBUM TOMORROW THAT YOU SHOULD SIT IN ON.
THAT'LL GIVE YOU AN IDEA OF OUR IMAGE.
OKAY.

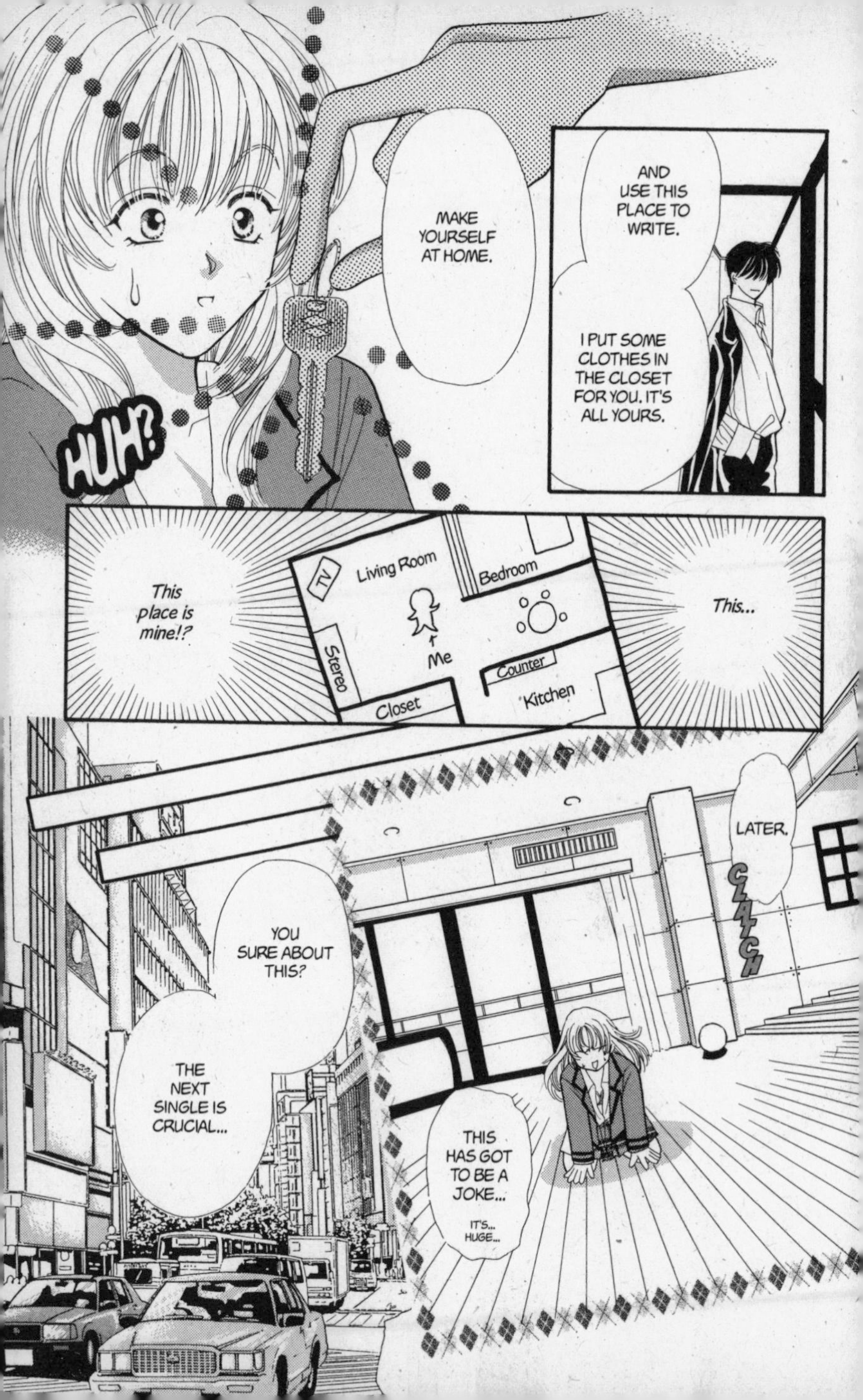
AND USE THIS PLACE TO WRITE.
I PUT SOME CLOTHES IN THE CLOSET FOR YOU. IT'S ALL YOURS.
MAKE YOURSELF AT HOME.
HUH?
This...
Living Room
Bedroom
TV
Stereo
Me
Counter
Kitchen
Closet
This place is mine!?
LATER.
CLATCH
THIS HAS GOT TO BE A JOKE...
IT'S... HUGE...
YOU SURE ABOUT THIS?
THE NEXT SINGLE IS CRUCIAL...

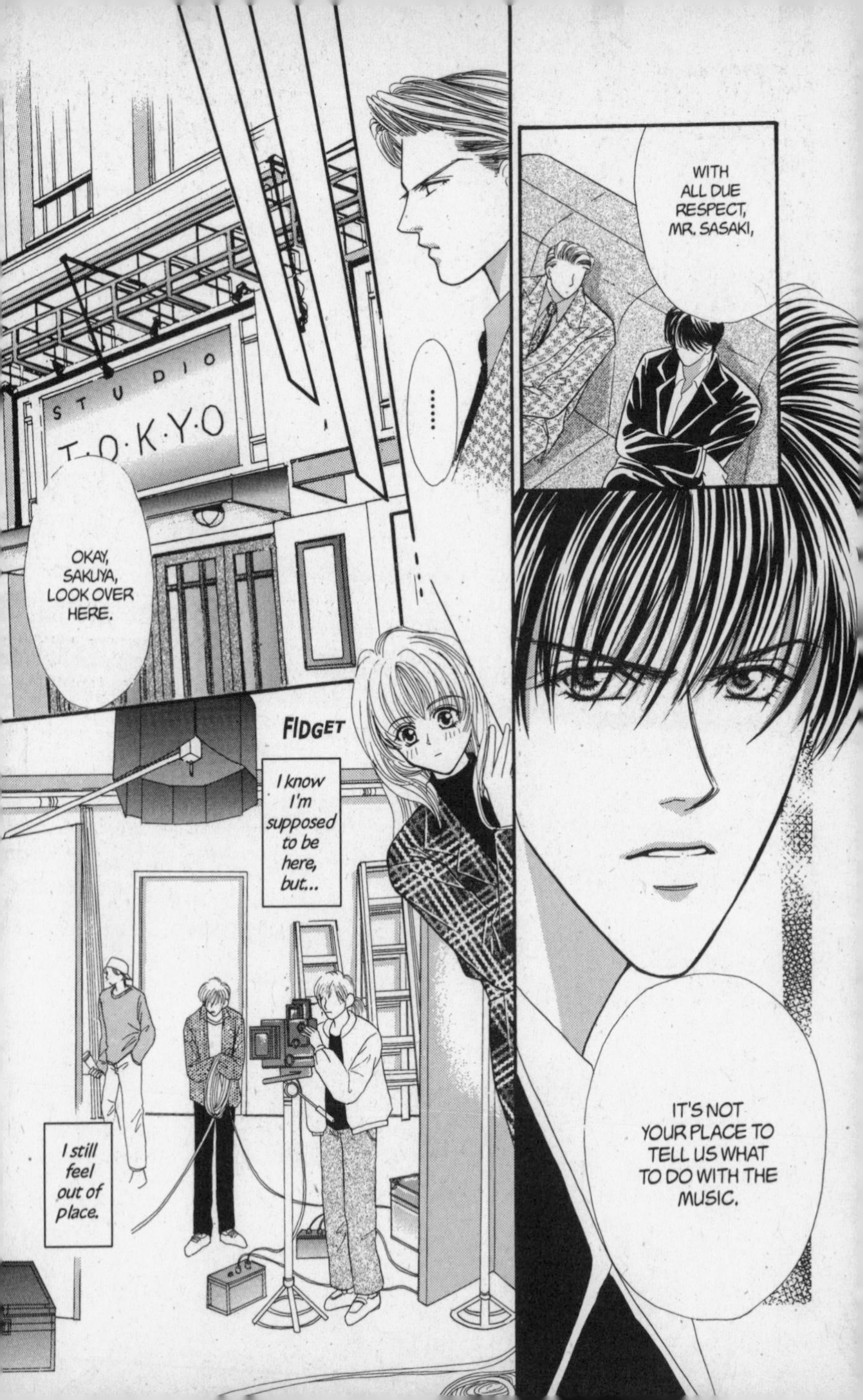
WITH ALL DUE RESPECT, MR. SASAKI,
IT'S NOT YOUR PLACE TO TELL US WHAT TO DO WITH THE MUSIC.
......
STUDIO T·O·K·Y·O
OKAY, SAKUYA, LOOK OVER HERE.
FIDGET
I know I'm supposed to be here, but...
I still feel out of place.

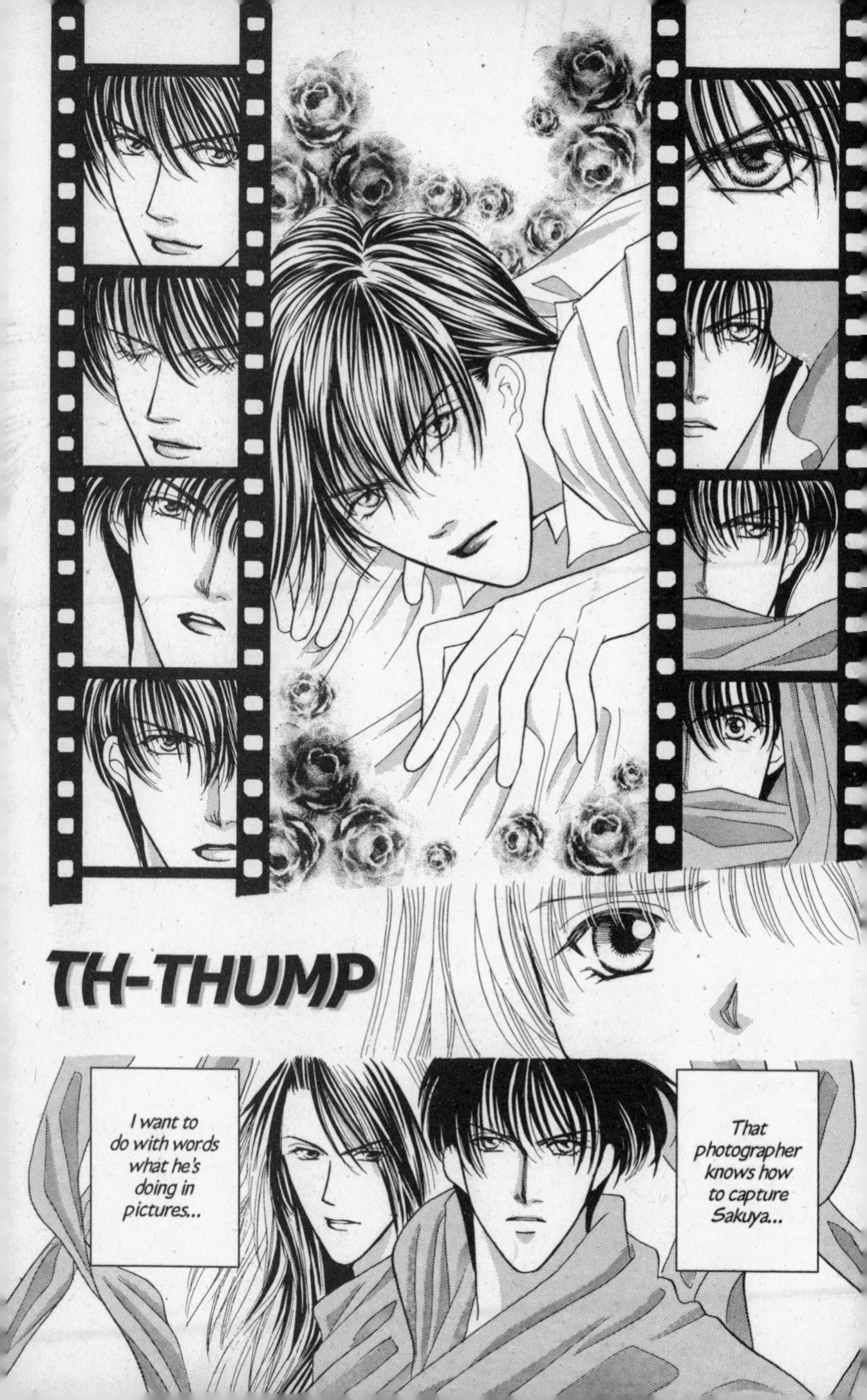
TH-THUMP
That photographer knows how to capture Sakuya...
I want to do with words what he's doing in pictures...

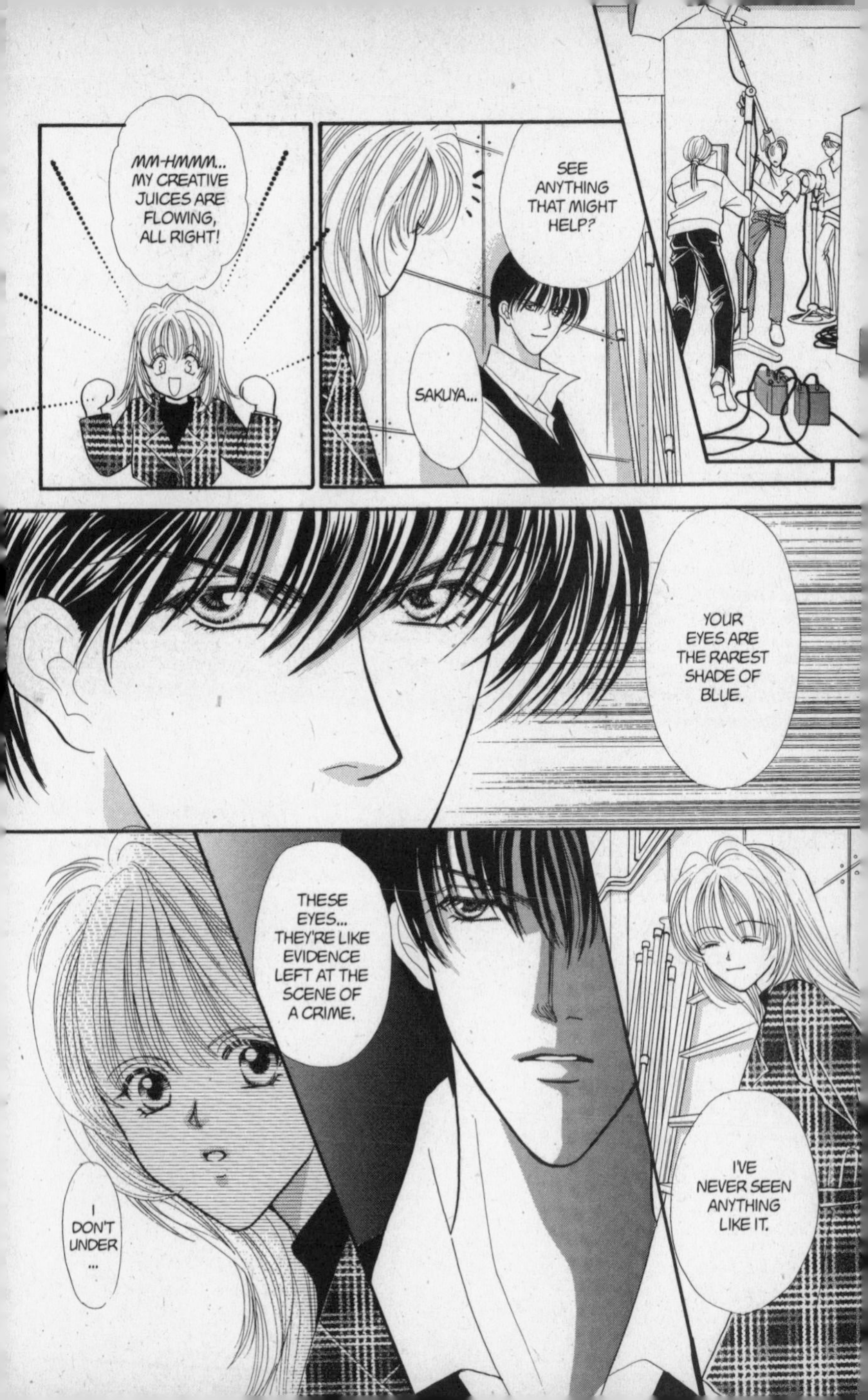
SEE ANYTHING THAT MIGHT HELP?
SAKUYA...
MM-HMMM... MY CREATIVE JUICES ARE FLOWING, ALL RIGHT!
YOUR EYES ARE THE RAREST SHADE OF BLUE.
THESE EYES... THEY'RE LIKE EVIDENCE LEFT AT THE SCENE OF A CRIME.
I'VE NEVER SEEN ANYTHING LIKE IT.
I DON'T UNDER ...

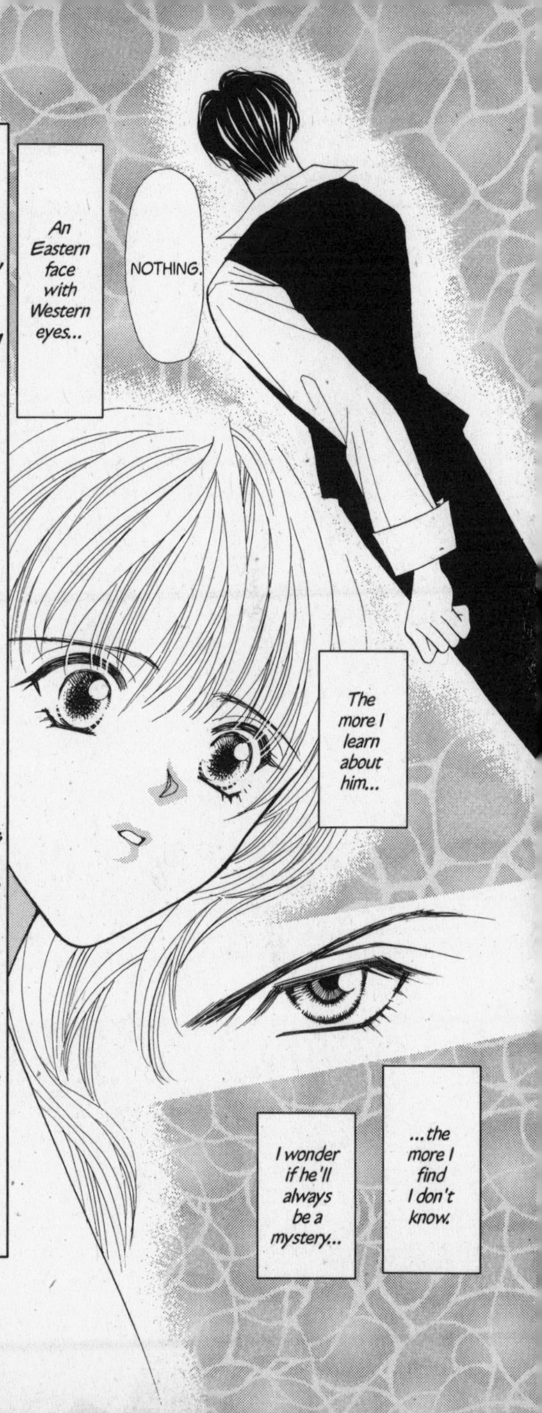
NOTHING.
An Eastern face with Western eyes...
The more I learn about him...
...the more I find I don't know.
I wonder if he'll always be a mystery...

(Continuation)

Like an investigative reporter, I grilled for details about recording artists - personality quirks, schedules, day-to-day life. And when I was done with that research - I did more! (When I started, I knew less about 'Visual bands' than I did about straight-up rock'n'roll, if you can believe it. I considered boy band TOKIO a rock band. Haha!)

Since so many of you wrote to insist that Sakuya was Ryuichi Kawamura, I looked into it. I started watching videos and soaps, buying CDs and magazines. I learned a lot. I looked into Hyde of L'ARC-EN-CIEL too, since Lucifer is a Visual band, as well. I bet that's why some of you thought Sakuya was Koshi Inaba of B'z...it makes sense. B'z has some sexy lyrics!! (Or maybe it was that Sakuya's hairstyle looks like Inaba's old one...?)

Around the time of "Risky", I fell madly in love with Inaba. The "Bad Communication" video was so hot I thought I was going to pass out! I still want to get my hands on that video. Anybody else remember when "Bad Communication" was used in a Fujitsu commercial...? Maybe I'm the only one who's that obsessed!

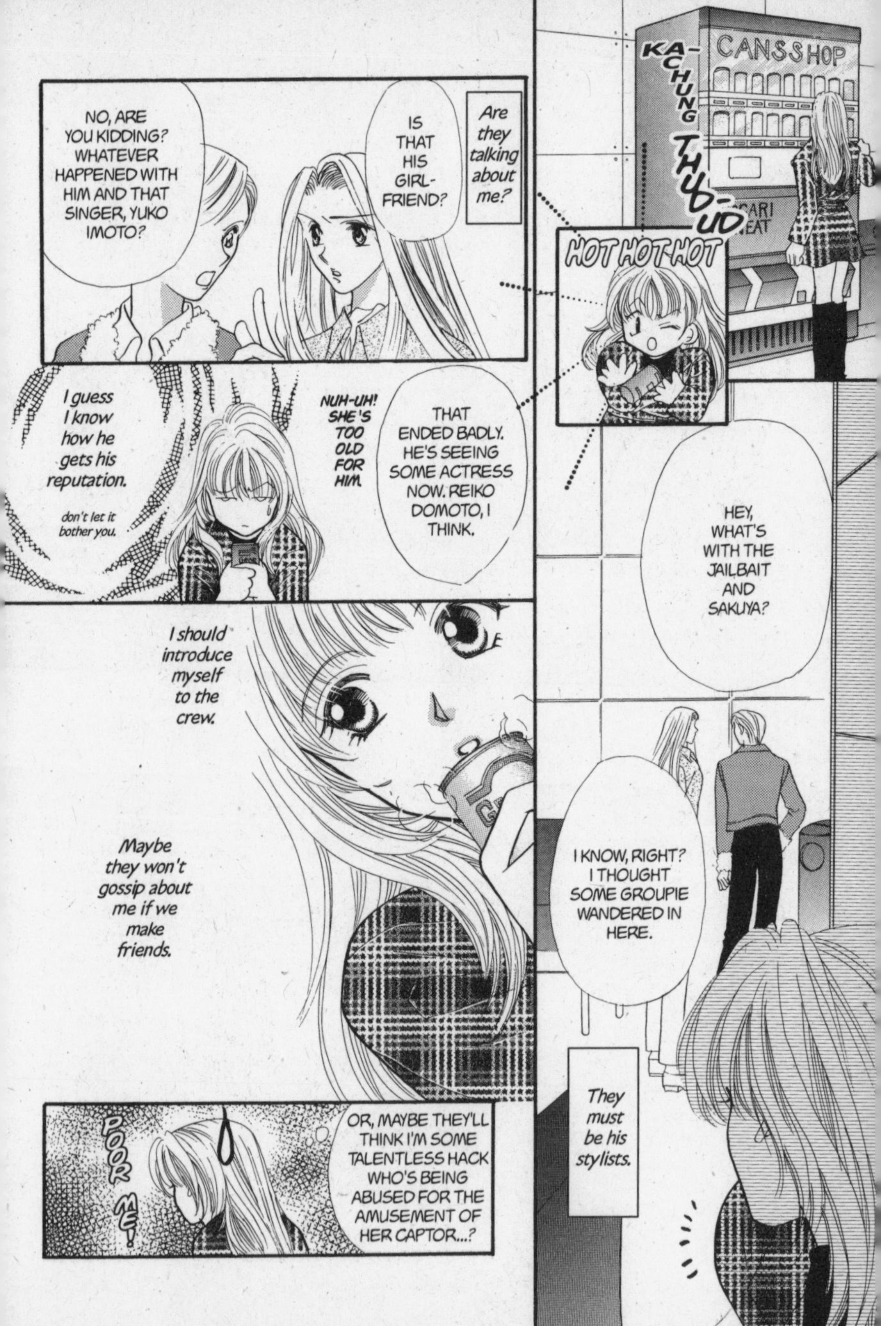

KA-CHUNG
THUD
CANSSHOP
HOT HOT HOT
HEY, WHAT'S WITH THE JAILBAIT AND SAKUYA?
I KNOW, RIGHT? I THOUGHT SOME GROUPIE WANDERED IN HERE.
They must be his stylists.
Are they talking about me?
IS THAT HIS GIRL-FRIEND?
NO, ARE YOU KIDDING? WHATEVER HAPPENED WITH HIM AND THAT SINGER, YUKO IMOTO?
THAT ENDED BADLY. HE'S SEEING SOME ACTRESS NOW. REIKO DOMOTO, I THINK.
NUH-UH! SHE'S TOO OLD FOR HIM.
I guess I know how he gets his reputation.
don't let it bother you.
I should introduce myself to the crew.
Maybe they won't gossip about me if we make friends.
OR, MAYBE THEY'LL THINK I'M SOME TALENTLESS HACK WHO'S BEING ABUSED FOR THE AMUSEMENT OF HER CAPTOR...?
POOR ME!

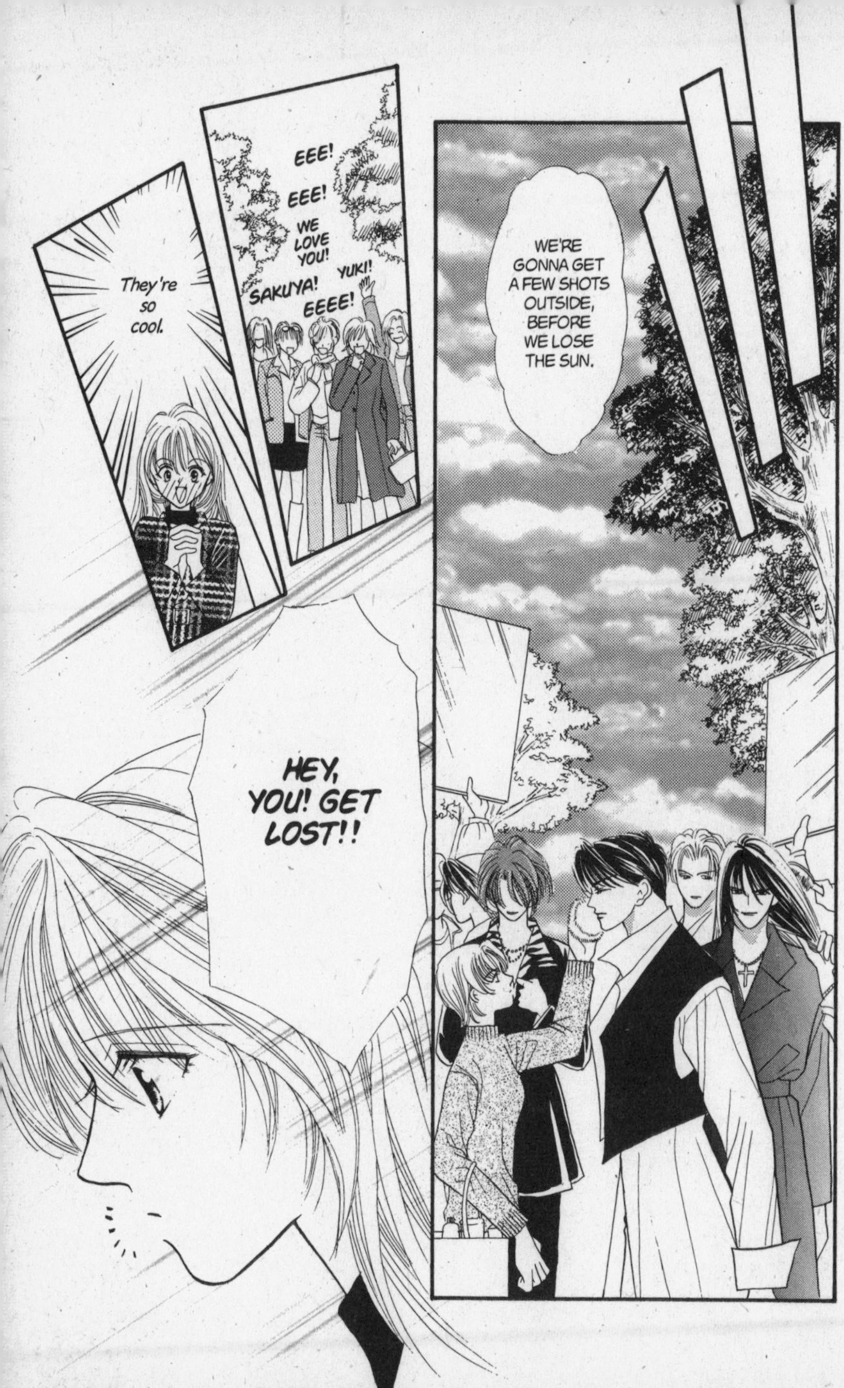
WE'RE GONNA GET A FEW SHOTS OUTSIDE, BEFORE WE LOSE THE SUN.
EEE!
EEE!
WE LOVE YOU!
YUKI!
SAKUYA!
EEEE!
They're so cool.
HEY, YOU! GET LOST!!

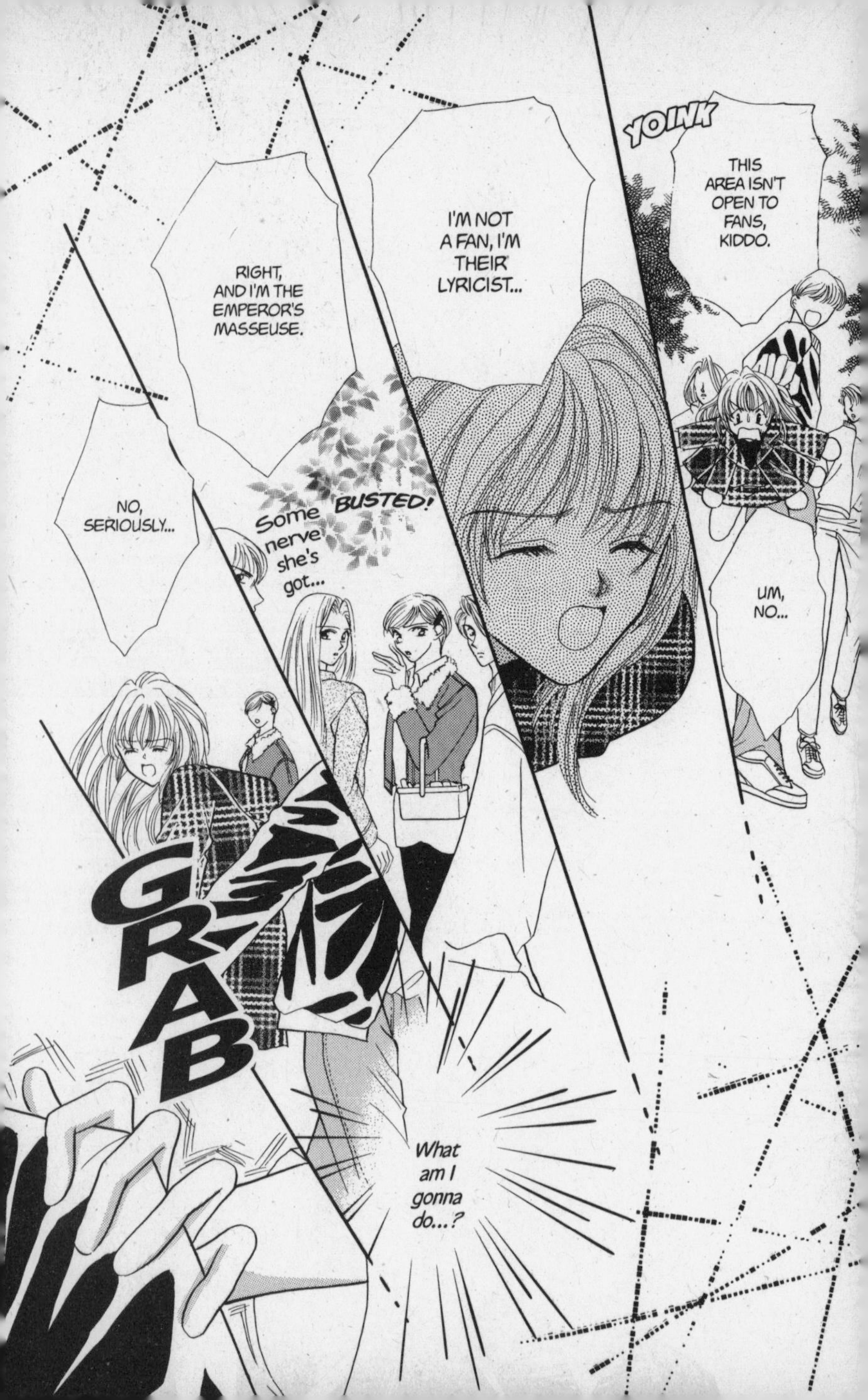
YOINK
THIS AREA ISN'T OPEN TO FANS, KIDDO.
UM, NO...
I'M NOT A FAN, I'M THEIR LYRICIST...
BUSTED!
RIGHT, AND I'M THE EMPEROR'S MASSEUSE.
Some nerve she's got...
NO, SERIOUSLY...
GRAB
What am I gonna do...?

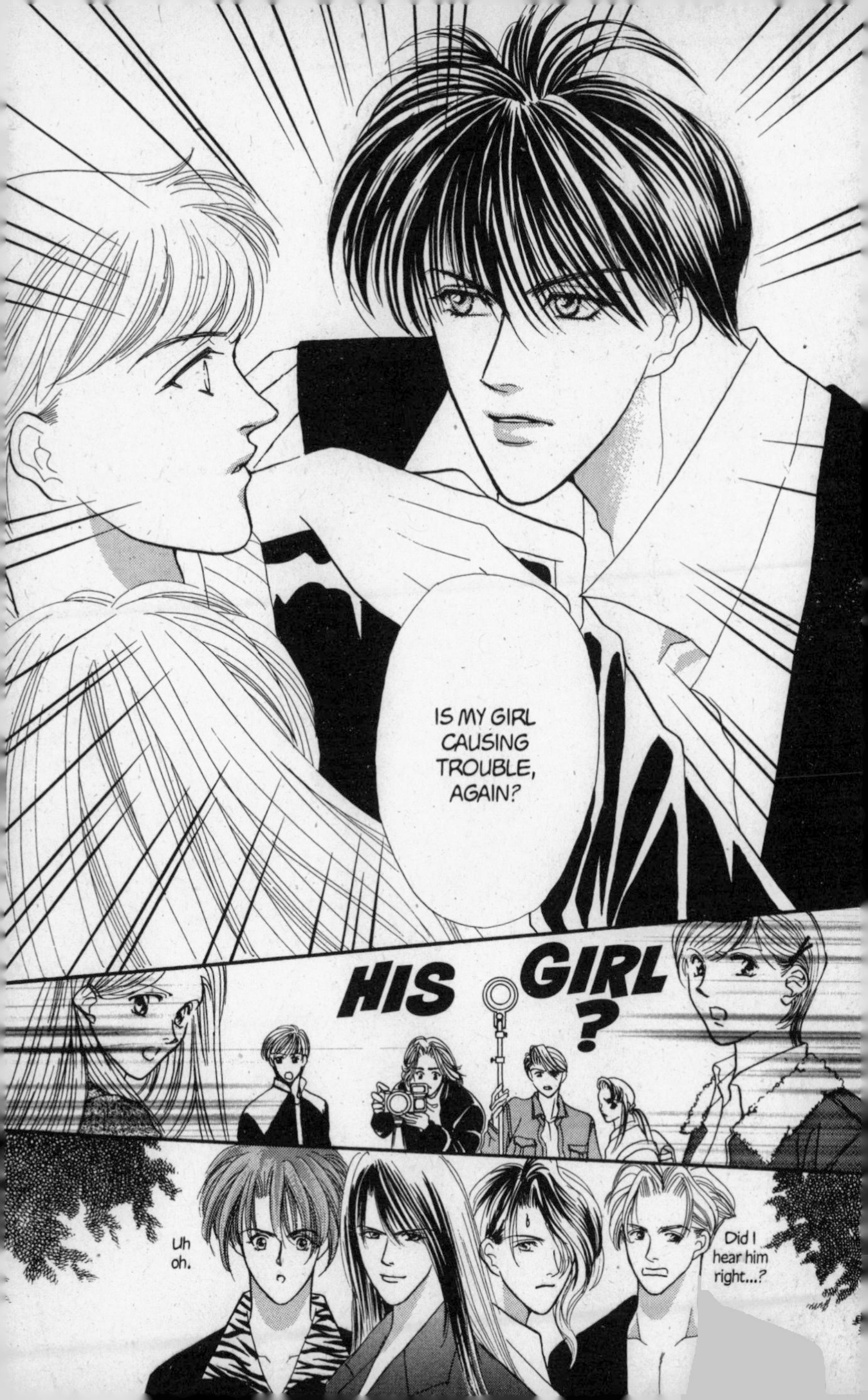
IS MY GIRL CAUSING TROUBLE, AGAIN?
HIS GIRL ?
Did I hear him right...?
Uh oh.

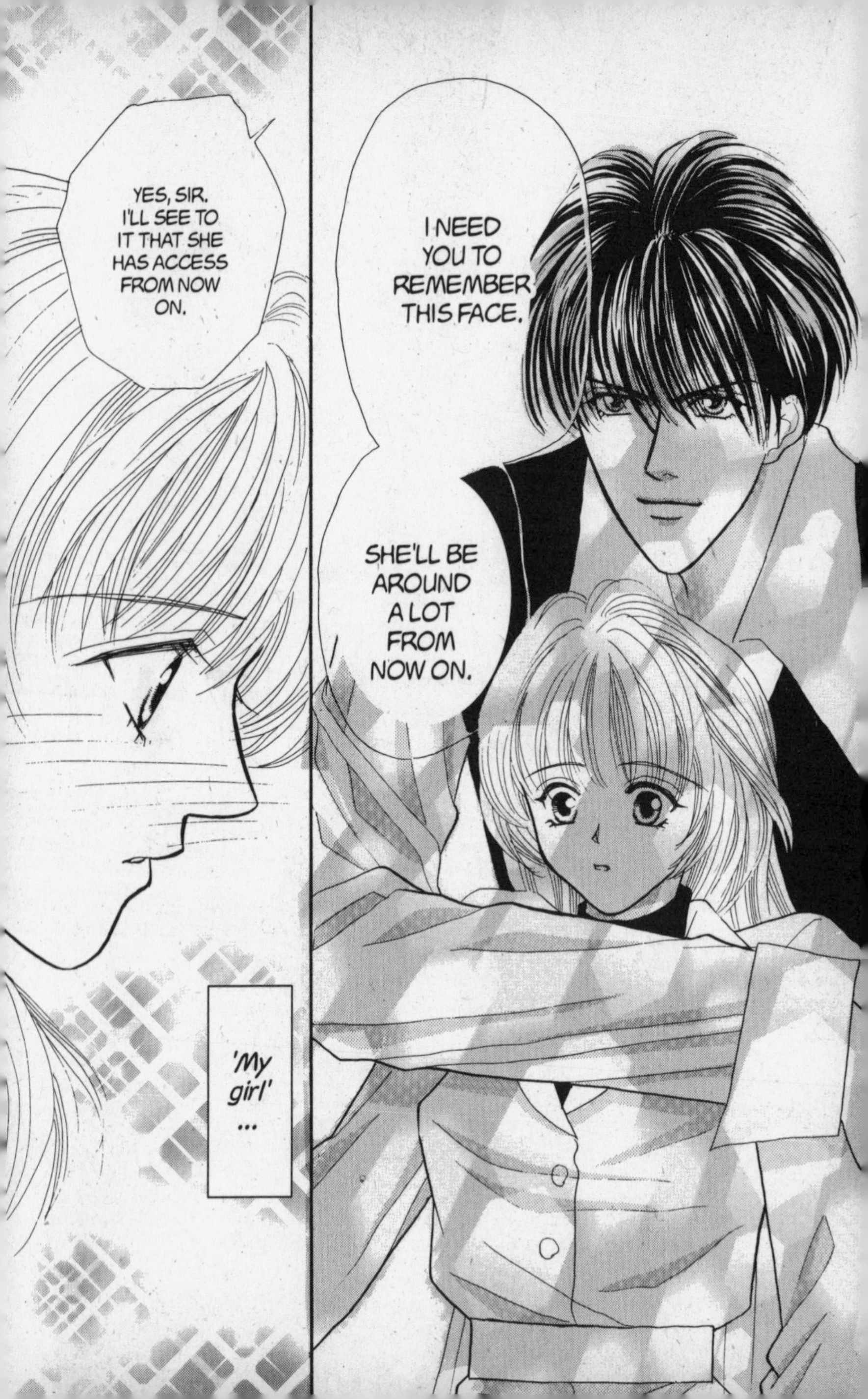
I NEED YOU TO REMEMBER THIS FACE.
SHE'LL BE AROUND A LOT FROM NOW ON.
YES, SIR. I'LL SEE TO IT THAT SHE HAS ACCESS FROM NOW ON.
'My girl' ...

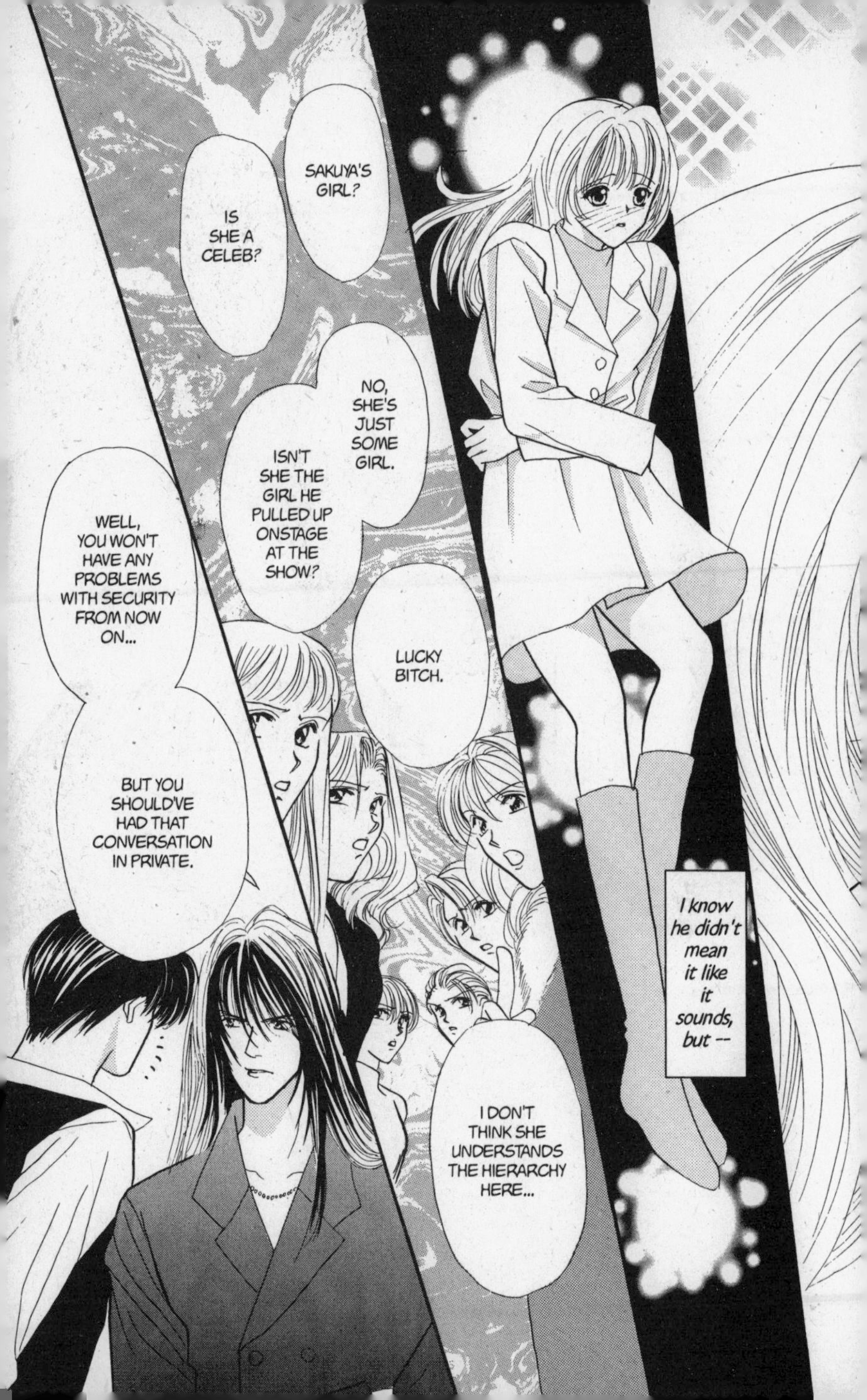

I know he didn't mean it like it sounds, but --
SAKUYA'S GIRL?
IS SHE A CELEB?
NO, SHE'S JUST SOME GIRL.
ISN'T SHE THE GIRL HE PULLED UP ONSTAGE AT THE SHOW?
LUCKY BITCH.
I DON'T THINK SHE UNDERSTANDS THE HIERARCHY HERE...
WELL, YOU WON'T HAVE ANY PROBLEMS WITH SECURITY FROM NOW ON...
BUT YOU SHOULD'VE HAD THAT CONVERSATION IN PRIVATE.

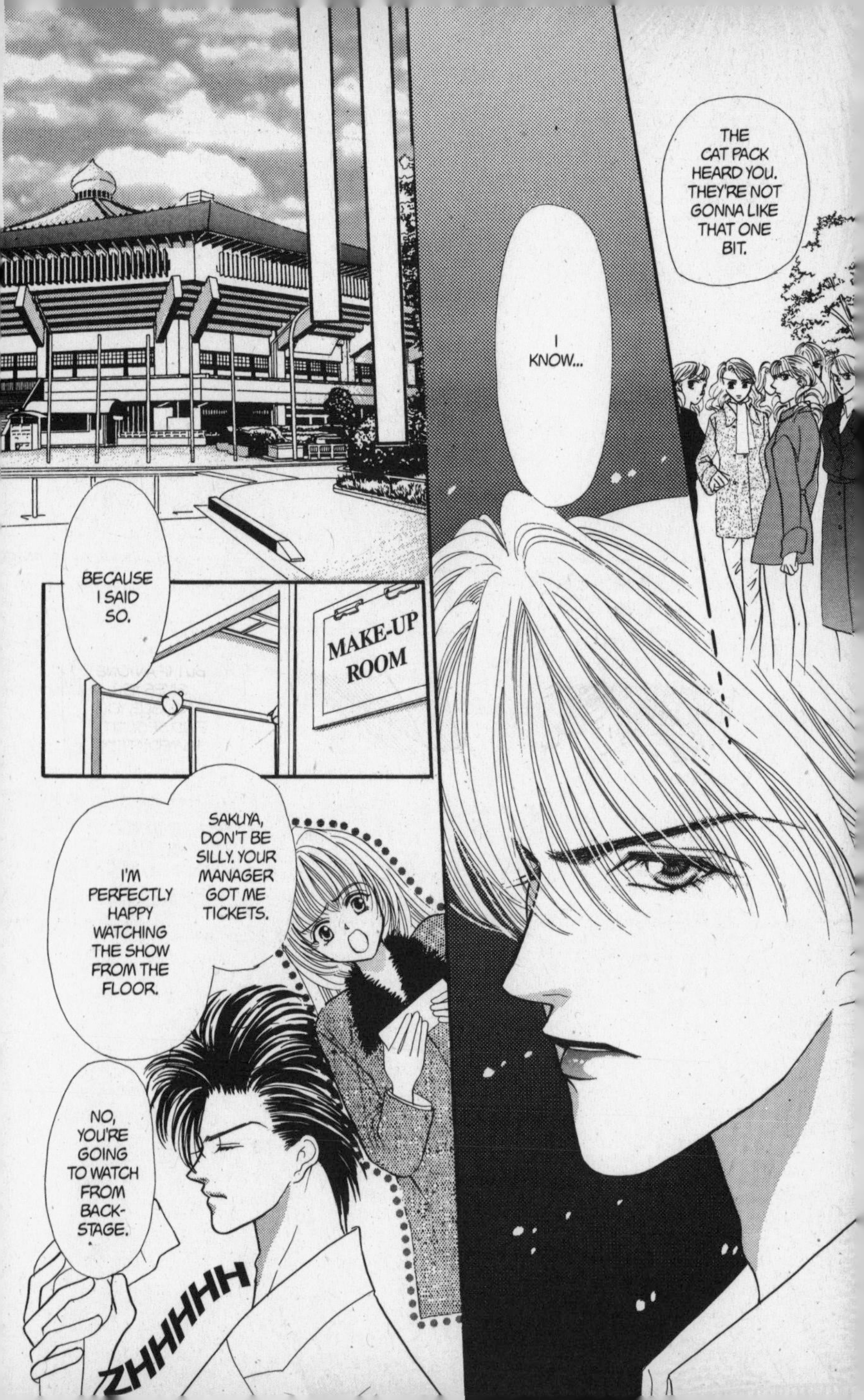
THE CAT PACK HEARD YOU. THEY'RE NOT GONNA LIKE THAT ONE BIT.
I KNOW...
BECAUSE I SAID SO.
MAKE-UP ROOM
SAKUYA, DON'T BE SILLY. YOUR MANAGER GOT ME TICKETS.
I'M PERFECTLY HAPPY WATCHING THE SHOW FROM THE FLOOR.
NO, YOU'RE GOING TO WATCH FROM BACK-STAGE.
ZHHHHH

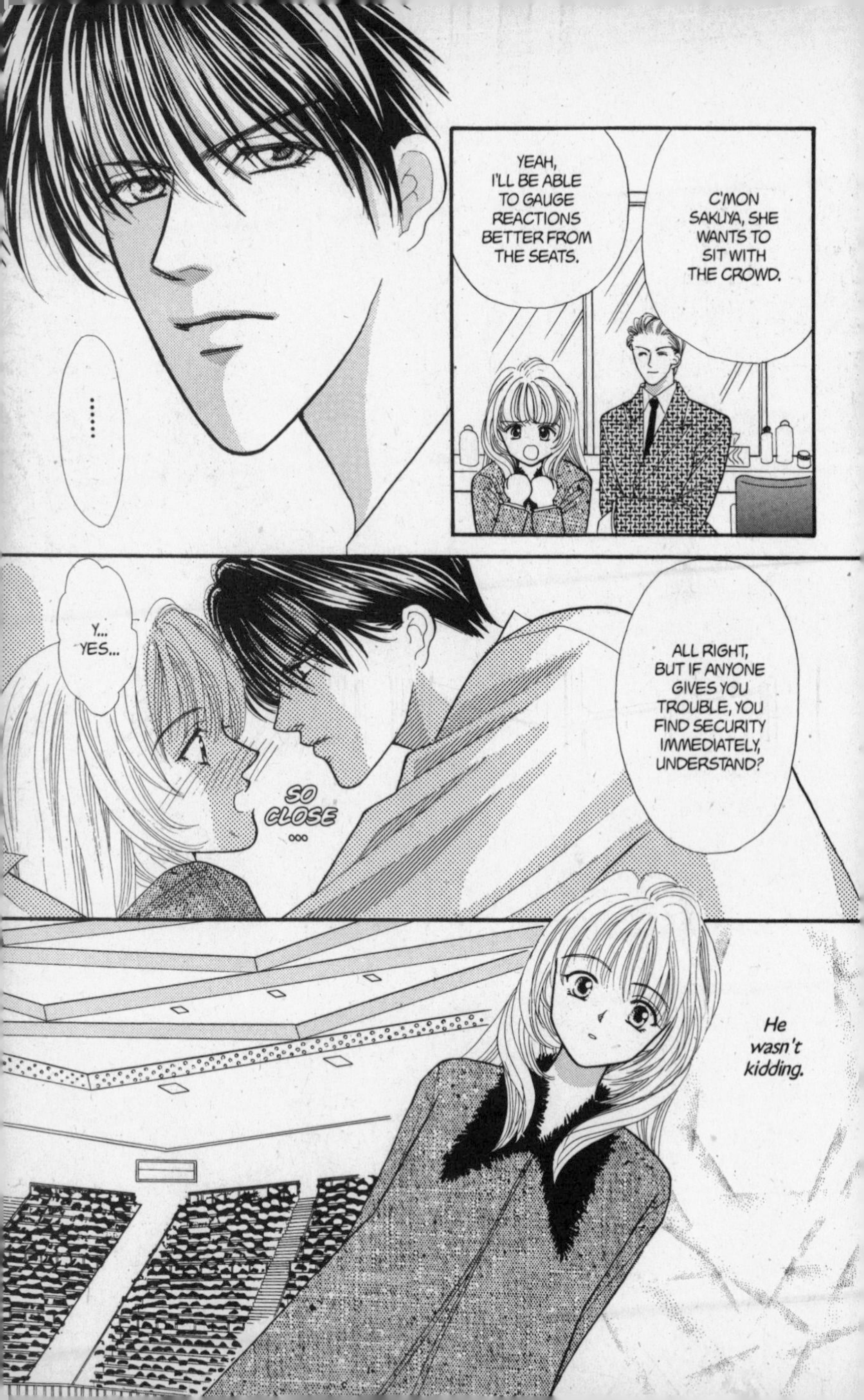
C'MON SAKUYA, SHE WANTS TO SIT WITH THE CROWD.
YEAH, I'LL BE ABLE TO GAUGE REACTIONS BETTER FROM THE SEATS.
......
ALL RIGHT, BUT IF ANYONE GIVES YOU TROUBLE, YOU FIND SECURITY IMMEDIATELY, UNDERSTAND?
SO CLOSE ...
Y... YES...
He wasn't kidding.

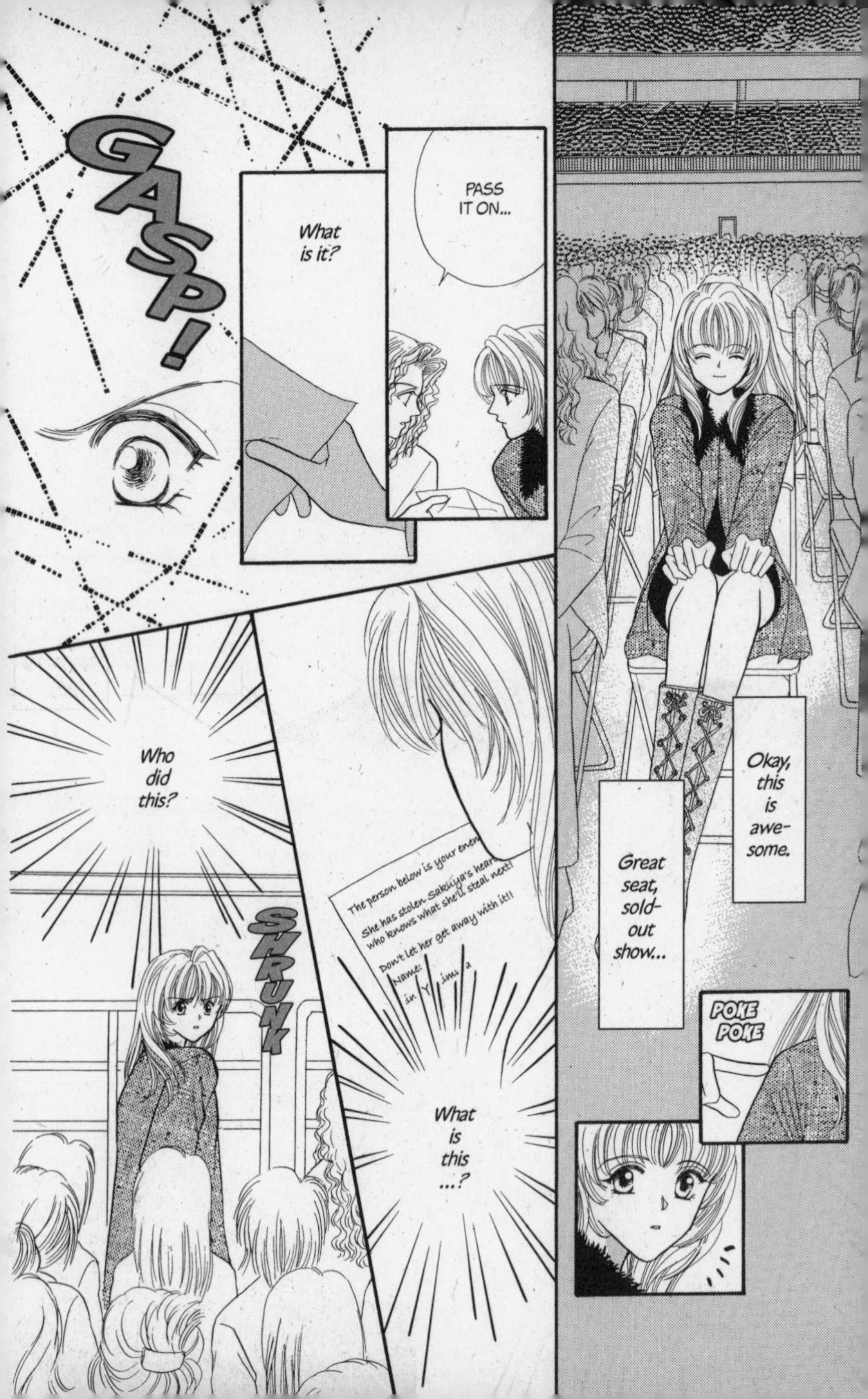
Okay, this is awe-some.
Great seat, sold-out show...
POKE POKE
PASS IT ON...
What is it?
GASP!
who knows what she'll steal next!
Don't let her get away with it!!
Name:
What is this ...?
Who did this?
SHRUNK

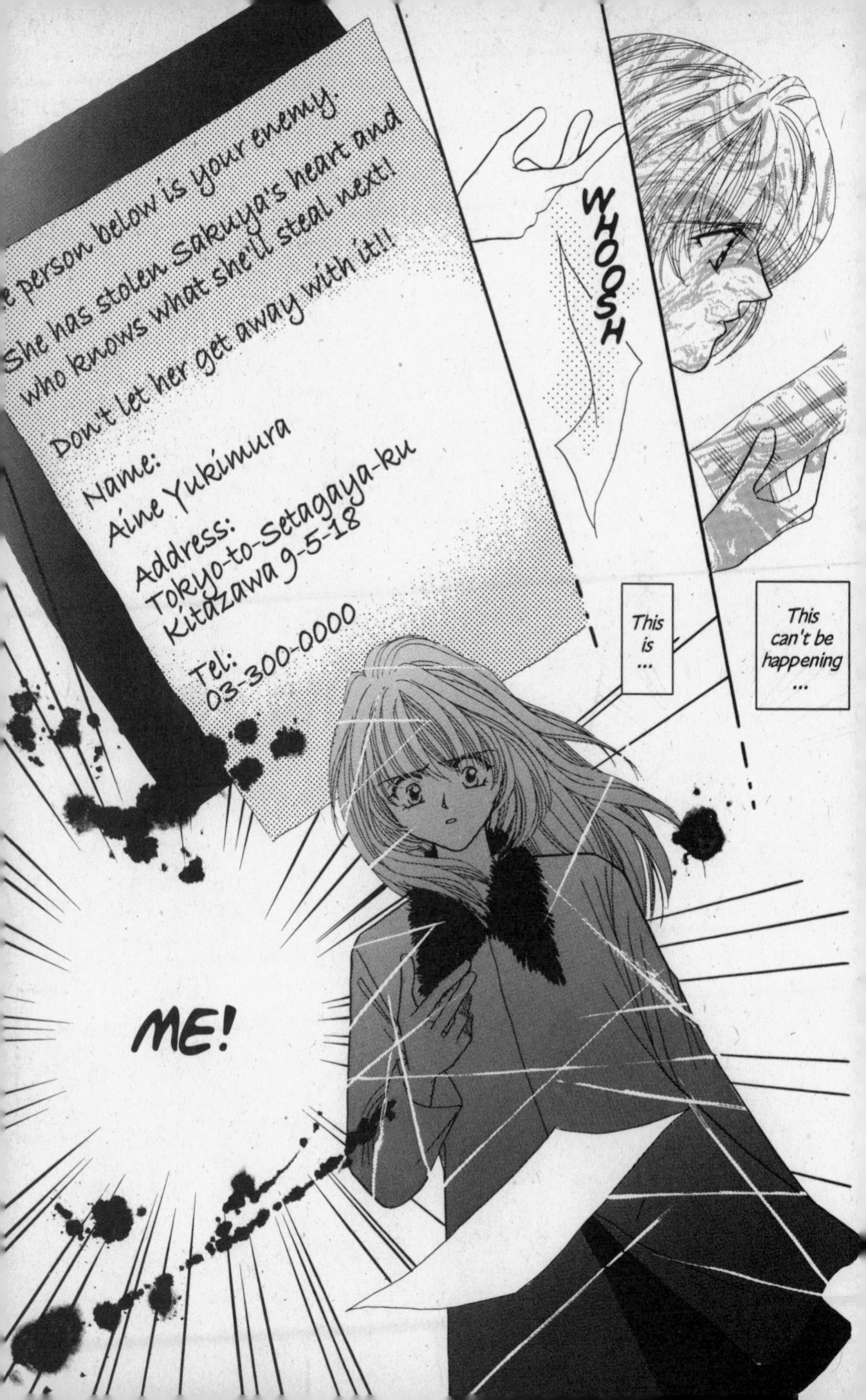
e person below is your enemy.
She has stolen Sakuya's heart and
who knows what she'll steal next!
Don't let her get away with it!!
Name:
Aine Yukimura
Address:
Tokyo-to-Setagaya-ku
Kitazawa 9-5-18
Tel:
03-300-0000
WHOOSH
This can't be happening...
This is...
ME!

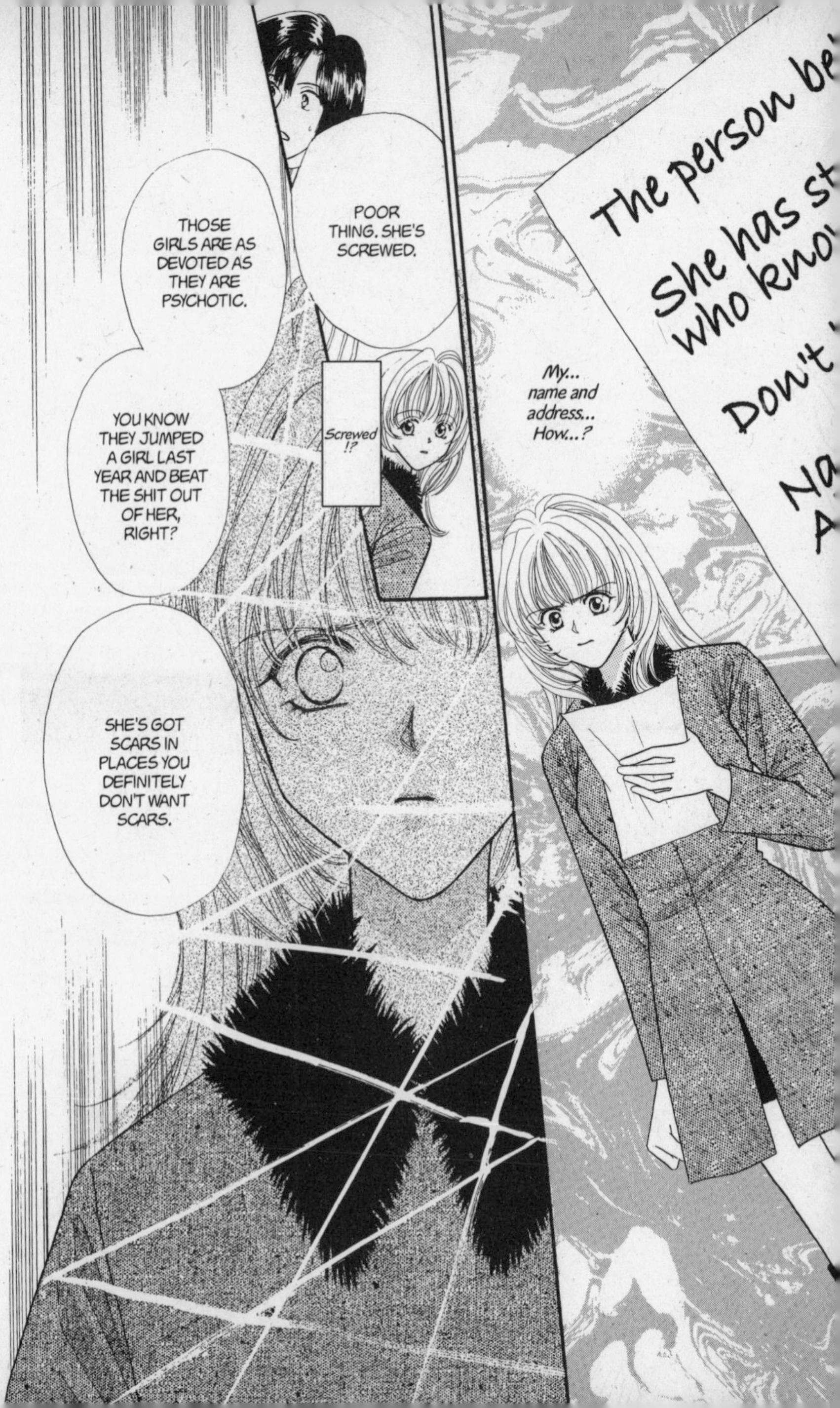
The person
She has
who
Don't
My... name and address... How...?
POOR THING. SHE'S SCREWED.
Screwed!?
THOSE GIRLS ARE AS DEVOTED AS THEY ARE PSYCHOTIC.
YOU KNOW THEY JUMPED A GIRL LAST YEAR AND BEAT THE SHIT OUT OF HER, RIGHT?
SHE'S GOT SCARS IN PLACES YOU DEFINITELY DON'T WANT SCARS.

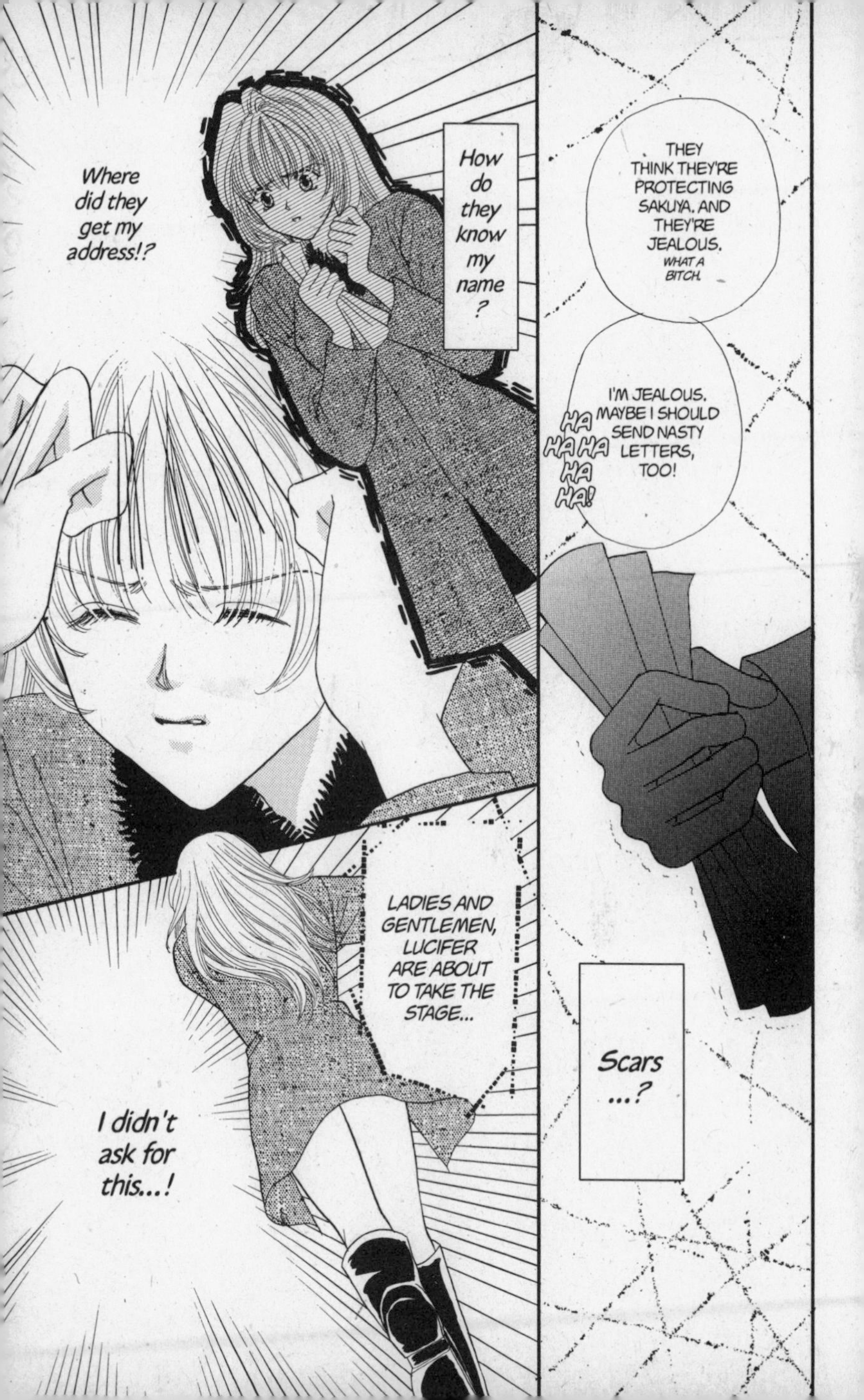
THEY THINK THEY'RE PROTECTING SAKUYA. AND THEY'RE JEALOUS.
WHAT A BITCH.
I'M JEALOUS. MAYBE I SHOULD SEND NASTY LETTERS, TOO!
HA HA HA HA HA!
Scars ...?
How do they know my name?
Where did they get my address!?
LADIES AND GENTLEMEN, LUCIFER ARE ABOUT TO TAKE THE STAGE...
I didn't ask for this...!

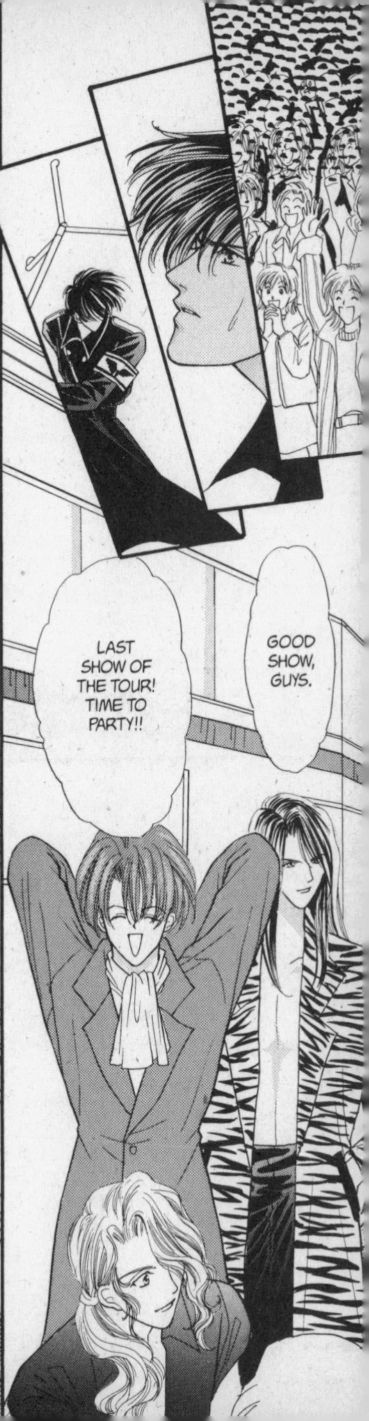
GOOD SHOW, GUYS.
LAST SHOW OF THE TOUR! TIME TO PARTY!!

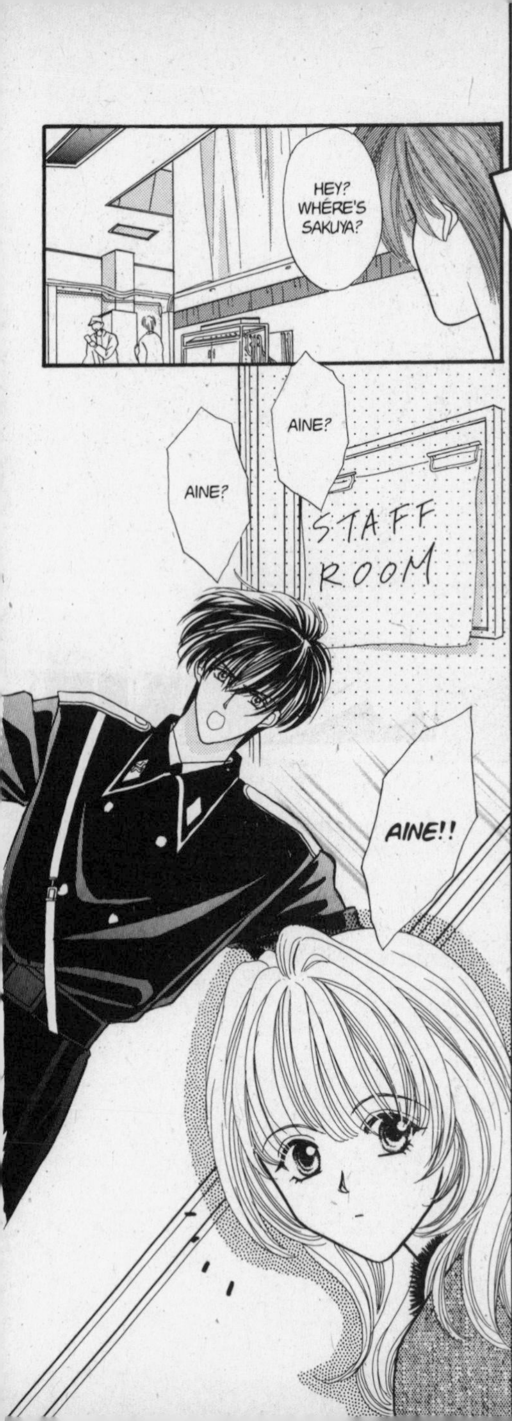
HEY? WHERE'S SAKUYA?
AINE?
AINE?
STAFF ROOM
AINE!!

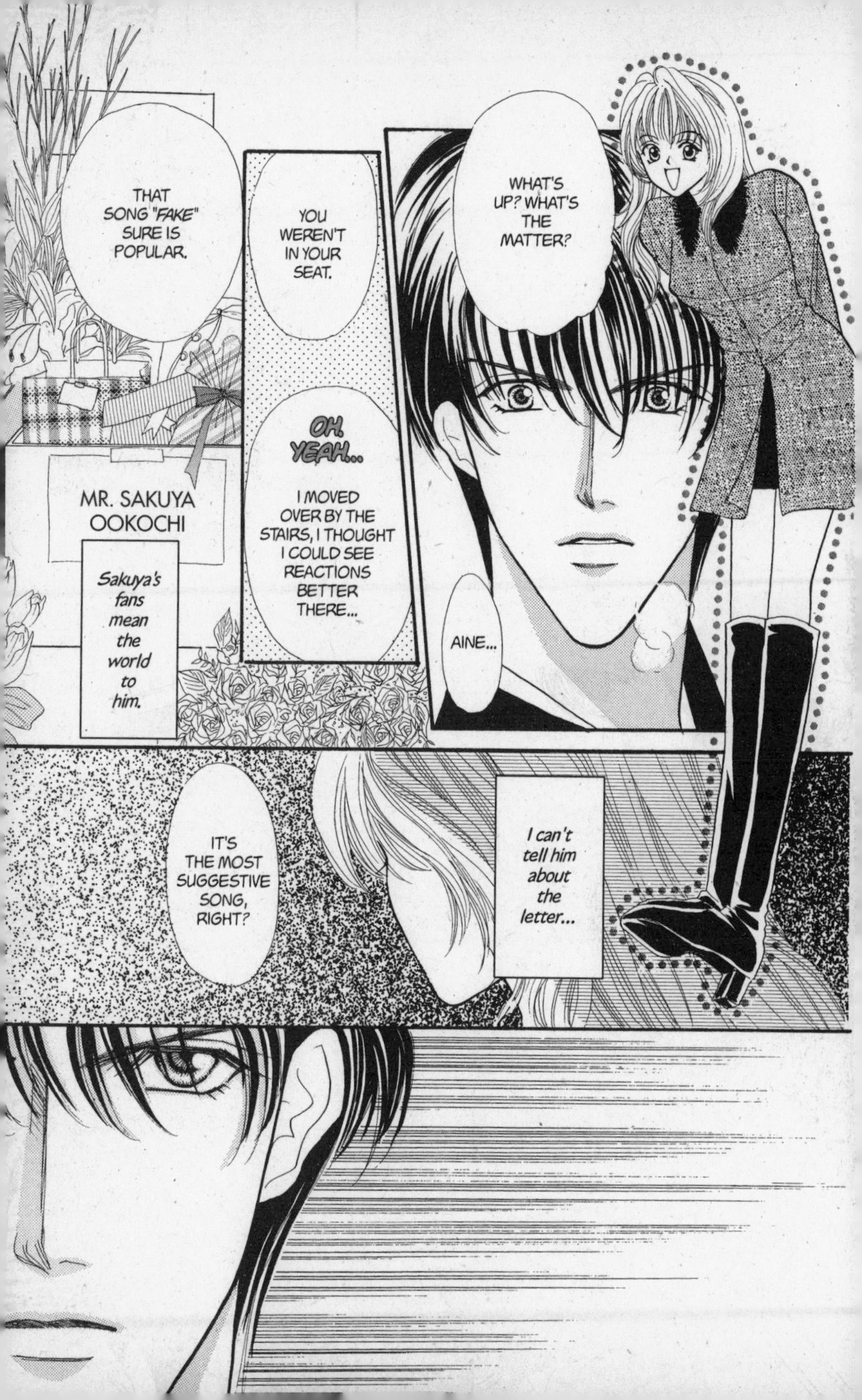
WHAT'S UP? WHAT'S THE MATTER?
AINE...
YOU WEREN'T IN YOUR SEAT.
OH. YEAH...
I MOVED OVER BY THE STAIRS, I THOUGHT I COULD SEE REACTIONS BETTER THERE...
THAT SONG "FAKE" SURE IS POPULAR.
MR. SAKUYA OOKOCHI
Sakuya's fans mean the world to him.
I can't tell him about the letter...
IT'S THE MOST SUGGESTIVE SONG, RIGHT?

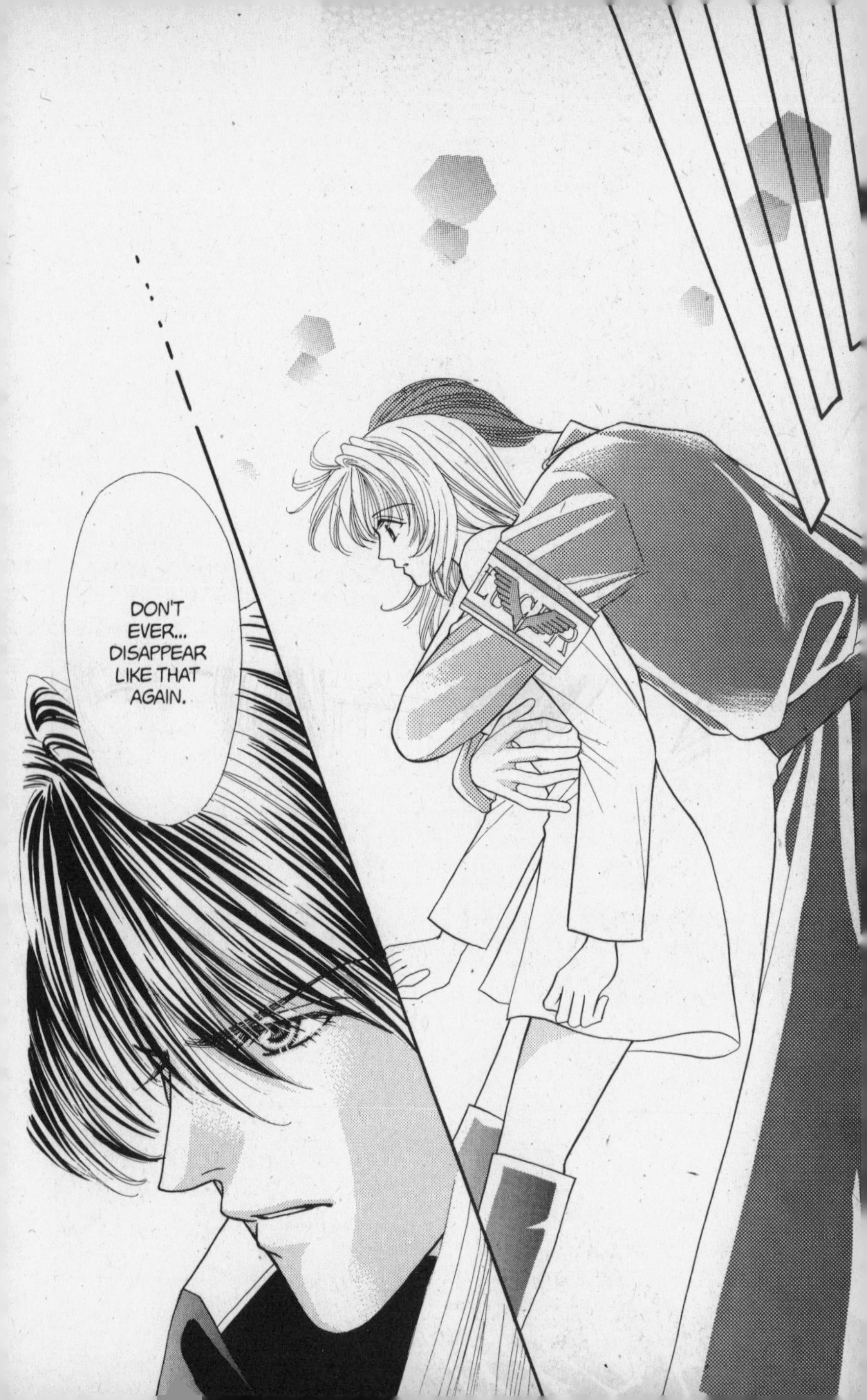
DON'T EVER... DISAPPEAR LIKE THAT AGAIN.

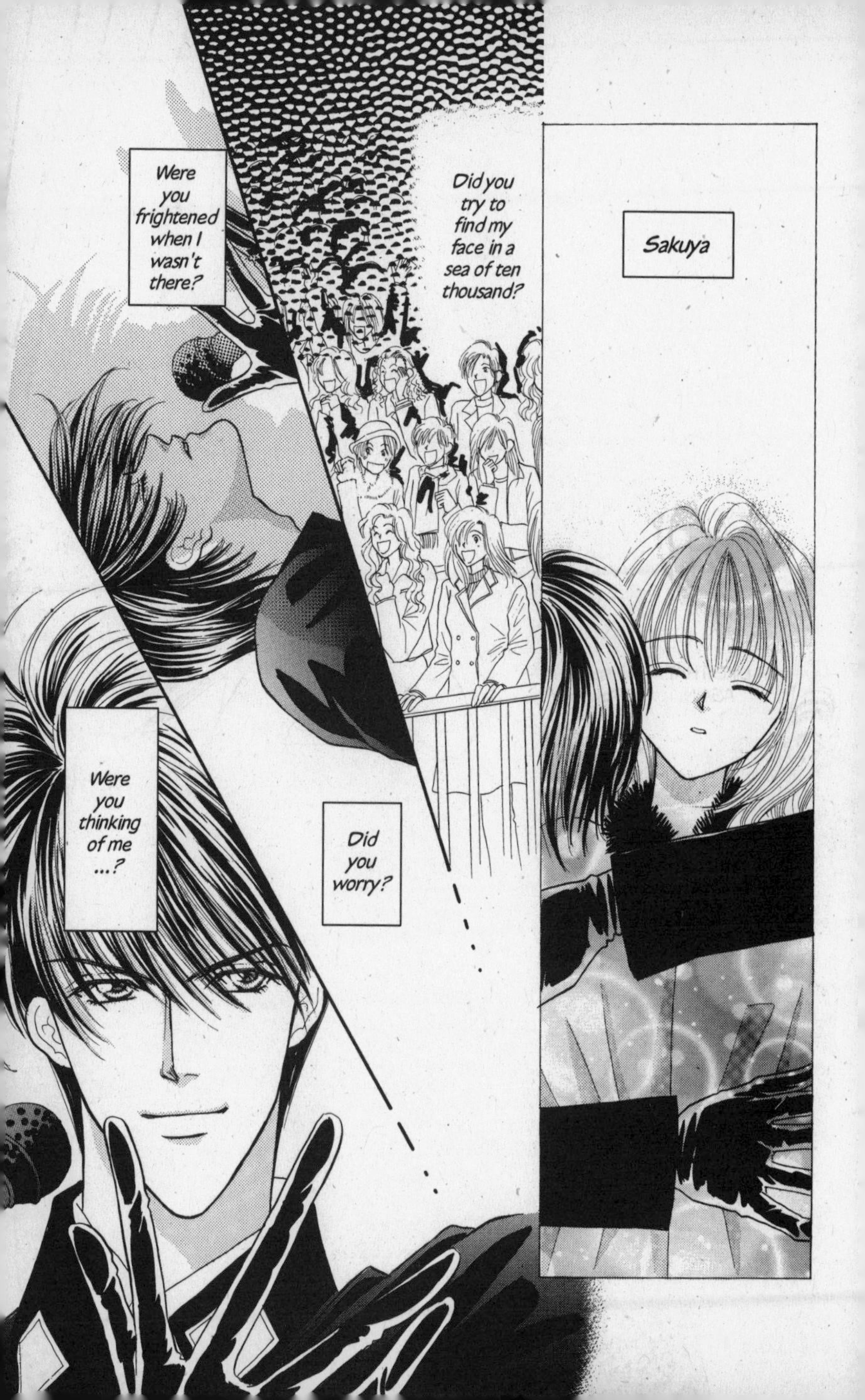
Sakuya
Did you try to find my face in a sea of ten thousand?
Were you frightened when I wasn't there?
Did you worry?
Were you thinking of me ...?

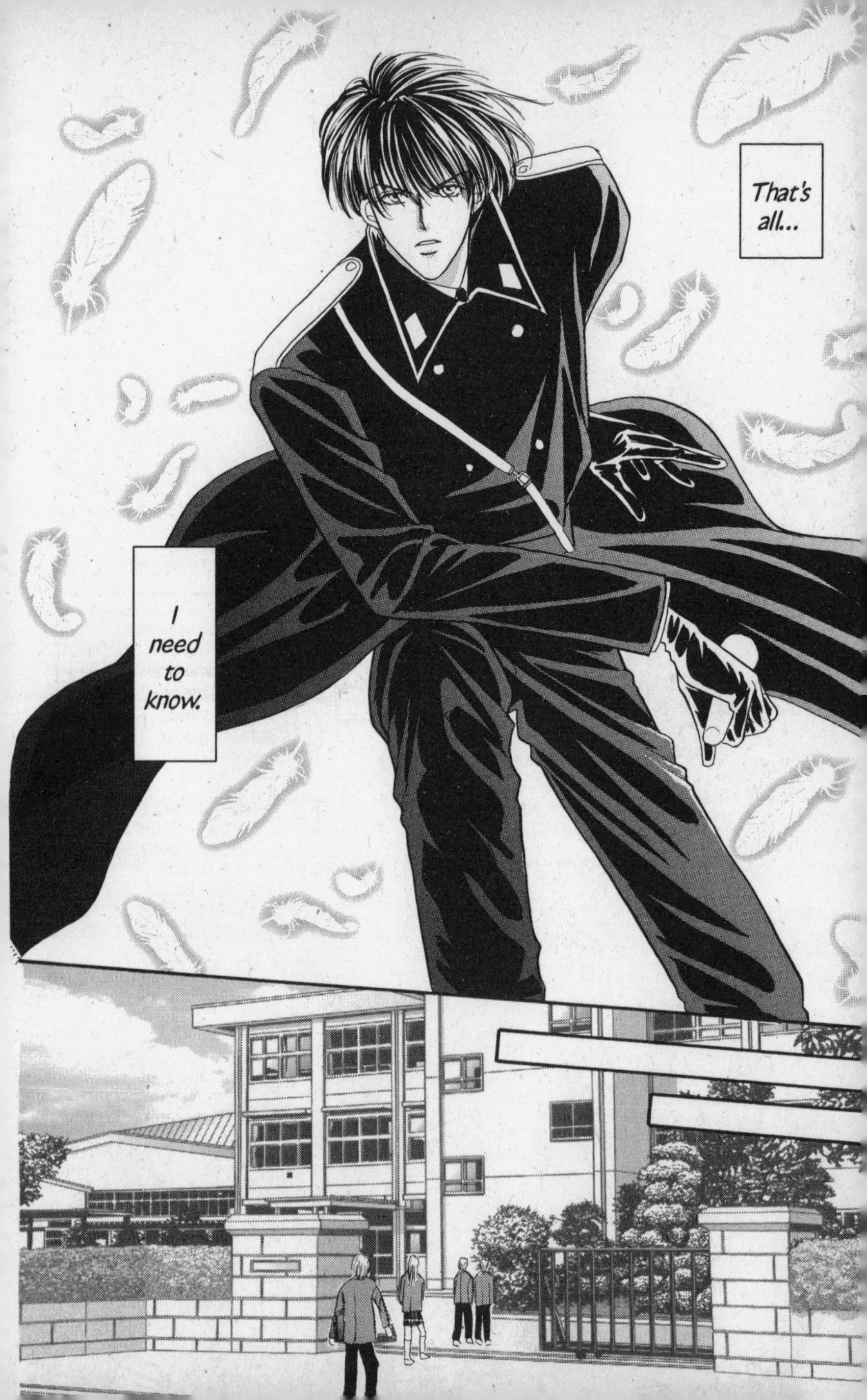
That's all...
I need to know.

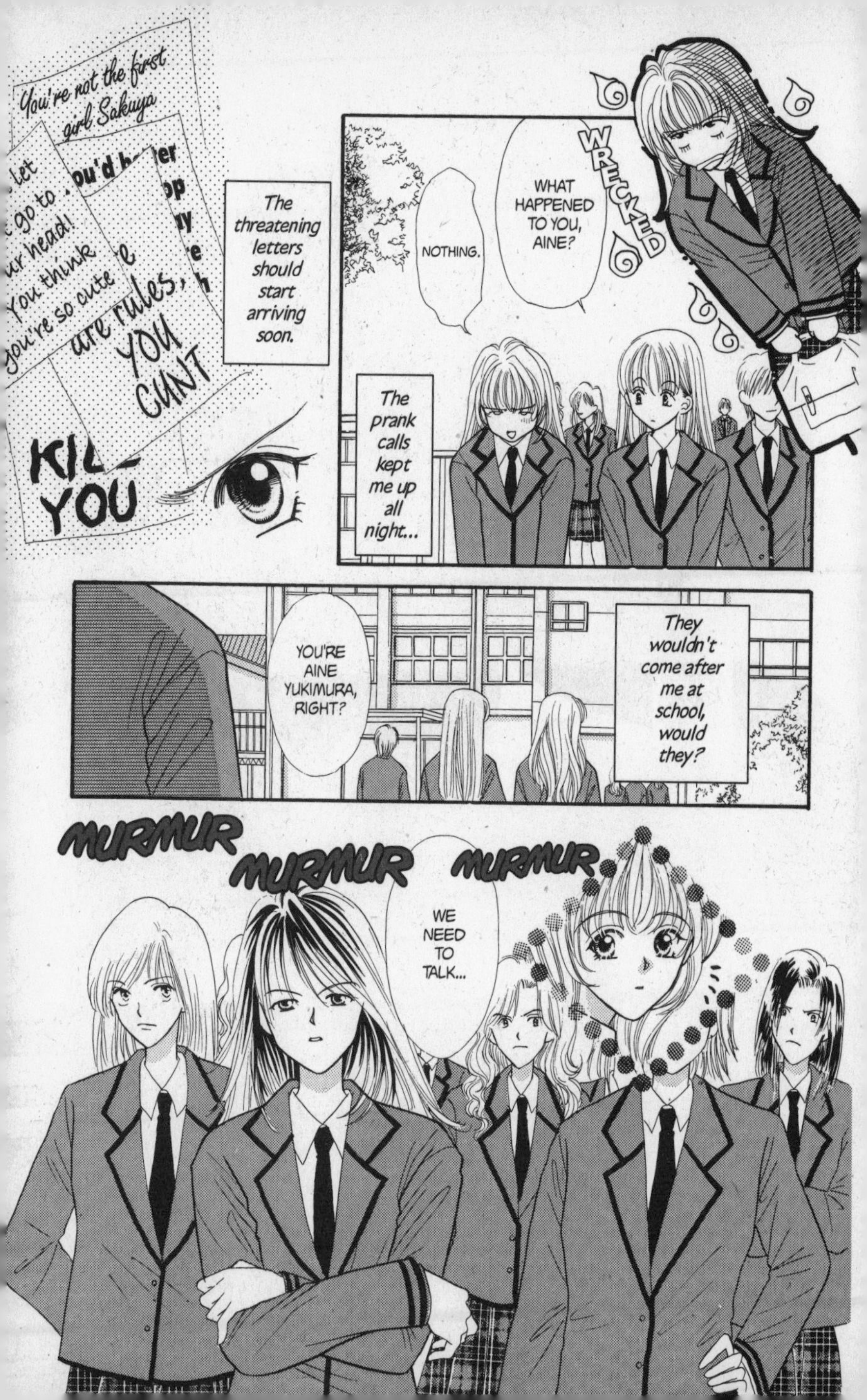
WRECKED
WHAT HAPPENED TO YOU, AINE?
NOTHING.
The prank calls kept me up all night...
The threatening letters should start arriving soon.
You're not the first girl Sakuya
You think you're so cute
are rules, YOU CUNT
YOU
They wouldn't come after me at school, would they?
YOU'RE AINE YUKIMURA, RIGHT?
MURMUR
MURMUR
MURMUR
WE NEED TO TALK...

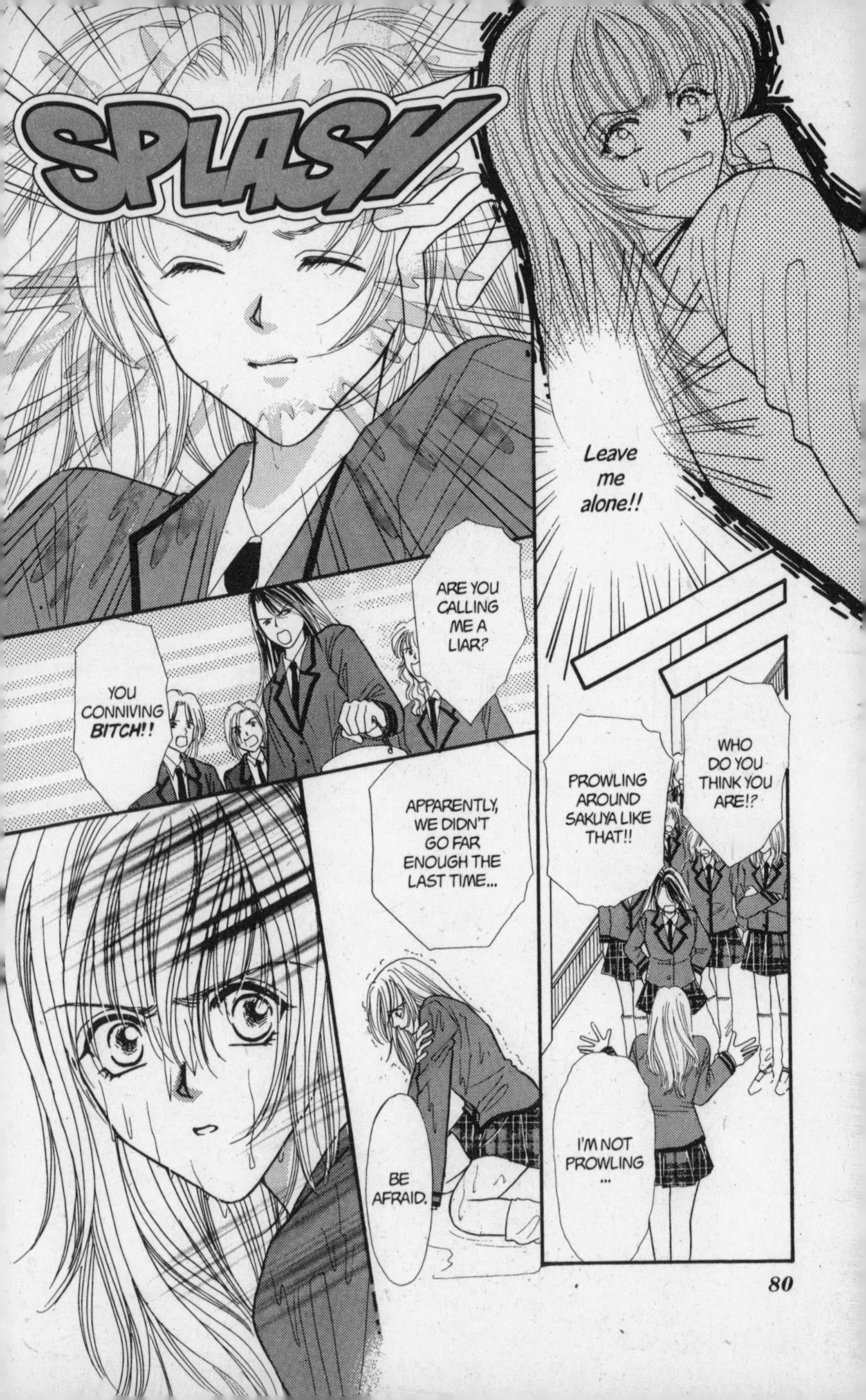
Leave me alone!!
SPLASH
WHO DO YOU THINK YOU ARE!?
PROWLING AROUND SAKUYA LIKE THAT!!
I'M NOT PROWLING ...
ARE YOU CALLING ME A LIAR?
YOU CONNIVING BITCH!!
APPARENTLY, WE DIDN'T GO FAR ENOUGH THE LAST TIME...
BE AFRAID.

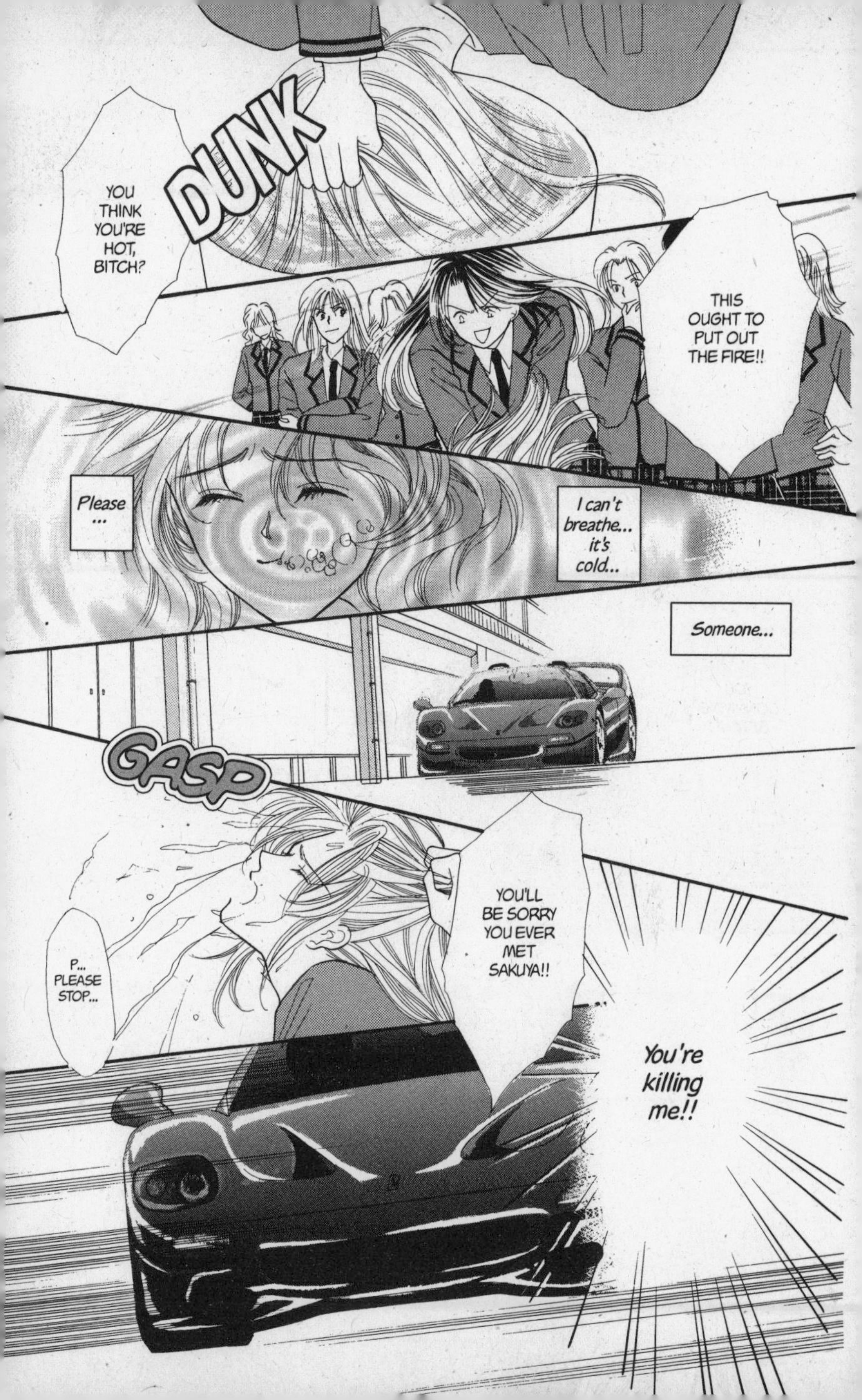
DUNK
YOU THINK YOU'RE HOT, BITCH?
THIS OUGHT TO PUT OUT THE FIRE!!
I can't breathe... it's cold...
Please ...
Someone...
GASP
YOU'LL BE SORRY YOU EVER MET SAKUYA!!
P... PLEASE STOP...
You're killing me!!

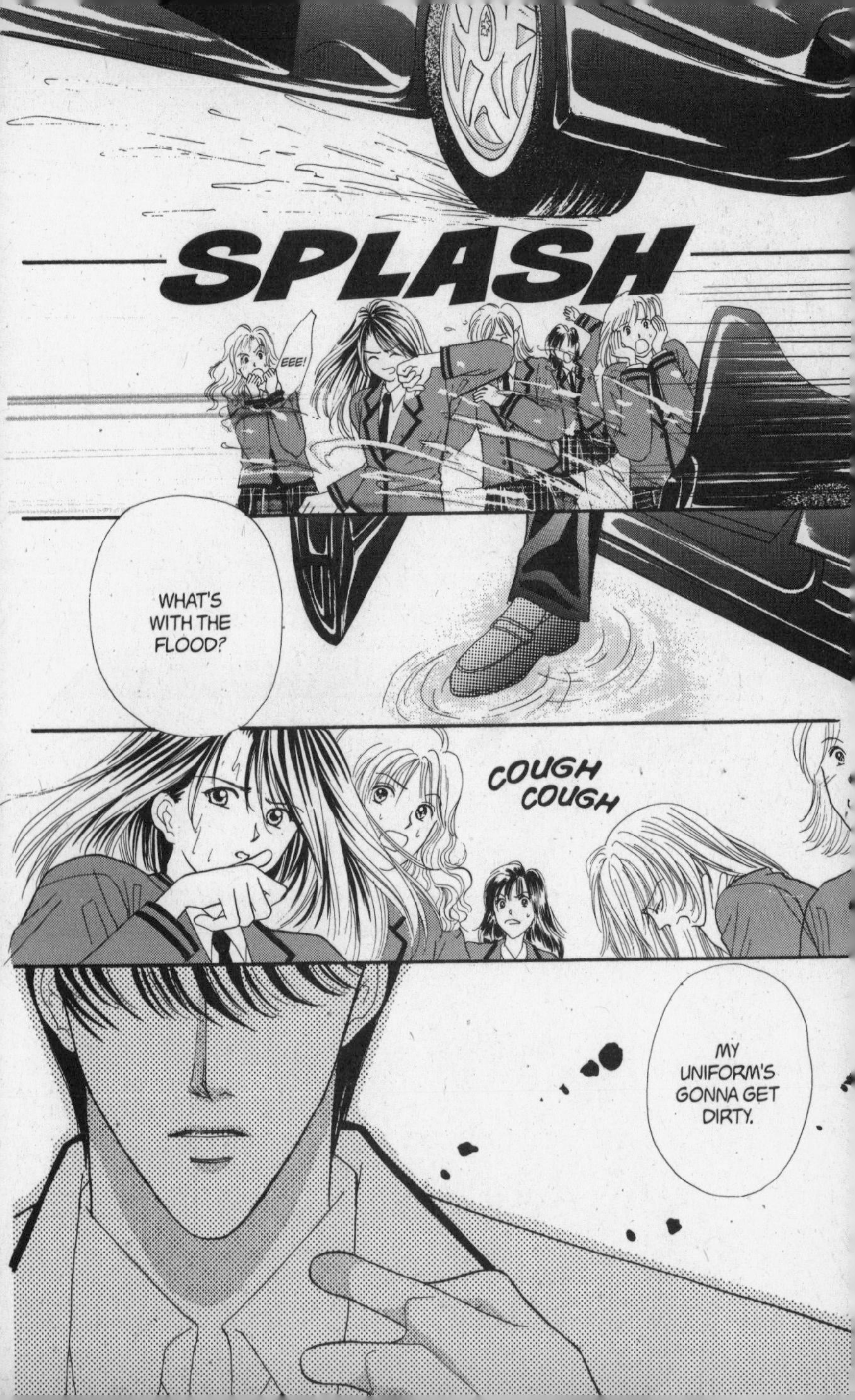
SPLASH
EEE!
WHAT'S WITH THE FLOOD?
COUGH COUGH
MY UNIFORM'S GONNA GET DIRTY.

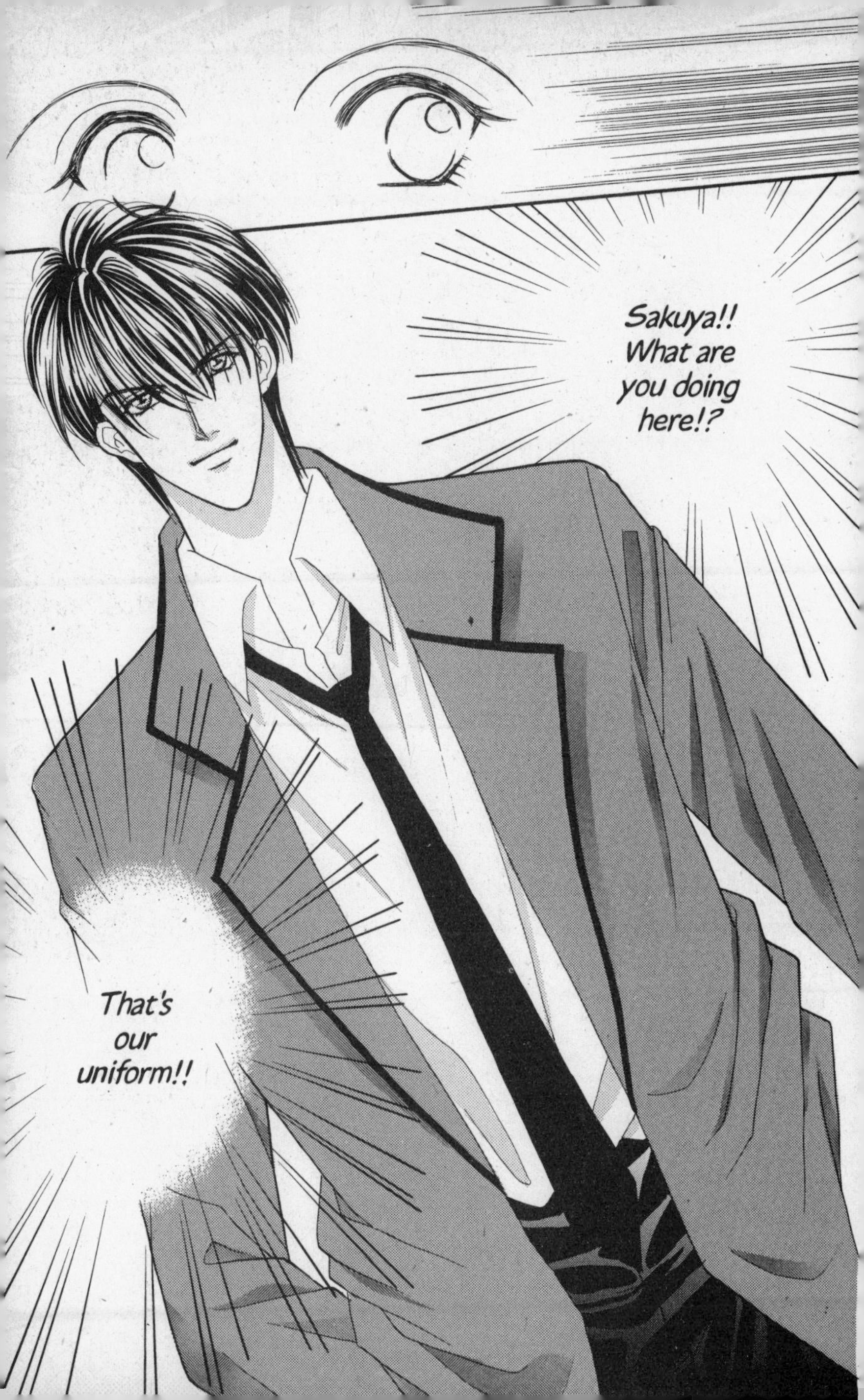
Sakuya!! What are you doing here!?
That's our uniform!!

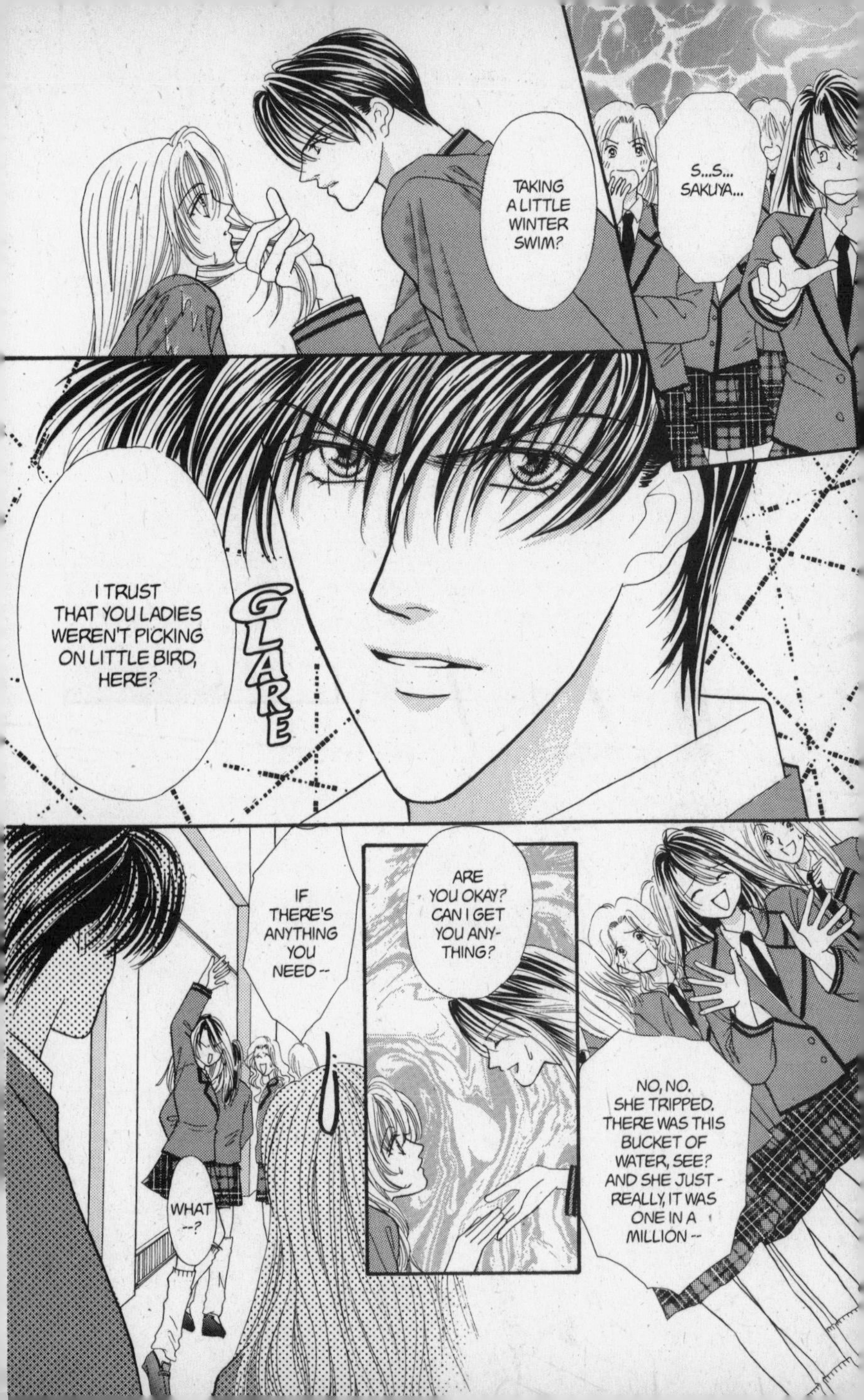
S...S... SAKUYA...
TAKING A LITTLE WINTER SWIM?
I TRUST THAT YOU LADIES WEREN'T PICKING ON LITTLE BIRD, HERE?
GLARE
NO, NO. SHE TRIPPED. THERE WAS THIS BUCKET OF WATER, SEE? AND SHE JUST - REALLY, IT WAS ONE IN A MILLION --
ARE YOU OKAY? CAN I GET YOU ANY-THING?
IF THERE'S ANYTHING YOU NEED --
WHAT --?

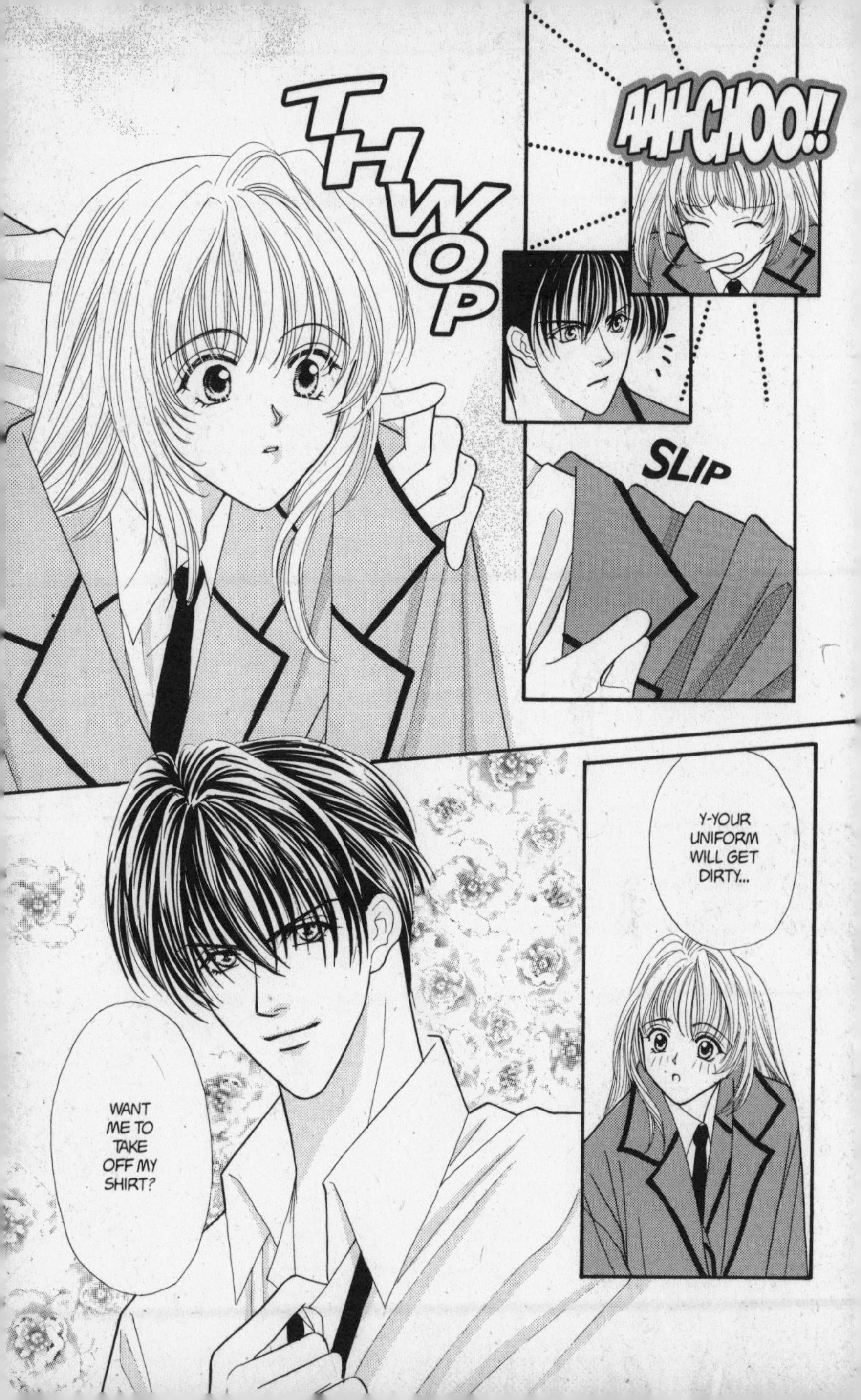
AAH-CHOO!!
SLIP
THWOP
Y-YOUR UNIFORM WILL GET DIRTY...
WANT ME TO TAKE OFF MY SHIRT?

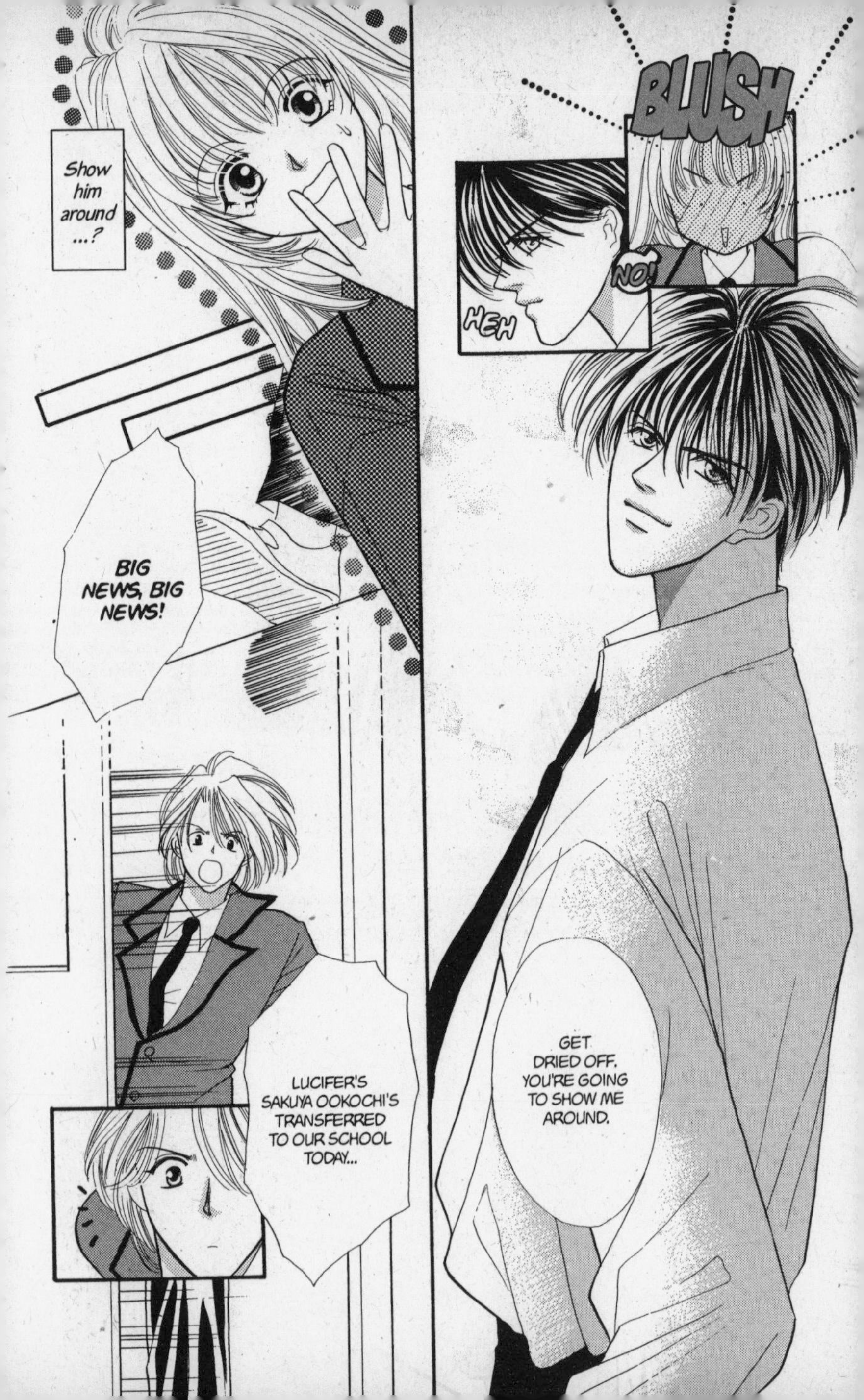
BLUSH
NO!
HEH
GET DRIED OFF. YOU'RE GOING TO SHOW ME AROUND.
Show him around ...?
BIG NEWS, BIG NEWS!
LUCIFER'S SAKUYA OOKOCHI'S TRANSFERRED TO OUR SCHOOL TODAY...

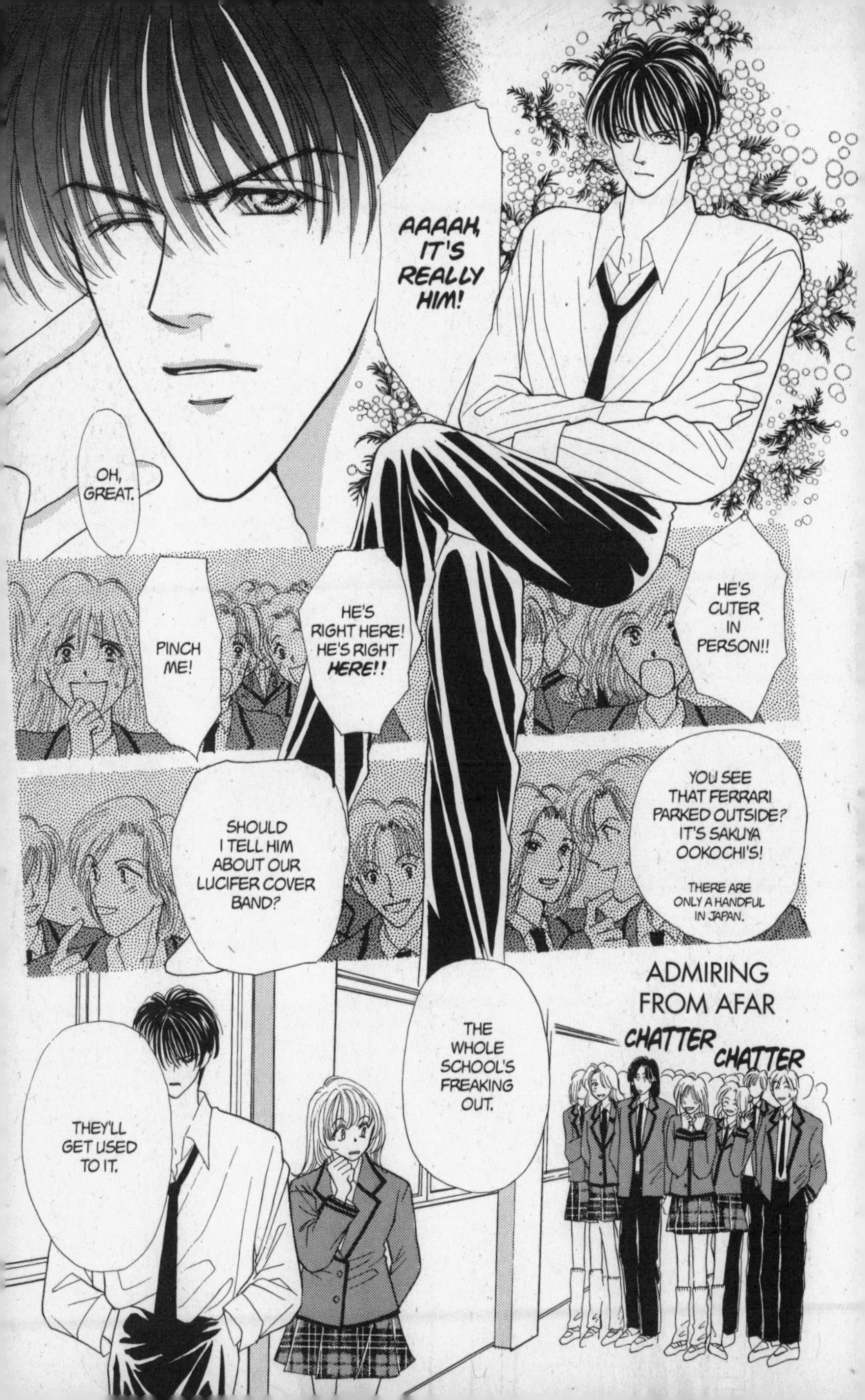
AAAAH, IT'S REALLY HIM!
OH, GREAT.
HE'S CUTER IN PERSON!!
HE'S RIGHT HERE! HE'S RIGHT HERE!!
PINCH ME!
YOU SEE THAT FERRARI PARKED OUTSIDE? IT'S SAKUYA OOKOCHI'S!
THERE ARE ONLY A HANDFUL IN JAPAN.
SHOULD I TELL HIM ABOUT OUR LUCIFER COVER BAND?
ADMIRING FROM AFAR
CHATTER CHATTER
THE WHOLE SCHOOL'S FREAKING OUT.
THEY'LL GET USED TO IT.

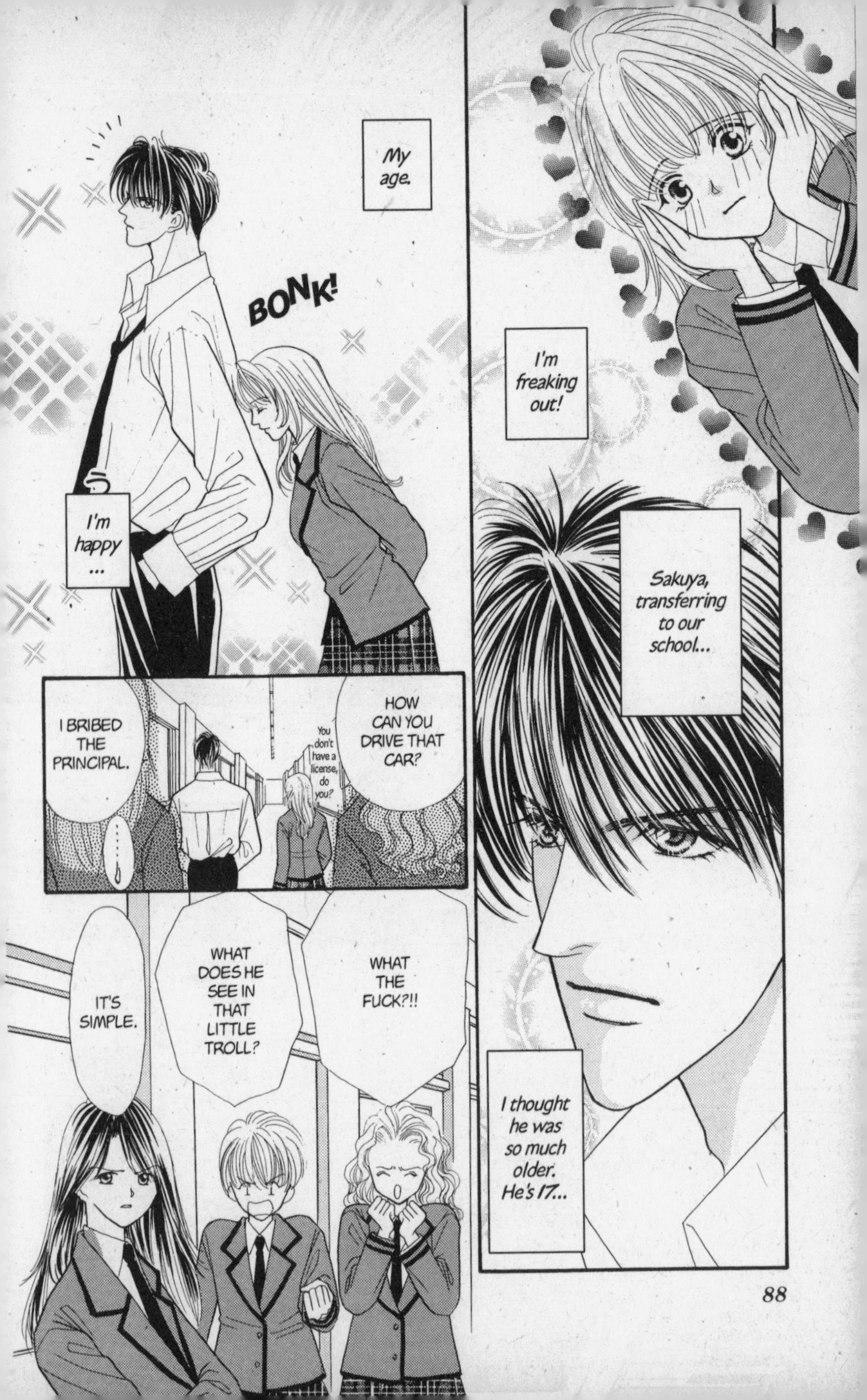
I'm freaking out!
Sakuya, transferring to our school...
I thought he was so much older. He's 17...
My age.
BONK!
I'm happy ...
HOW CAN YOU DRIVE THAT CAR?
You don't have a license, do you?
I BRIBED THE PRINCIPAL.
......
WHAT THE FUCK?!!
WHAT DOES HE SEE IN THAT LITTLE TROLL?
IT'S SIMPLE.

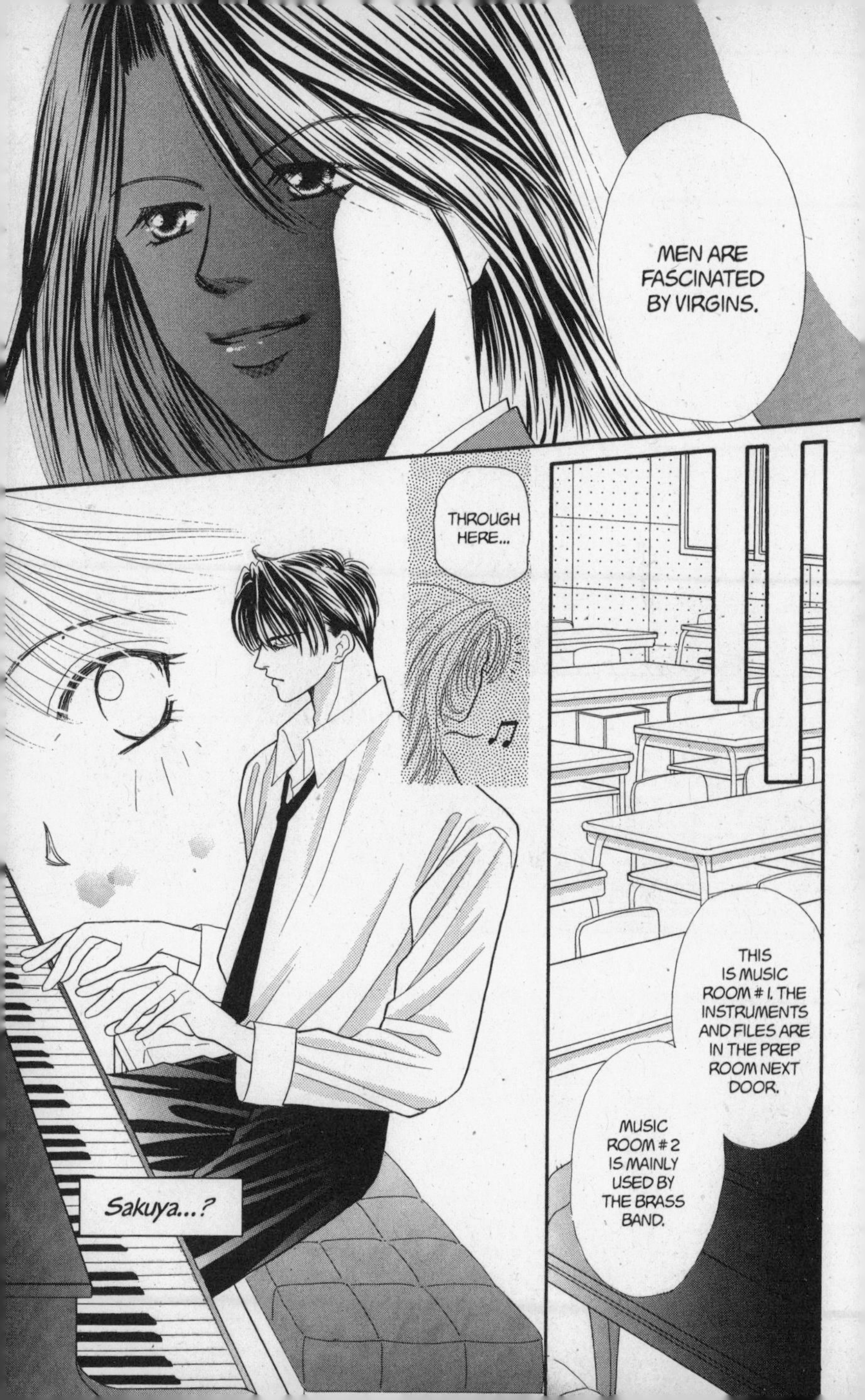
MEN ARE FASCINATED BY VIRGINS.
THIS IS MUSIC ROOM # 1. THE INSTRUMENTS AND FILES ARE IN THE PREP ROOM NEXT DOOR.
MUSIC ROOM # 2 IS MAINLY USED BY THE BRASS BAND.
THROUGH HERE...
Sakuya...?

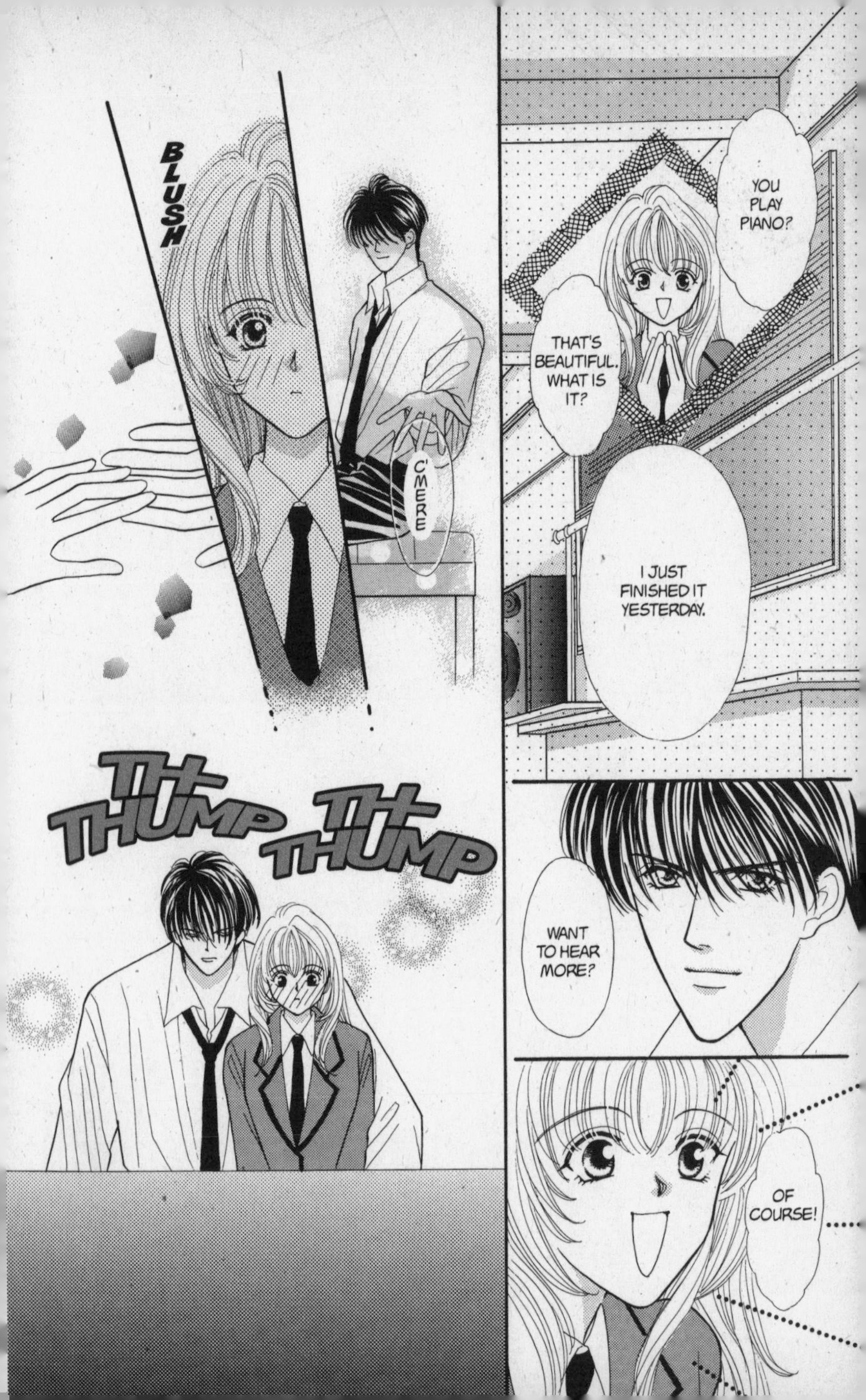
YOU PLAY PIANO?
THAT'S BEAUTIFUL. WHAT IS IT?
I JUST FINISHED IT YESTERDAY.
WANT TO HEAR MORE?
OF COURSE!
C'MERE
BLUSH
TH-THUMP TH-THUMP

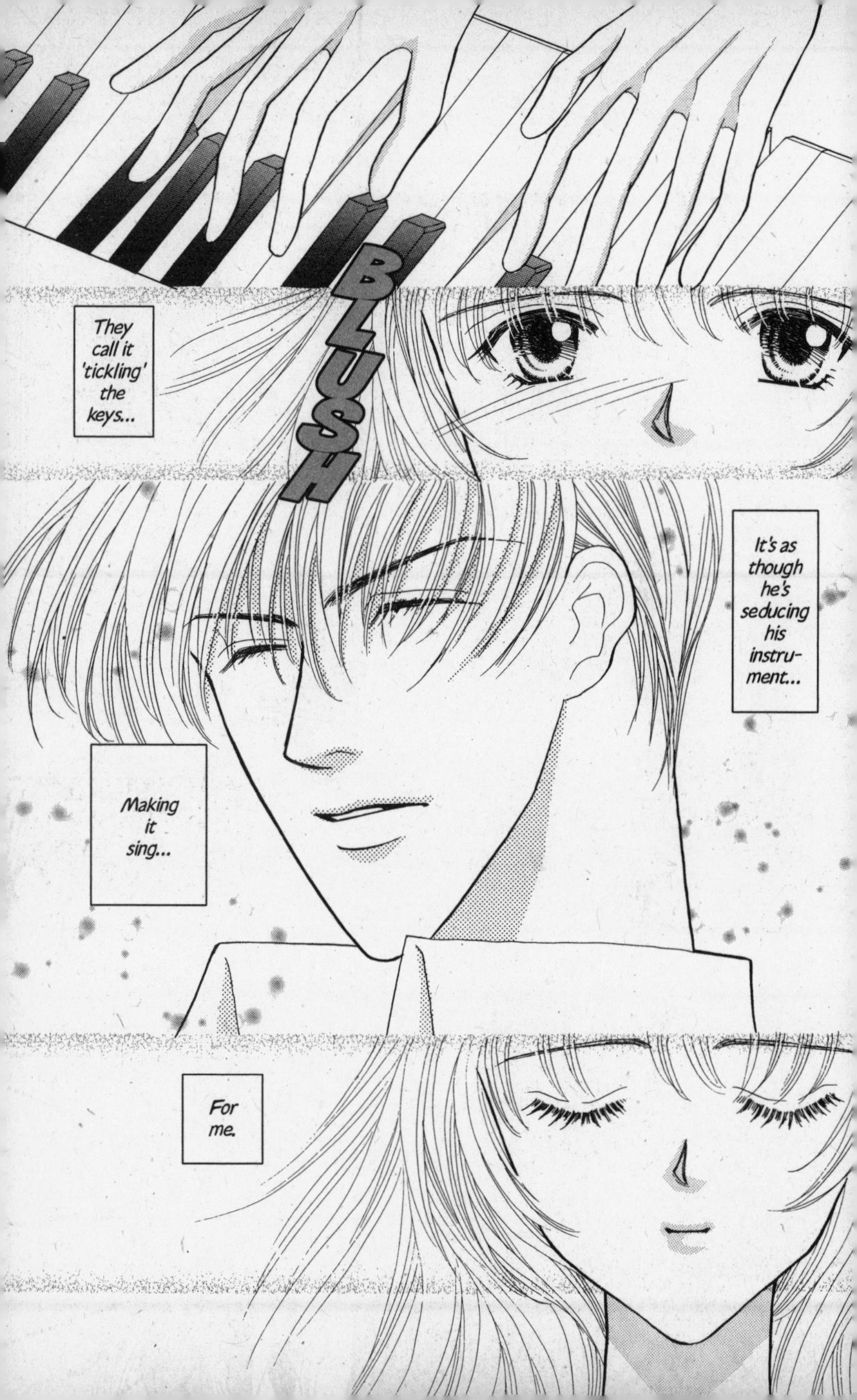
BLUSH
They call it 'tickling' the keys...
It's as though he's seducing his instrument...
Making it sing...
For me.

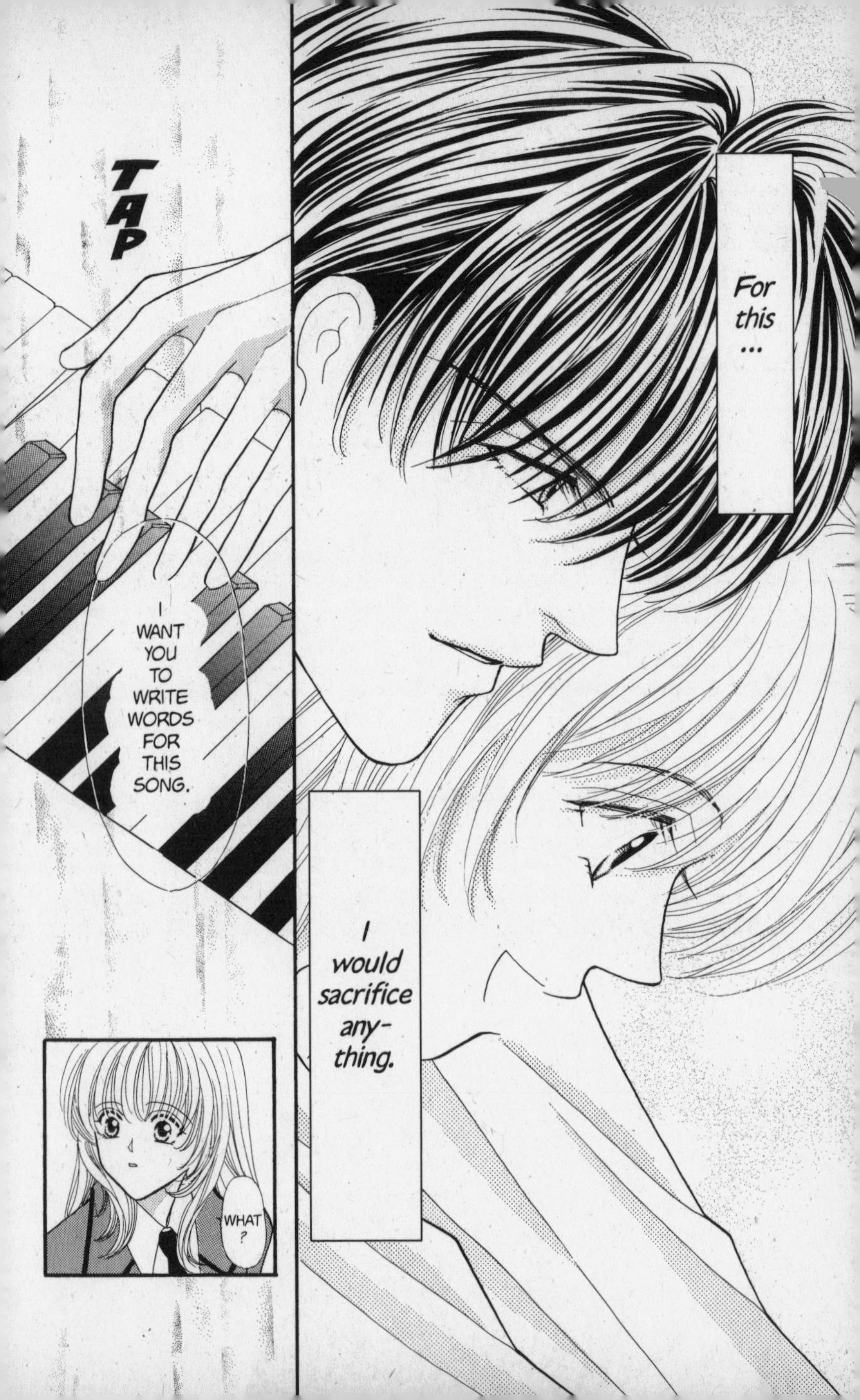
For this ...
I would sacrifice any-thing.
TAP
I WANT YOU TO WRITE WORDS FOR THIS SONG.
WHAT?

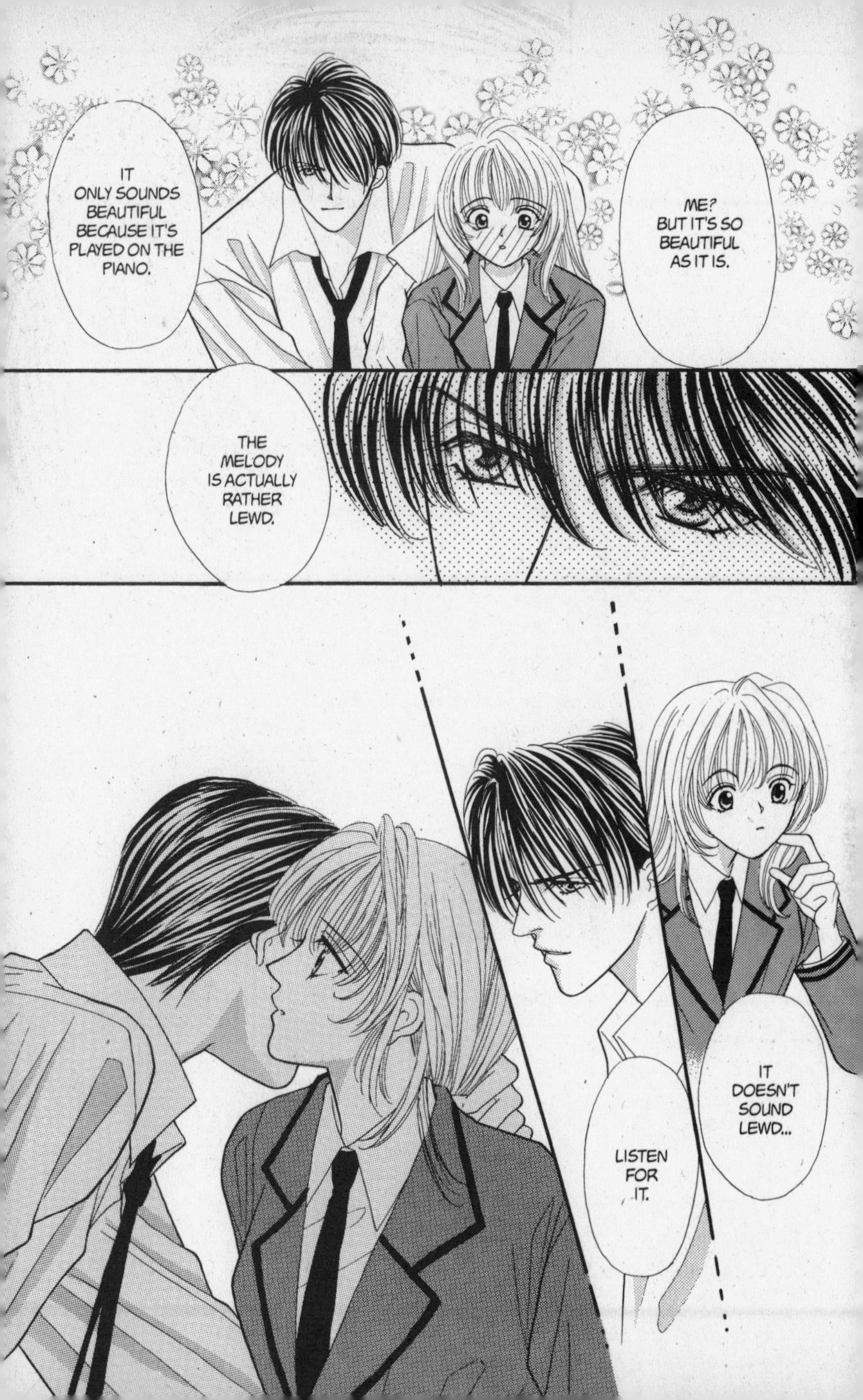
ME? BUT IT'S SO BEAUTIFUL AS IT IS.
IT ONLY SOUNDS BEAUTIFUL BECAUSE IT'S PLAYED ON THE PIANO.
THE MELODY IS ACTUALLY RATHER LEWD.
IT DOESN'T SOUND LEWD...
LISTEN FOR IT.

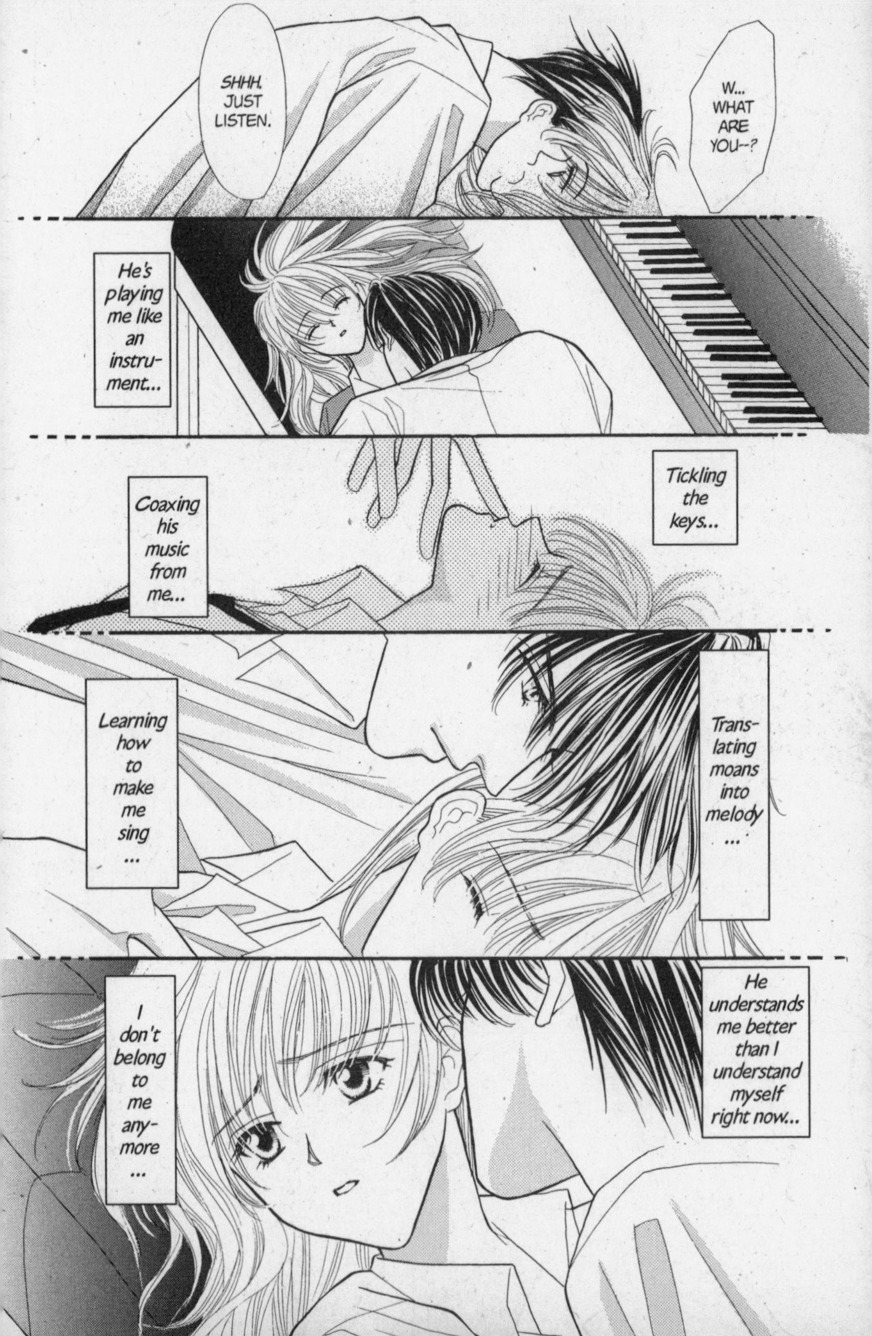
W... WHAT ARE YOU--?
SHHH. JUST LISTEN.
He's playing me like an instrument...
Tickling the keys...
Coaxing his music from me...
Translating moans into melody...
Learning how to make me sing...
He understands me better than I understand myself right now...
I don't belong to me anymore...

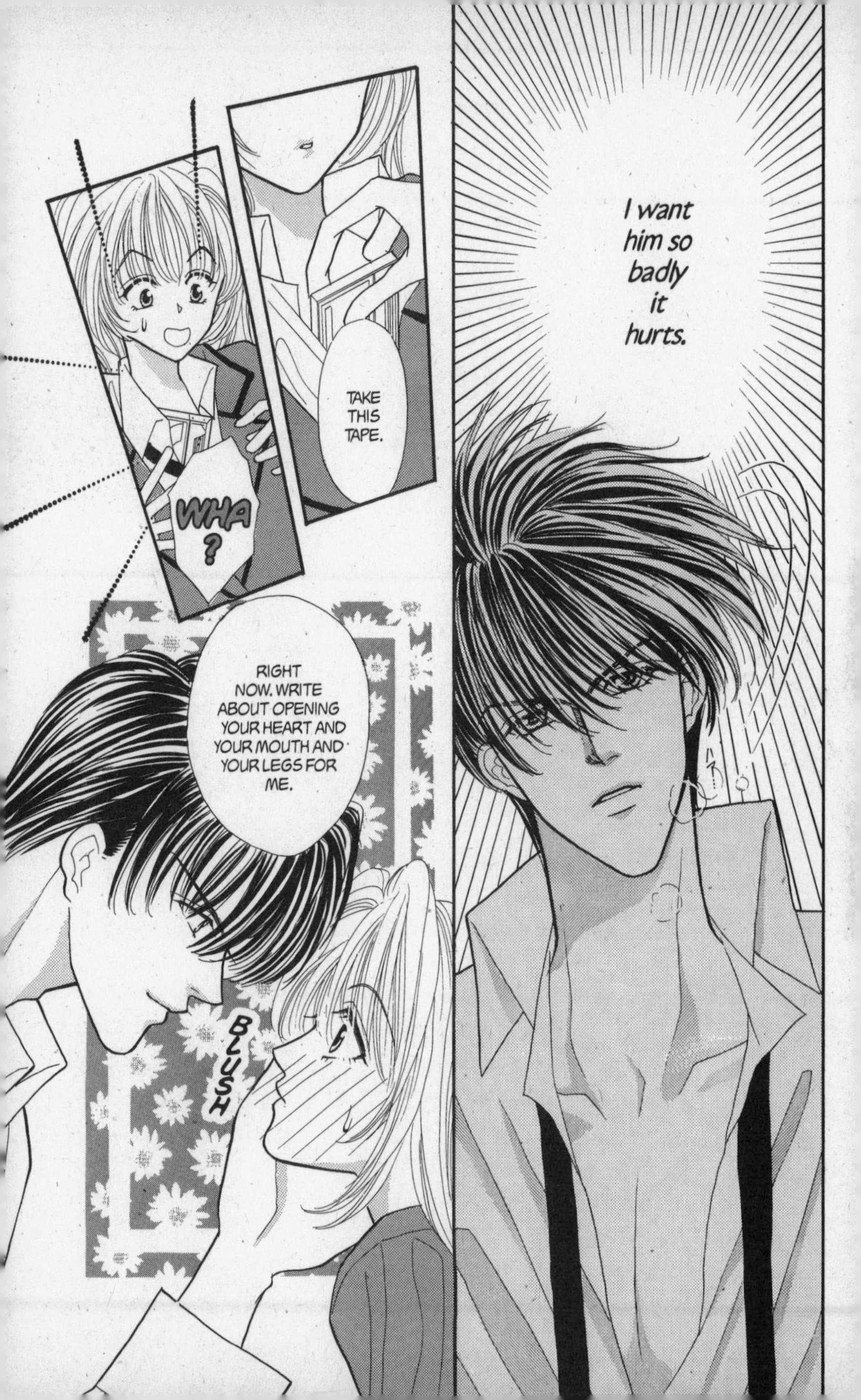
I want him so badly it hurts.
TAKE THIS TAPE.
WHA ?
RIGHT NOW. WRITE ABOUT OPENING YOUR HEART AND YOUR MOUTH AND YOUR LEGS FOR ME.
BLUSH

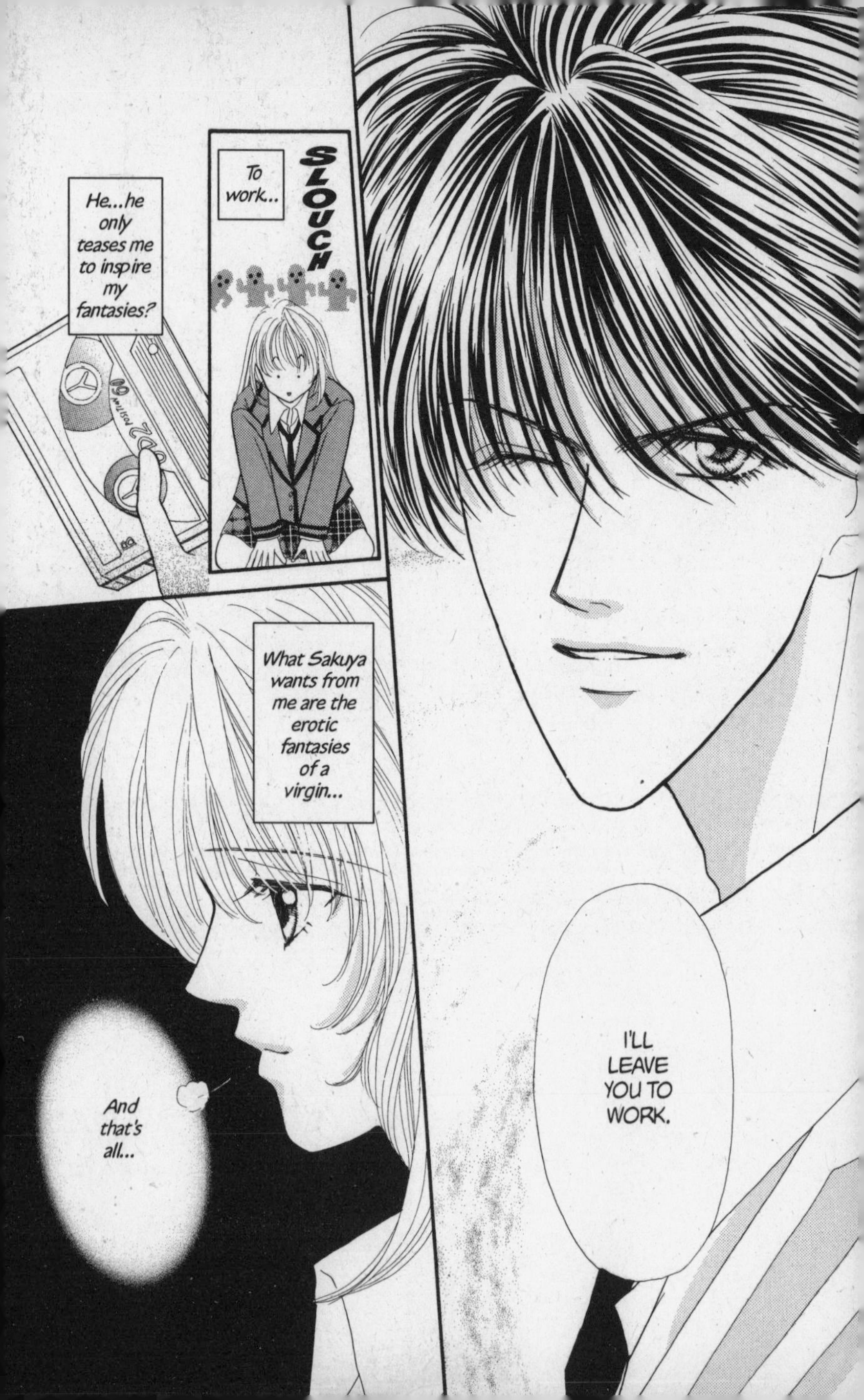
I'LL LEAVE YOU TO WORK.
To work...
SLOUCH
He...he only teases me to inspire my fantasies?
What Sakuya wants from me are the erotic fantasies of a virgin...
And that's all...

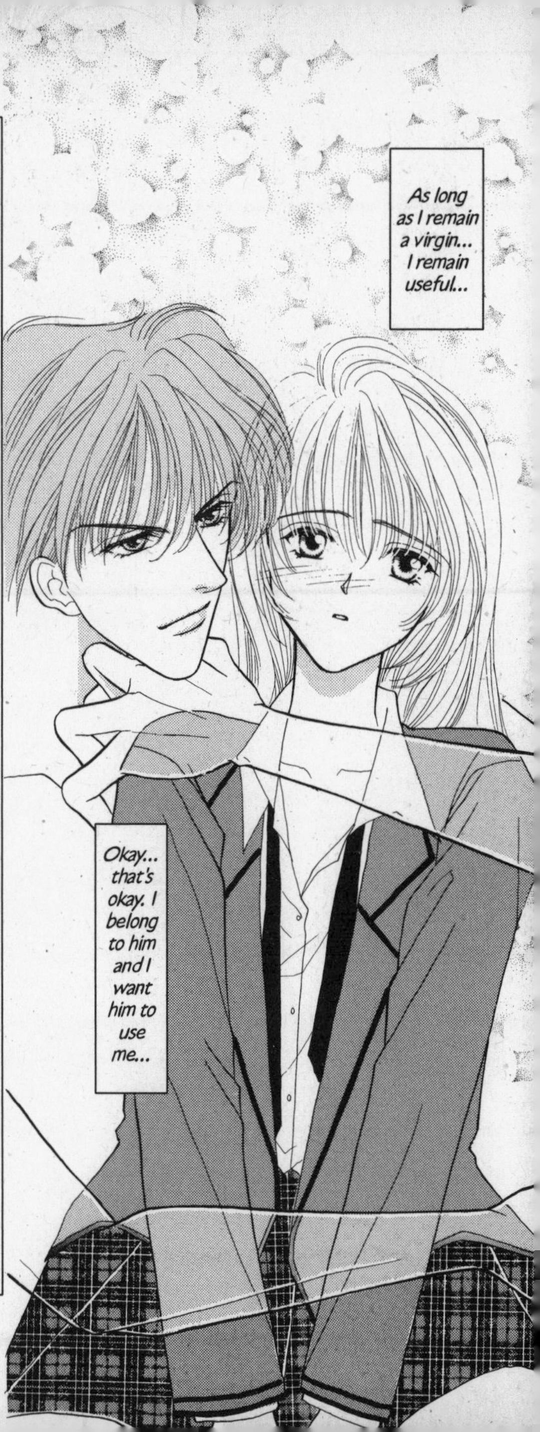
As long as I remain a virgin... I remain useful...
Okay... that's okay. I belong to him and I want him to use me...

Speaking of Visual bands, how about BUCK-TICK? I worship vocalist Atsushi Sakurai. He is the best singer I've ever heard! He communicates so much with the tone of his voice. And those lyrics!! Come to think of it, Lucifer might write naughty lyrics because Buck- Tick's made me climb the walls.

By the way, I'm often asked, 'Who writes the lyrics used in the comic?' The answer is: I do! It nearly kills me every time I have to do it. They take me about five hours each. I couldn't do it if I had to worry about a melody. (A few people have written music to go with the lyrics and they've sent me tapes. I've got talented fans!)

Speaking of good songs, I've listened to a lot of music since starting this project but Ryuichi Kawamura's song "Glass" is AMAZING. I highly recommend you check it out. DENKI GROOVE'S "Shangri-La" is also great. Have you seen the video? Takkyu Ishino has such a creepy grin...Oh, and speaking of videos...

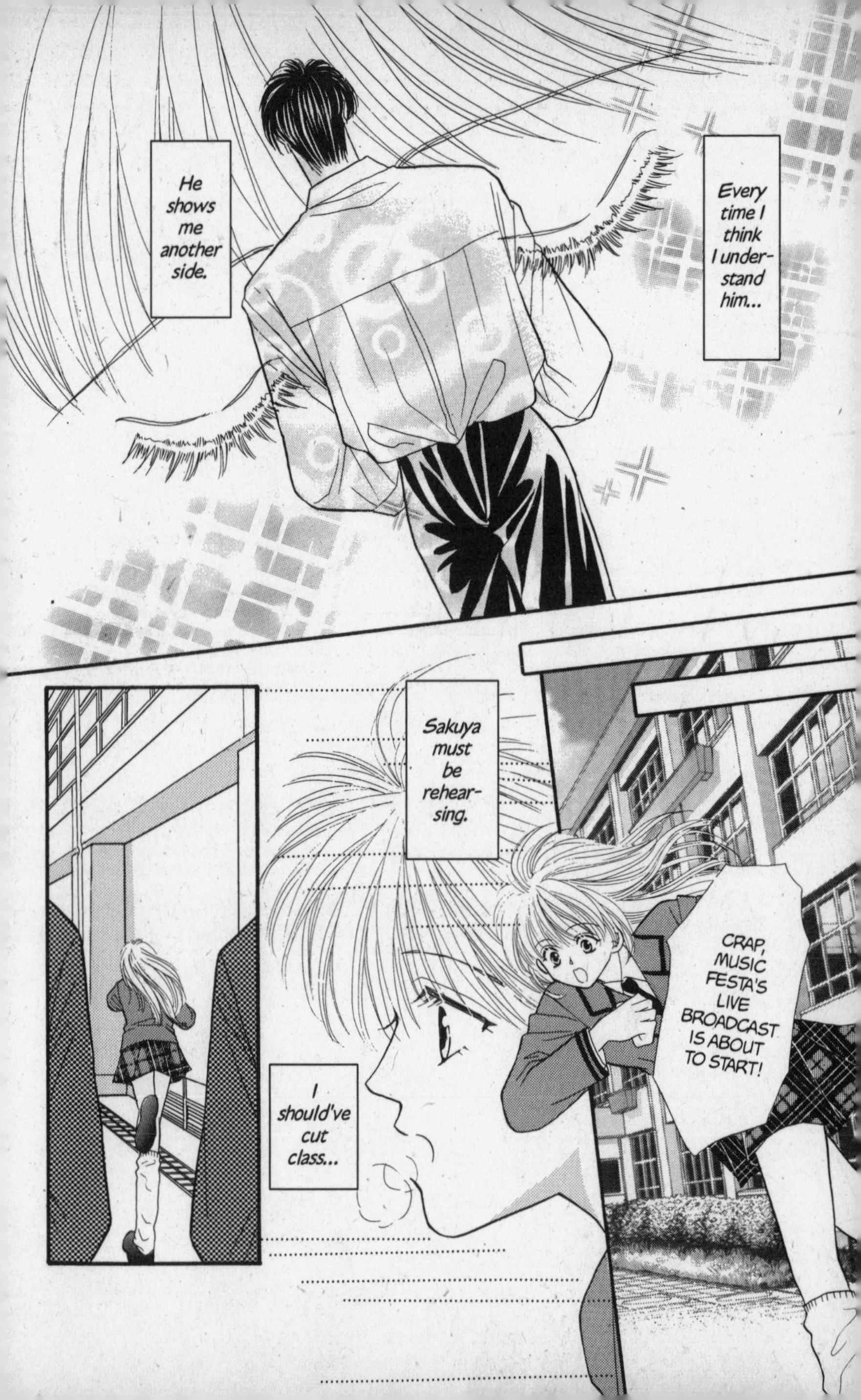
Every time I think I under-stand him...
He shows me another side.
CRAP, MUSIC FESTA'S LIVE BROADCAST IS ABOUT TO START!
Sakuya must be rehear-sing.
I should've cut class...

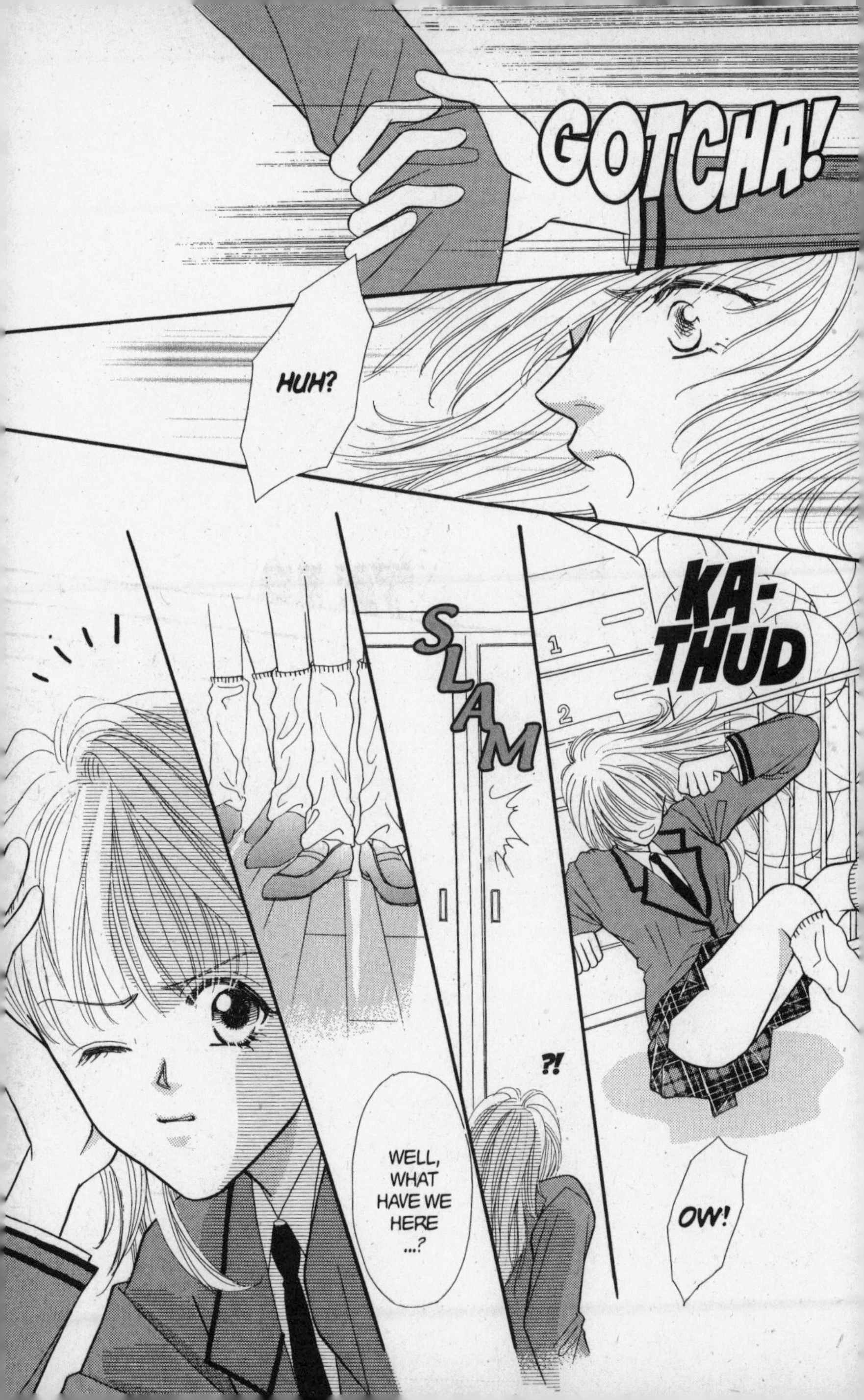
GOTCHA!
HUH?
KA-THUD
OW!
SLAM
?!
WELL, WHAT HAVE WE HERE ...?

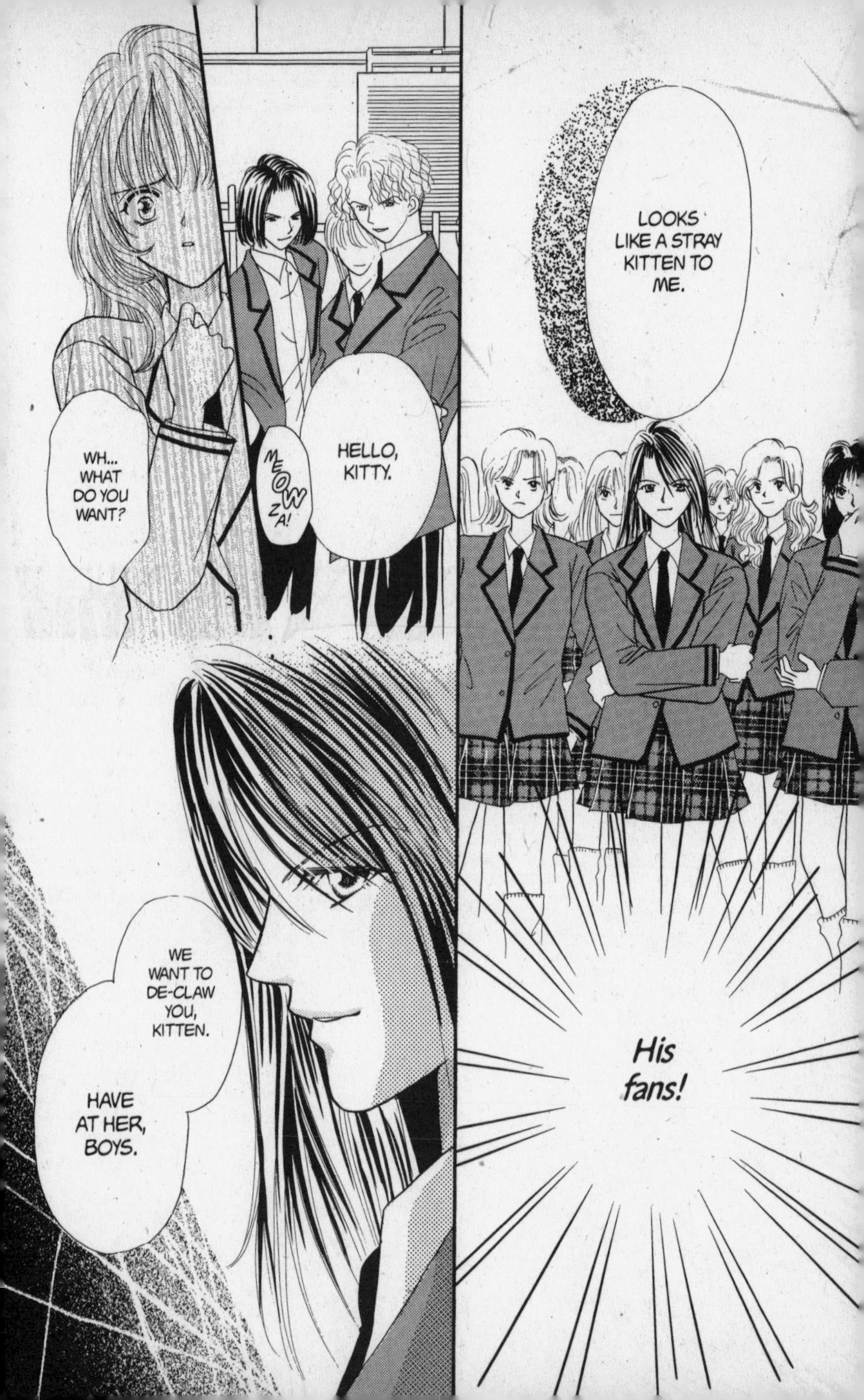
LOOKS LIKE A STRAY KITTEN TO ME.
His fans!
HELLO, KITTY.
MEOWZA!
WH... WHAT DO YOU WANT?
WE WANT TO DE-CLAW YOU, KITTEN.
HAVE AT HER, BOYS.

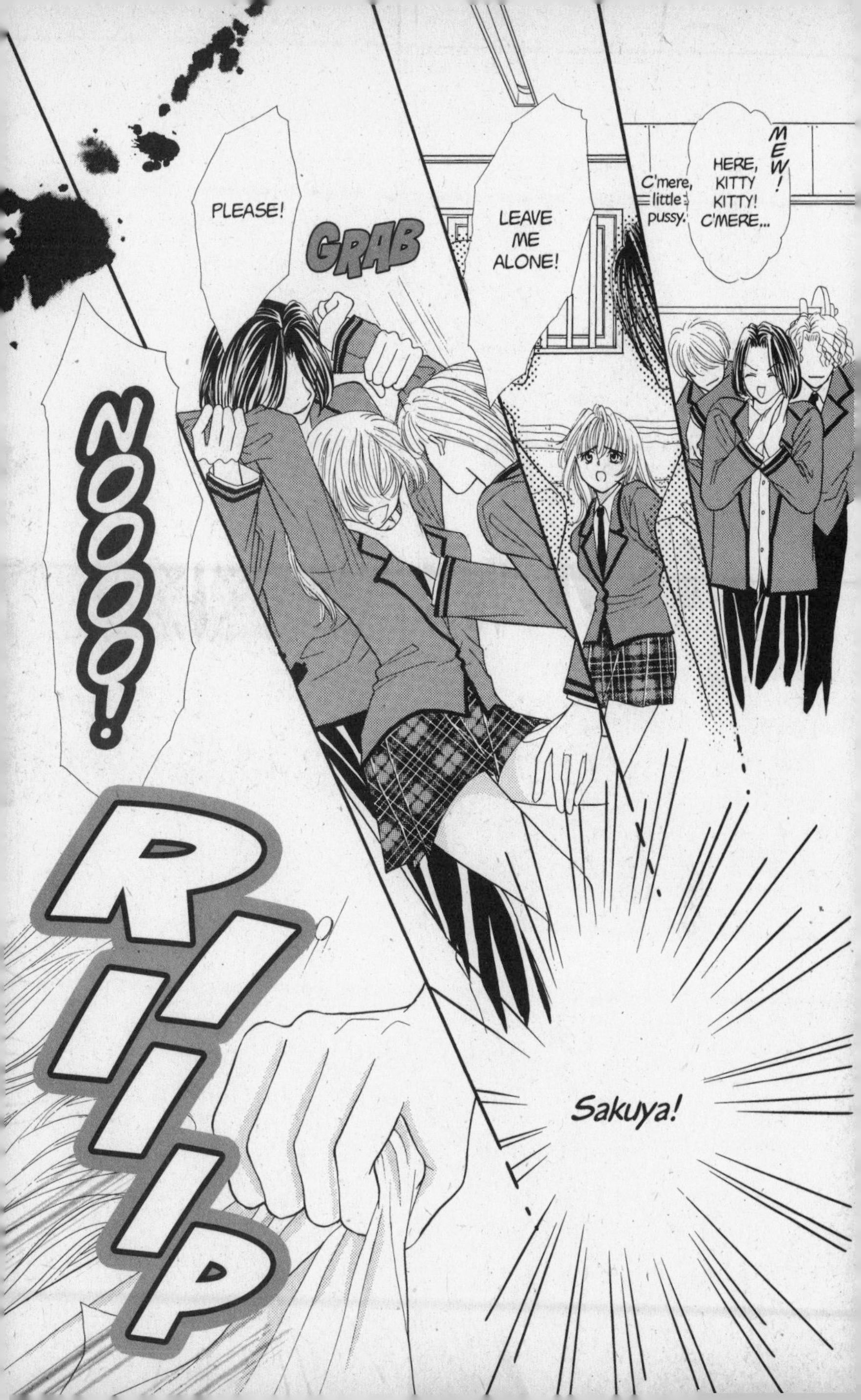
MEW!
HERE, KITTY KITTY! C'MERE...
C'mere, little pussy.
LEAVE ME ALONE!
GRAB
PLEASE!
NOOOO!
Sakuya!
RIIIP

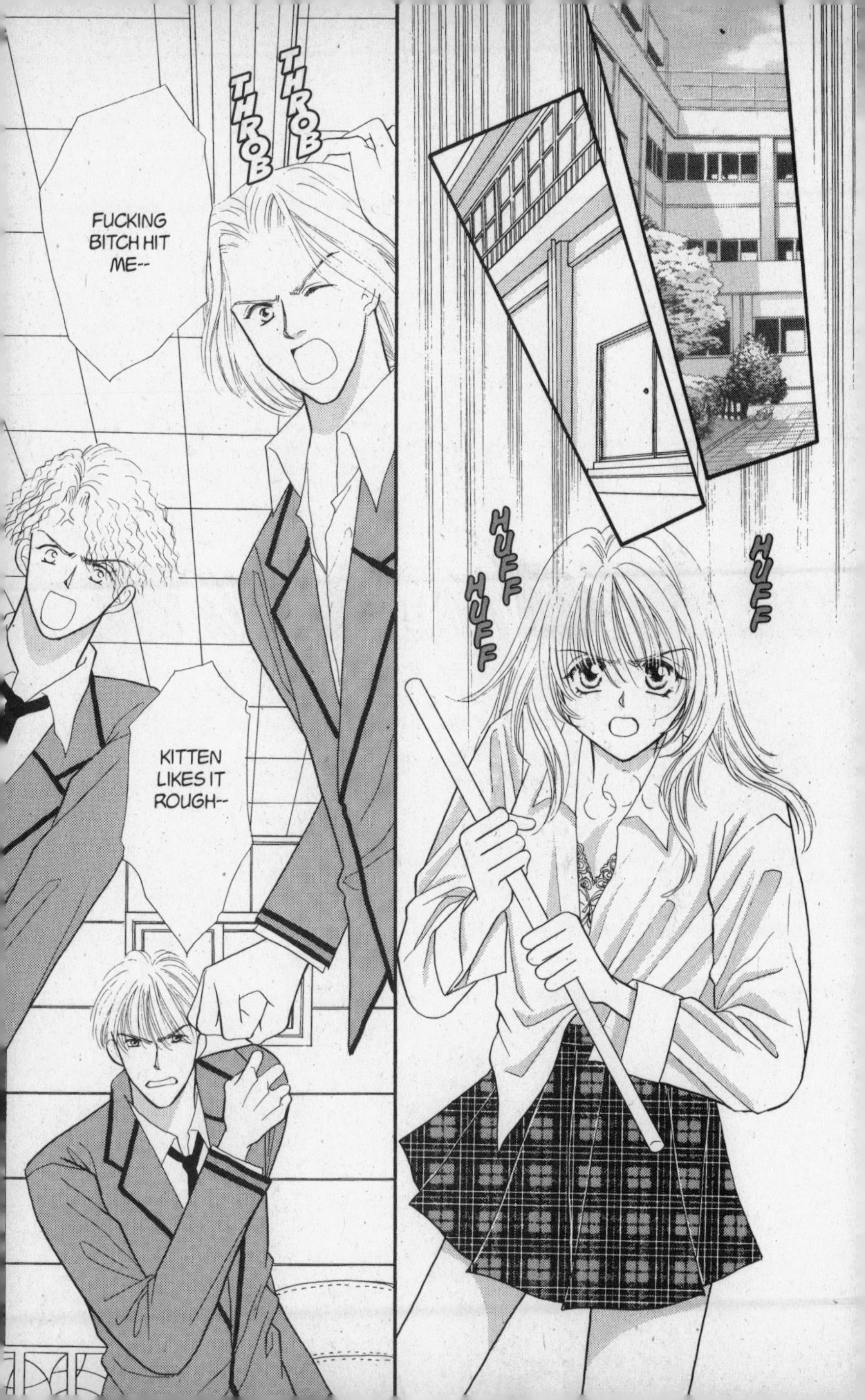
HUFF
HUFF
HUFF
THROB
THROB
FUCKING BITCH HIT ME--
KITTEN LIKES IT ROUGH--

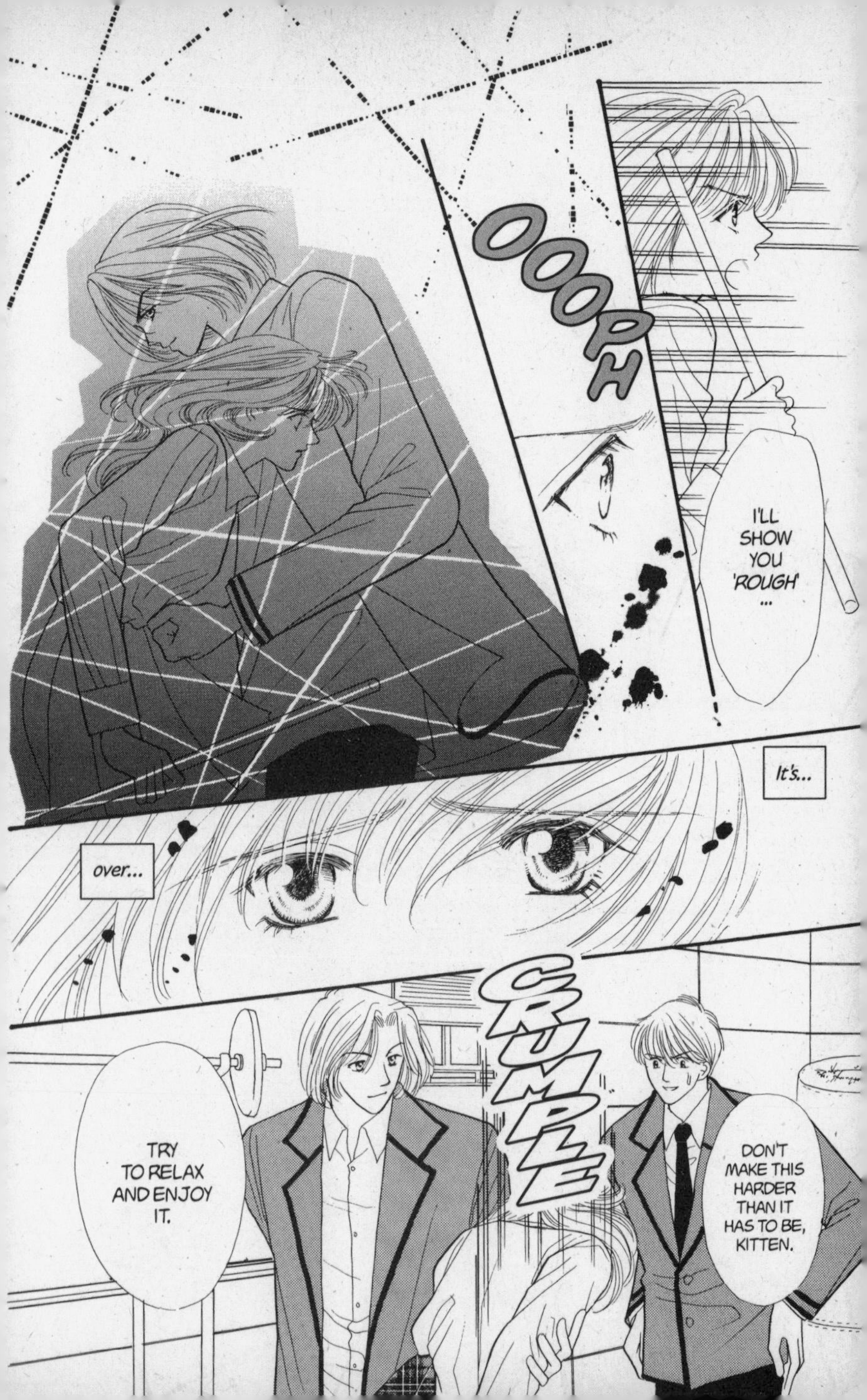
I'LL SHOW YOU 'ROUGH'...
OOOPH
It's...
over...
CRUMPLE
DON'T MAKE THIS HARDER THAN IT HAS TO BE, KITTEN.
TRY TO RELAX AND ENJOY IT.

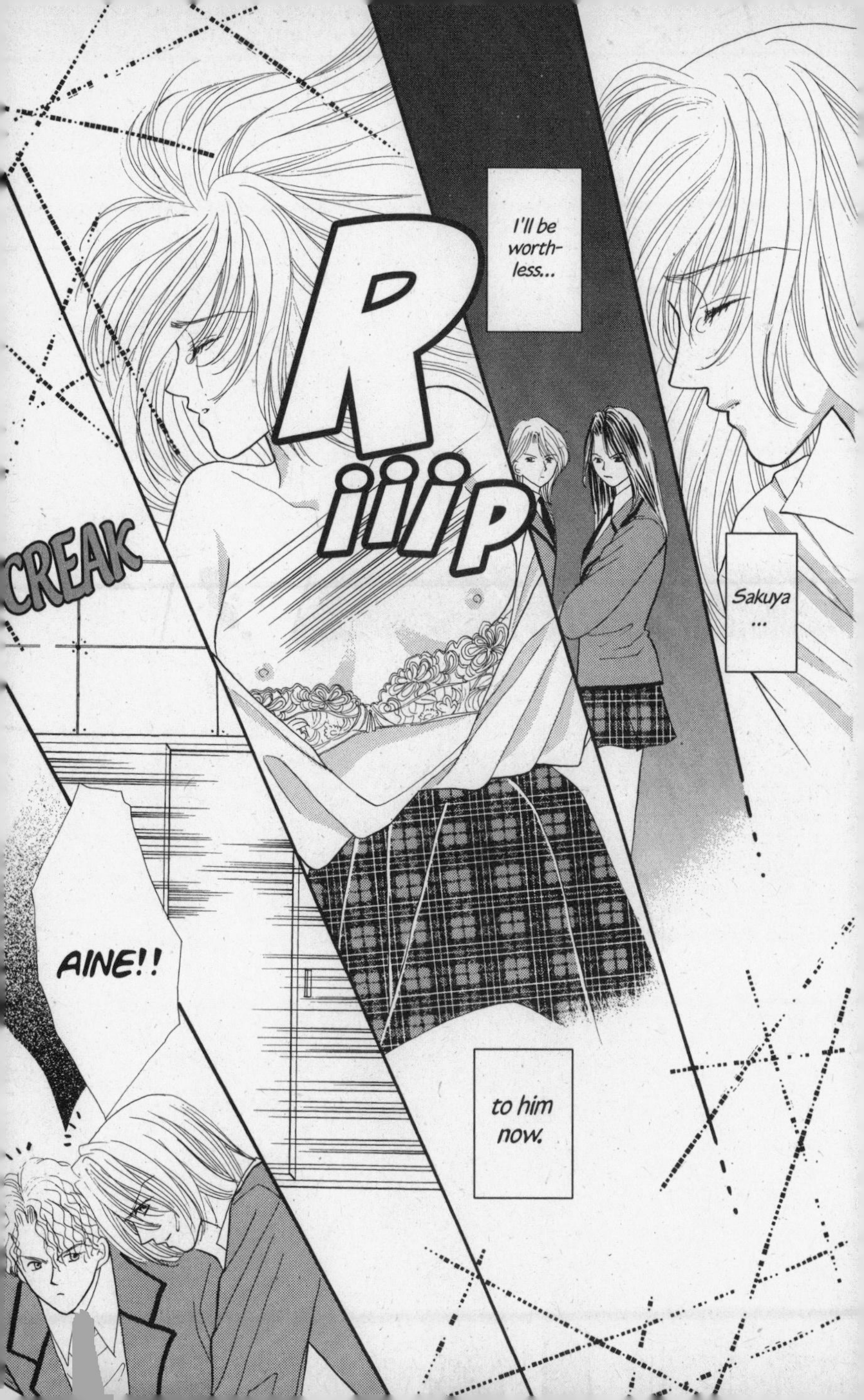
Sakuya
...
I'll be worth-less...
R iiip
CREAK
to him now.
AINE!!

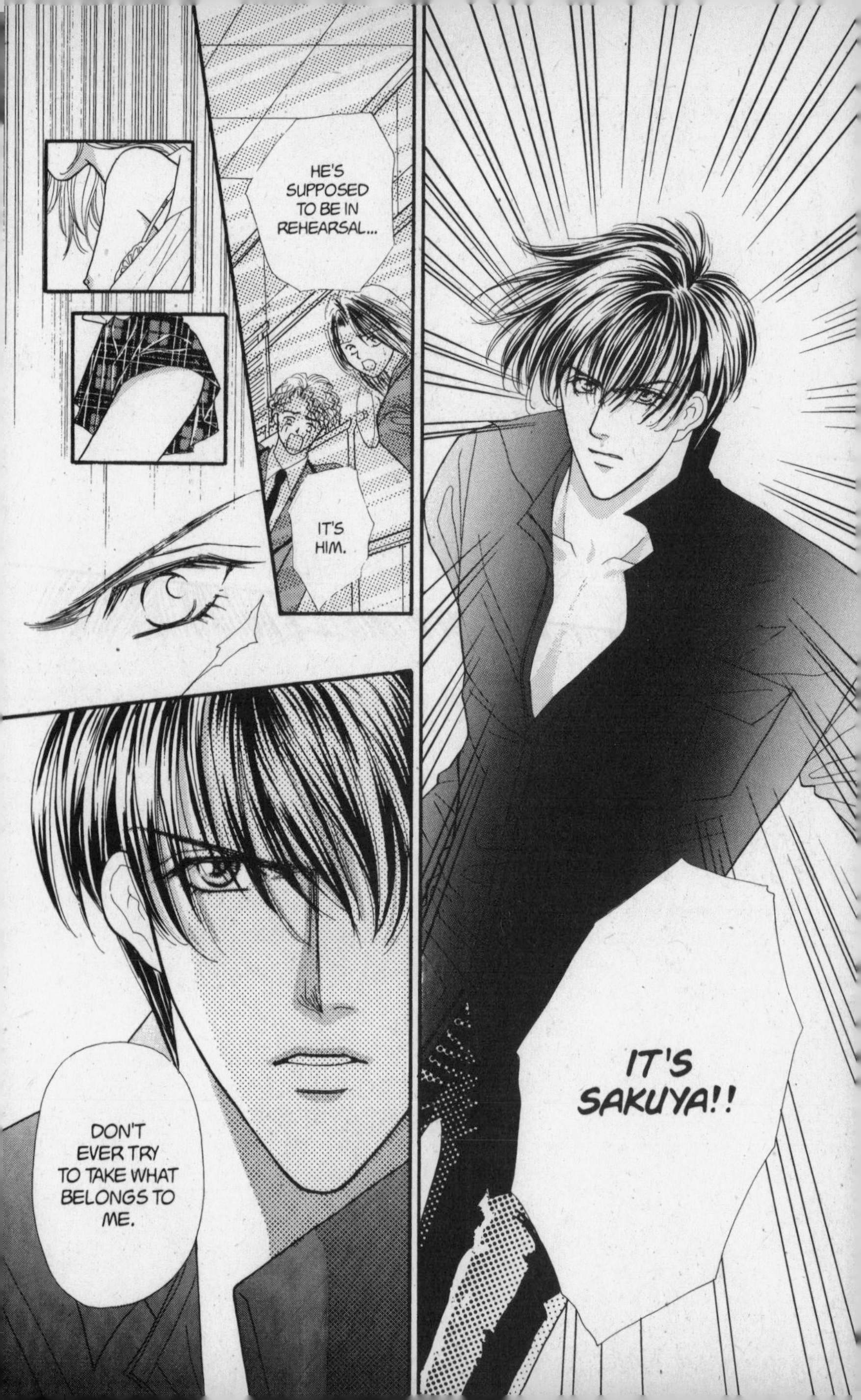
IT'S SAKUYA!!
HE'S SUPPOSED TO BE IN REHEARSAL...
IT'S HIM.
DON'T EVER TRY TO TAKE WHAT BELONGS TO ME.

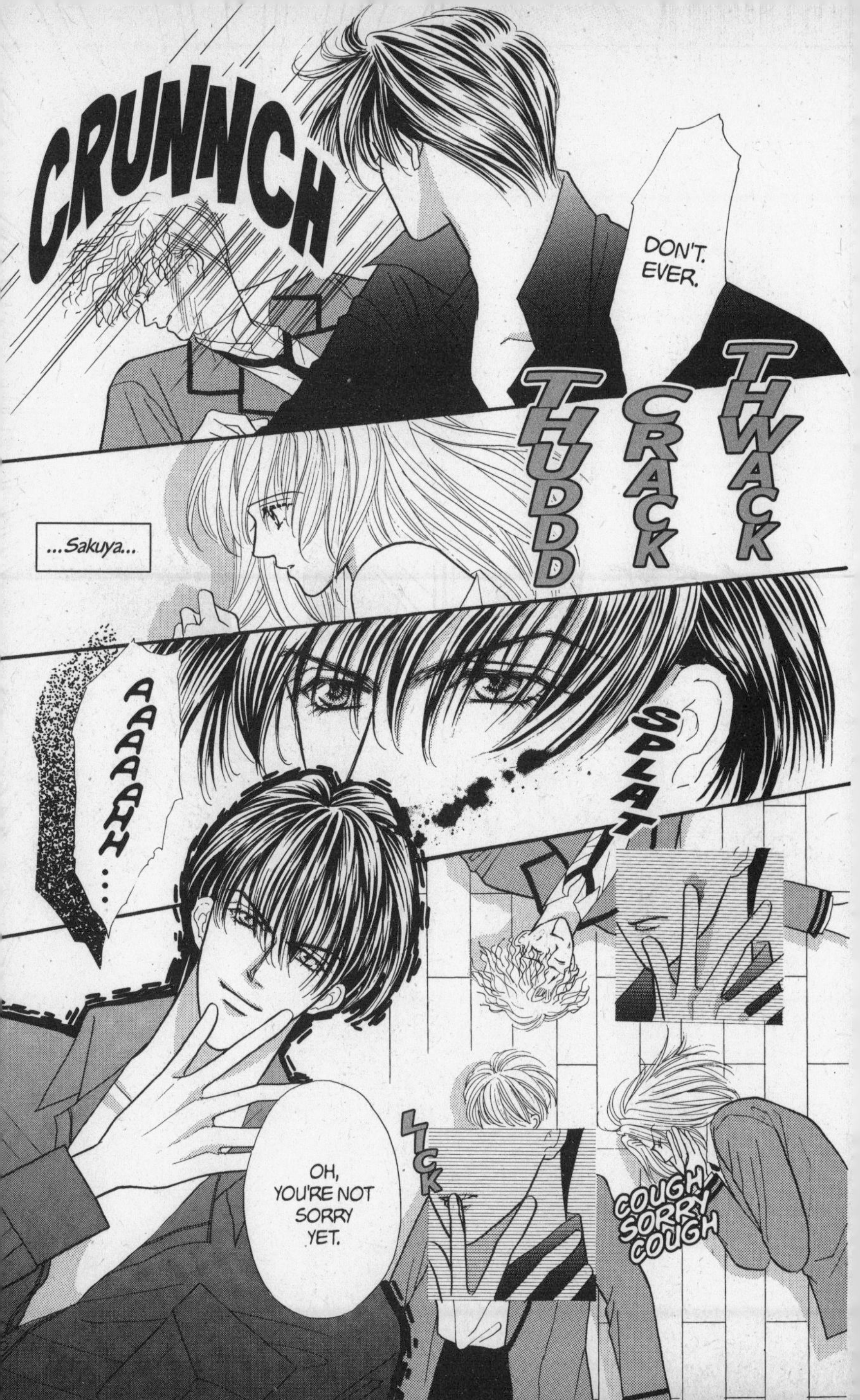
DON'T. EVER.
CRUNNCH
THWACK
CRACK
THUDD
...Sakuya...
SPLAT
AAAAAAH...
COUGH SORRY COUGH
LICK
OH, YOU'RE NOT SORRY YET.

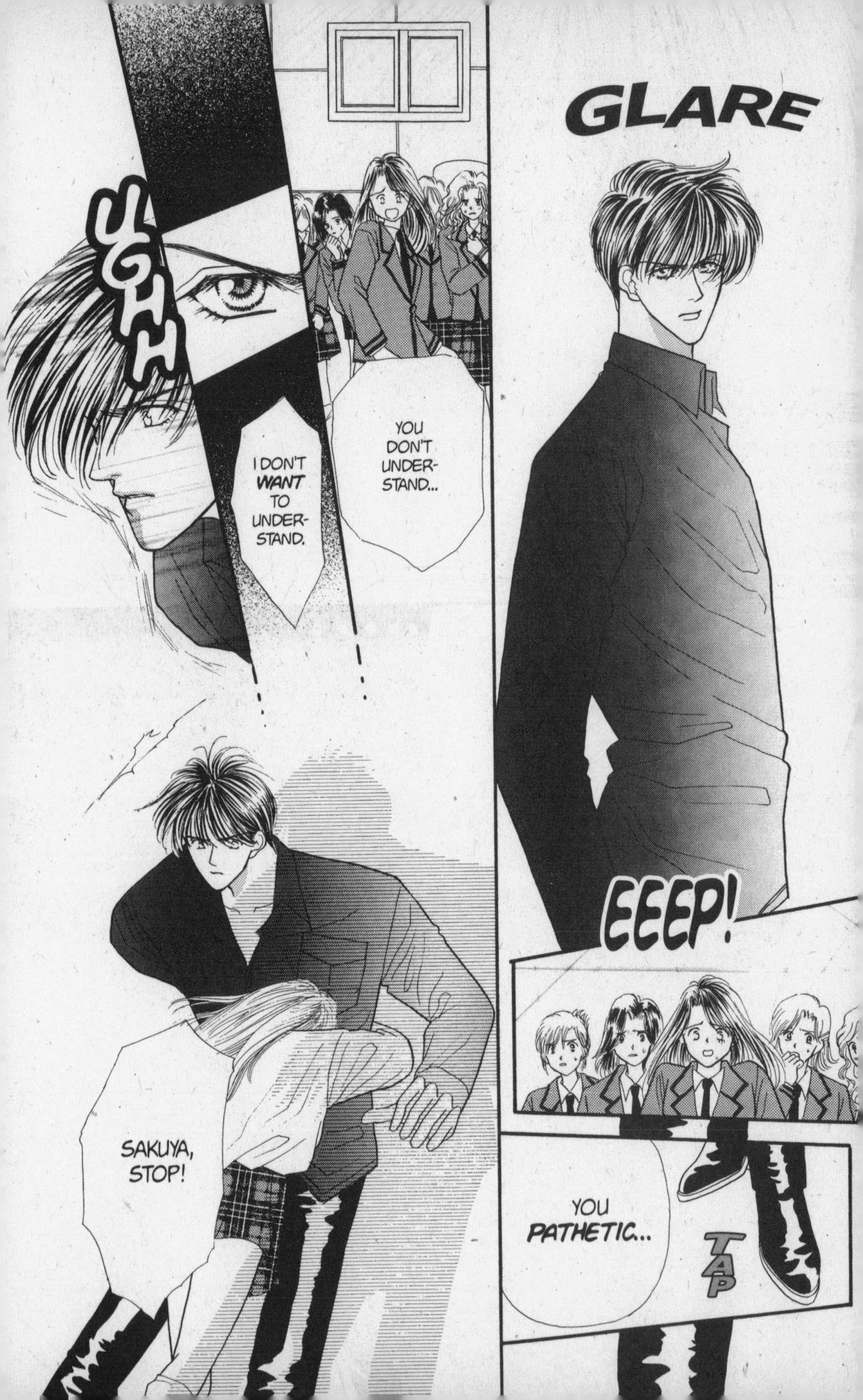
GLARE
EEEP!
YOU PATHETIC...
TAP
YOU DON'T UNDER-STAND...
UGHH
I DON'T WANT TO UNDER-STAND.
SAKUYA, STOP!

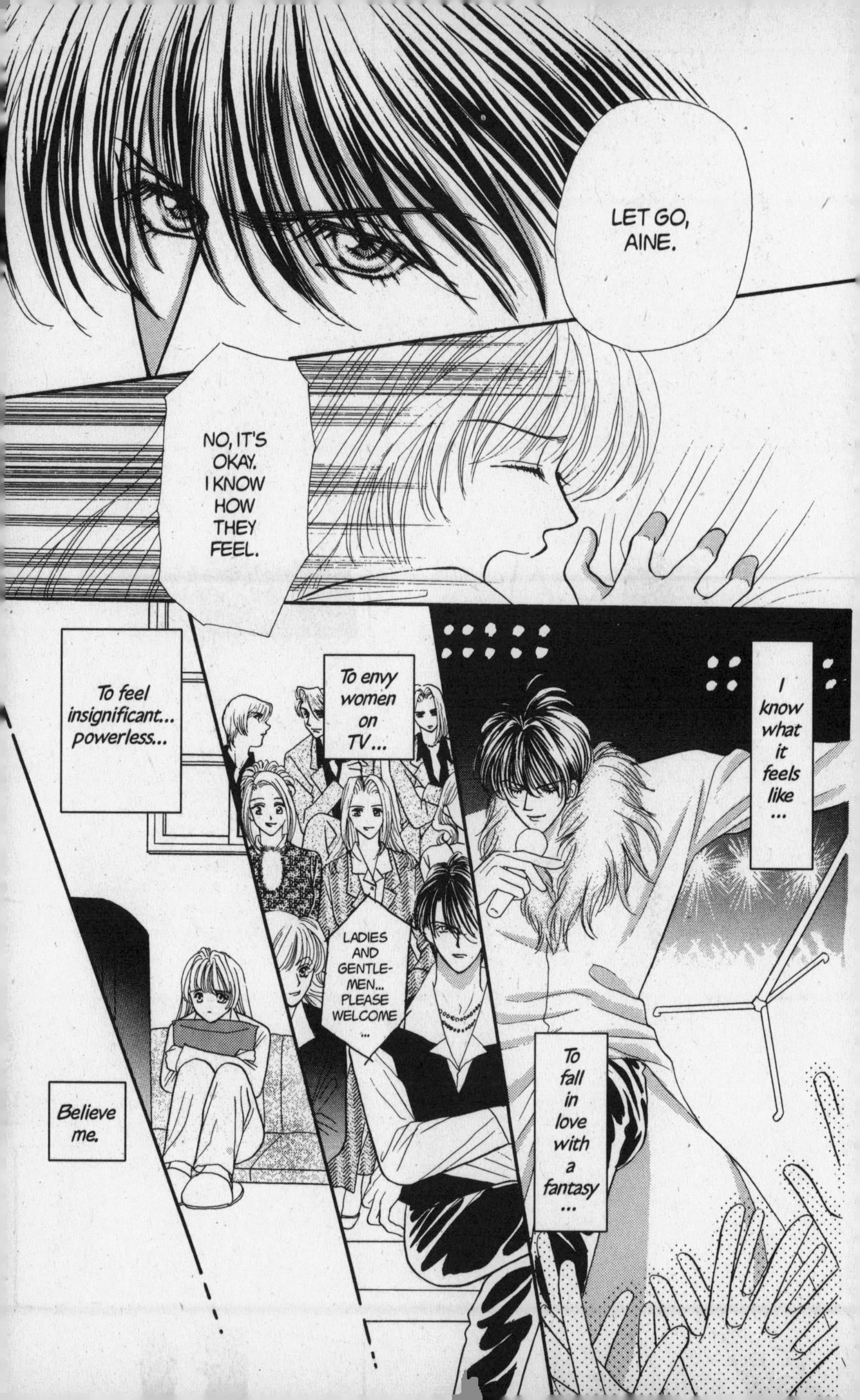
LET GO, AINE.
NO, IT'S OKAY. I KNOW HOW THEY FEEL.
I know what it feels like ...
To fall in love with a fantasy ...
To envy women on TV ...
LADIES AND GENTLE-MEN... PLEASE WELCOME ...
To feel insignificant... powerless...
Believe me.

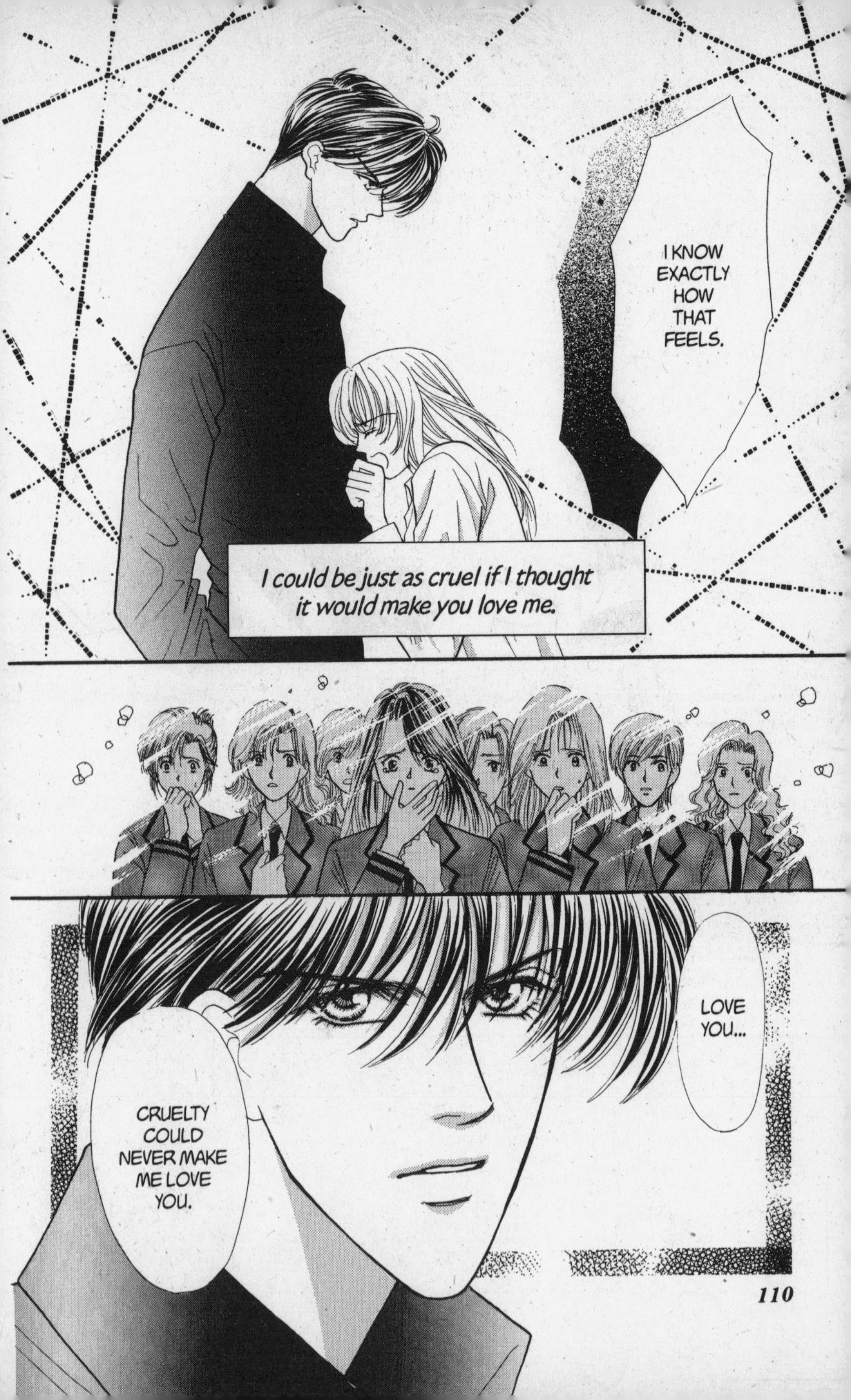
I KNOW EXACTLY HOW THAT FEELS.
I could be just as cruel if I thought it would make you love me.
LOVE YOU...
CRUELTY COULD NEVER MAKE ME LOVE YOU.

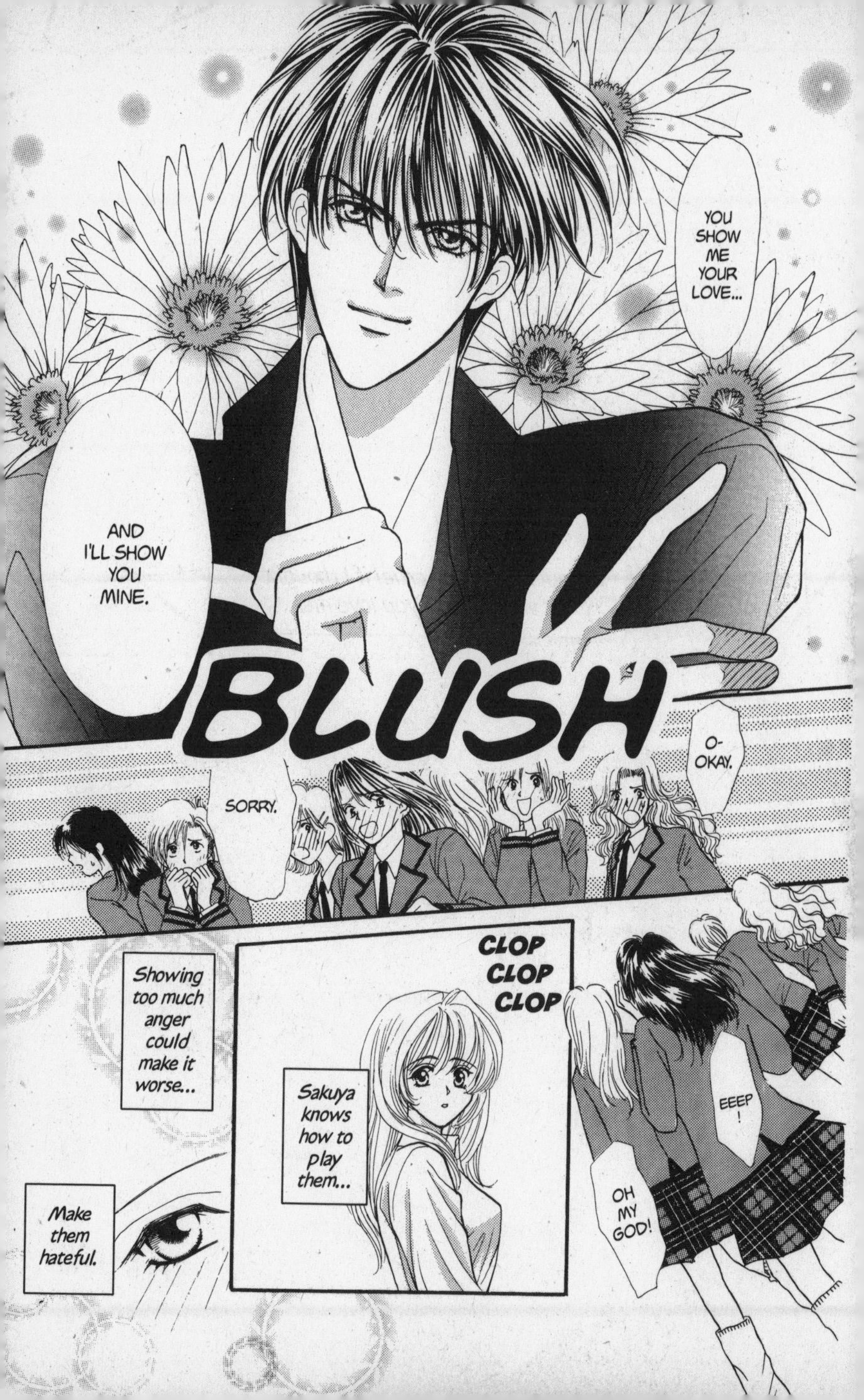
YOU SHOW ME YOUR LOVE...
AND I'LL SHOW YOU MINE.
BLUSH
O-OKAY.
SORRY.
EEEP!
OH MY GOD!
CLOP CLOP CLOP
Sakuya knows how to play them...
Showing too much anger could make it worse...
Make them hateful.

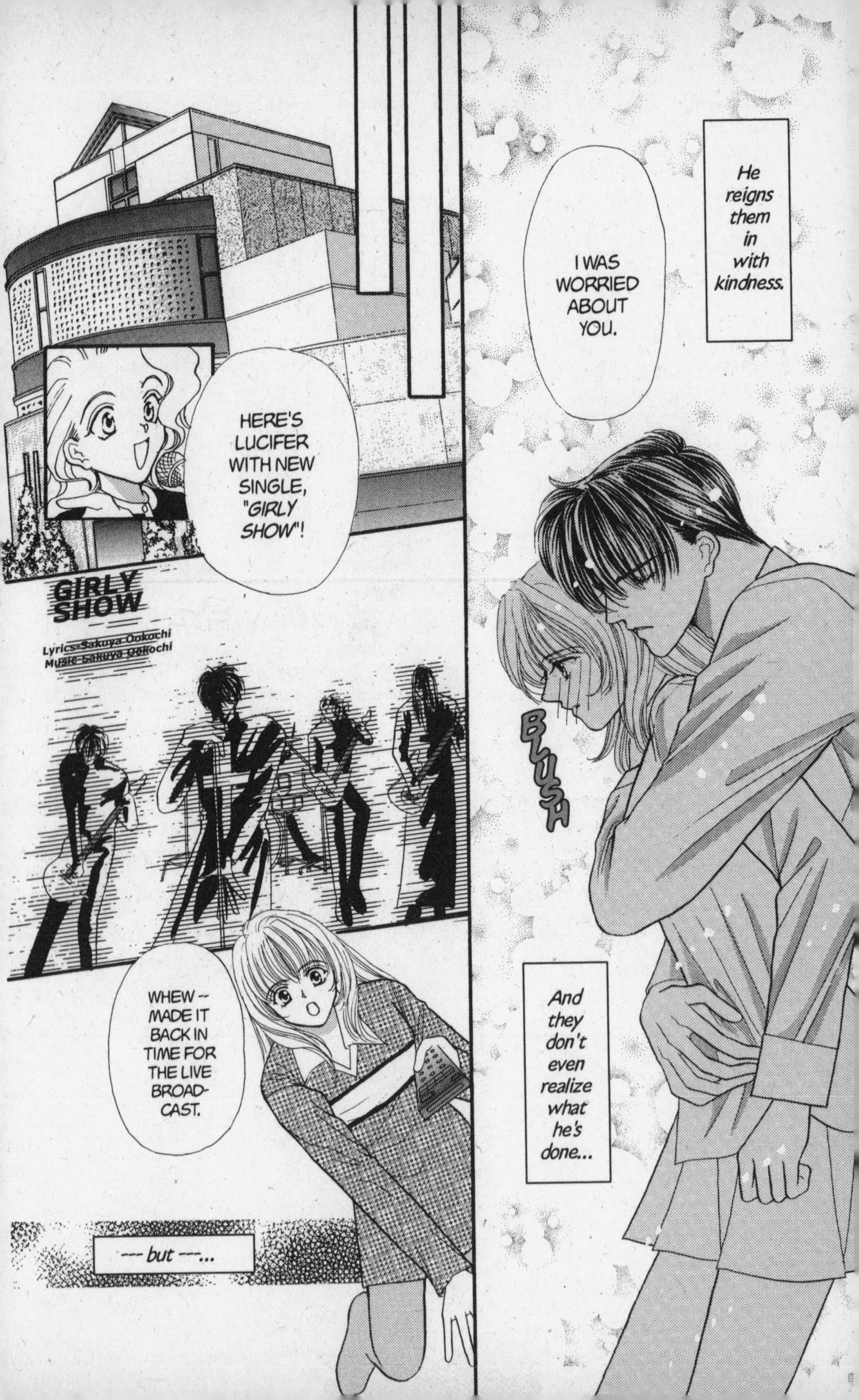
He reigns them in with kindness.
I WAS WORRIED ABOUT YOU.
BLUSH
And they don't even realize what he's done...
HERE'S LUCIFER WITH NEW SINGLE, "GIRLY SHOW"!
GIRLY SHOW
Lyrics-Sakuya Ookochi
Music-Sakuya Ookochi
WHEW -- MADE IT BACK IN TIME FOR THE LIVE BROAD-CAST.
--- but ---...

Have you seen Hakuei's video for "NUDE"? So! Hot! (Those ARE contact lenses he's wearing, right?)

L'Arc-en-Ciel's "LIES AND TRUTH" video is a MASTERPIECE. And Yellow Monkey's videos are cool -- they're made in the American style. Videos and photos in magazines inspire me to draw. Like, 'I want to draw these eyes' or I want to use certain colors.

If I'm offered a color issue, I'm thinking of styling it like a CD cover. Of course, my skills aren't quite there yet. I mean, I've got ideas but I still hate drawing in color.

Speaking of color, many of you send in your print-clubs with your letters...

(to be continued)

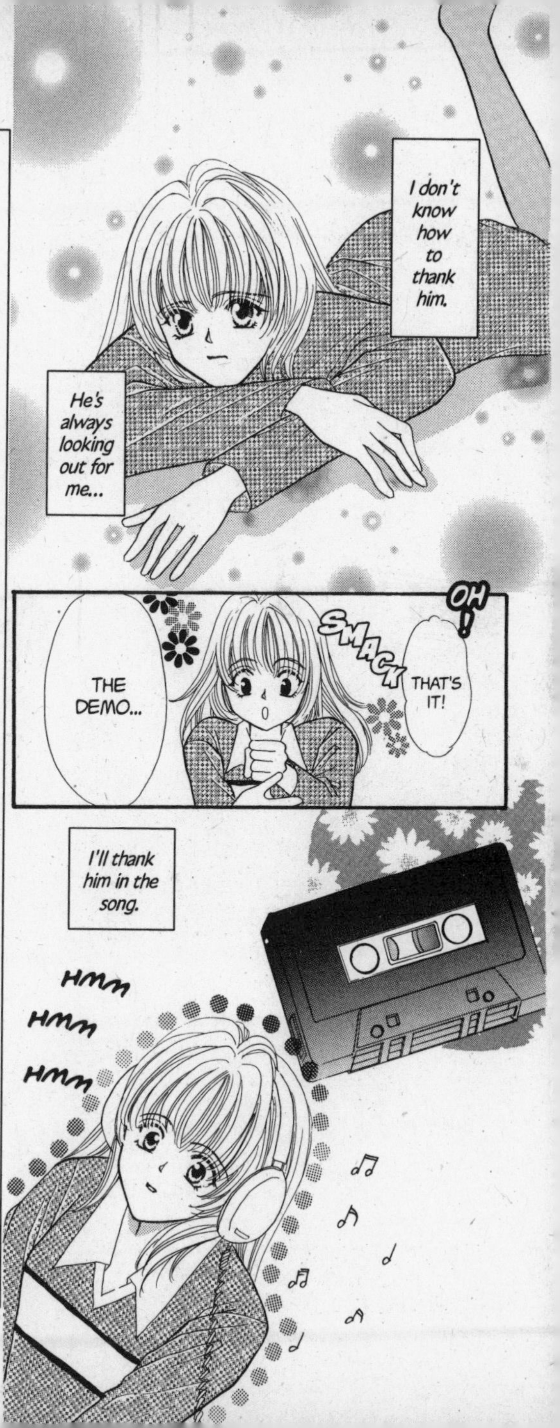
I don't know how to thank him.
He's always looking out for me...
OH!
SMACK
THAT'S IT!
THE DEMO...
I'll thank him in the song.
HMM
HMM
HMM

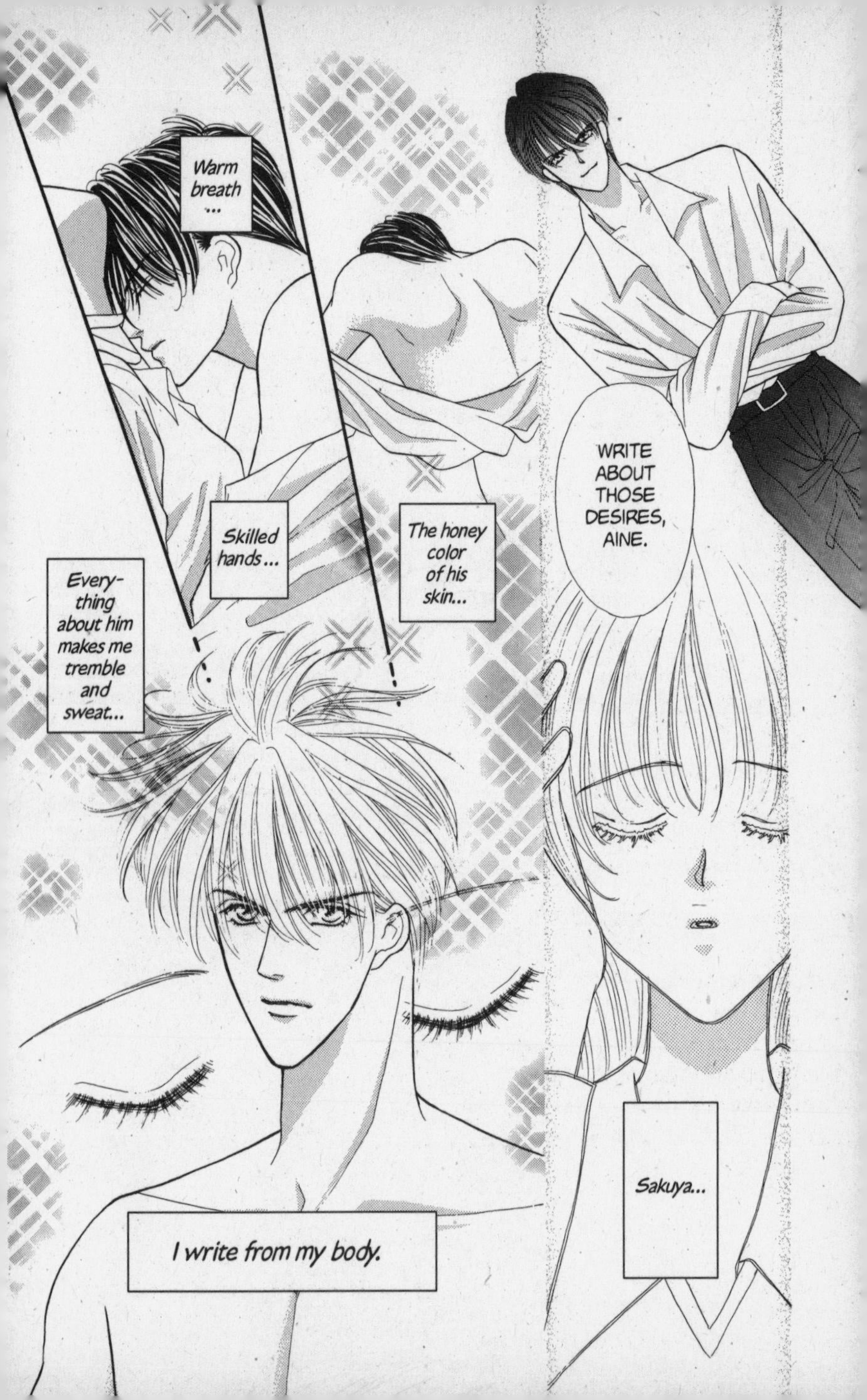
WRITE ABOUT THOSE DESIRES, AINE.
Sakuya...
The honey color of his skin...
Warm breath...
Skilled hands...
Every-thing about him makes me tremble and sweat...
I write from my body.

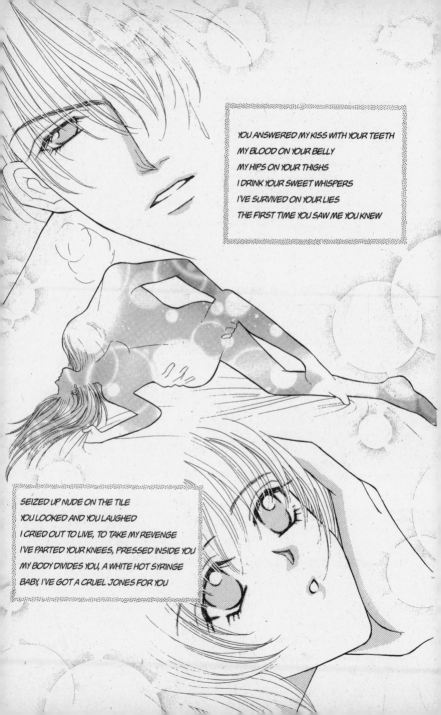

YOU ANSWERED MY KISS WITH YOUR TEETH
MY BLOOD ON YOUR BELLY
MY HIPS ON YOUR THIGHS
I DRINK YOUR SWEET WHISPERS
I'VE SURVIVED ON YOUR LIES
THE FIRST TIME YOU SAW ME YOU KNEW

SEIZED UP NUDE ON THE TILE
YOU LOOKED AND YOU LAUGHED
I CRIED OUT TO LIVE, TO TAKE MY REVENGE
I'VE PARTED YOUR KNEES, PRESSED INSIDE YOU
MY BODY DIVIDES YOU, A WHITE HOT SYRINGE
BABY, I'VE GOT A CRUEL JONES FOR YOU

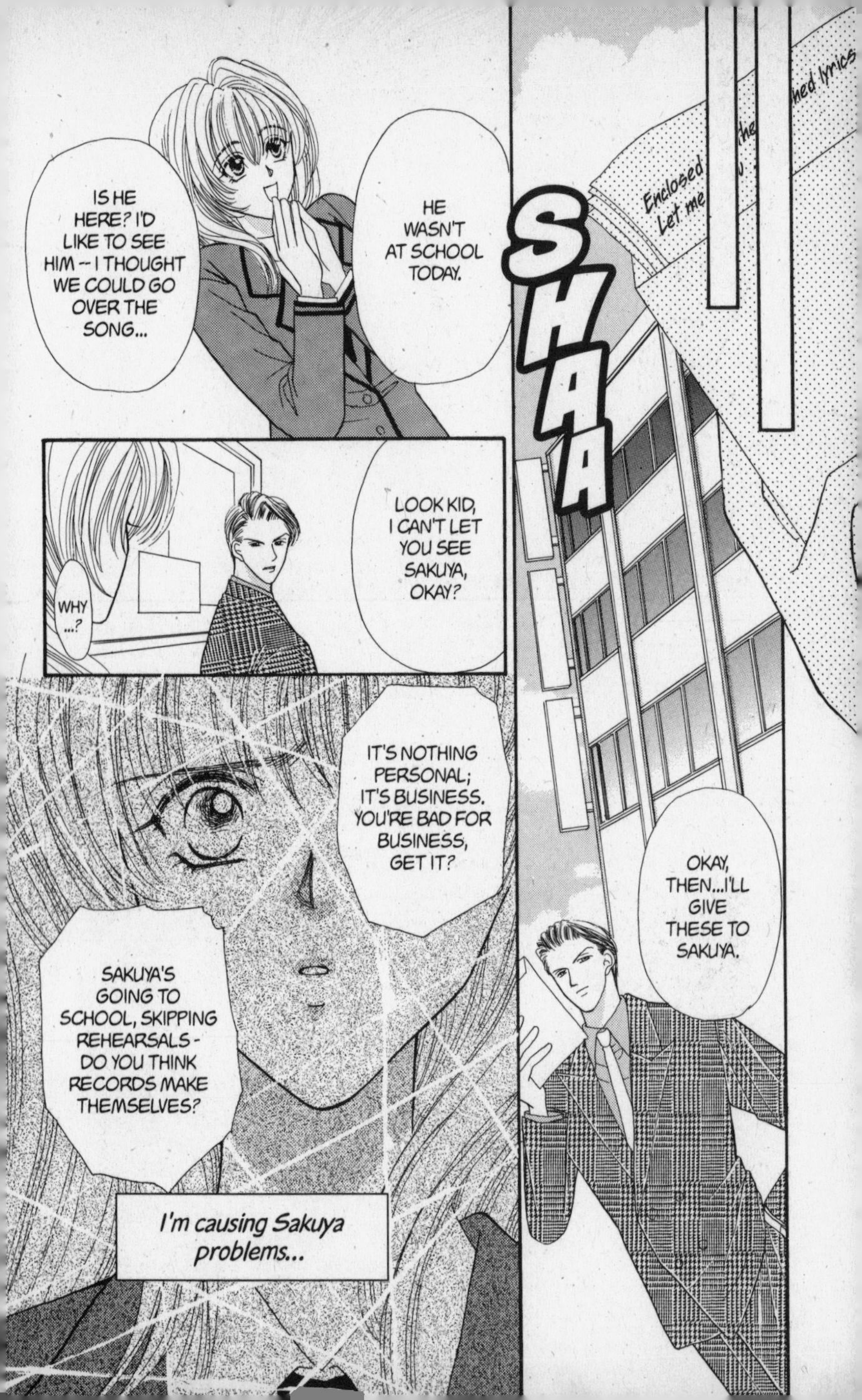
Enclosed
Let me
SHAA
OKAY, THEN...I'LL GIVE THESE TO SAKUYA.
HE WASN'T AT SCHOOL TODAY.
IS HE HERE? I'D LIKE TO SEE HIM -- I THOUGHT WE COULD GO OVER THE SONG...
LOOK KID, I CAN'T LET YOU SEE SAKUYA, OKAY?
WHY ...?
IT'S NOTHING PERSONAL; IT'S BUSINESS. YOU'RE BAD FOR BUSINESS, GET IT?
SAKUYA'S GOING TO SCHOOL, SKIPPING REHEARSALS - DO YOU THINK RECORDS MAKE THEMSELVES?
I'm causing Sakuya problems...

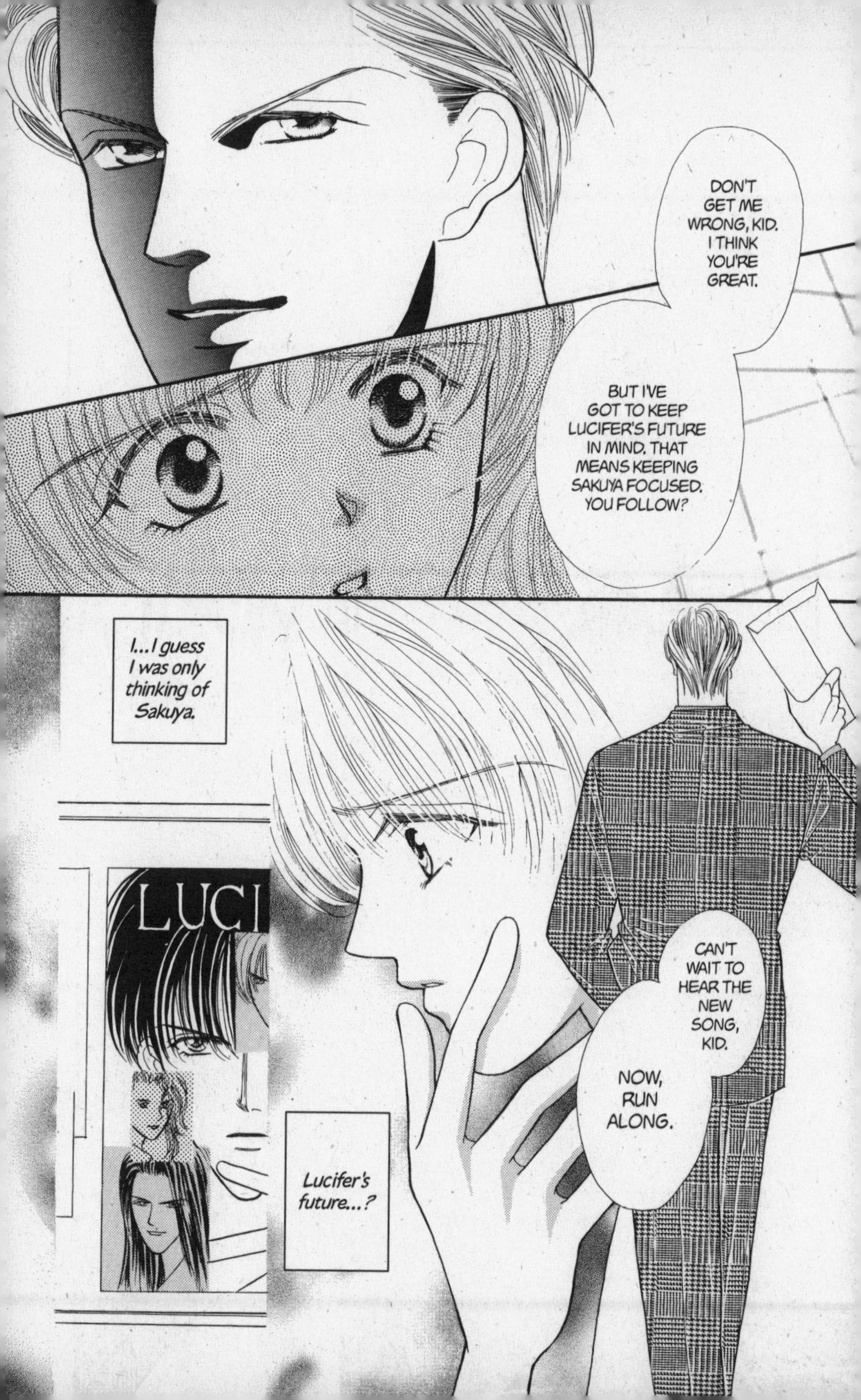
DON'T GET ME WRONG, KID. I THINK YOU'RE GREAT.
BUT I'VE GOT TO KEEP LUCIFER'S FUTURE IN MIND. THAT MEANS KEEPING SAKUYA FOCUSED. YOU FOLLOW?
CAN'T WAIT TO HEAR THE NEW SONG, KID.
NOW, RUN ALONG.
I...I guess I was only thinking of Sakuya.
LUCI
Lucifer's future...?

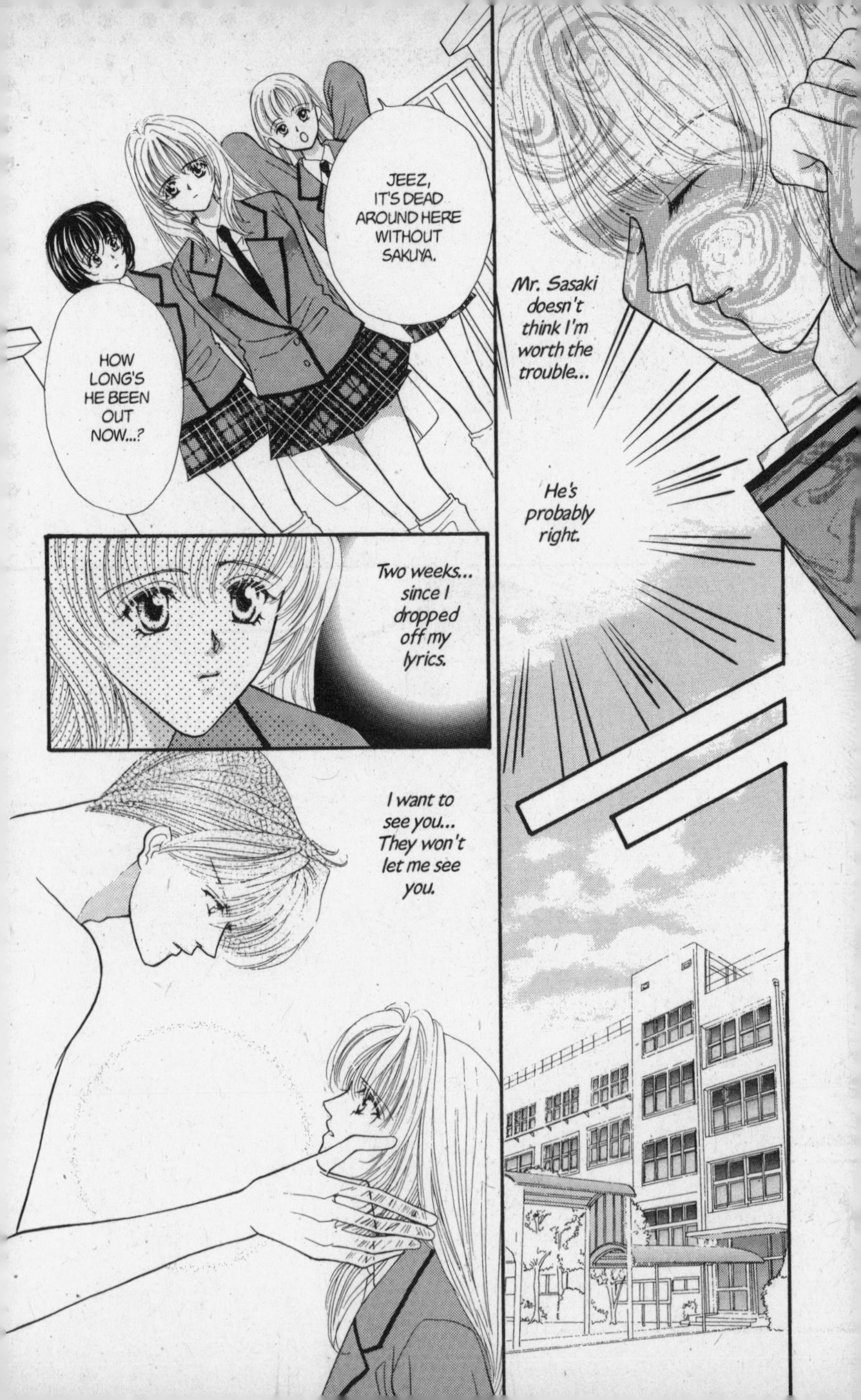
Mr. Sasaki doesn't think I'm worth the trouble...
He's probably right.
JEEZ, IT'S DEAD AROUND HERE WITHOUT SAKUYA.
HOW LONG'S HE BEEN OUT NOW...?
Two weeks... since I dropped off my lyrics.
I want to see you... They won't let me see you.

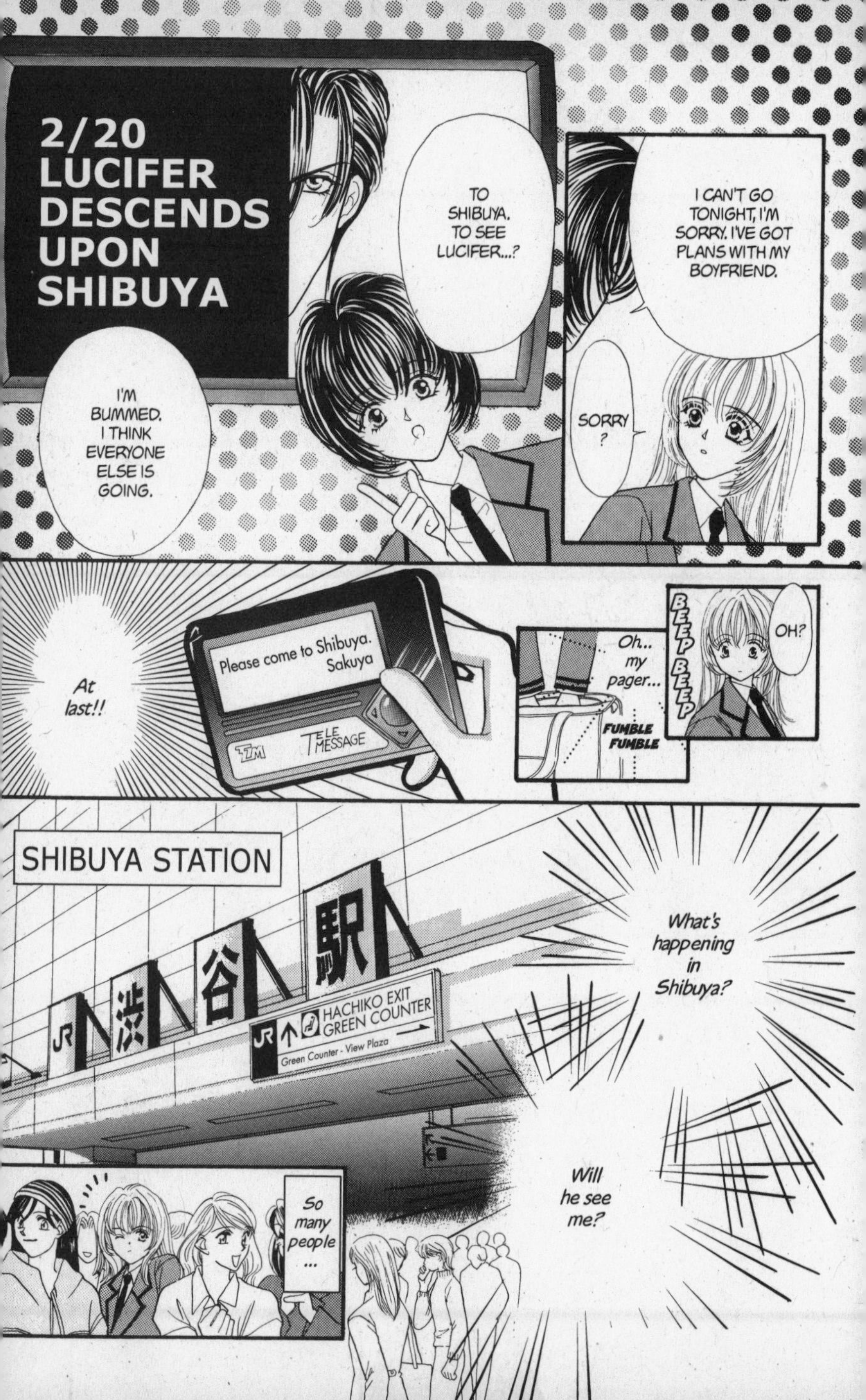
I CAN'T GO TONIGHT, I'M SORRY. I'VE GOT PLANS WITH MY BOYFRIEND.
SORRY?
2/20 LUCIFER DESCENDS UPON SHIBUYA
TO SHIBUYA. TO SEE LUCIFER...?
I'M BUMMED. I THINK EVERYONE ELSE IS GOING.
OH?
BEEP BEEP
Oh... my pager...
FUMBLE FUMBLE
Please come to Shibuya. Sakuya
TELE MESSAGE
TLM
At last!!
What's happening in Shibuya?
SHIBUYA STATION
JR 渋谷駅
JR HACHIKO EXIT GREEN COUNTER
Green Counter - View Plaza
Will he see me?
So many people ...

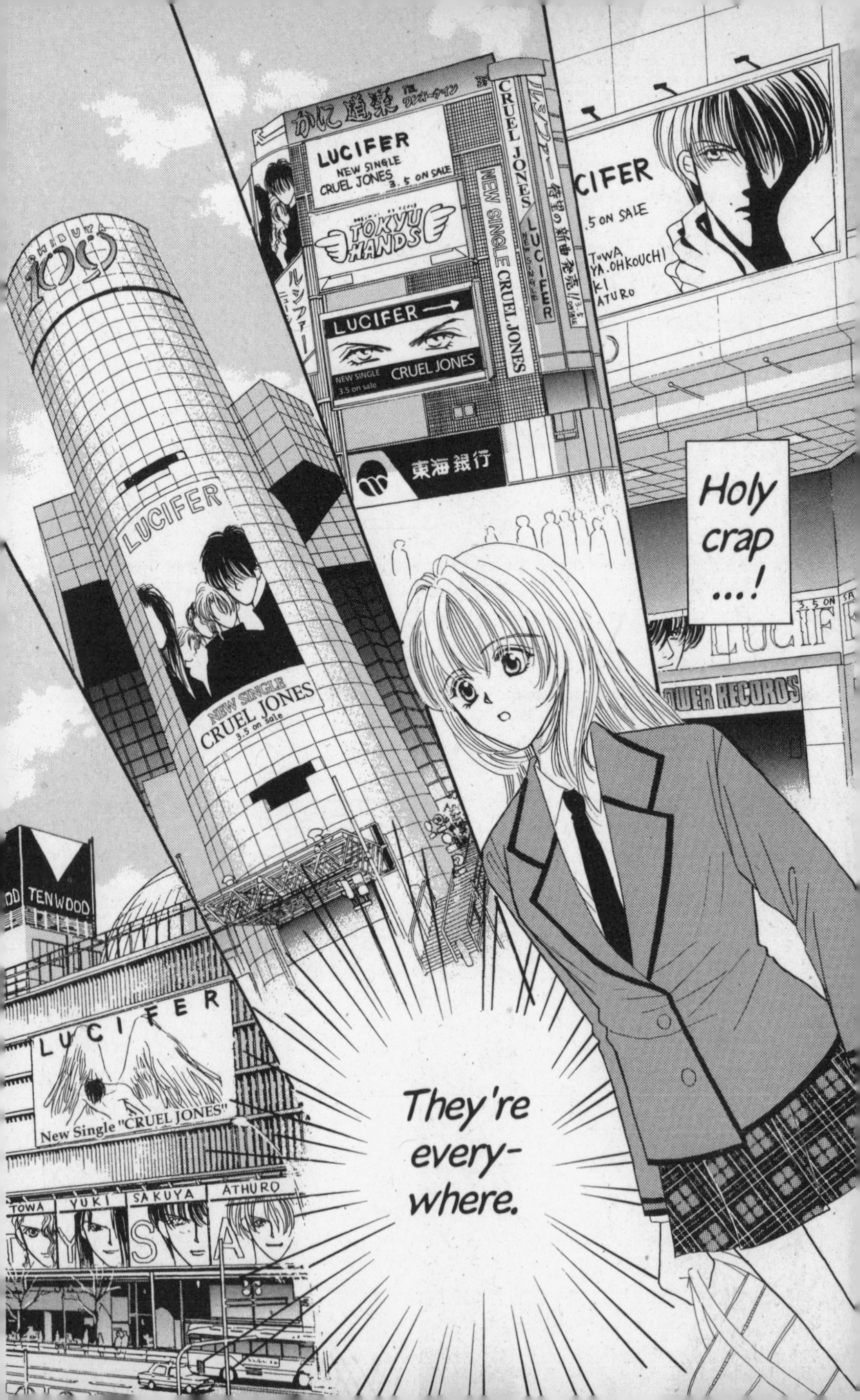
CIFER
.5 ON SALE
TOWA
YA.OHKOUCHI
Holy crap ...!
3.5 ON SA
OWER RECORDS
かに道楽
LUCIFER
NEW SINGLE
CRUEL JONES
3.5 ON SALE
TOKYU HANDS
LUCIFER
CRUEL JONES
NEW SINGLE
3.5 on sale
NEW SINGLE CRUEL JONES
CRUEL JONES
LUCIFER
東海銀行
LUCIFER
NEW SINGLE
CRUEL JONES
3.5 on sale
TENWOOD
LUCIFER
New Single "CRUEL JONES"
TOWA
YUKI
SAKUYA
ATHURO
They're every-where.

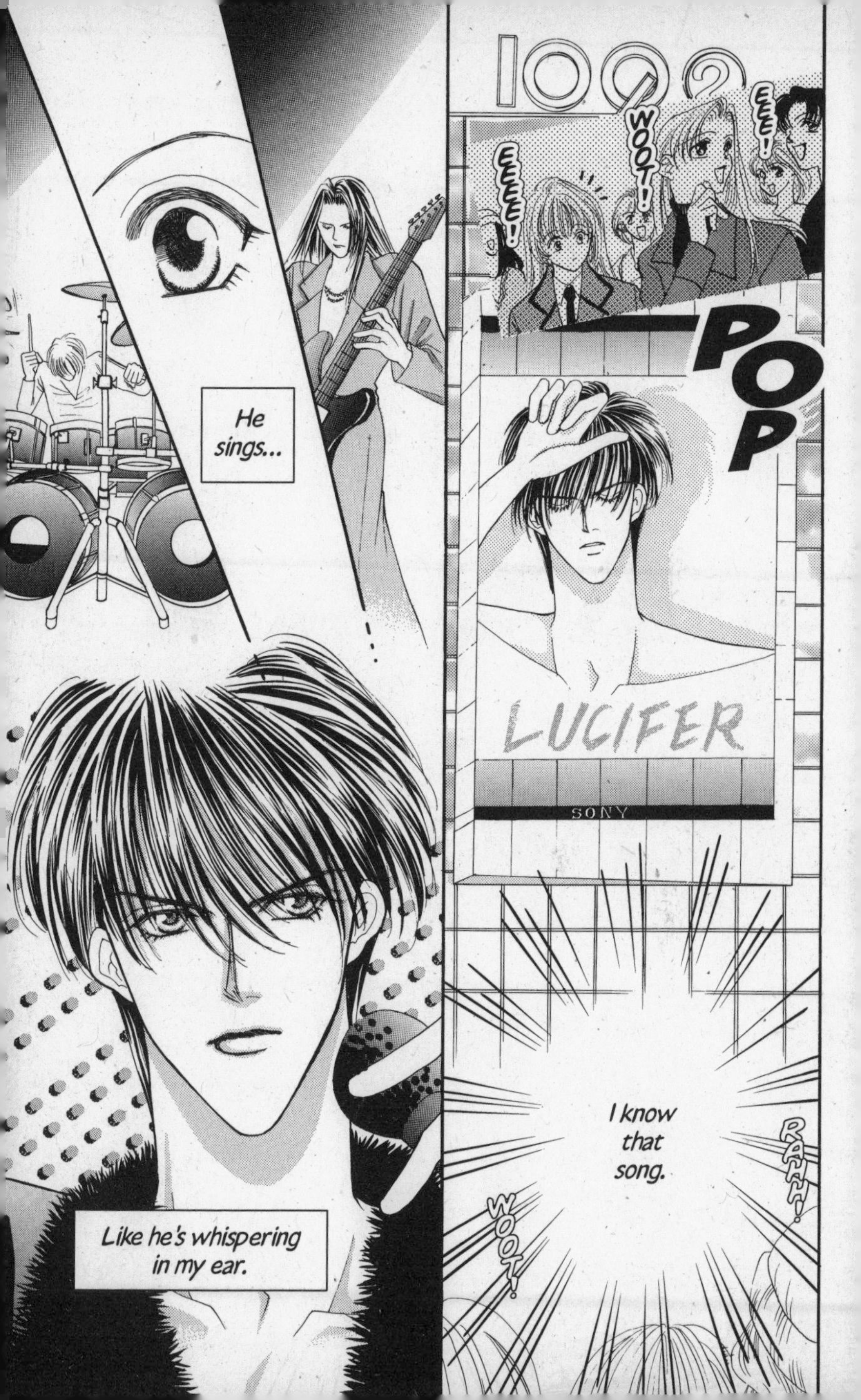
EEE!
WOOT!
EEEE!
POP
LUCIFER
SONY
I know that song.
RAHH!
WOOT!
He sings...
Like he's whispering in my ear.

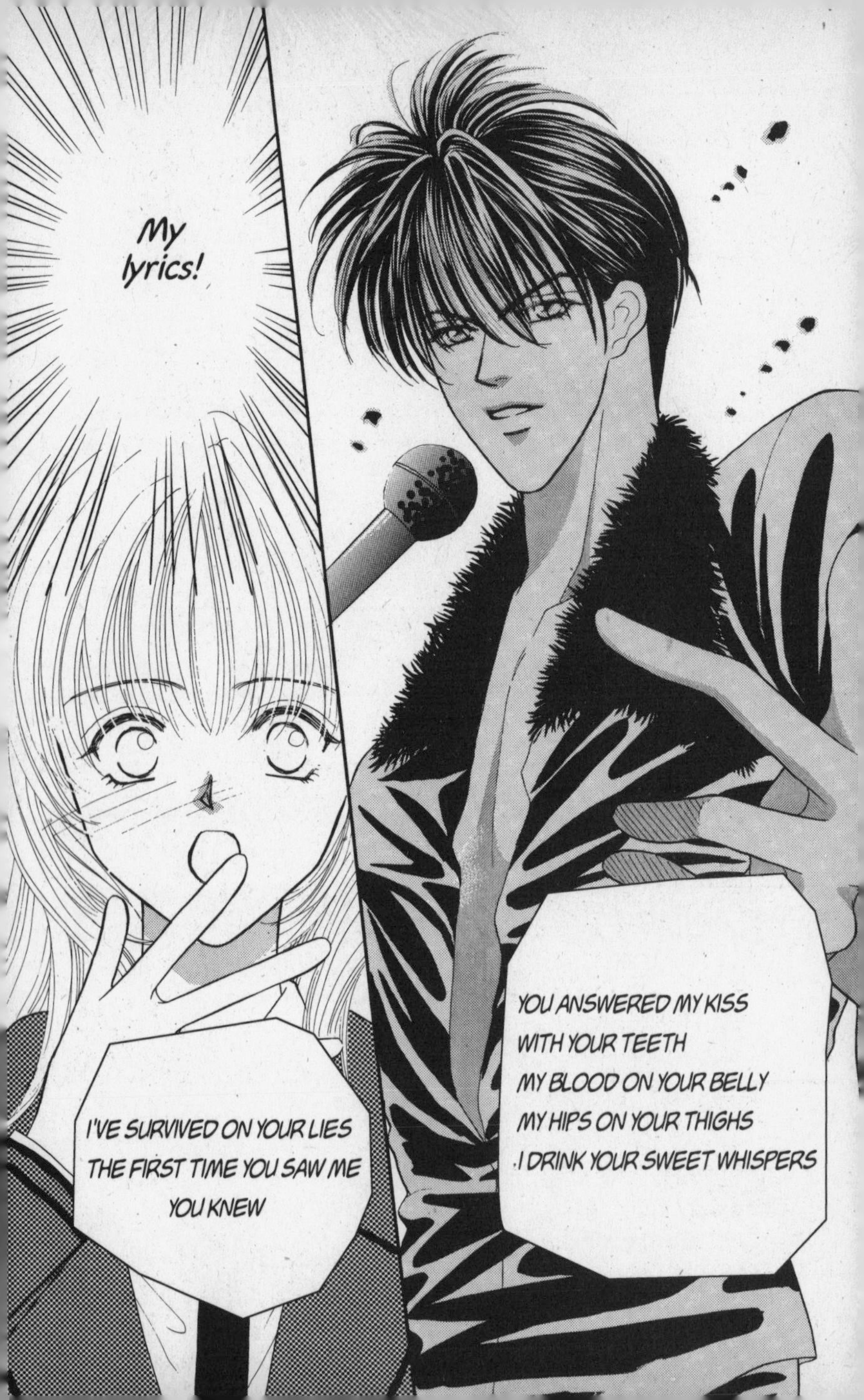
YOU ANSWERED MY KISS WITH YOUR TEETH MY BLOOD ON YOUR BELLY MY HIPS ON YOUR THIGHS I DRINK YOUR SWEET WHISPERS
My lyrics!
I'VE SURVIVED ON YOUR LIES THE FIRST TIME YOU SAW ME YOU KNEW

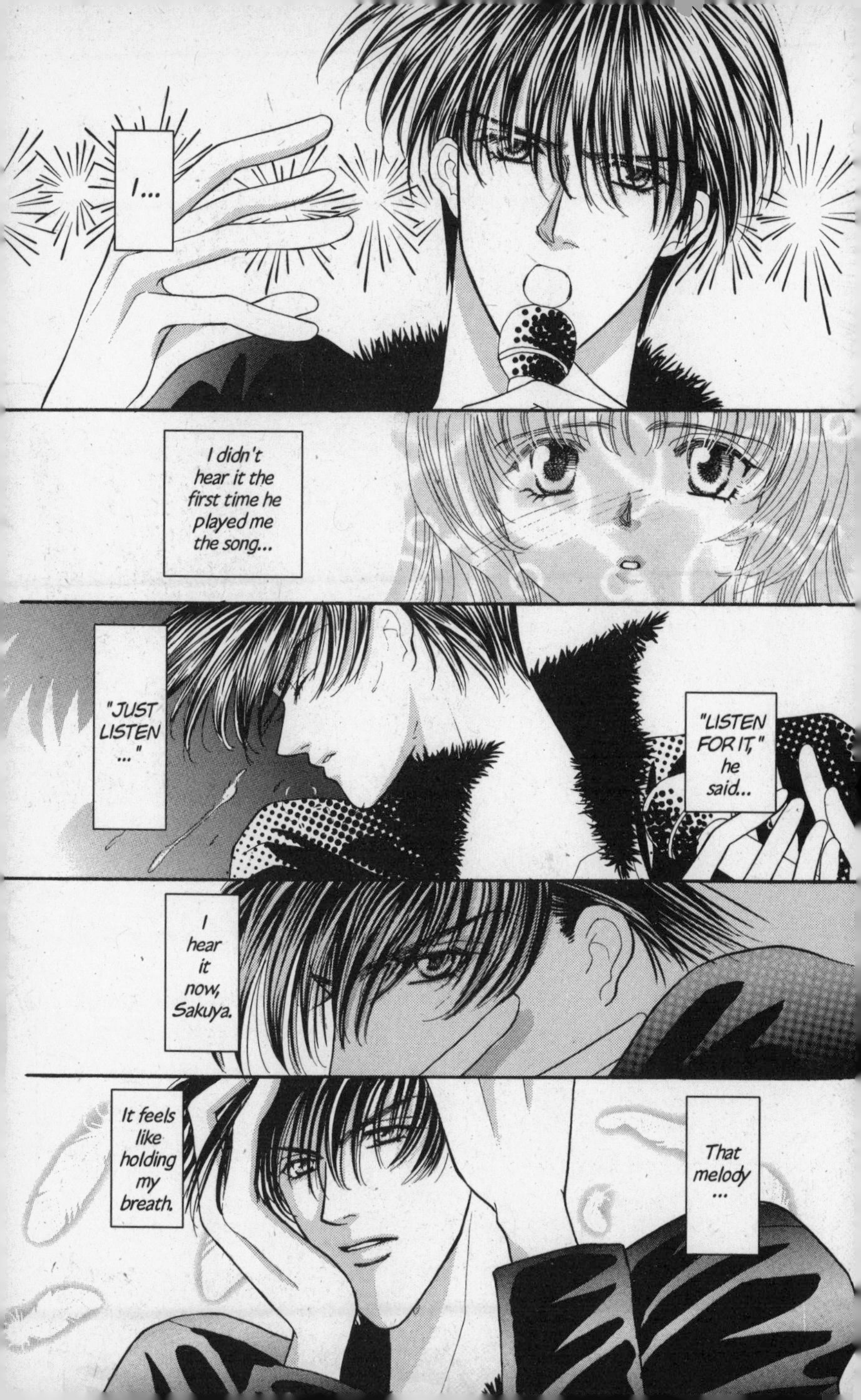
I...
I didn't hear it the first time he played me the song...
"LISTEN FOR IT," he said...
"JUST LISTEN ..."
I hear it now, Sakuya.
That melody ...
It feels like holding my breath.

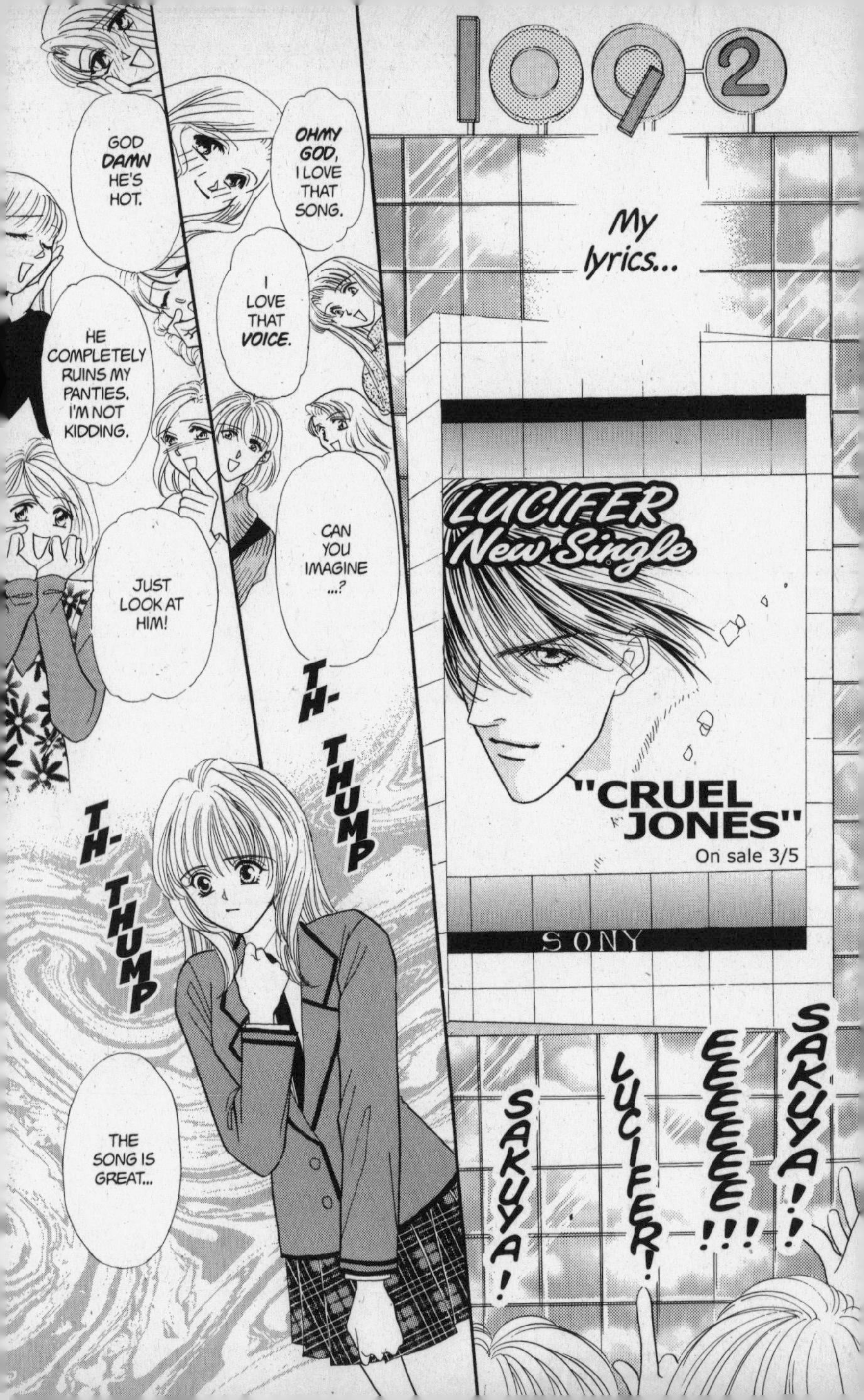
My lyrics...
LUCIFER New Single
"CRUEL JONES"
On sale 3/5
SONY
SAKUYA!!
EEEEEE!!!
LUCIFER!
SAKUYA!
OHMY GOD, I LOVE THAT SONG.
I LOVE THAT VOICE.
CAN YOU IMAGINE ...?
TH-THUMP
GOD DAMN HE'S HOT.
HE COMPLETELY RUINS MY PANTIES. I'M NOT KIDDING.
JUST LOOK AT HIM!
TH-THUMP
THE SONG IS GREAT...

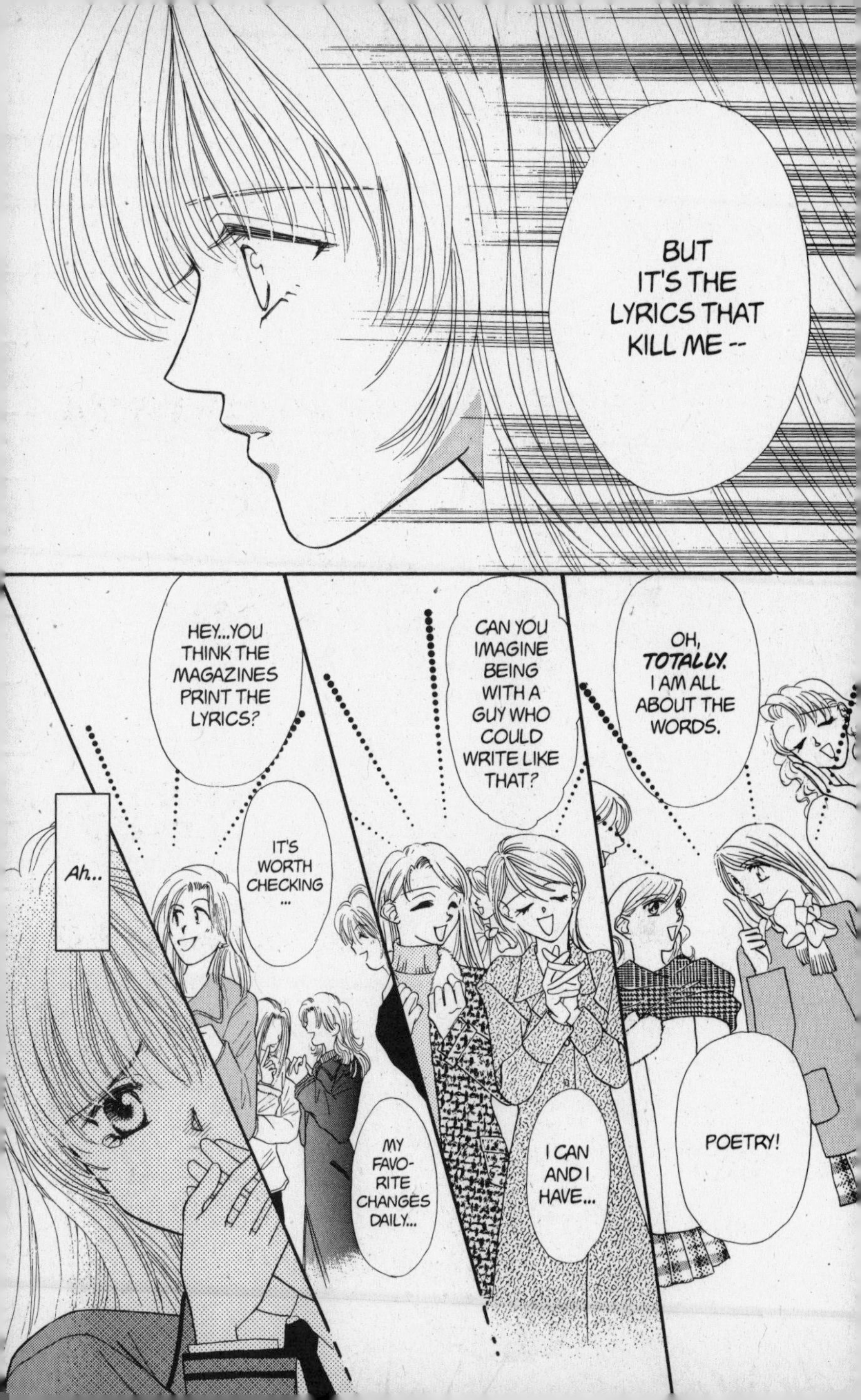
BUT IT'S THE LYRICS THAT KILL ME --
OH, ***TOTALLY.*** I AM ALL ABOUT THE WORDS.
POETRY!
CAN YOU IMAGINE BEING WITH A GUY WHO COULD WRITE LIKE THAT?
I CAN AND I HAVE...
HEY...YOU THINK THE MAGAZINES PRINT THE LYRICS?
IT'S WORTH CHECKING ...
MY FAVO-RITE CHANGES DAILY...
Ah...

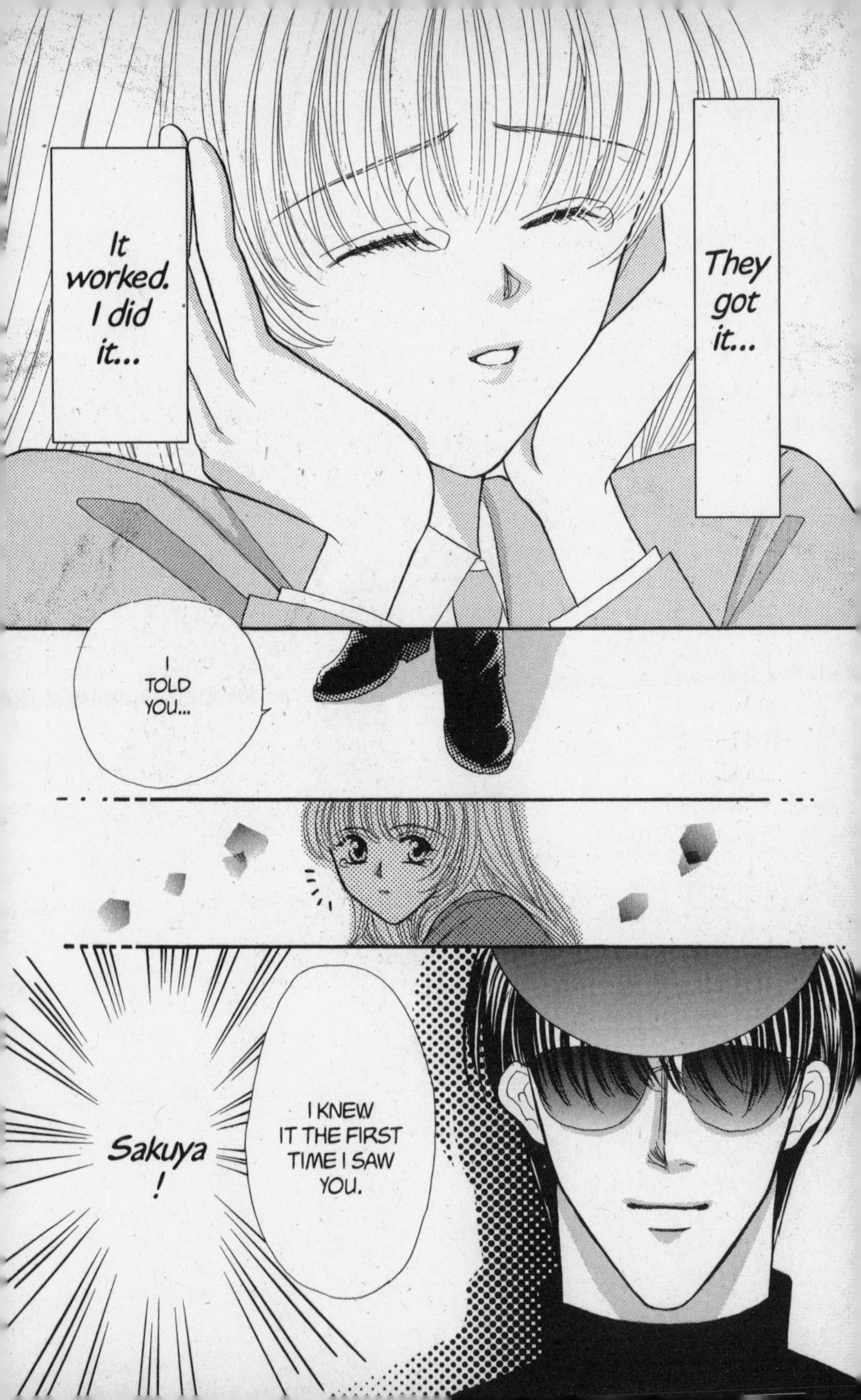

They got it...
It worked. I did it...
I TOLD YOU...
I KNEW IT THE FIRST TIME I SAW YOU.
Sakuya!

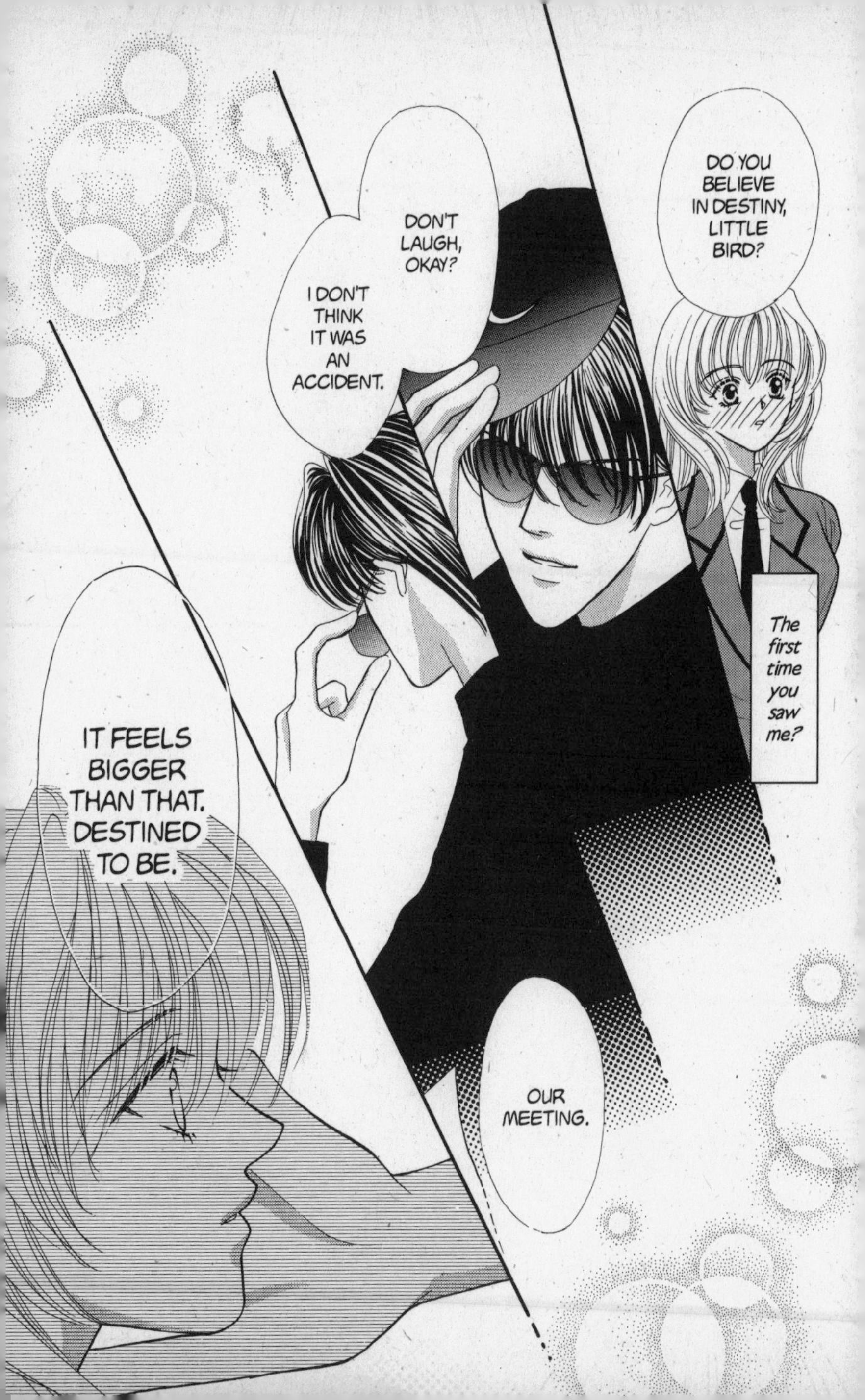
DO YOU BELIEVE IN DESTINY, LITTLE BIRD?
The first time you saw me?
DON'T LAUGH, OKAY?
I DON'T THINK IT WAS AN ACCIDENT.
OUR MEETING.
IT FEELS BIGGER THAN THAT. DESTINED TO BE.

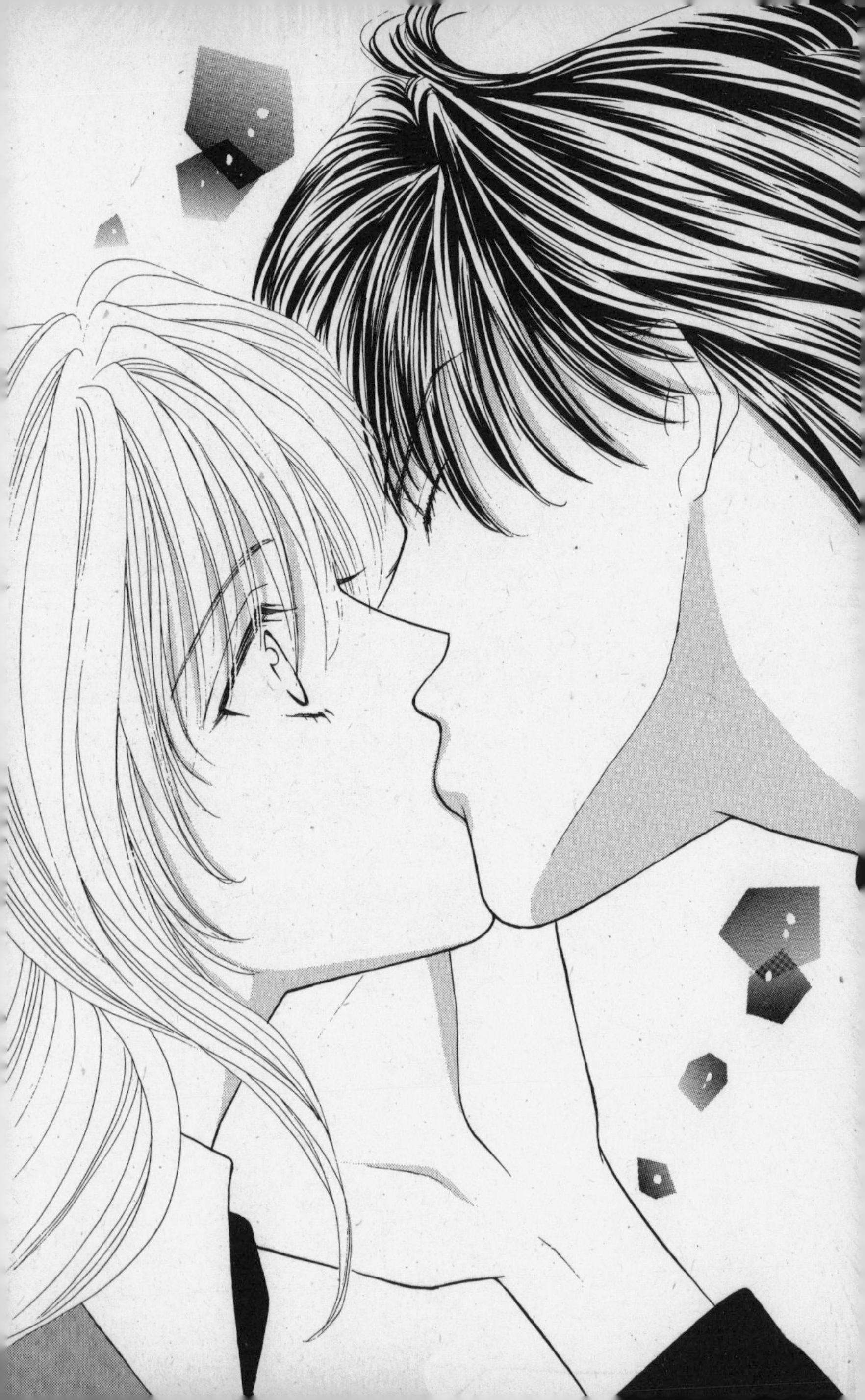

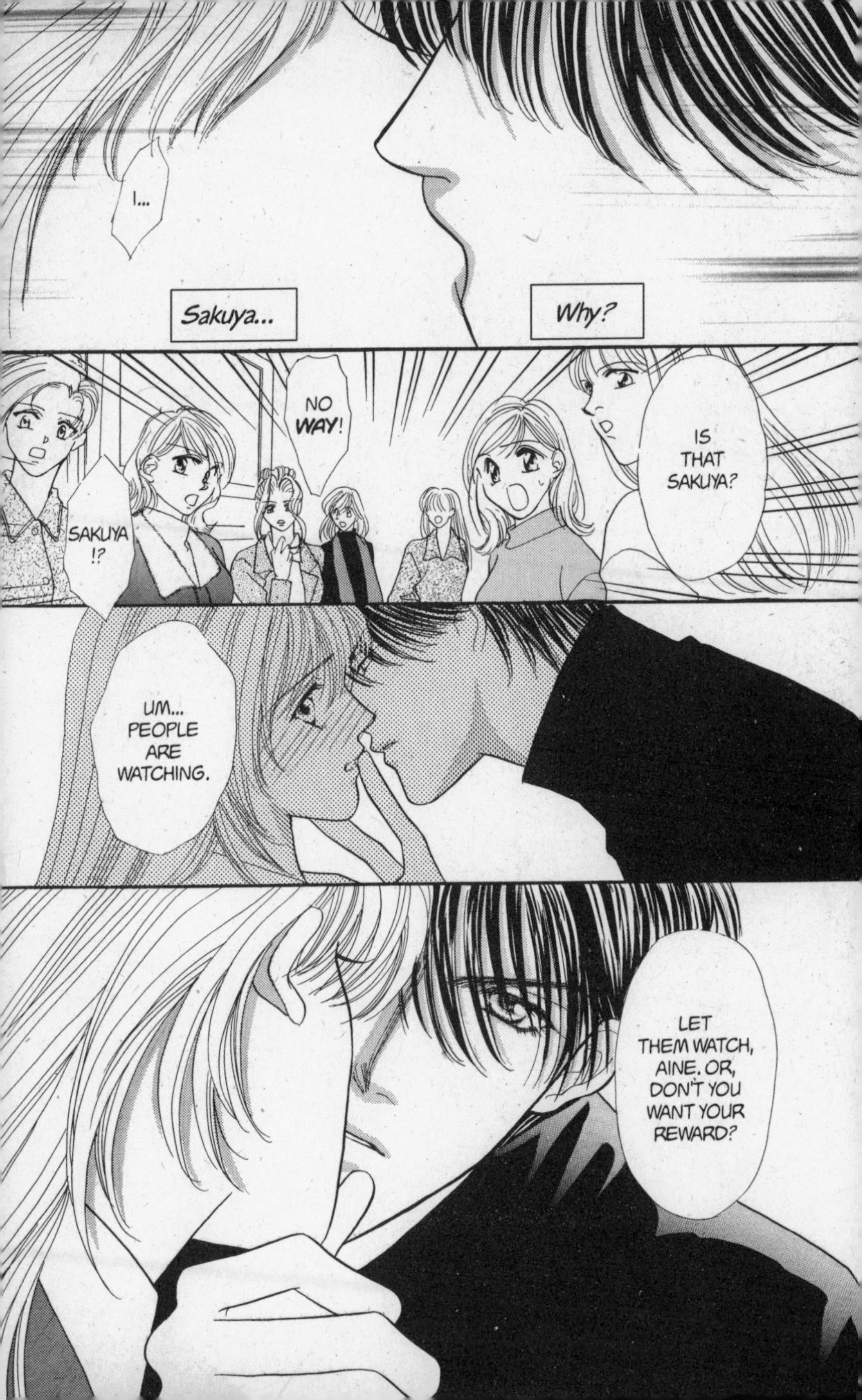
I...
Sakuya...
Why?
IS THAT SAKUYA?
NO WAY!
SAKUYA!?
UM... PEOPLE ARE WATCHING.
LET THEM WATCH, AINE. OR, DON'T YOU WANT YOUR REWARD?

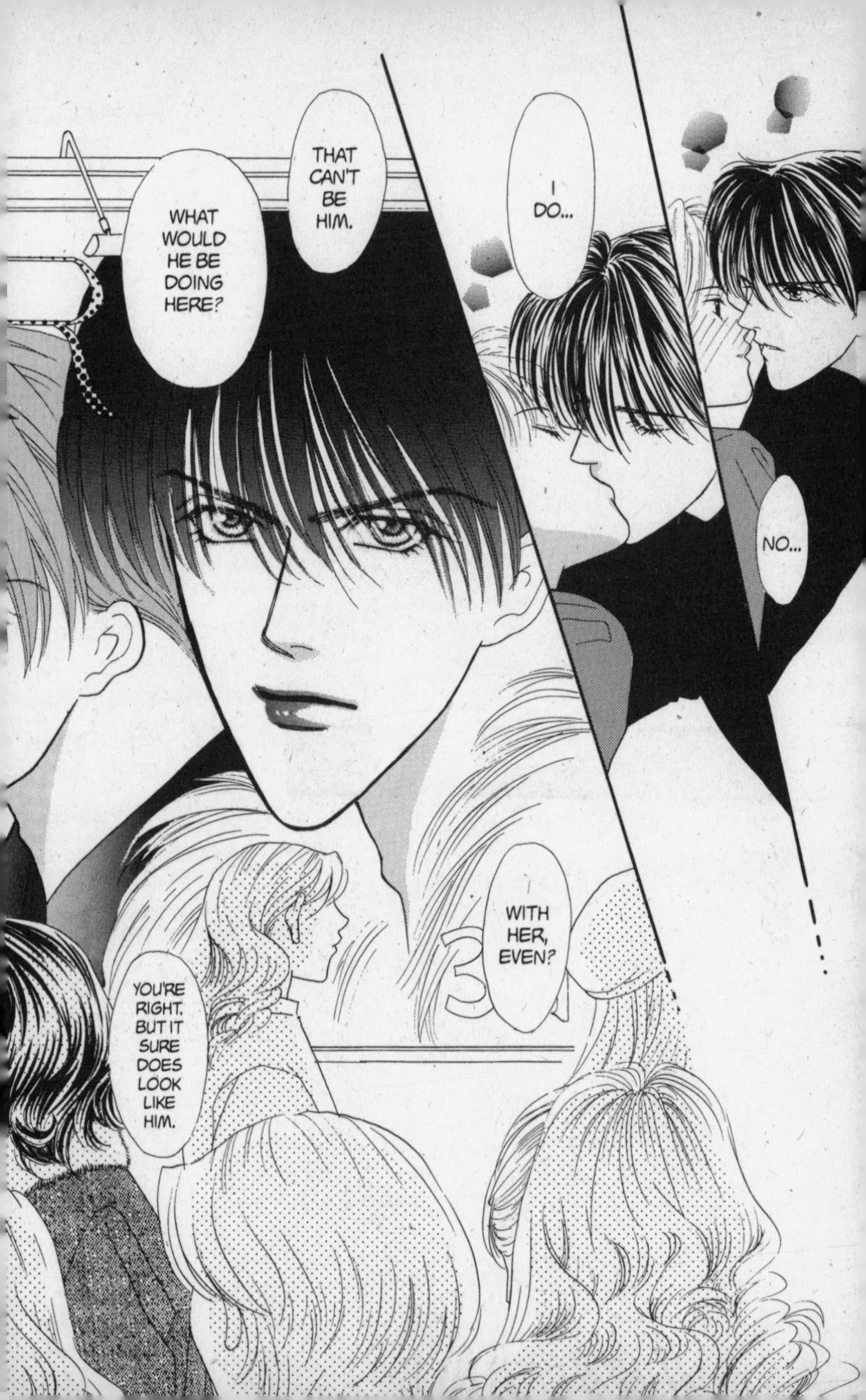
NO...
I DO...
THAT CAN'T BE HIM.
WHAT WOULD HE BE DOING HERE?
WITH HER, EVEN?
YOU'RE RIGHT. BUT IT SURE DOES LOOK LIKE HIM.

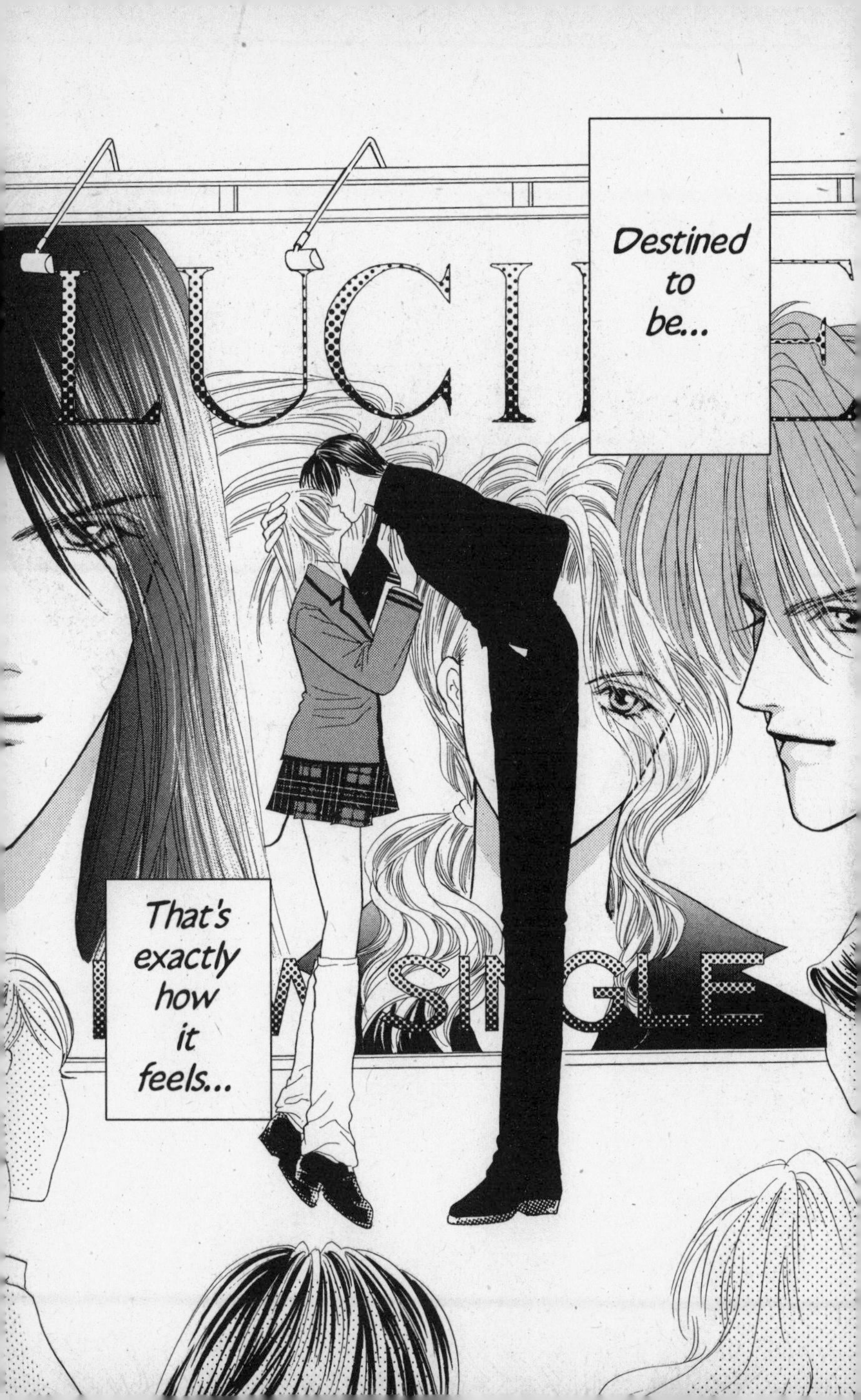
Destined to be...
SINGLE
That's exactly how it feels...

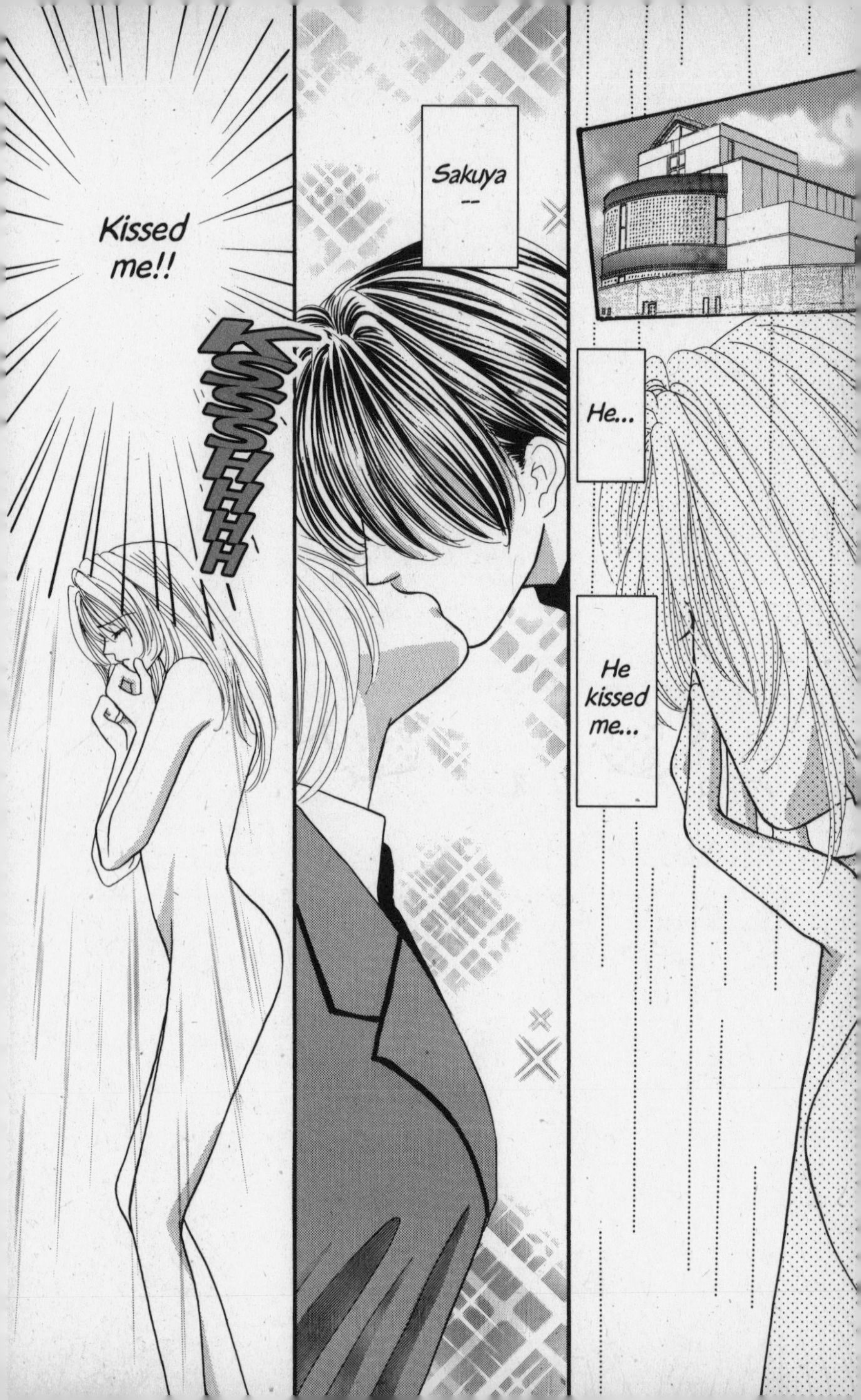
He...
He kissed me...
Sakuya --
Kissed me!!
KSSSHHHH

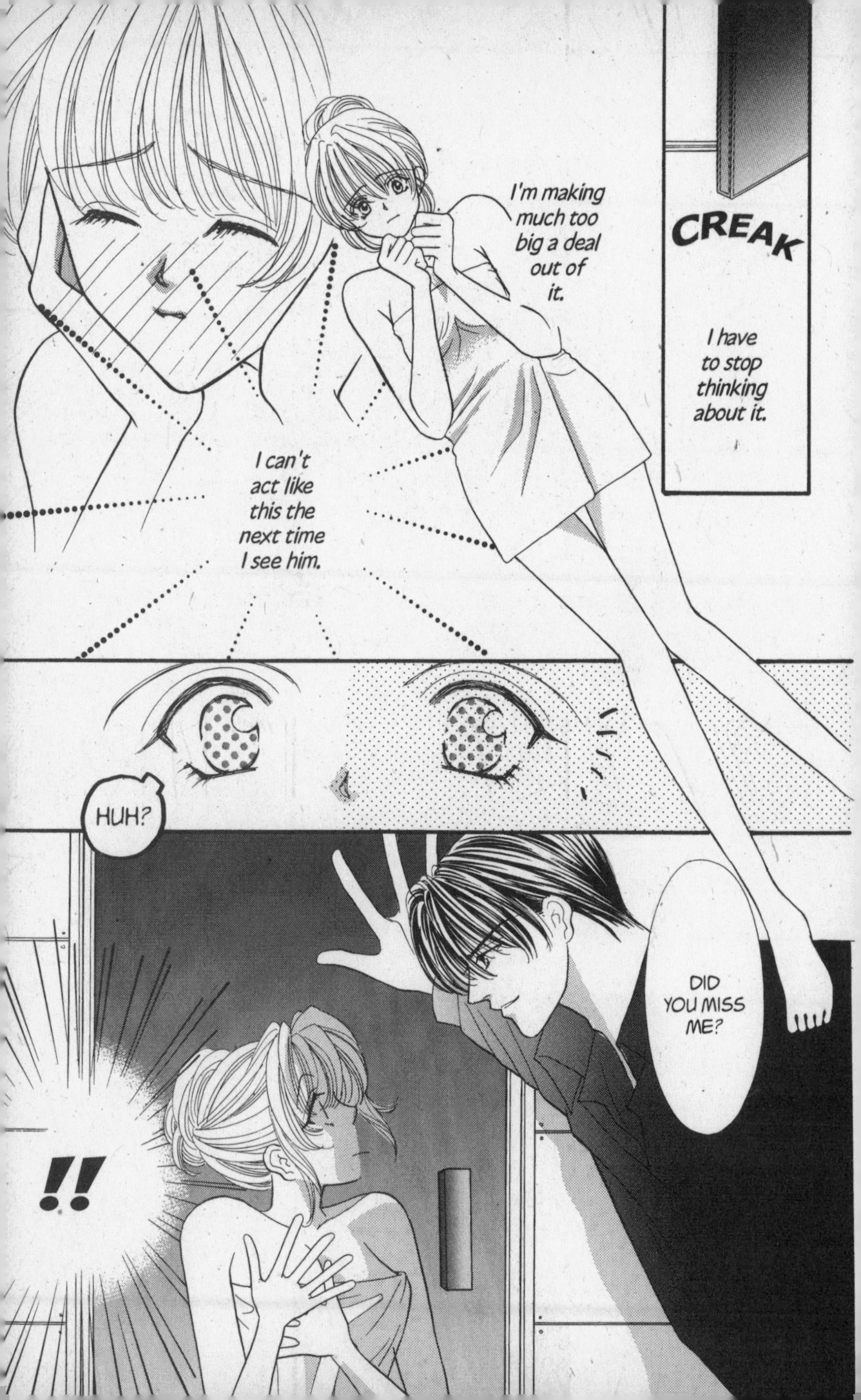
CREAK
I have to stop thinking about it.
I'm making much too big a deal out of it.
I can't act like this the next time I see him.
HUH?
DID YOU MISS ME?
!!

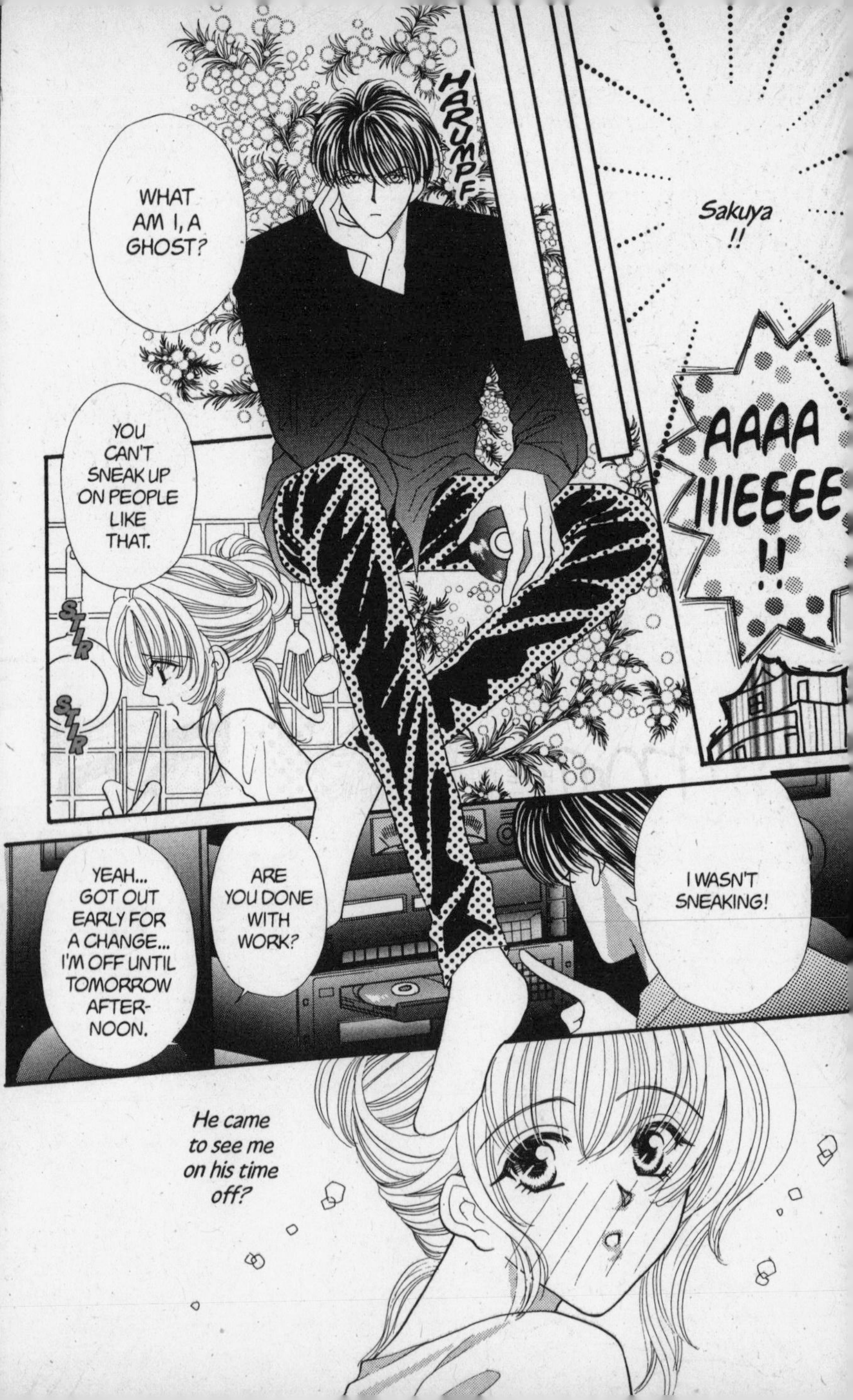
Sakuya !!
AAAA IIIEEEE !!
HARUMPF
WHAT AM I, A GHOST?
YOU CAN'T SNEAK UP ON PEOPLE LIKE THAT.
STIR
STIR
I WASN'T SNEAKING!
ARE YOU DONE WITH WORK?
YEAH... GOT OUT EARLY FOR A CHANGE... I'M OFF UNTIL TOMORROW AFTER-NOON.
He came to see me on his time off?

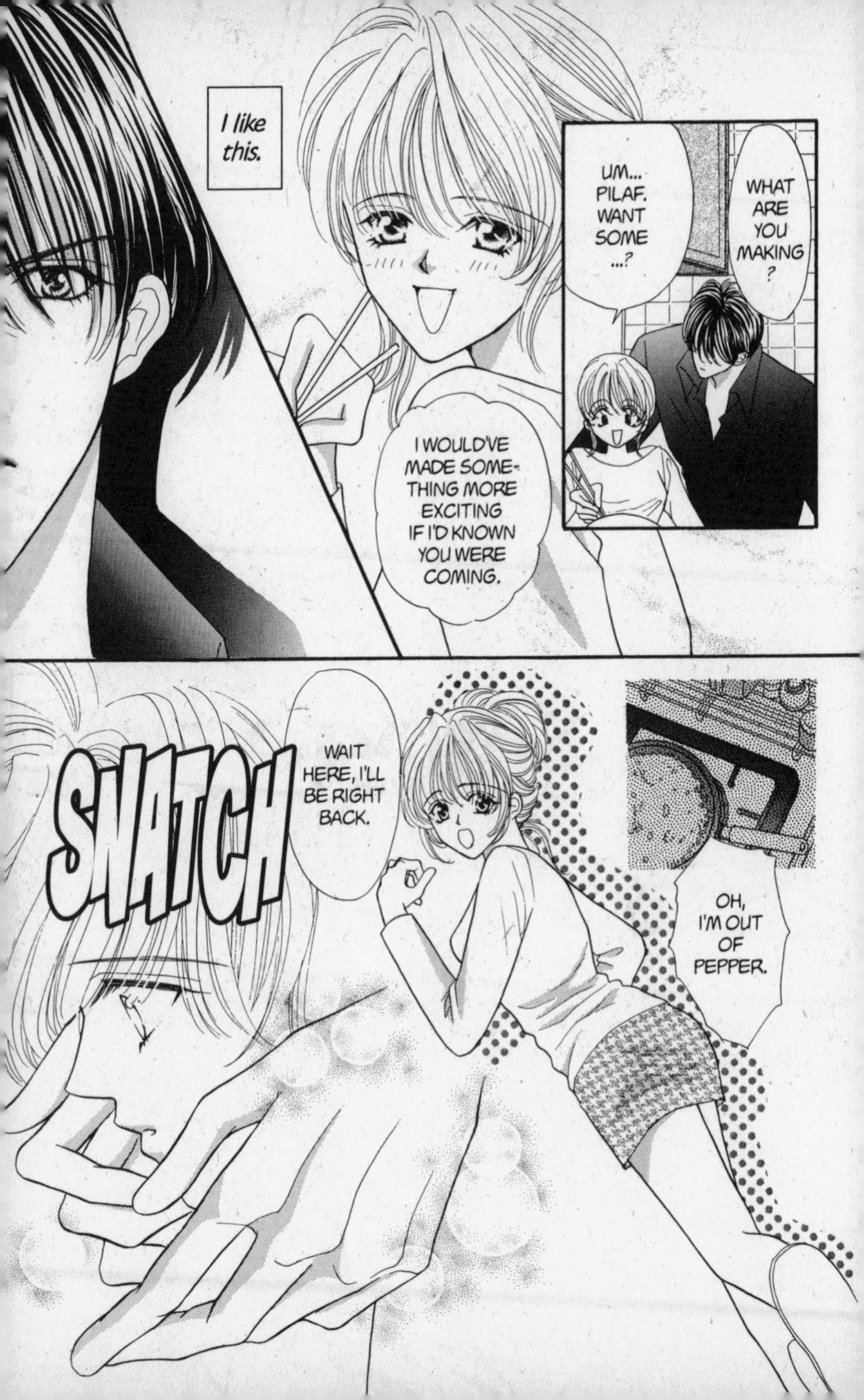
WHAT ARE YOU MAKING?
UM... PILAF. WANT SOME...?
I WOULD'VE MADE SOMETHING MORE EXCITING IF I'D KNOWN YOU WERE COMING.
I like this.
OH, I'M OUT OF PEPPER.
WAIT HERE, I'LL BE RIGHT BACK.
SNATCH

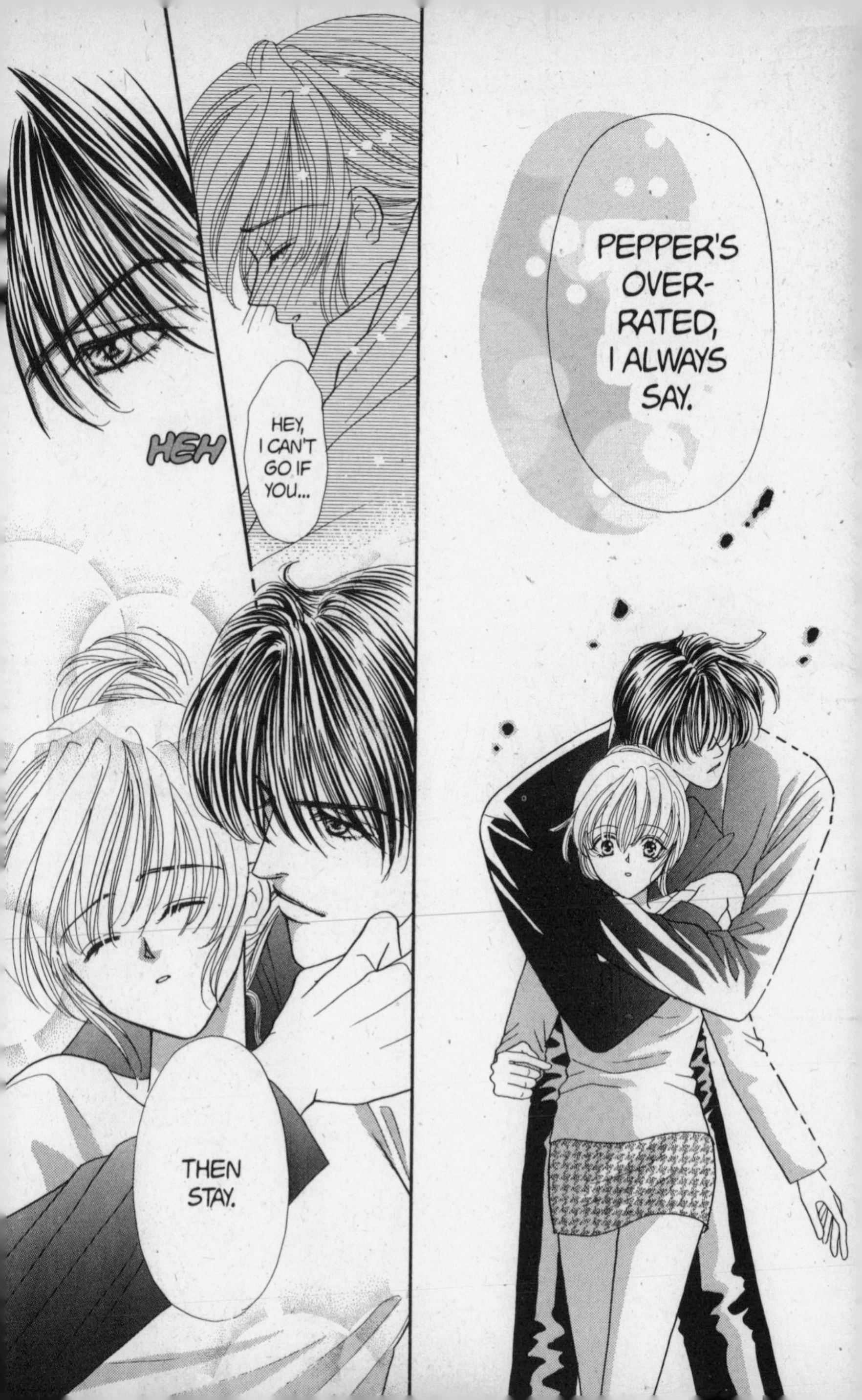
PEPPER'S OVER-RATED, I ALWAYS SAY.
HEH
HEY, I CAN'T GO IF YOU...
THEN STAY.

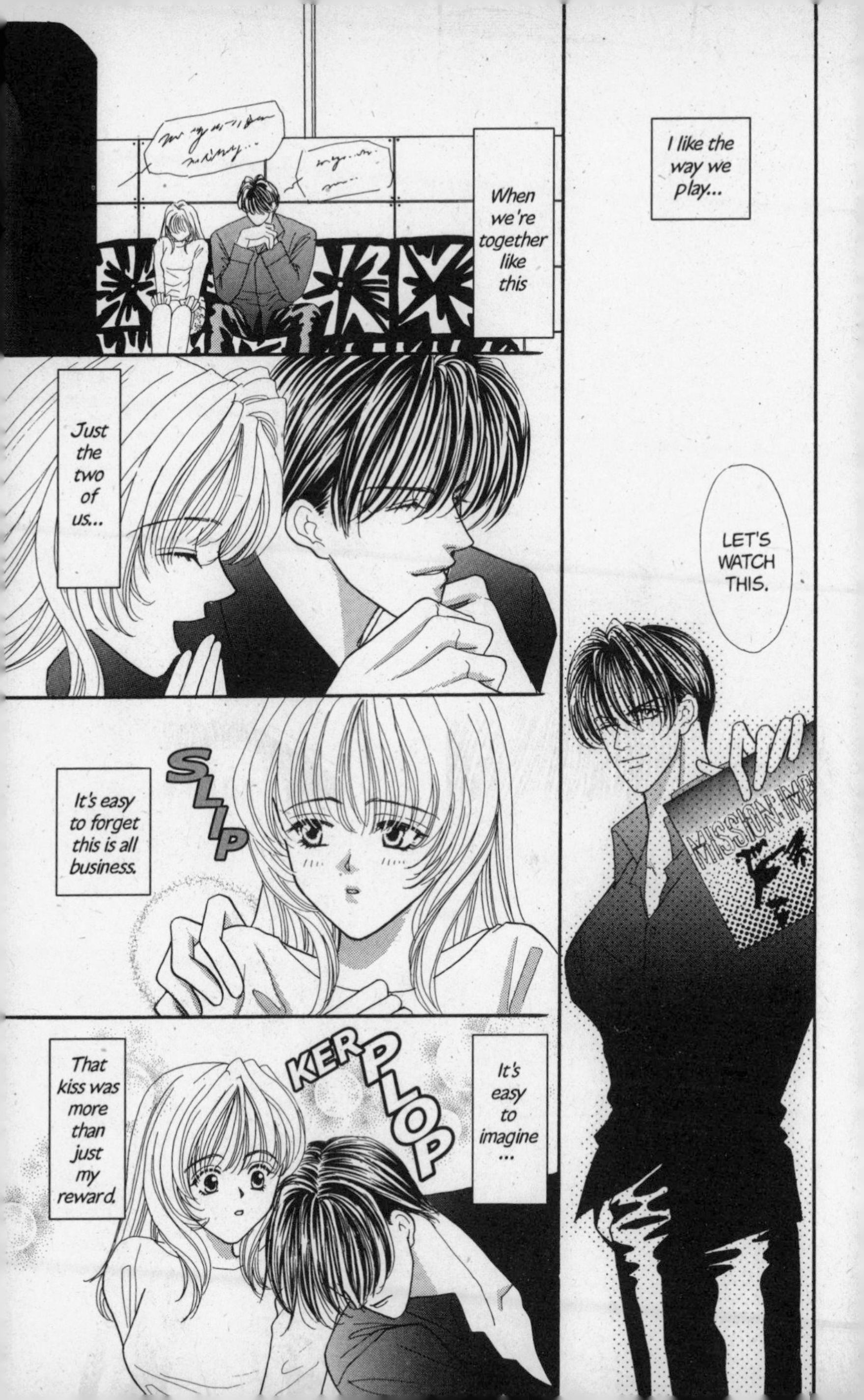
I like the way we play...
LET'S WATCH THIS.
MISSION: IMP
When we're together like this
Just the two of us...
SLIP
It's easy to forget this is all business.
It's easy to imagine...
KERPLOP
That kiss was more than just my reward.

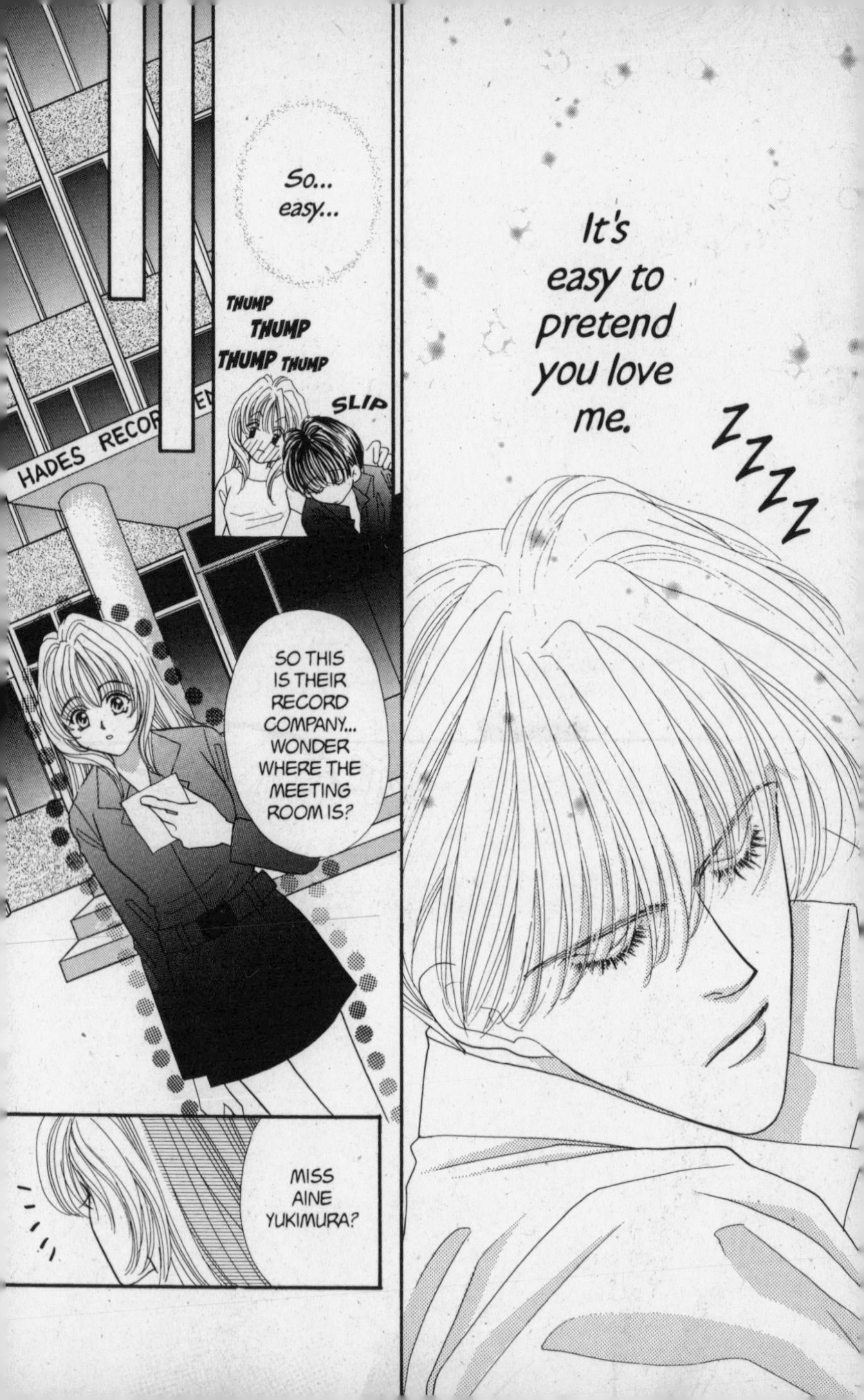

It's easy to pretend you love me.
ZZZZ
So... easy...
THUMP THUMP THUMP THUMP
SLIP
HADES RECOR
SO THIS IS THEIR RECORD COMPANY... WONDER WHERE THE MEETING ROOM IS?
MISS AINE YUKIMURA?

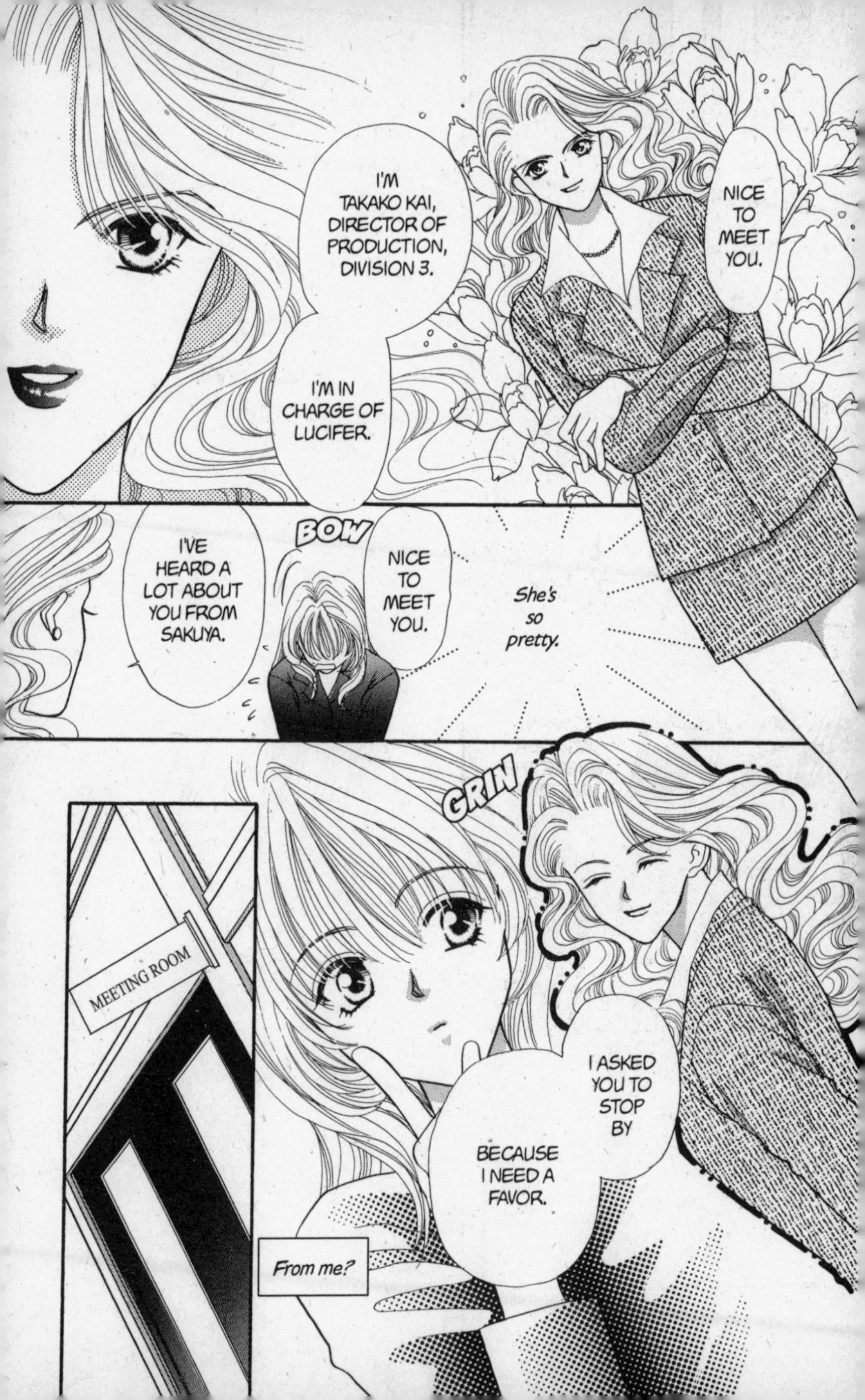
NICE TO MEET YOU.
I'M TAKAKO KAI, DIRECTOR OF PRODUCTION, DIVISION 3.
I'M IN CHARGE OF LUCIFER.
She's so pretty.
BOW
NICE TO MEET YOU.
I'VE HEARD A LOT ABOUT YOU FROM SAKUYA.
GRIN
I ASKED YOU TO STOP BY
BECAUSE I NEED A FAVOR.
From me?
MEETING ROOM

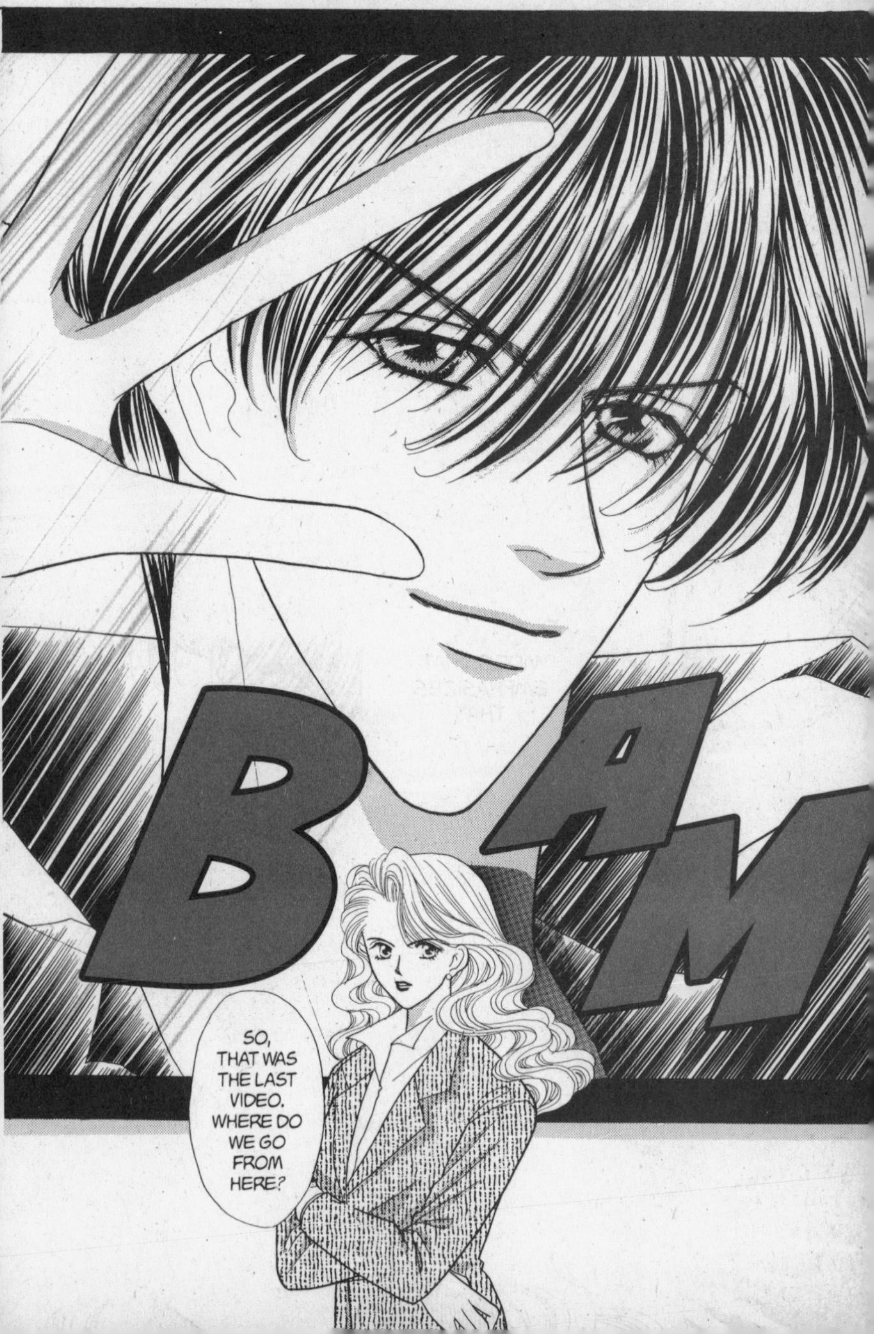
BAM
SO, THAT WAS THE LAST VIDEO. WHERE DO WE GO FROM HERE?

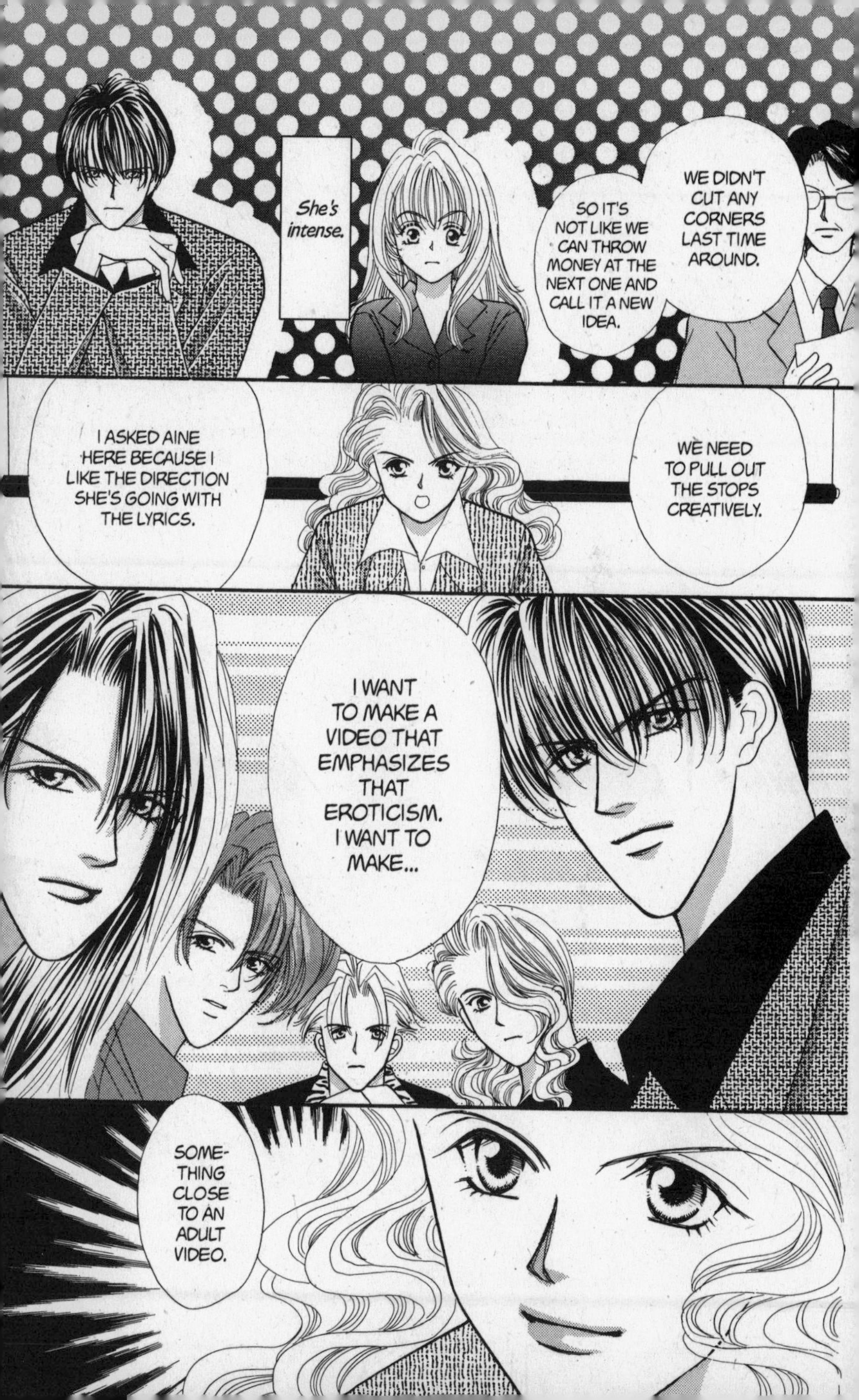
WE DIDN'T CUT ANY CORNERS LAST TIME AROUND.
SO IT'S NOT LIKE WE CAN THROW MONEY AT THE NEXT ONE AND CALL IT A NEW IDEA.
She's intense.
WE NEED TO PULL OUT THE STOPS CREATIVELY.
I ASKED AINE HERE BECAUSE I LIKE THE DIRECTION SHE'S GOING WITH THE LYRICS.
I WANT TO MAKE A VIDEO THAT EMPHASIZES THAT EROTICISM. I WANT TO MAKE...
SOME-THING CLOSE TO AN ADULT VIDEO.

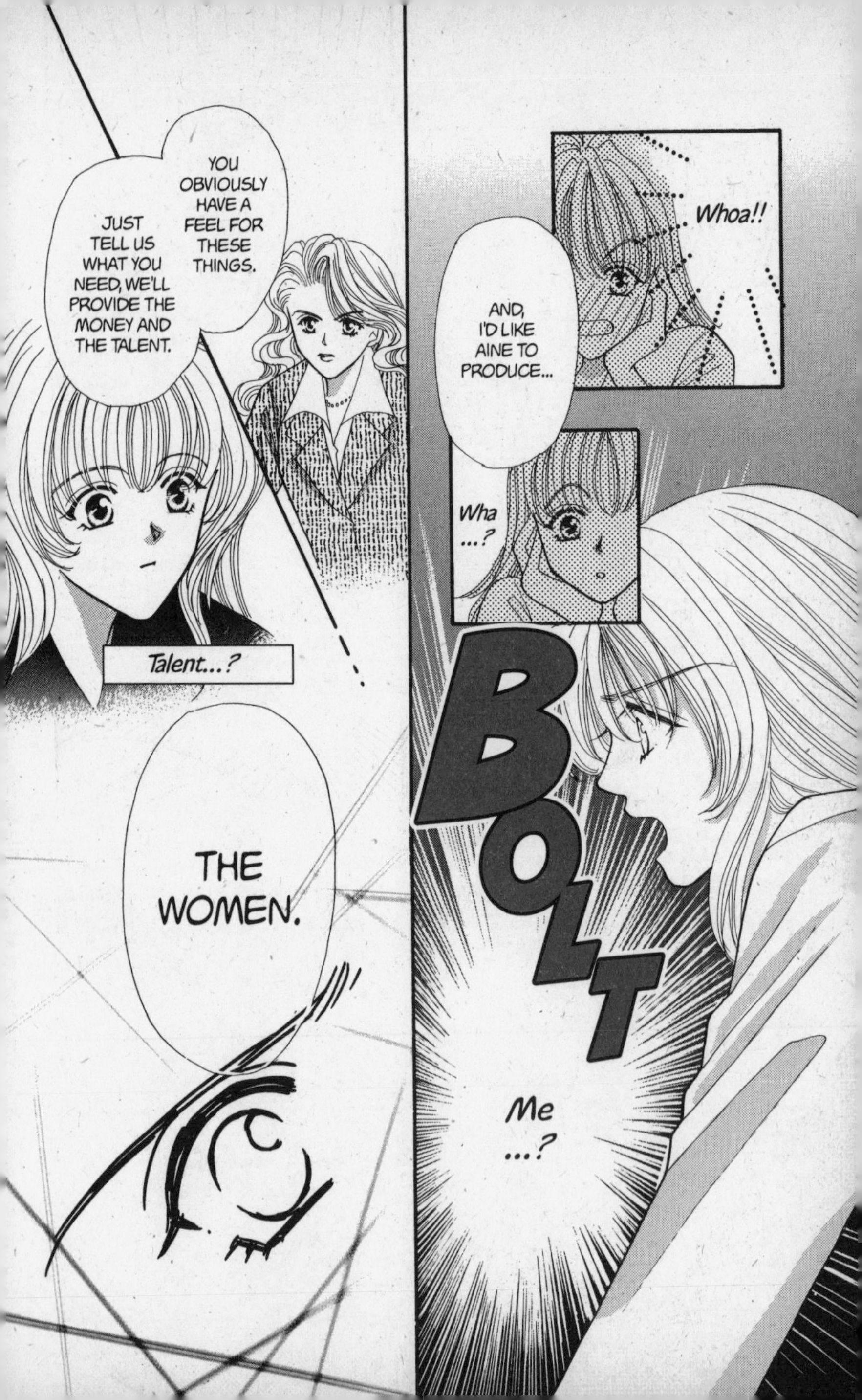
Whoa!!
AND, I'D LIKE AINE TO PRODUCE...
Wha ...?
BOLT
Me ...?
YOU OBVIOUSLY HAVE A FEEL FOR THESE THINGS. JUST TELL US WHAT YOU NEED, WE'LL PROVIDE THE MONEY AND THE TALENT.
Talent...?
THE WOMEN.

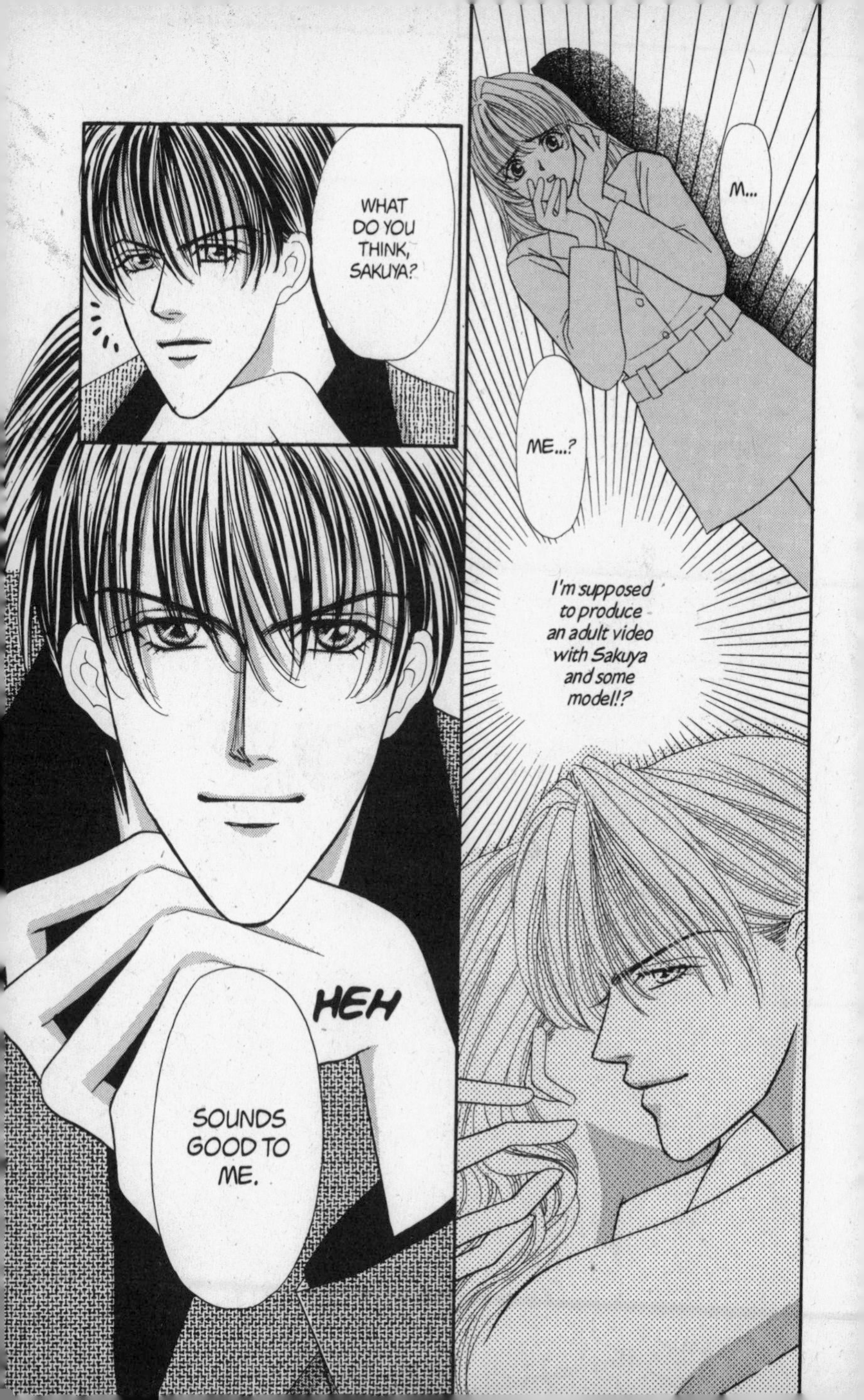
M...
ME...?
I'm supposed to produce an adult video with Sakuya and some model!?
WHAT DO YOU THINK, SAKUYA?
HEH
SOUNDS GOOD TO ME.

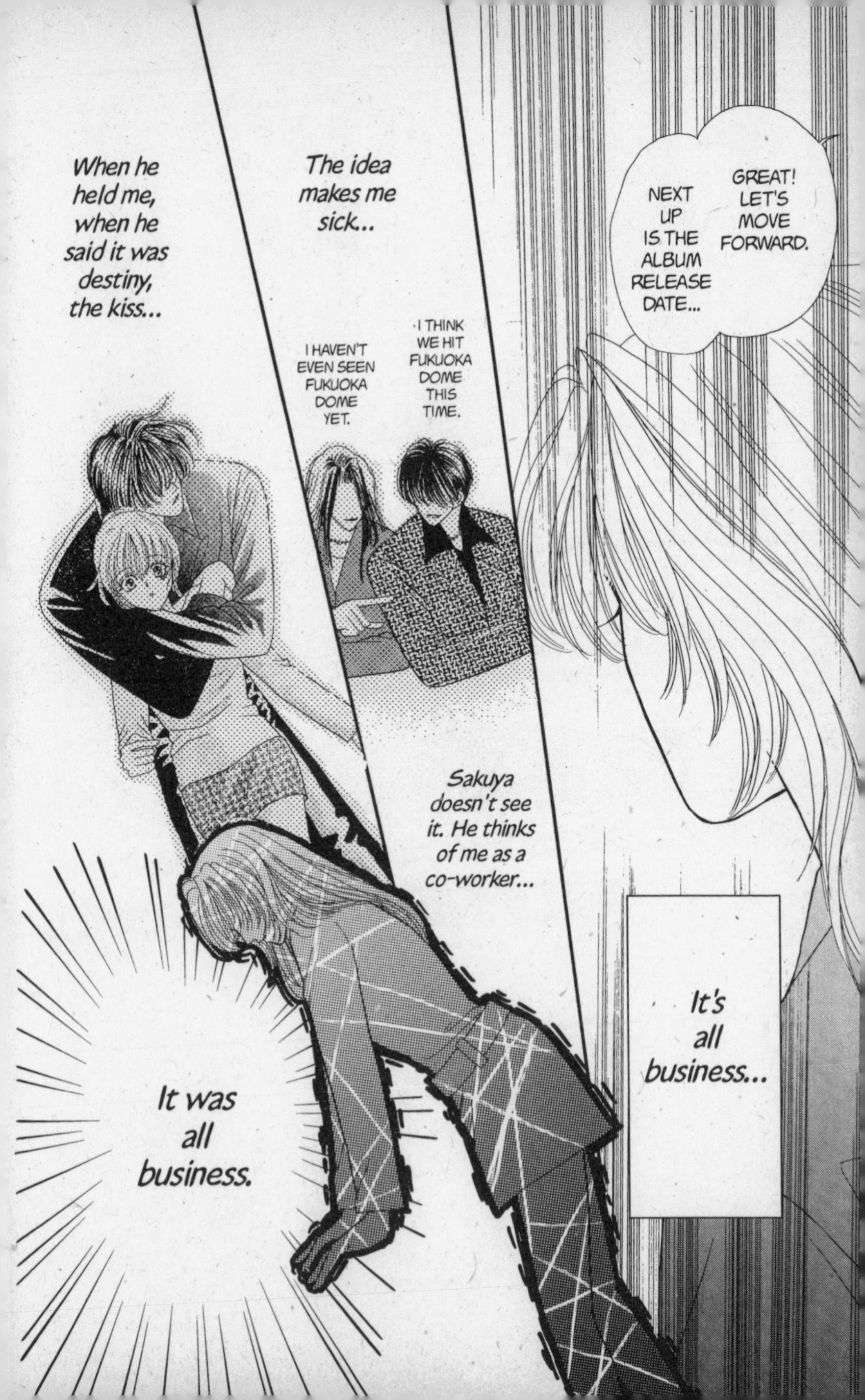
GREAT! LET'S MOVE FORWARD.
NEXT UP IS THE ALBUM RELEASE DATE...
It's all business...
The idea makes me sick...
I THINK WE HIT FUKUOKA DOME THIS TIME.
I HAVEN'T EVEN SEEN FUKUOKA DOME YET.
Sakuya doesn't see it. He thinks of me as a co-worker...
When he held me, when he said it was destiny, the kiss...
It was all business.

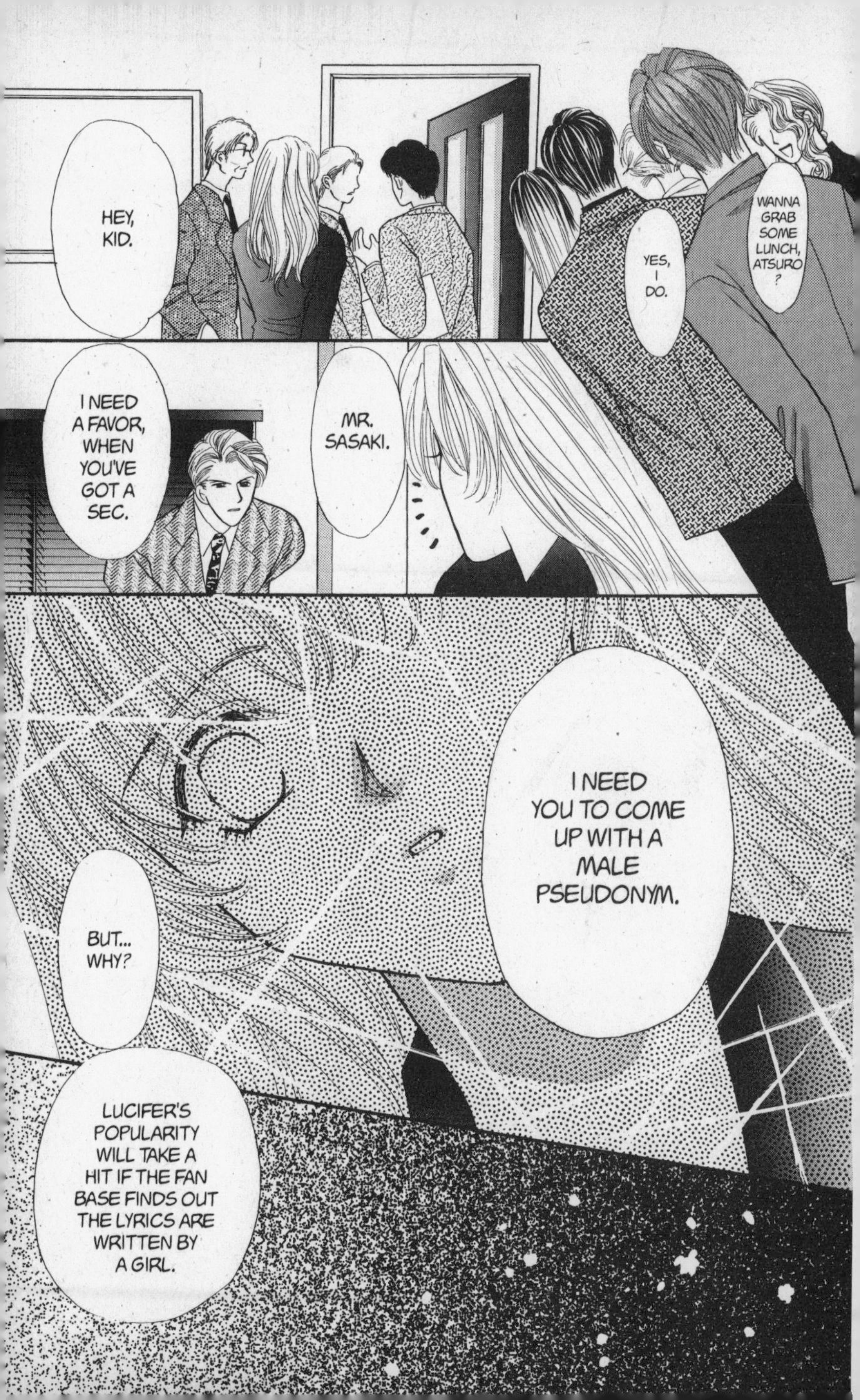
WANNA GRAB SOME LUNCH, ATSURO?
YES, I DO.
HEY, KID.
MR. SASAKI.
I NEED A FAVOR, WHEN YOU'VE GOT A SEC.
I NEED YOU TO COME UP WITH A MALE PSEUDONYM.
BUT... WHY?
LUCIFER'S POPULARITY WILL TAKE A HIT IF THE FAN BASE FINDS OUT THE LYRICS ARE WRITTEN BY A GIRL.

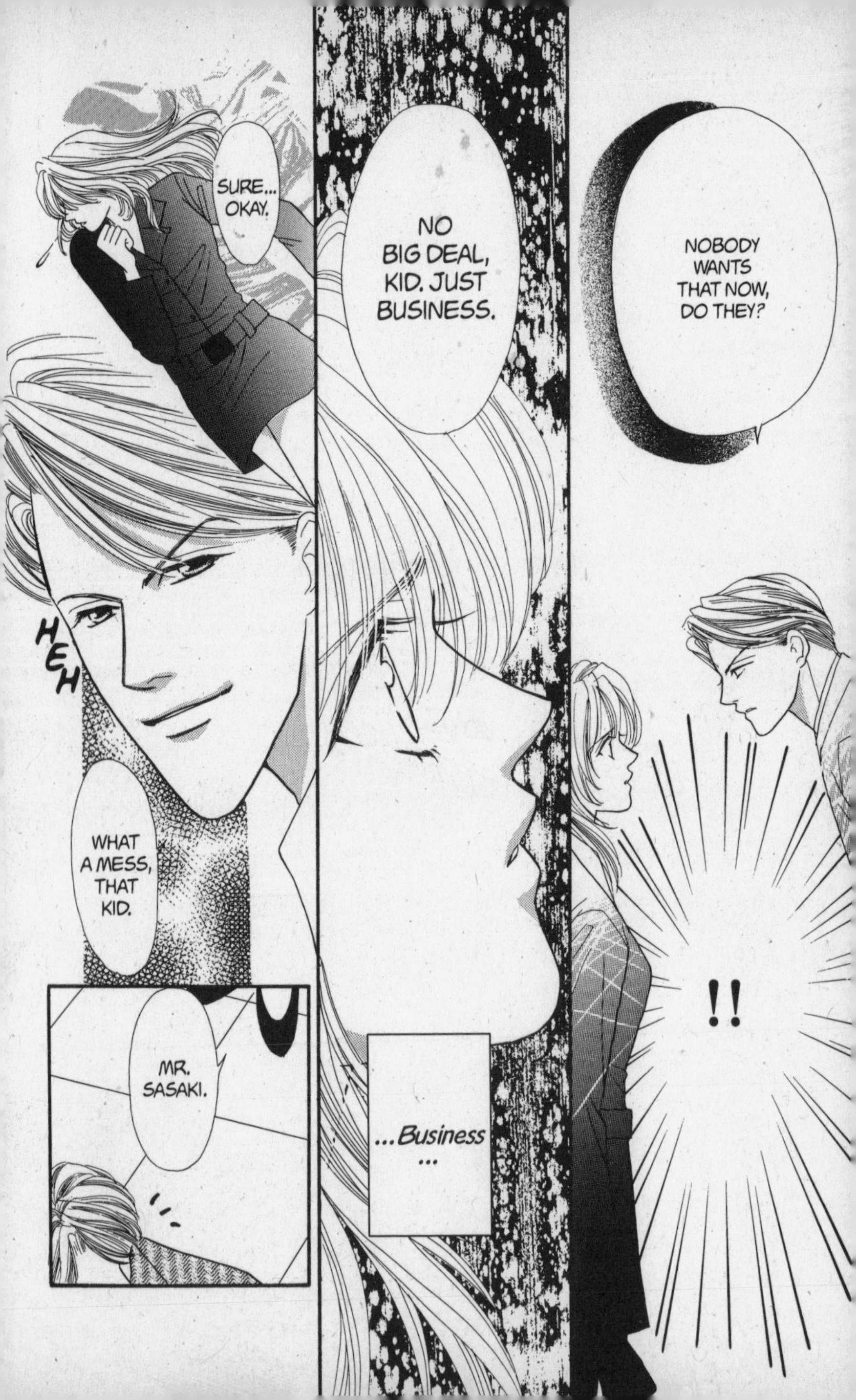
NOBODY WANTS THAT NOW, DO THEY?
!!
NO BIG DEAL, KID. JUST BUSINESS.
...Business ...
SURE... OKAY.
HEH
WHAT A MESS, THAT KID.
MR. SASAKI.

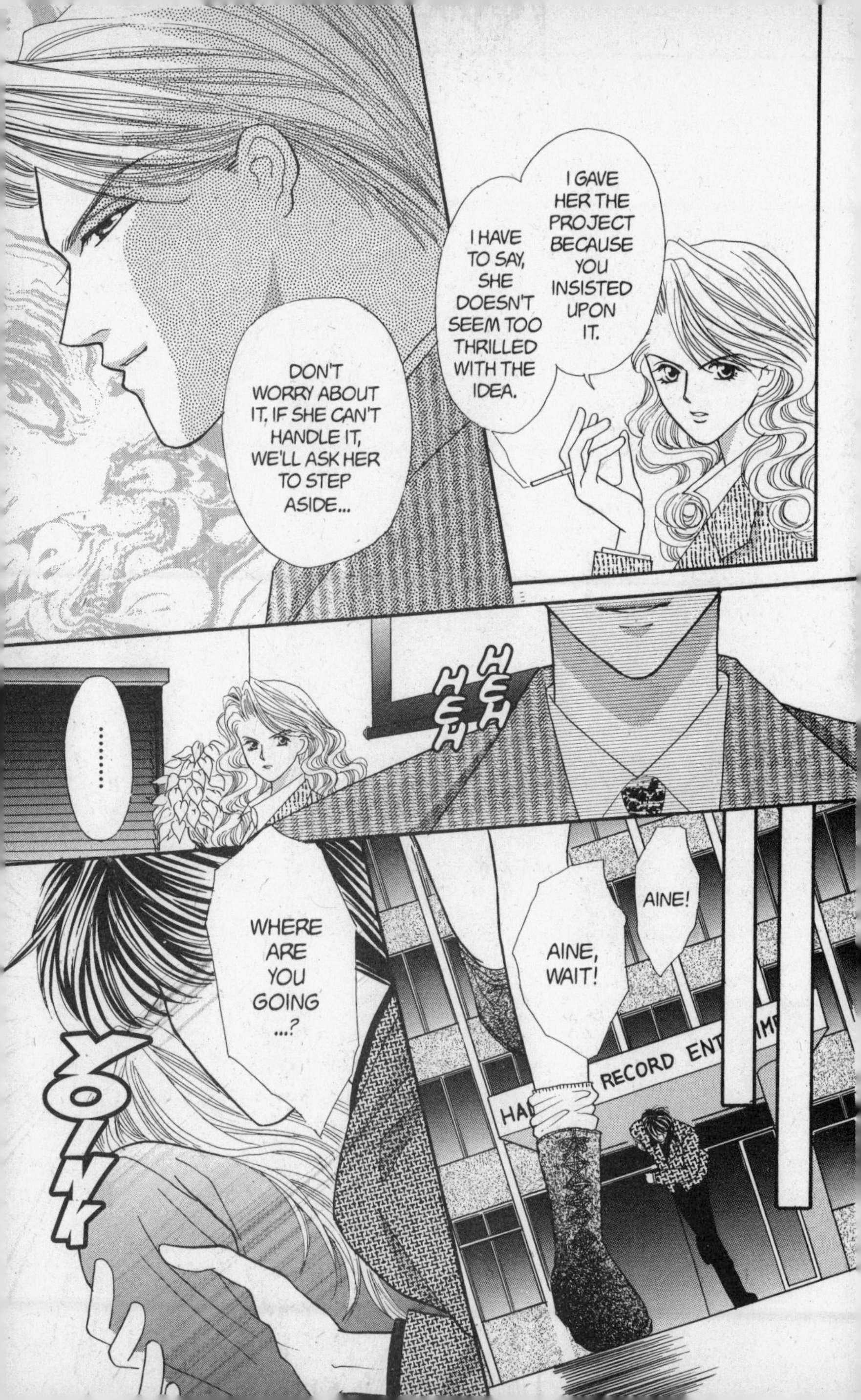
I GAVE HER THE PROJECT BECAUSE YOU INSISTED UPON IT.
I HAVE TO SAY, SHE DOESN'T SEEM TOO THRILLED WITH THE IDEA.
DON'T WORRY ABOUT IT, IF SHE CAN'T HANDLE IT, WE'LL ASK HER TO STEP ASIDE...
HEH HEH
......
AINE!
AINE, WAIT!
WHERE ARE YOU GOING ...?
YOINK

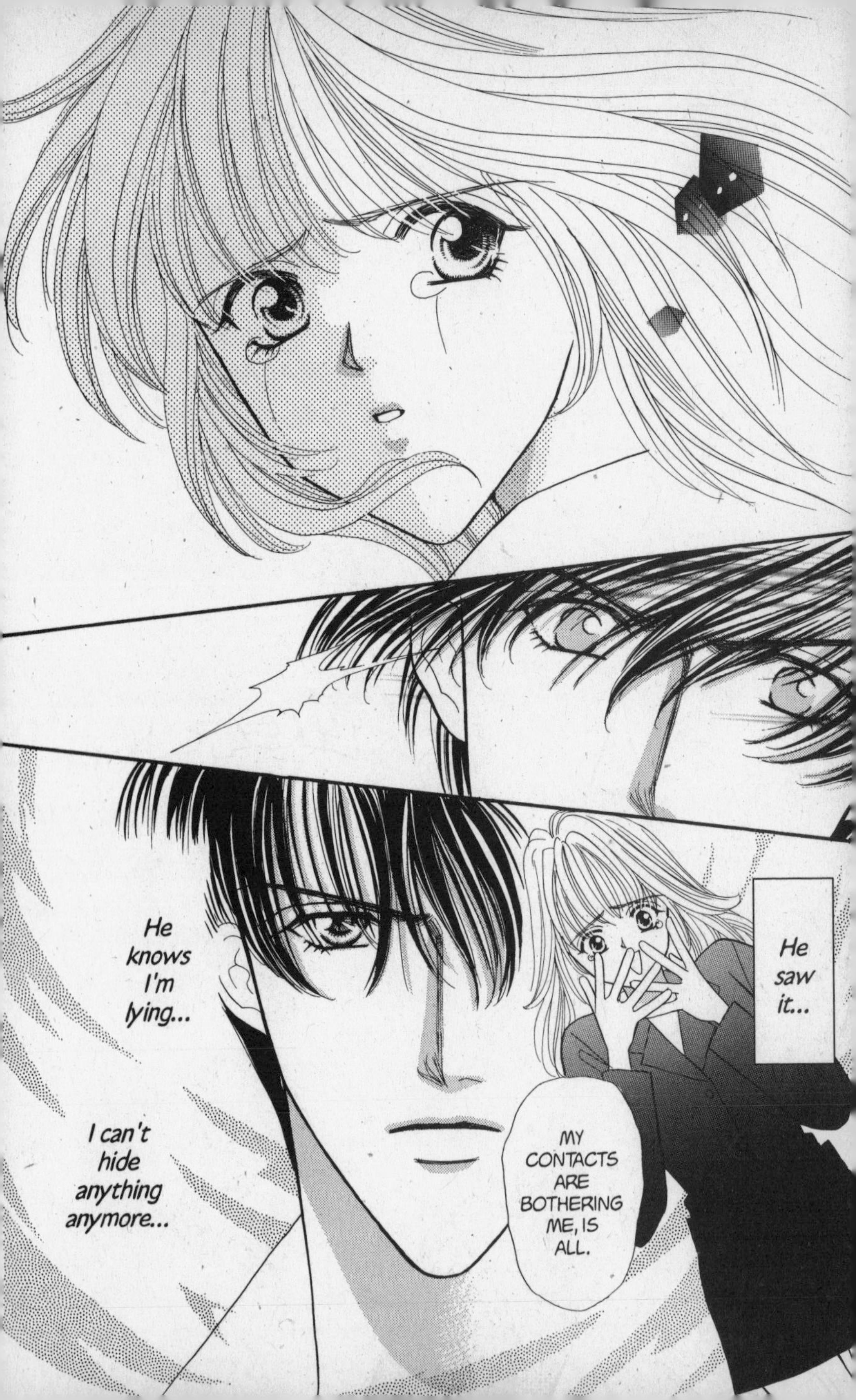
He saw it...
MY CONTACTS ARE BOTHERING ME, IS ALL.
He knows I'm lying...
I can't hide anything anymore...

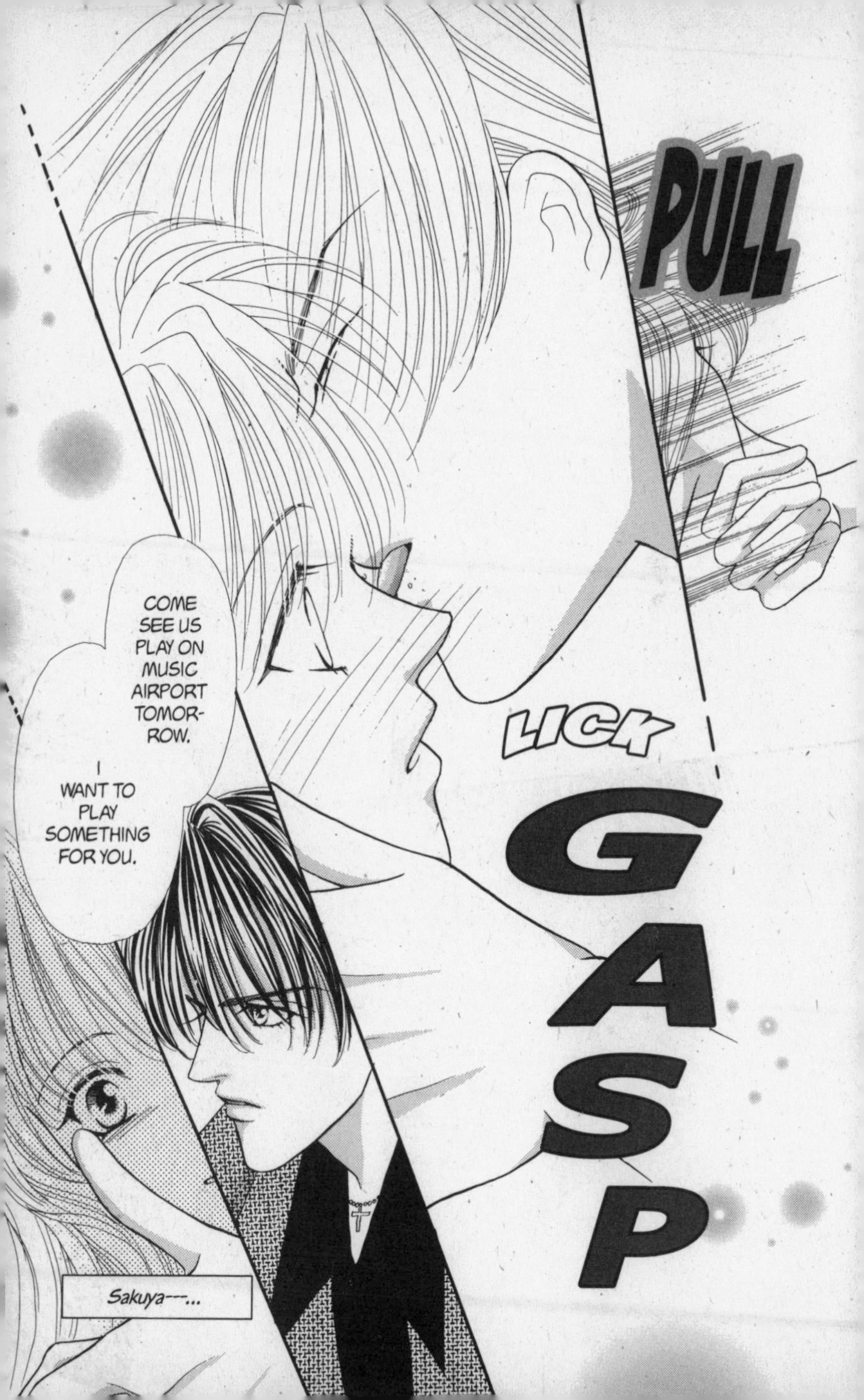
PULL
LICK
GASP
COME SEE US PLAY ON MUSIC AIRPORT TOMOR-ROW.
I WANT TO PLAY SOMETHING FOR YOU.
Sakuya---...

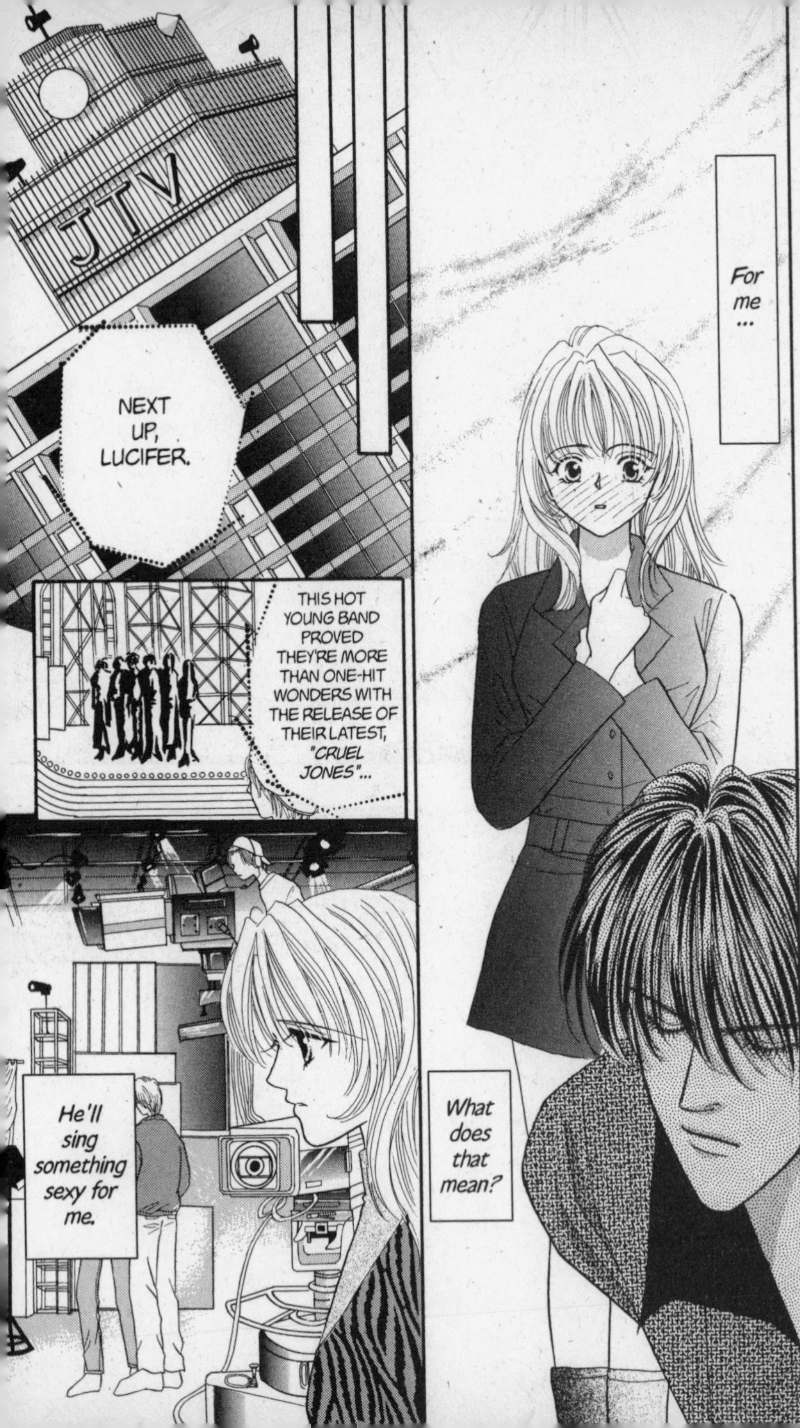
NEXT UP, LUCIFER.
THIS HOT YOUNG BAND PROVED THEY'RE MORE THAN ONE-HIT WONDERS WITH THE RELEASE OF THEIR LATEST, "CRUEL JONES"...
He'll sing something sexy for me.
For me ...
What does that mean?

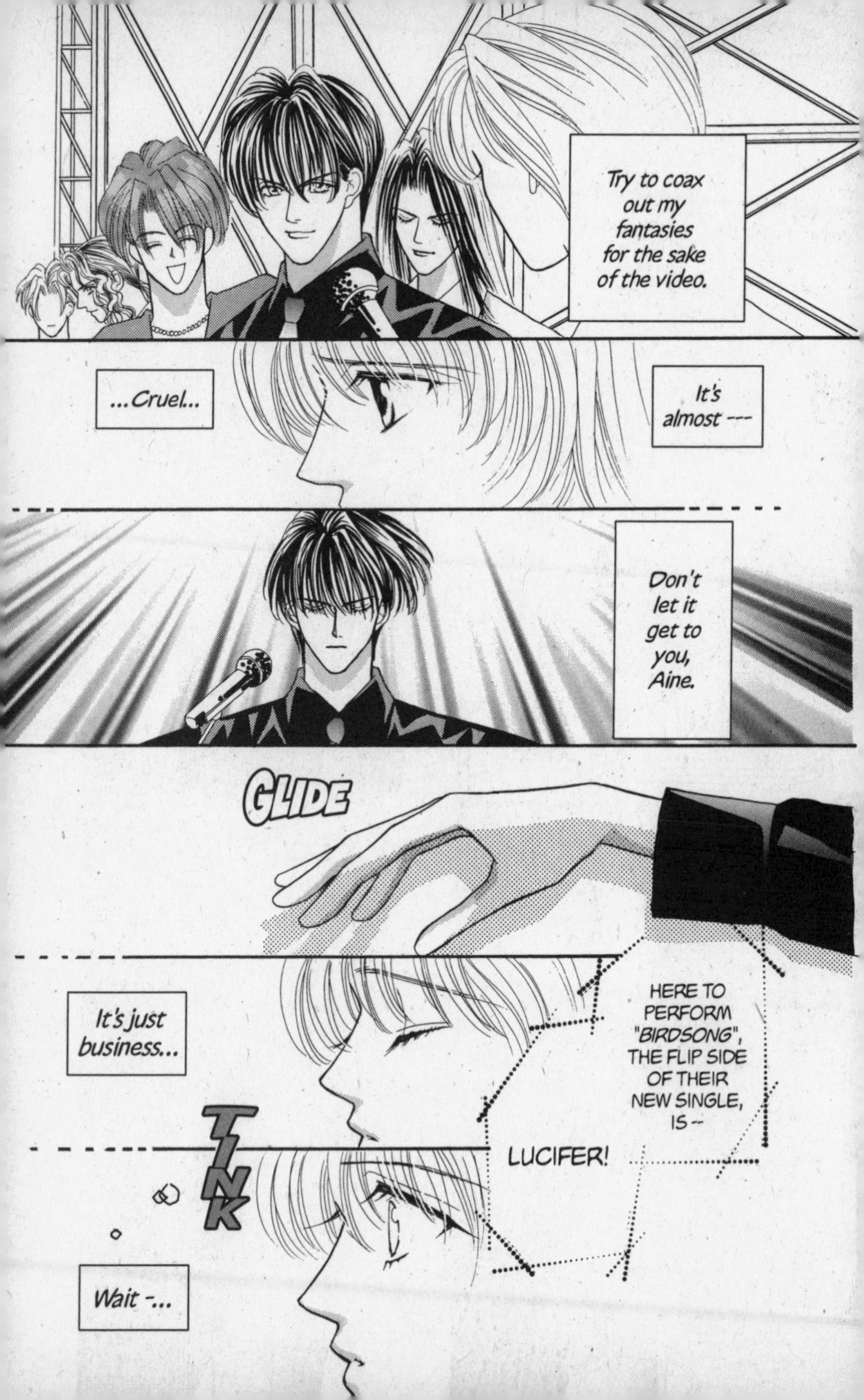
Try to coax out my fantasies for the sake of the video.
It's almost ---
...Cruel...
Don't let it get to you, Aine.
GLIDE
HERE TO PERFORM "BIRDSONG", THE FLIP SIDE OF THEIR NEW SINGLE, IS --
It's just business...
LUCIFER!
TINK
Wait -...

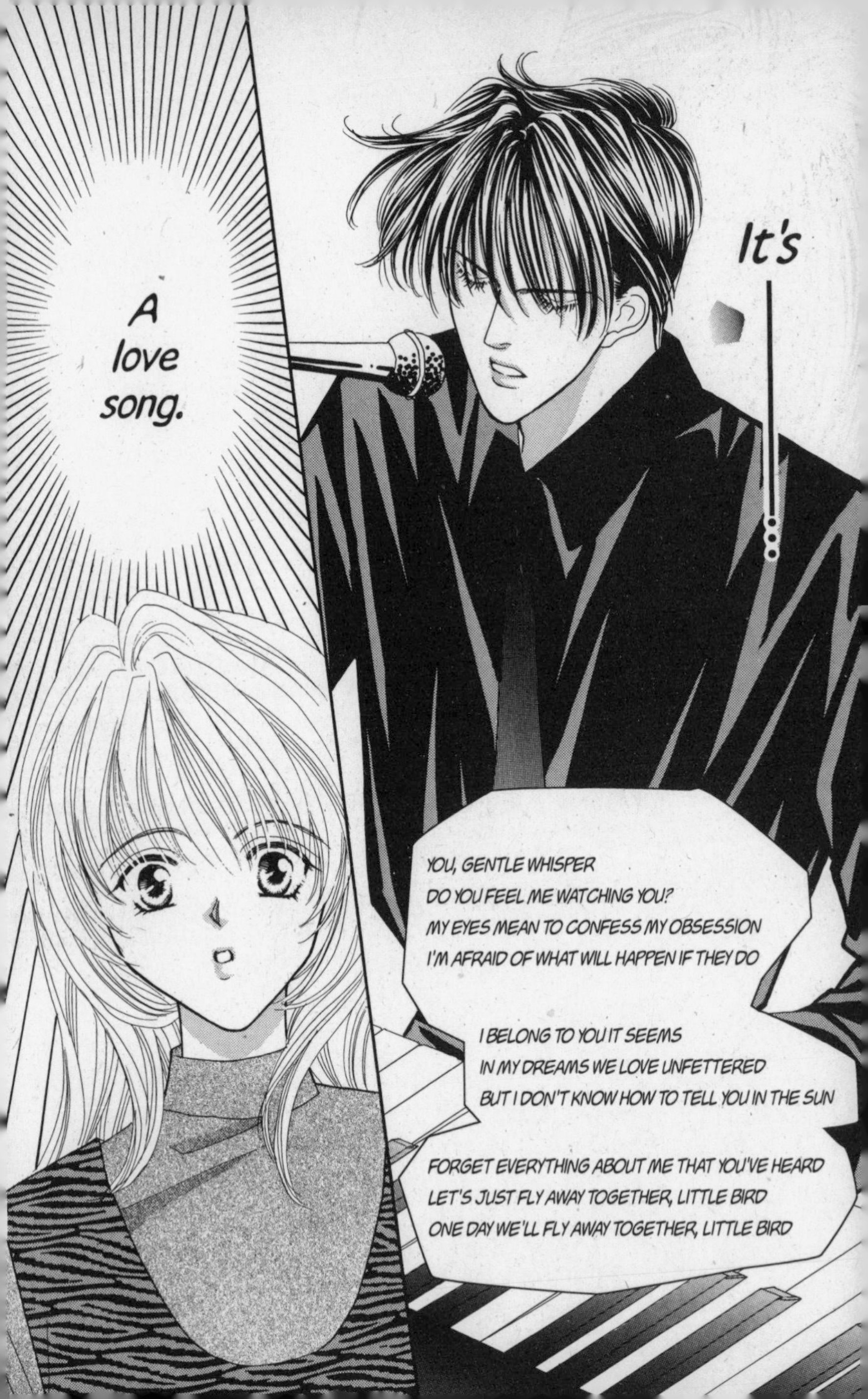
It's
YOU, GENTLE WHISPER
DO YOU FEEL ME WATCHING YOU?
MY EYES MEAN TO CONFESS MY OBSESSION
I'M AFRAID OF WHAT WILL HAPPEN IF THEY DO
I BELONG TO YOU IT SEEMS
IN MY DREAMS WE LOVE UNFETTERED
BUT I DON'T KNOW HOW TO TELL YOU IN THE SUN
FORGET EVERYTHING ABOUT ME THAT YOU'VE HEARD
LET'S JUST FLY AWAY TOGETHER, LITTLE BIRD
ONE DAY WE'LL FLY AWAY TOGETHER, LITTLE BIRD
A love song.

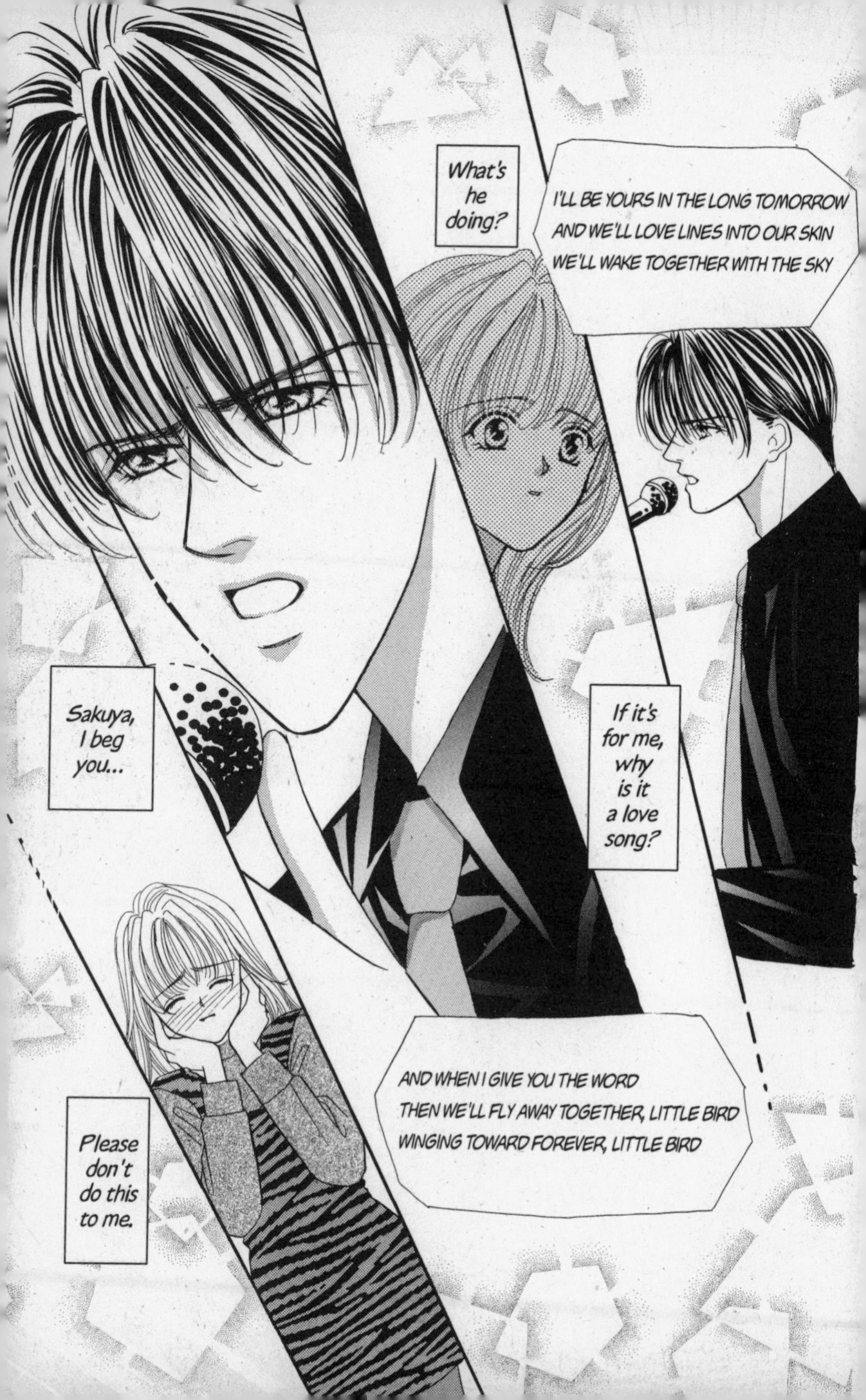
I'LL BE YOURS IN THE LONG TOMORROW AND WE'LL LOVE LINES INTO OUR SKIN WE'LL WAKE TOGETHER WITH THE SKY
What's he doing?
If it's for me, why is it a love song?
Sakuya, I beg you...
AND WHEN I GIVE YOU THE WORD THEN WE'LL FLY AWAY TOGETHER, LITTLE BIRD WINGING TOWARD FOREVER, LITTLE BIRD
Please don't do this to me.

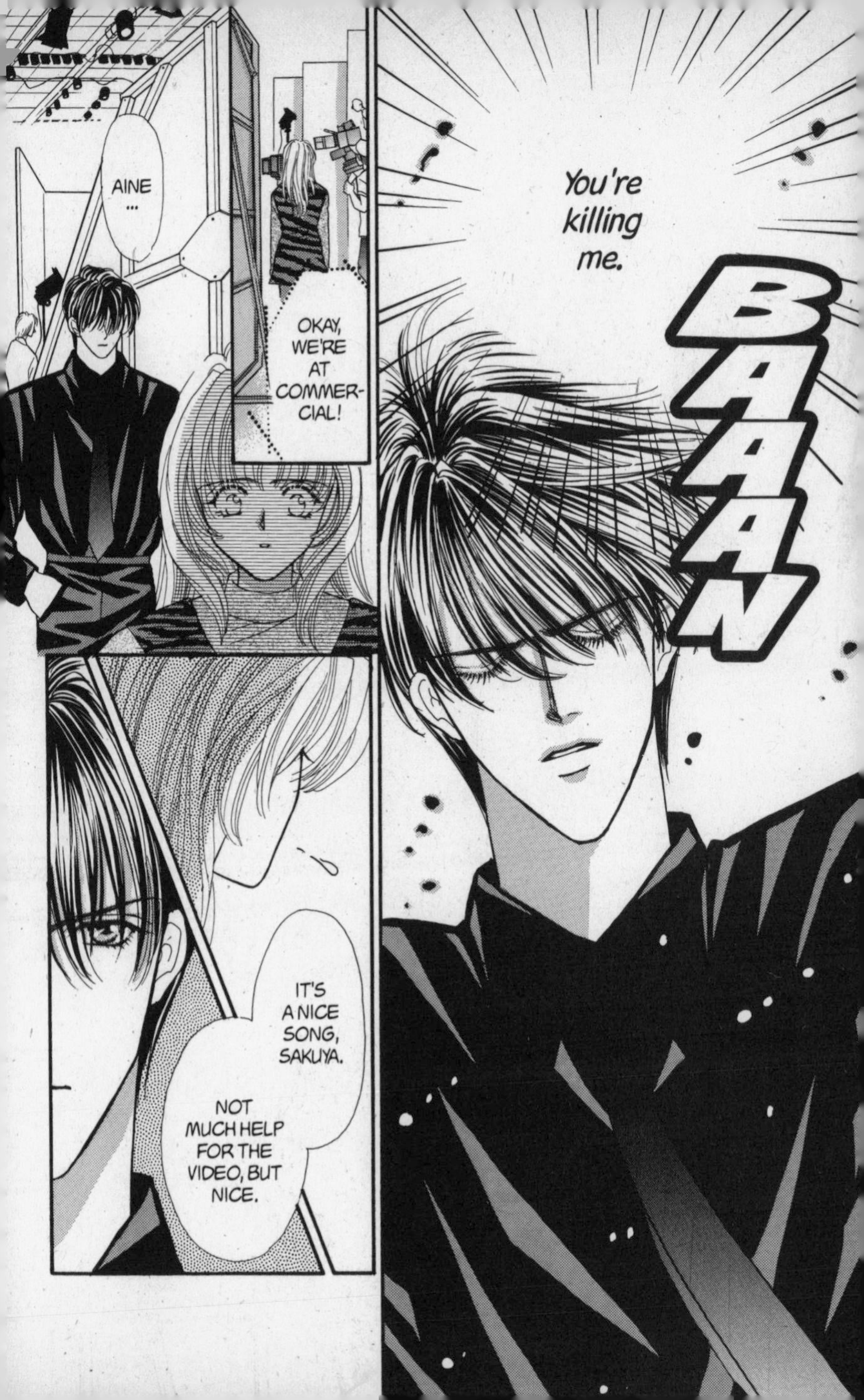
You're killing me.
BAAAN
OKAY, WE'RE AT COMMERCIAL!
AINE ...
IT'S A NICE SONG, SAKUYA.
NOT MUCH HELP FOR THE VIDEO, BUT NICE.

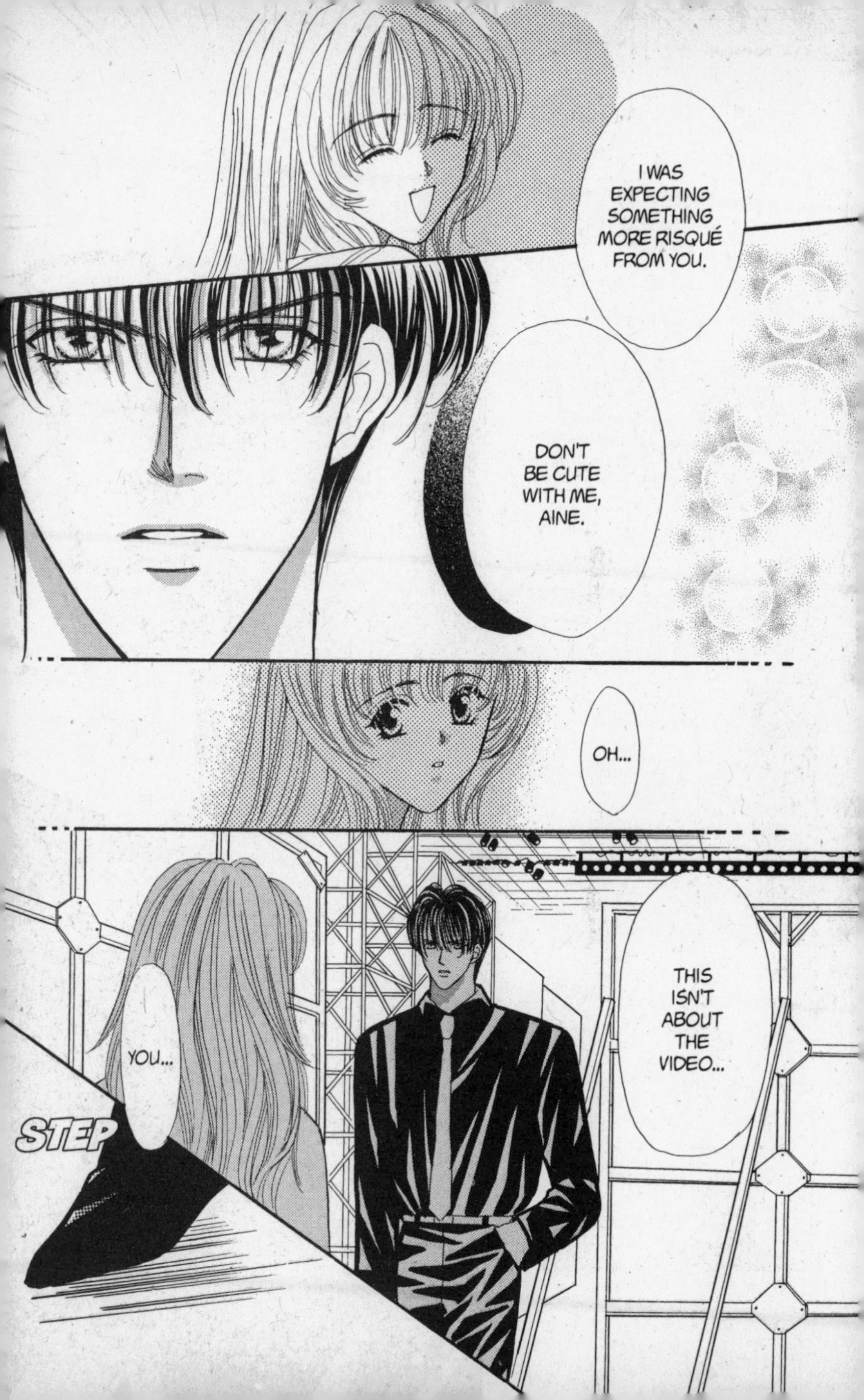
I WAS EXPECTING SOMETHING MORE RISQUÉ FROM YOU.
DON'T BE CUTE WITH ME, AINE.
OH...
THIS ISN'T ABOUT THE VIDEO...
YOU...
STEP

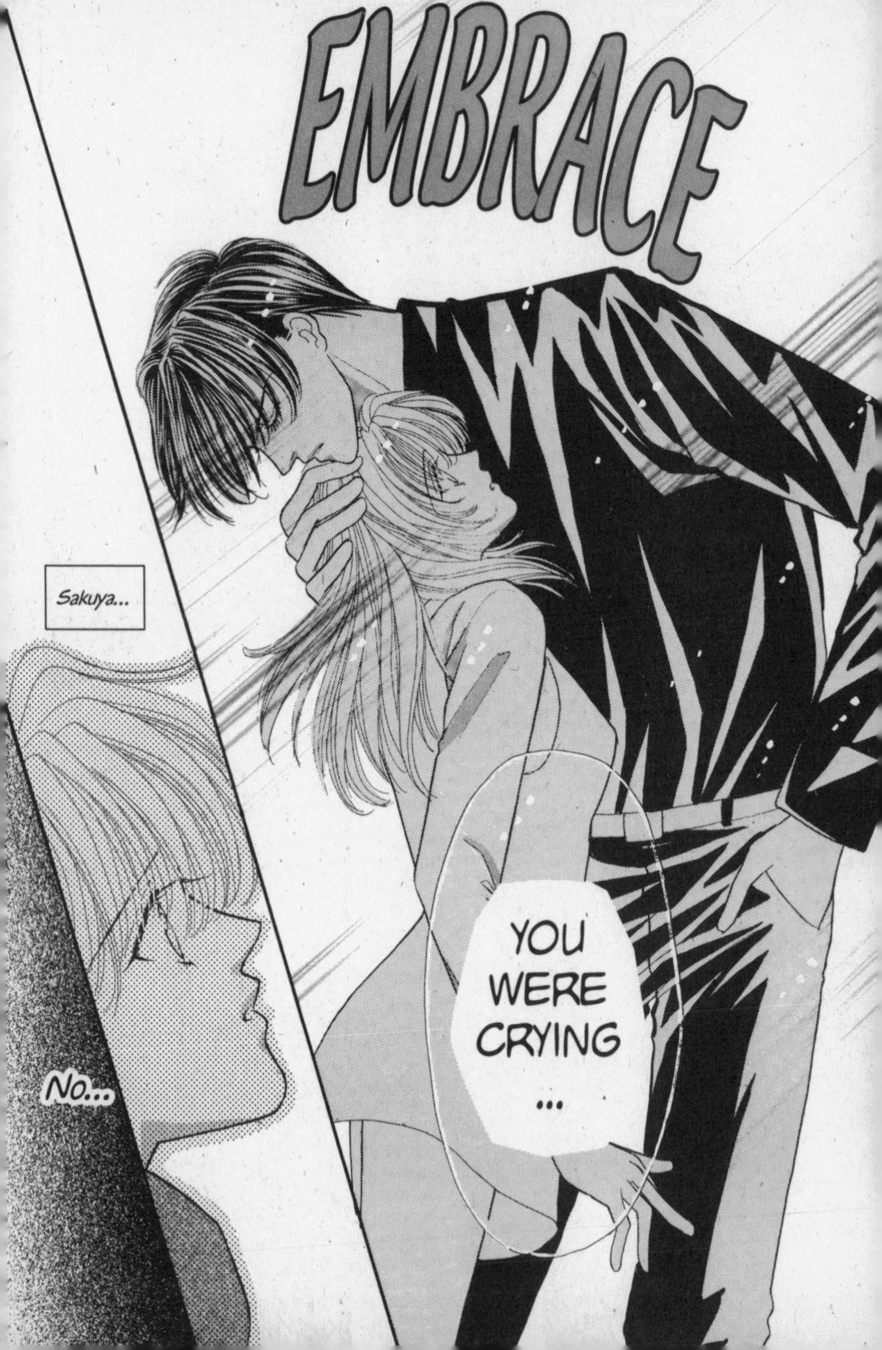
EMBRACE
YOU WERE CRYING ...
Sakuya...
No...

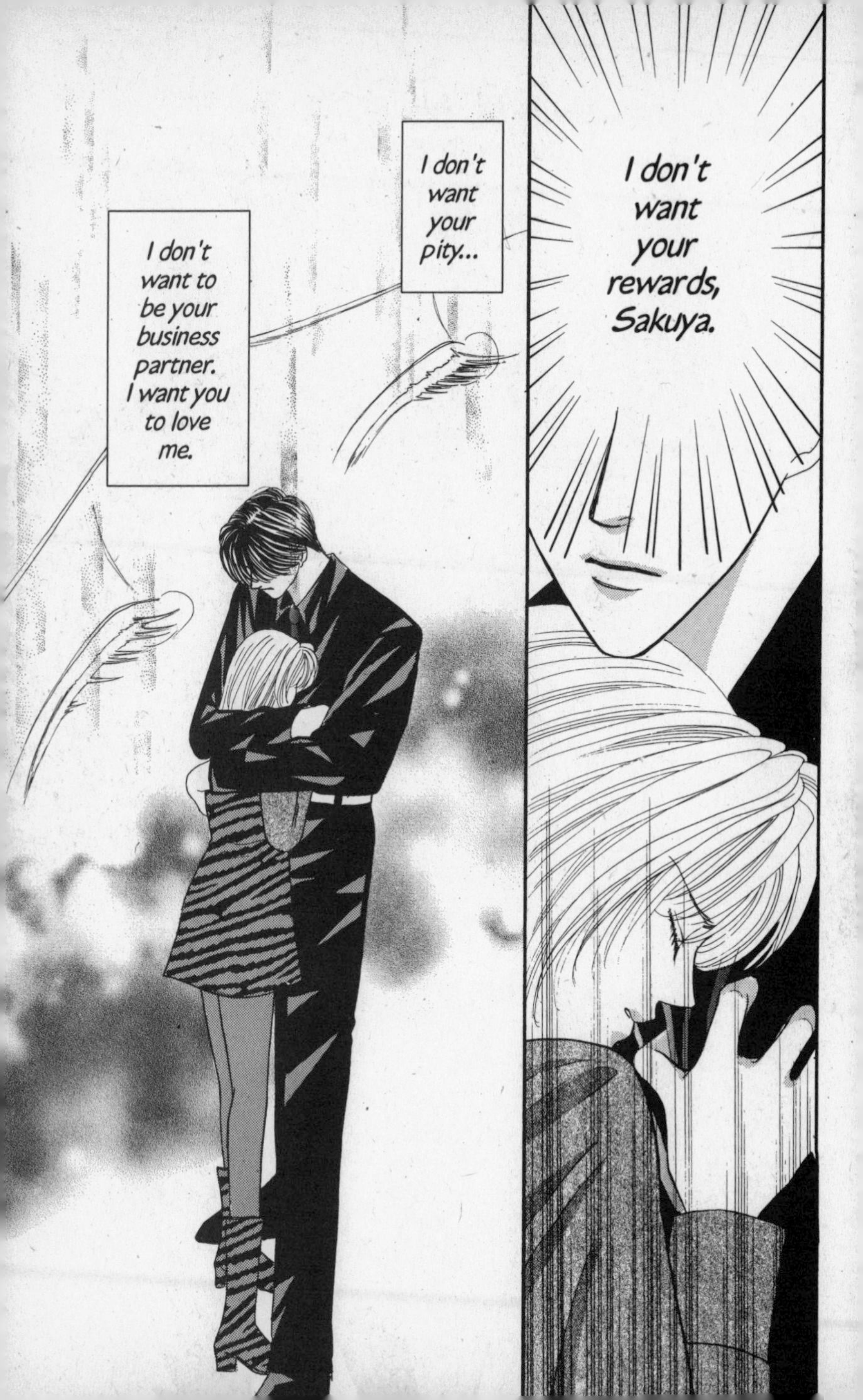
I don't want your rewards, Sakuya.
I don't want your pity...
I don't want to be your business partner. I want you to love me.

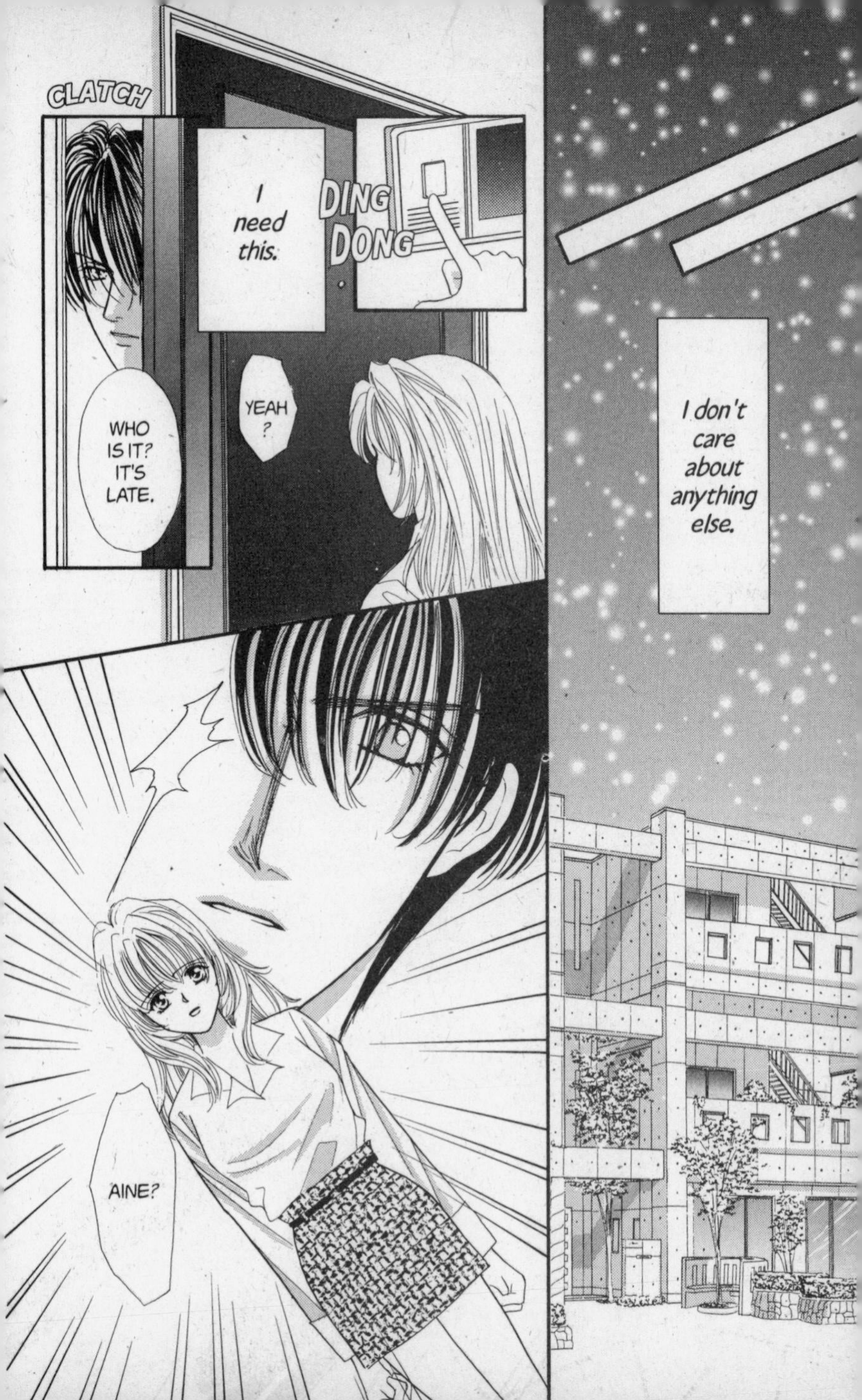
I don't care about anything else.
DING DONG
I need this.
CLATCH
WHO IS IT? IT'S LATE.
YEAH?
AINE?

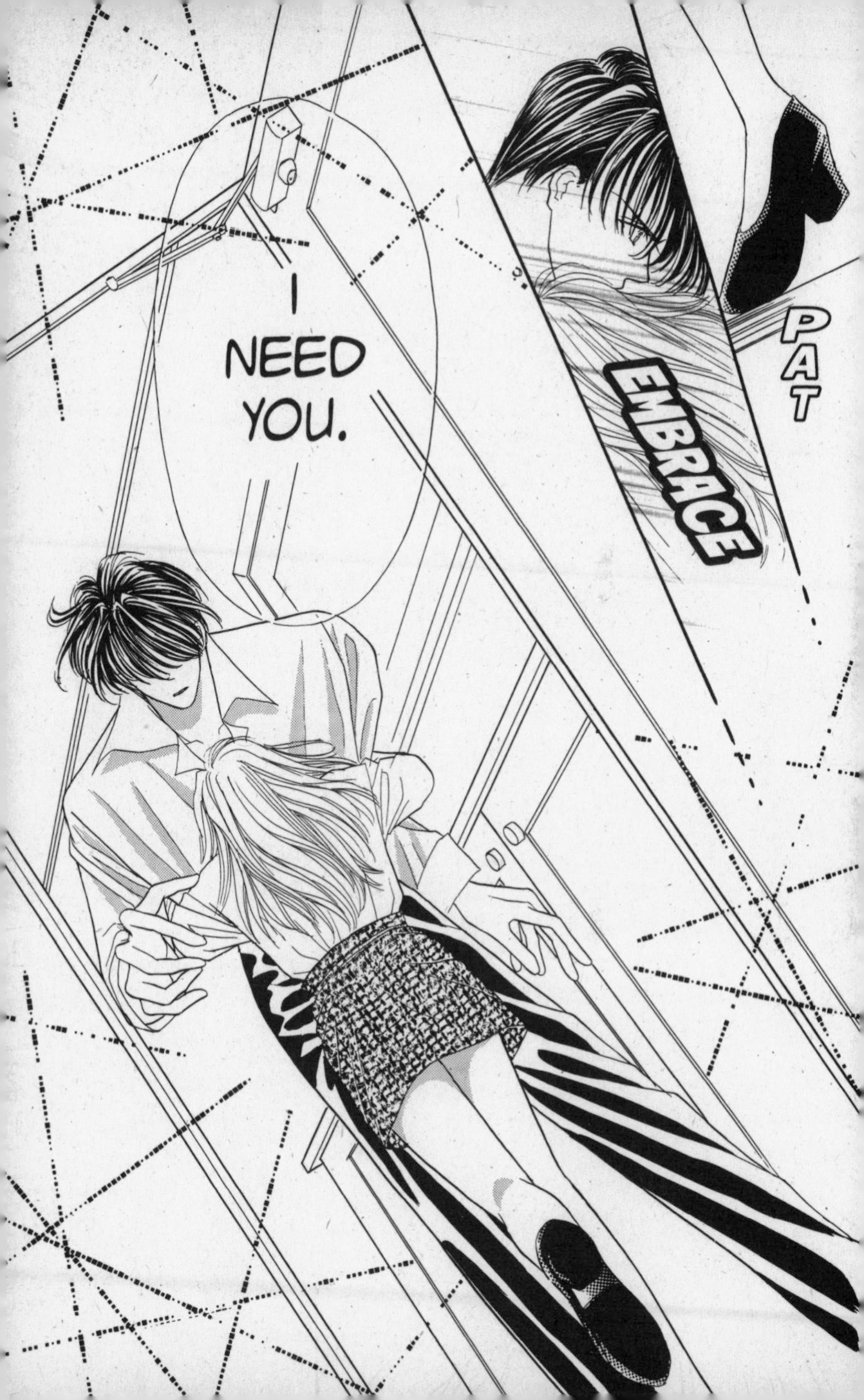
PAT
EMBRACE
I NEED YOU.

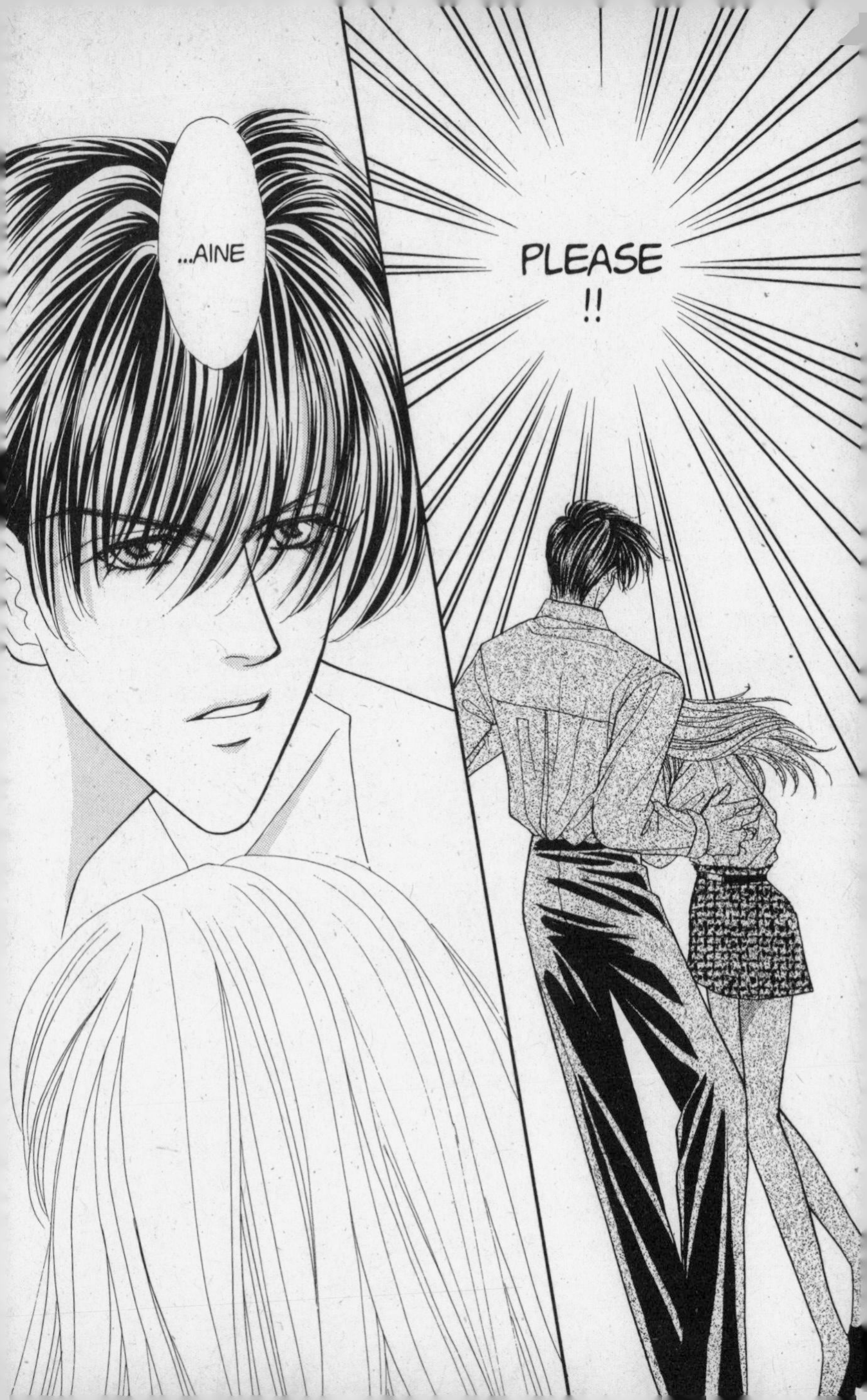
PLEASE !!
...AINE

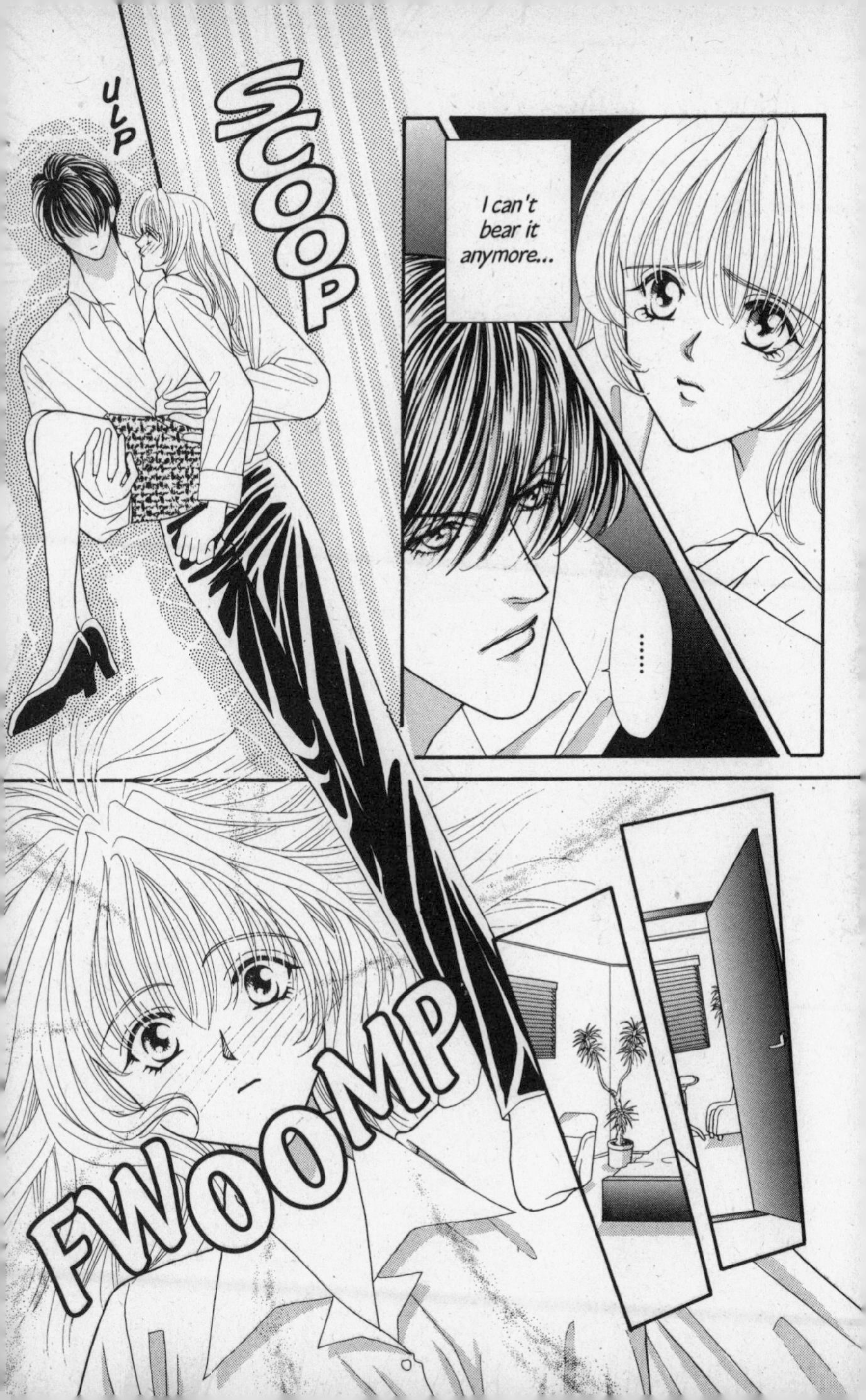
I can't bear it anymore...
......
ULP
SCOOP
FWOOMP

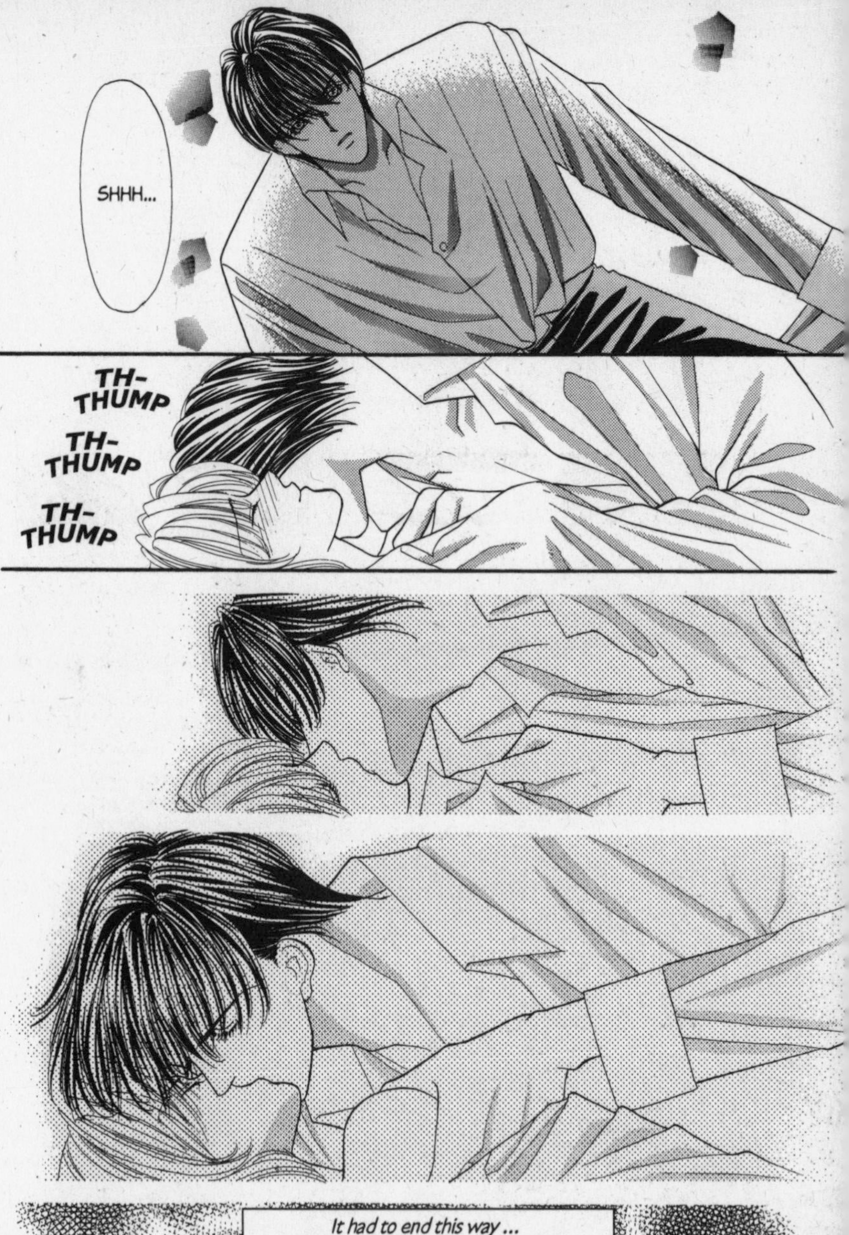
SHHH...
TH-THUMP
TH-THUMP
TH-THUMP
It had to end this way ...

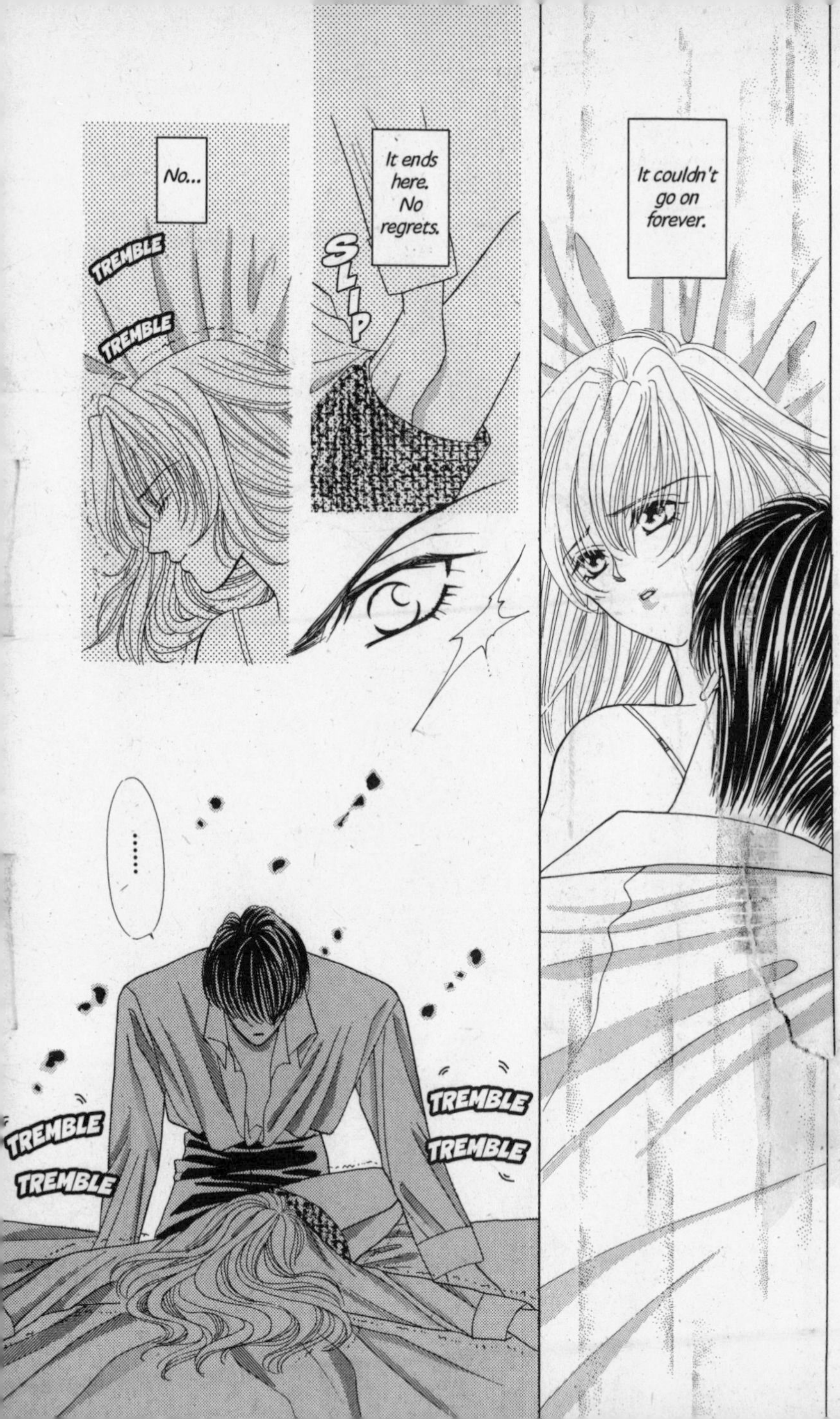
It couldn't go on forever.
It ends here. No regrets.
SLIP
No...
TREMBLE
TREMBLE
......
TREMBLE
TREMBLE
TREMBLE
TREMBLE

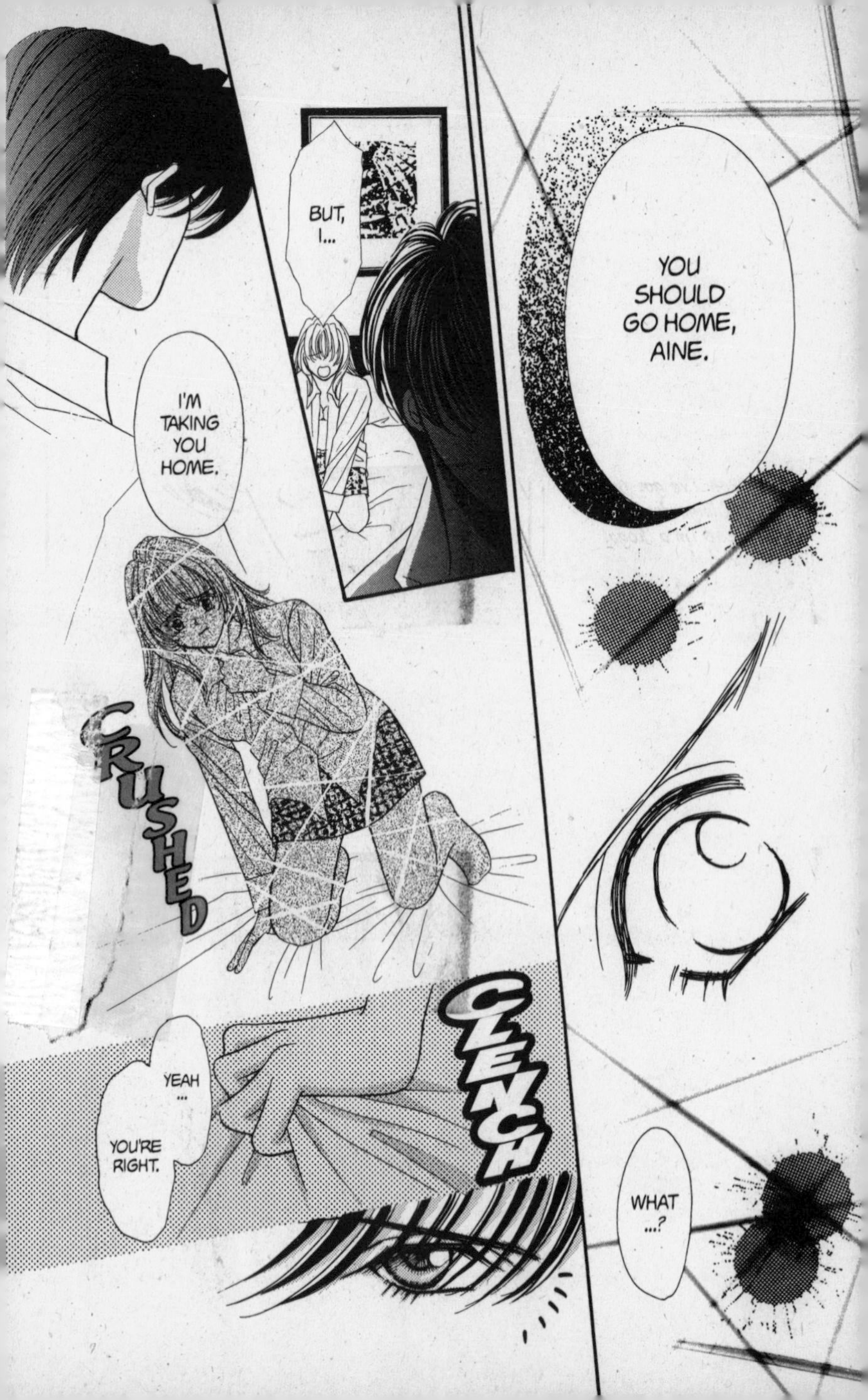
YOU SHOULD GO HOME, AINE.
WHAT ...?
BUT, I...
I'M TAKING YOU HOME.
CRUSHED
CLENCH
YEAH ... YOU'RE RIGHT.

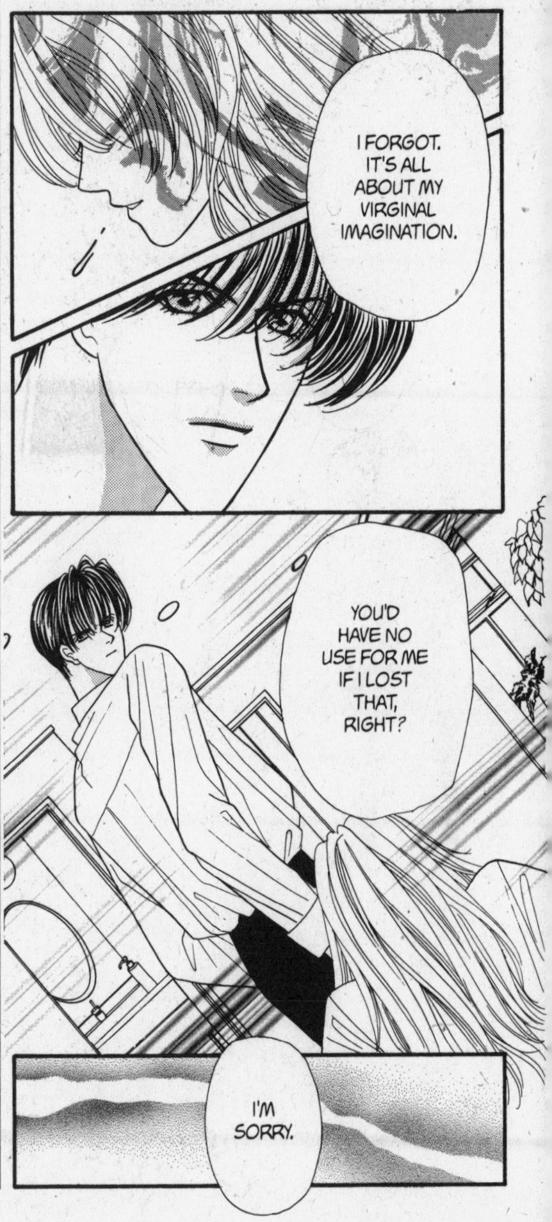
I FORGOT. IT'S ALL ABOUT MY VIRGINAL IMAGINATION.
YOU'D HAVE NO USE FOR ME IF I LOST THAT, RIGHT?
I'M SORRY.

Do you know what I do with them? No kidding: I stick them on my Hello Kitty filofax. There are so many cute frames these days. I even went to the Sanrio shop in Shibuya to take Hello Kitty print-clubs. I shouldn't be doing this at my age. I'm still acting like a high-schooler! I buy a lot of 'me Jane' and 'Jairo' clothes. I've got the kogal lingo down, too. I guess I'm a 'kogal wannabe'.

That's it for now... See you in volume 2!!

Special Thanks

Lyricist
- Tsuyoshi Aida

Sony Records
- Takako Kai

(Thank you so much for taking time out of your busy schedules to help me!)

Emiko Inoue

(Thank you for hooking me up. I still need to return your backstage pass, so let's go out for a drink? And don't forget the TOKIO concert...tickets are on me!)

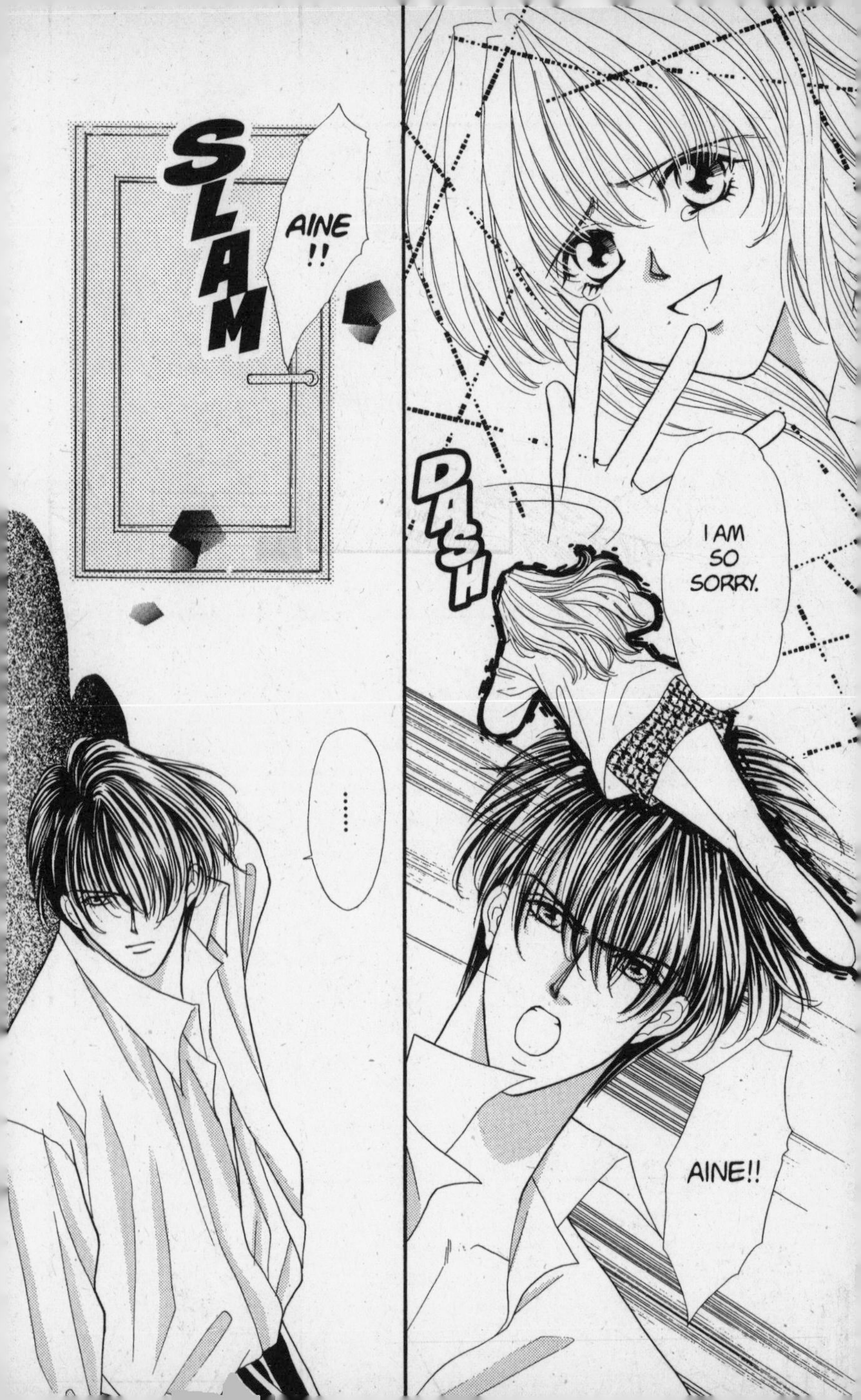
I AM SO SORRY.
DASH
AINE!!
AINE !!
SLAM
......

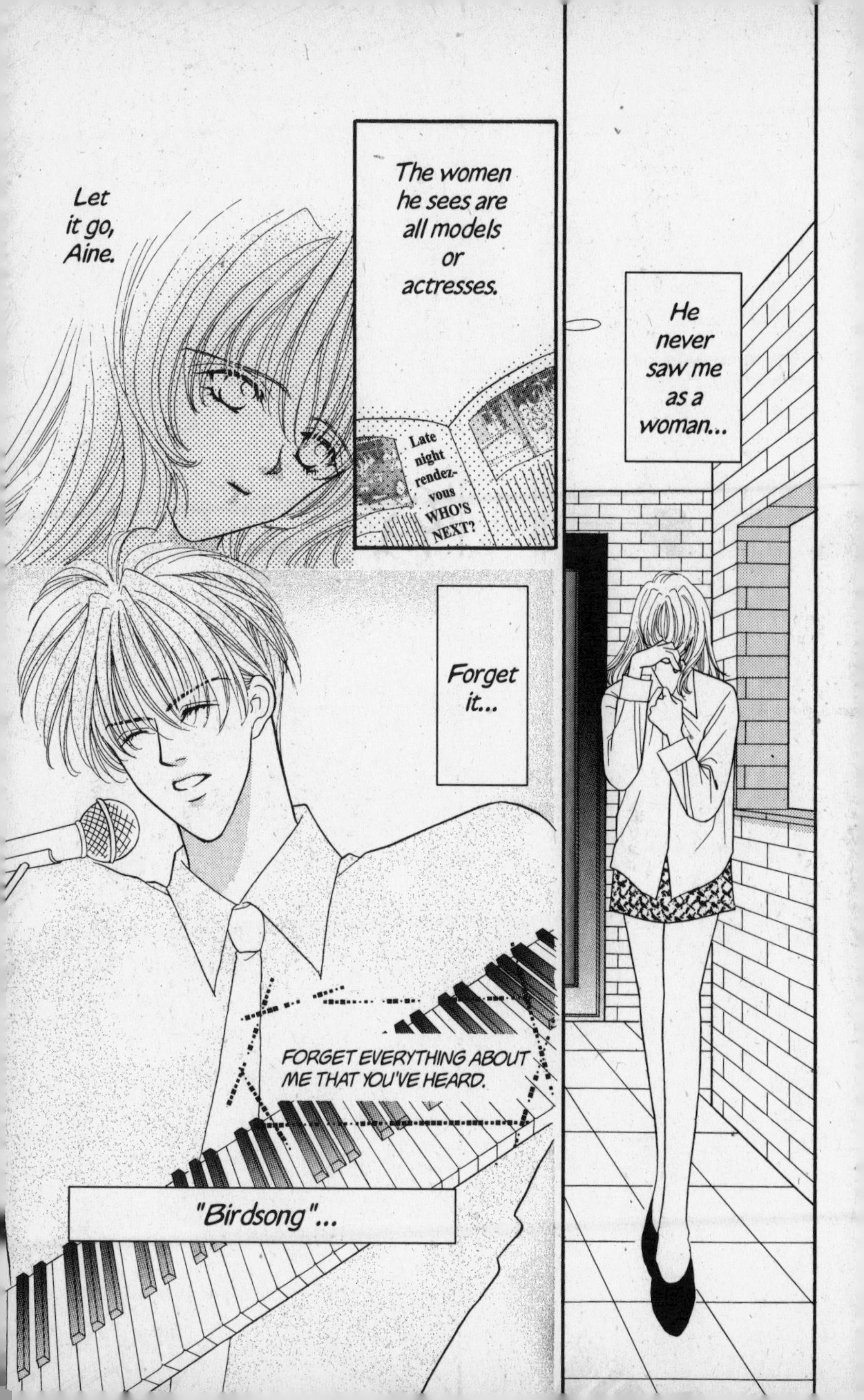
He never saw me as a woman...
The women he sees are all models or actresses.
Late night rendez-vous WHO'S NEXT?
Let it go, Aine.
Forget it...
FORGET EVERYTHING ABOUT ME THAT YOU'VE HEARD.
"Birdsong"...

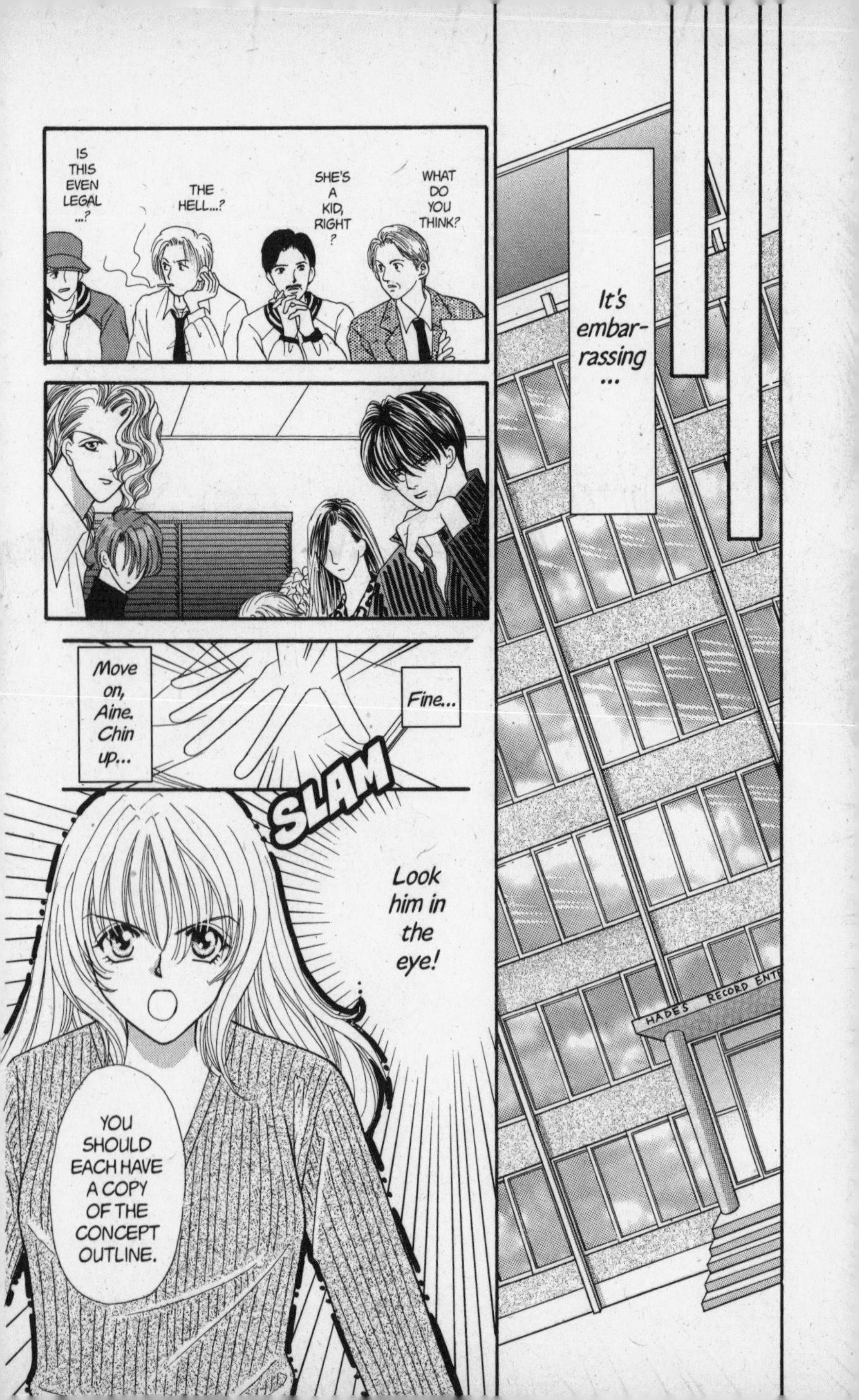
It's embarrassing...
WHAT DO YOU THINK?
SHE'S A KID, RIGHT?
THE HELL...?
IS THIS EVEN LEGAL...?
Fine...
Move on, Aine. Chin up...
SLAM
Look him in the eye!
YOU SHOULD EACH HAVE A COPY OF THE CONCEPT OUTLINE.

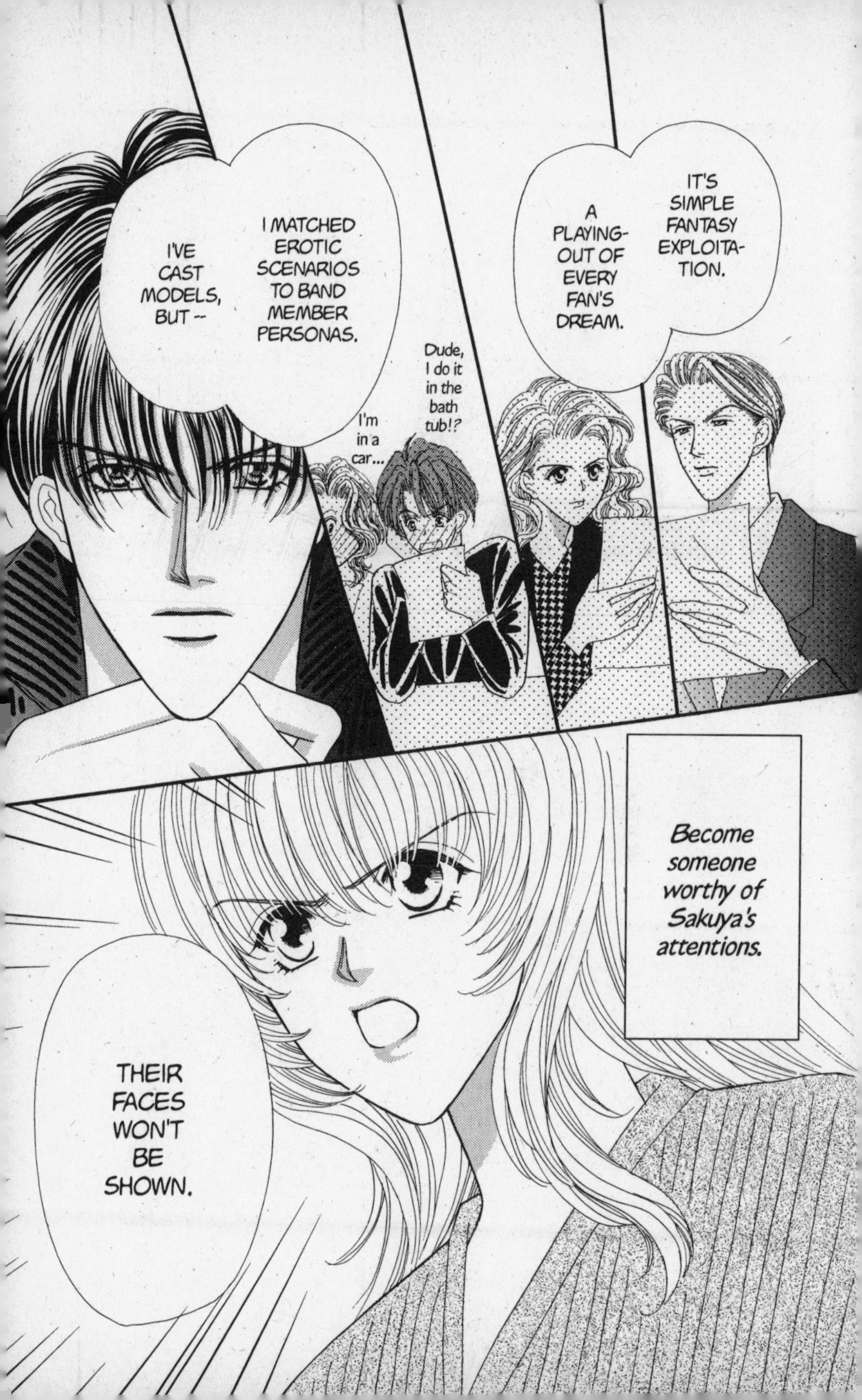
IT'S SIMPLE FANTASY EXPLOITA-TION.
A PLAYING-OUT OF EVERY FAN'S DREAM.
Dude, I do it in the bath tub!?
I'm in a car...
I MATCHED EROTIC SCENARIOS TO BAND MEMBER PERSONAS.
I'VE CAST MODELS, BUT --
Become someone worthy of Sakuya's attentions.
THEIR FACES WON'T BE SHOWN.

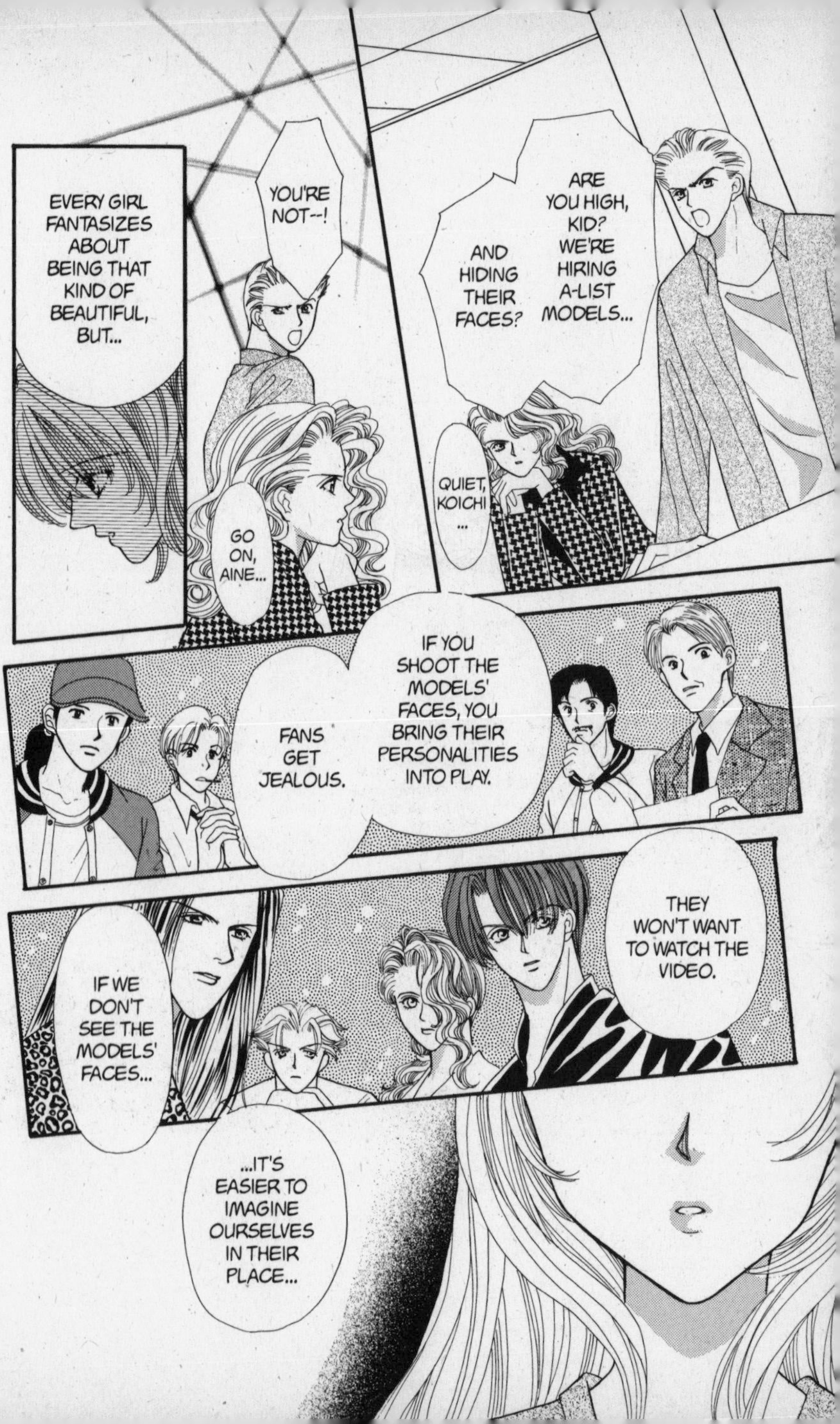
ARE YOU HIGH, KID? WE'RE HIRING A-LIST MODELS...
AND HIDING THEIR FACES?
QUIET, KOICHI ...
YOU'RE NOT--!
GO ON, AINE...
EVERY GIRL FANTASIZES ABOUT BEING THAT KIND OF BEAUTIFUL, BUT...
IF YOU SHOOT THE MODELS' FACES, YOU BRING THEIR PERSONALITIES INTO PLAY.
FANS GET JEALOUS.
THEY WON'T WANT TO WATCH THE VIDEO.
IF WE DON'T SEE THE MODELS' FACES...
...IT'S EASIER TO IMAGINE OURSELVES IN THEIR PLACE...

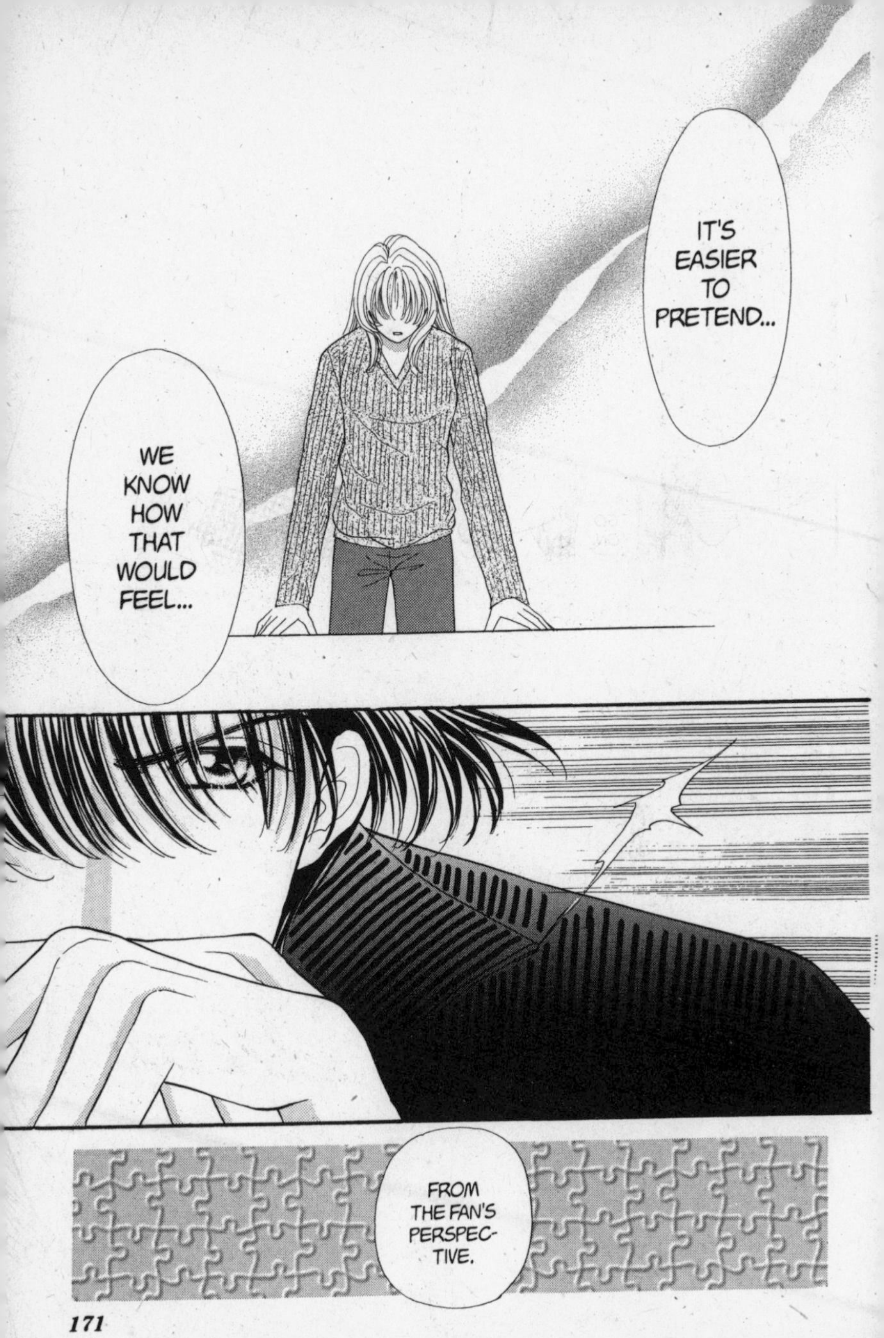
IT'S EASIER TO PRETEND...
WE KNOW HOW THAT WOULD FEEL...
FROM THE FAN'S PERSPEC-TIVE.

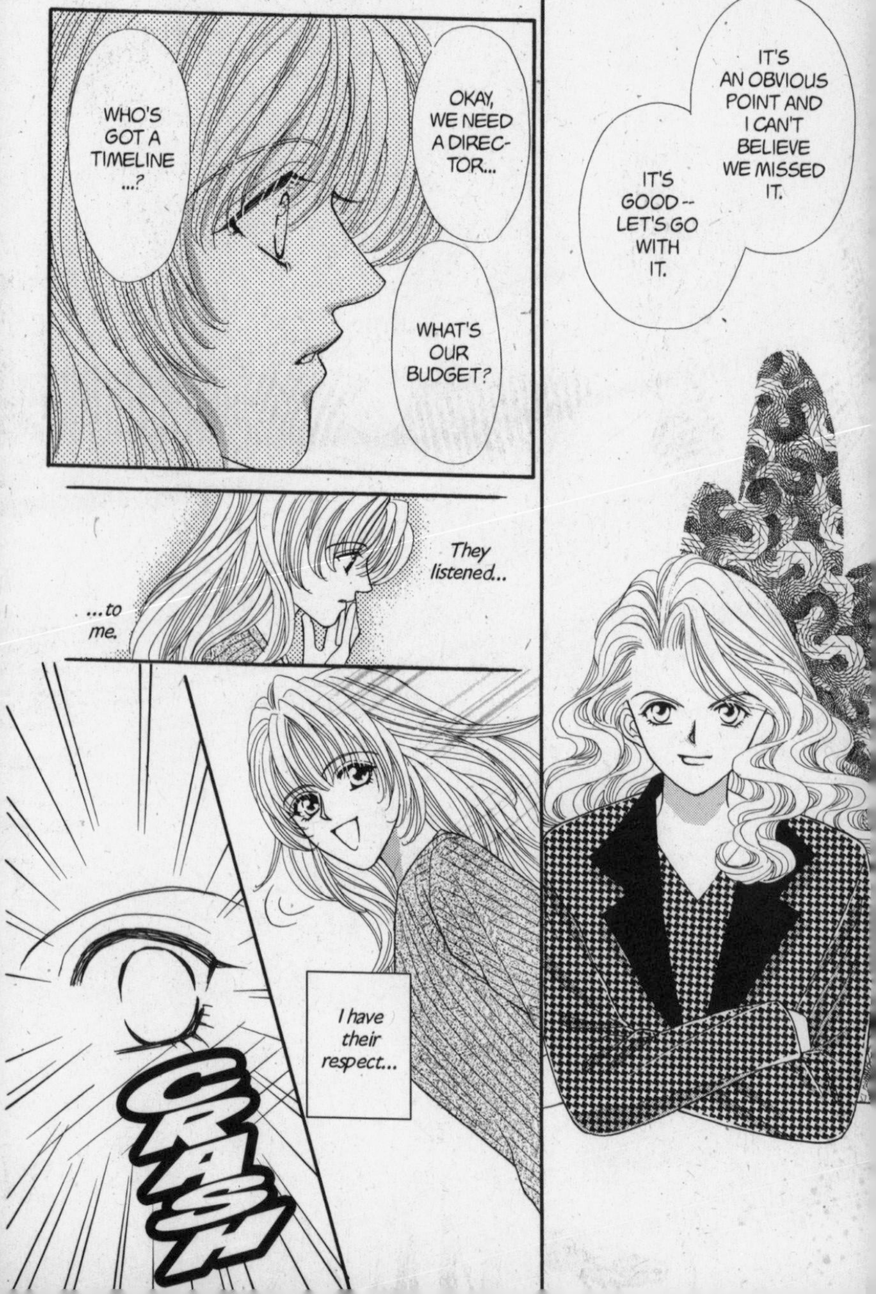
IT'S AN OBVIOUS POINT AND I CAN'T BELIEVE WE MISSED IT.
IT'S GOOD-- LET'S GO WITH IT.
OKAY, WE NEED A DIREC-TOR...
WHO'S GOT A TIMELINE ...?
WHAT'S OUR BUDGET?
They listened...
...to me.
I have their respect...
CRASH

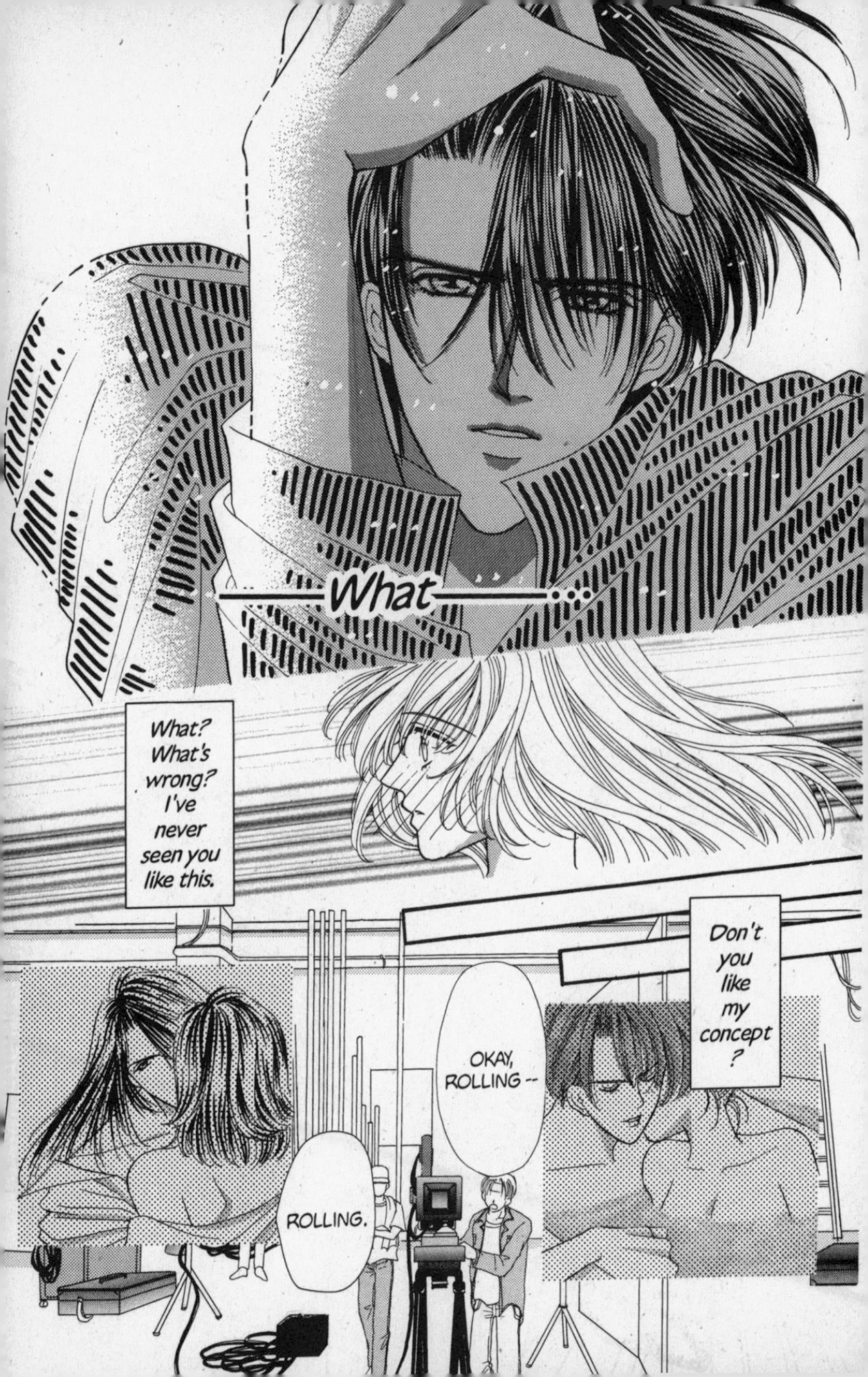
What——...
What? What's wrong? I've never seen you like this.
Don't you like my concept?
OKAY, ROLLING --
ROLLING.

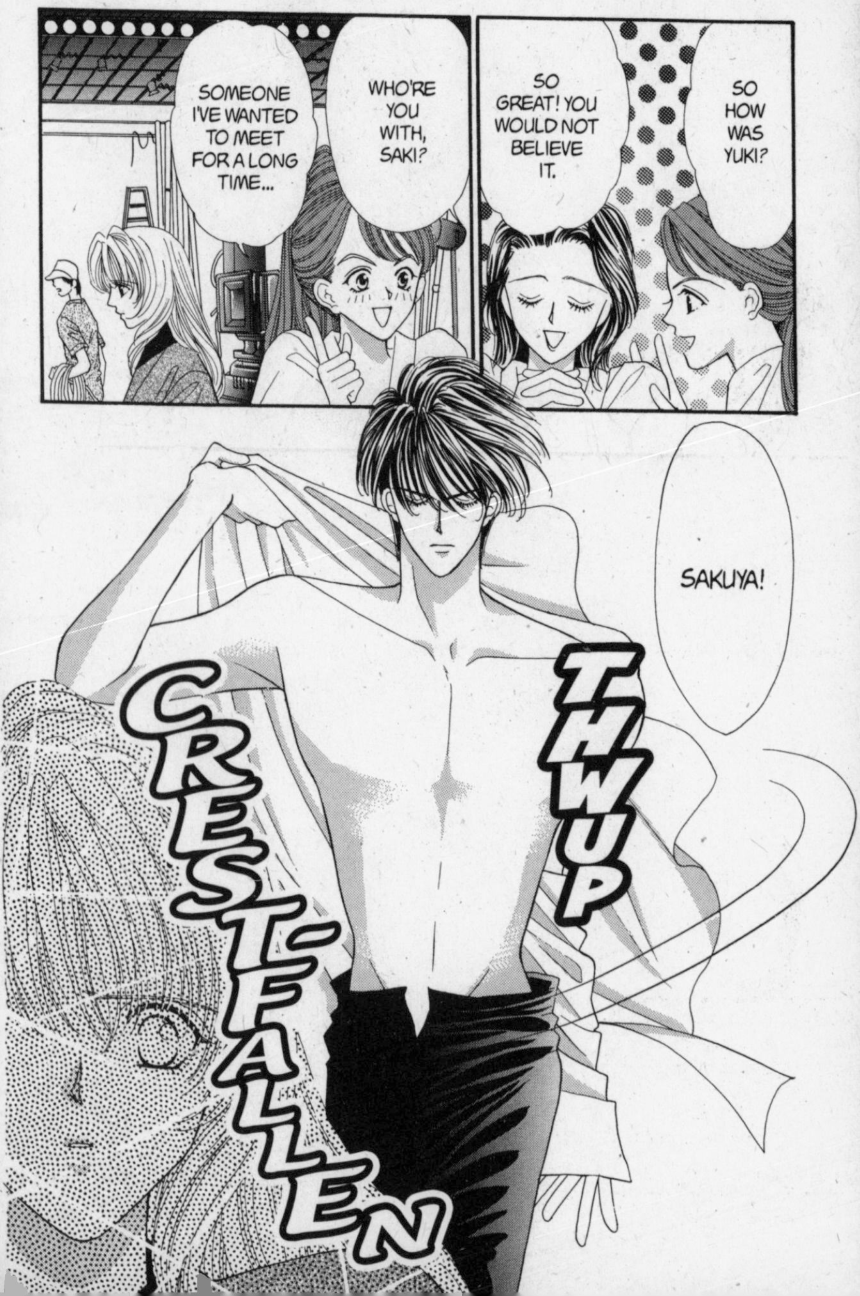
SO HOW WAS YUKI?
SO GREAT! YOU WOULD NOT BELIEVE IT.
WHO'RE YOU WITH, SAKI?
SOMEONE I'VE WANTED TO MEET FOR A LONG TIME...
SAKUYA!
THWUP
CREST-FALLEN

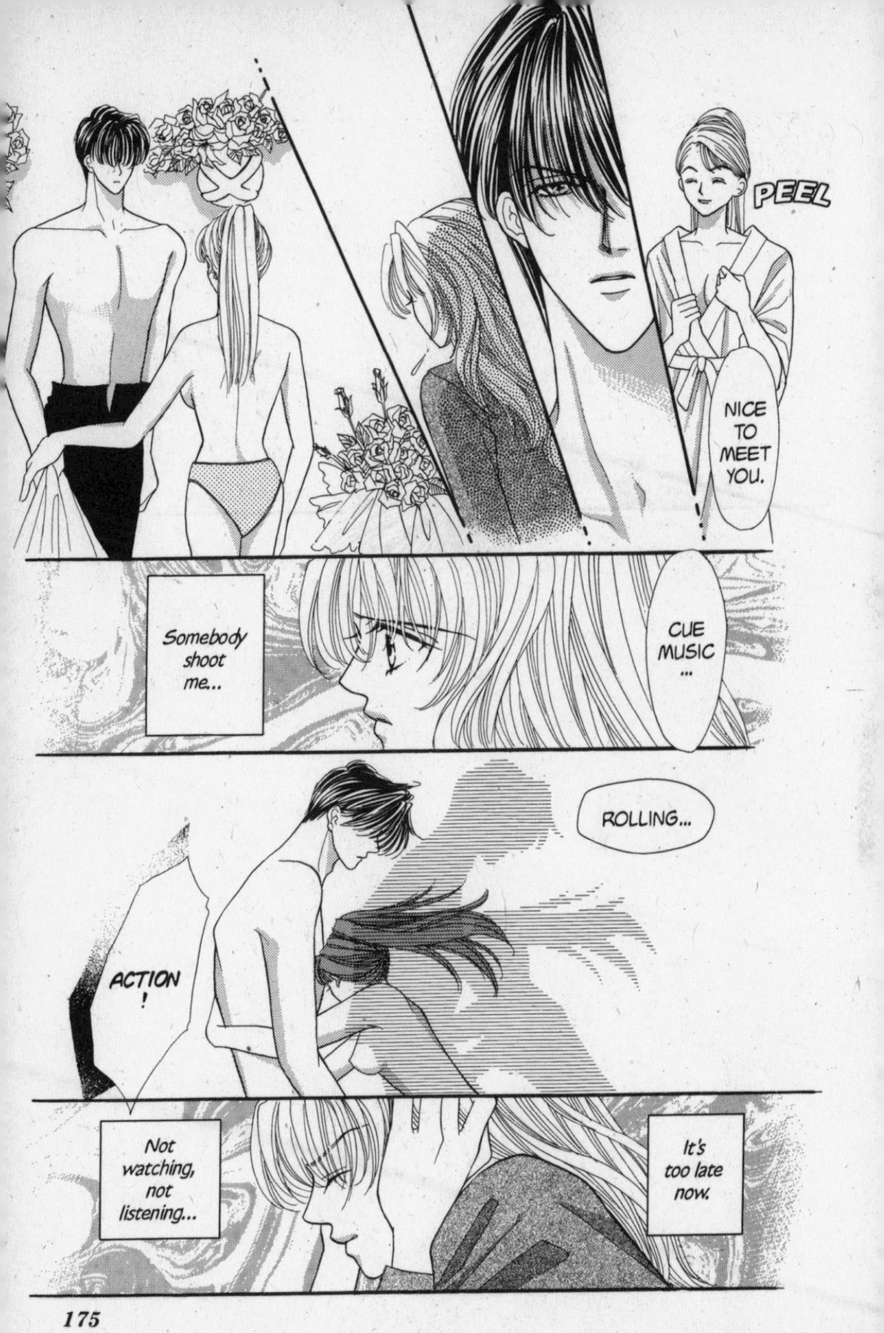
PEEL
NICE TO MEET YOU.
CUE MUSIC...
Somebody shoot me...
ROLLING...
ACTION!
It's too late now.
Not watching, not listening...

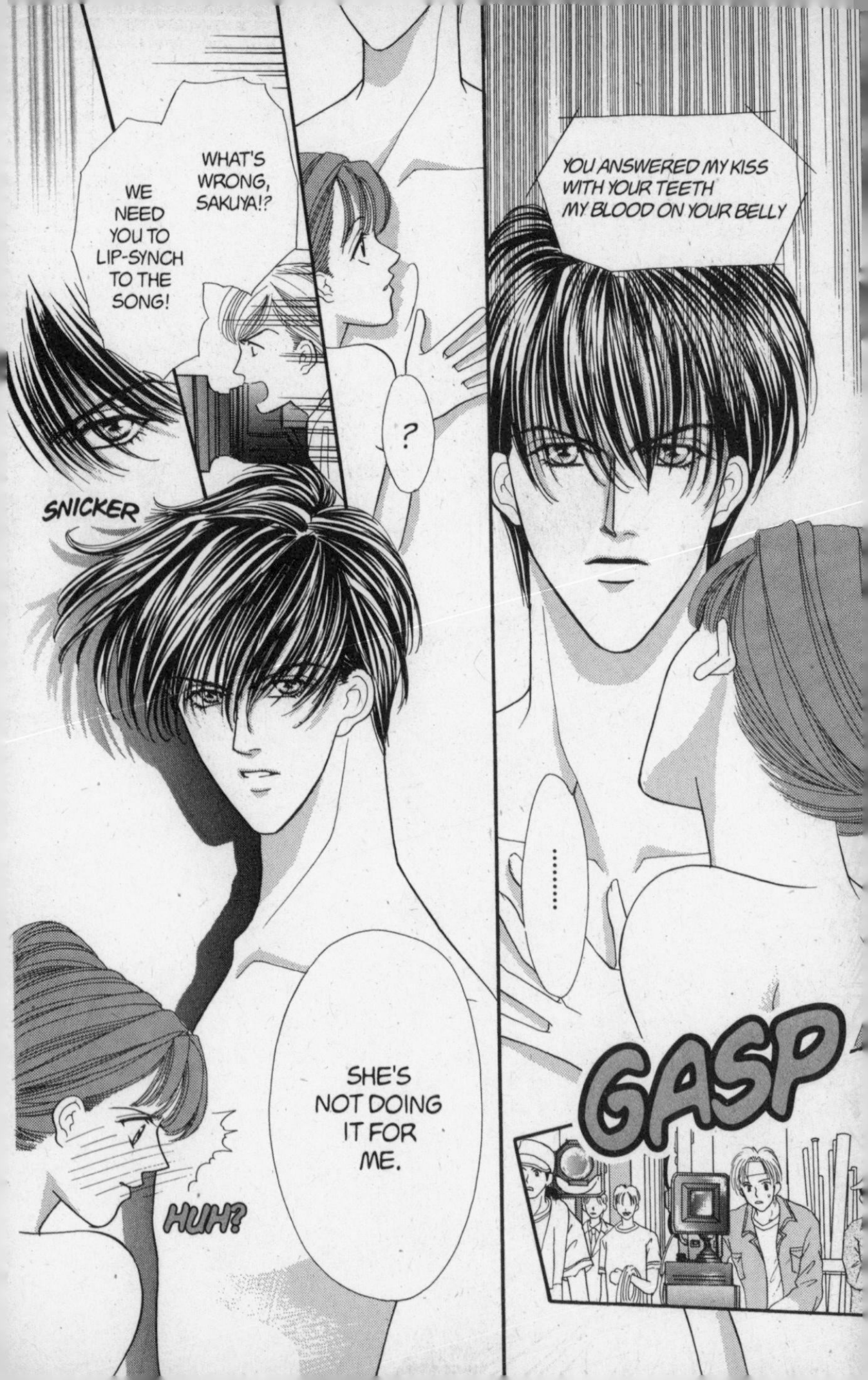
YOU ANSWERED MY KISS WITH YOUR TEETH MY BLOOD ON YOUR BELLY
......
GASP
WHAT'S WRONG, SAKUYA!?
WE NEED YOU TO LIP-SYNCH TO THE SONG!
?
SNICKER
SHE'S NOT DOING IT FOR ME.
HUH?

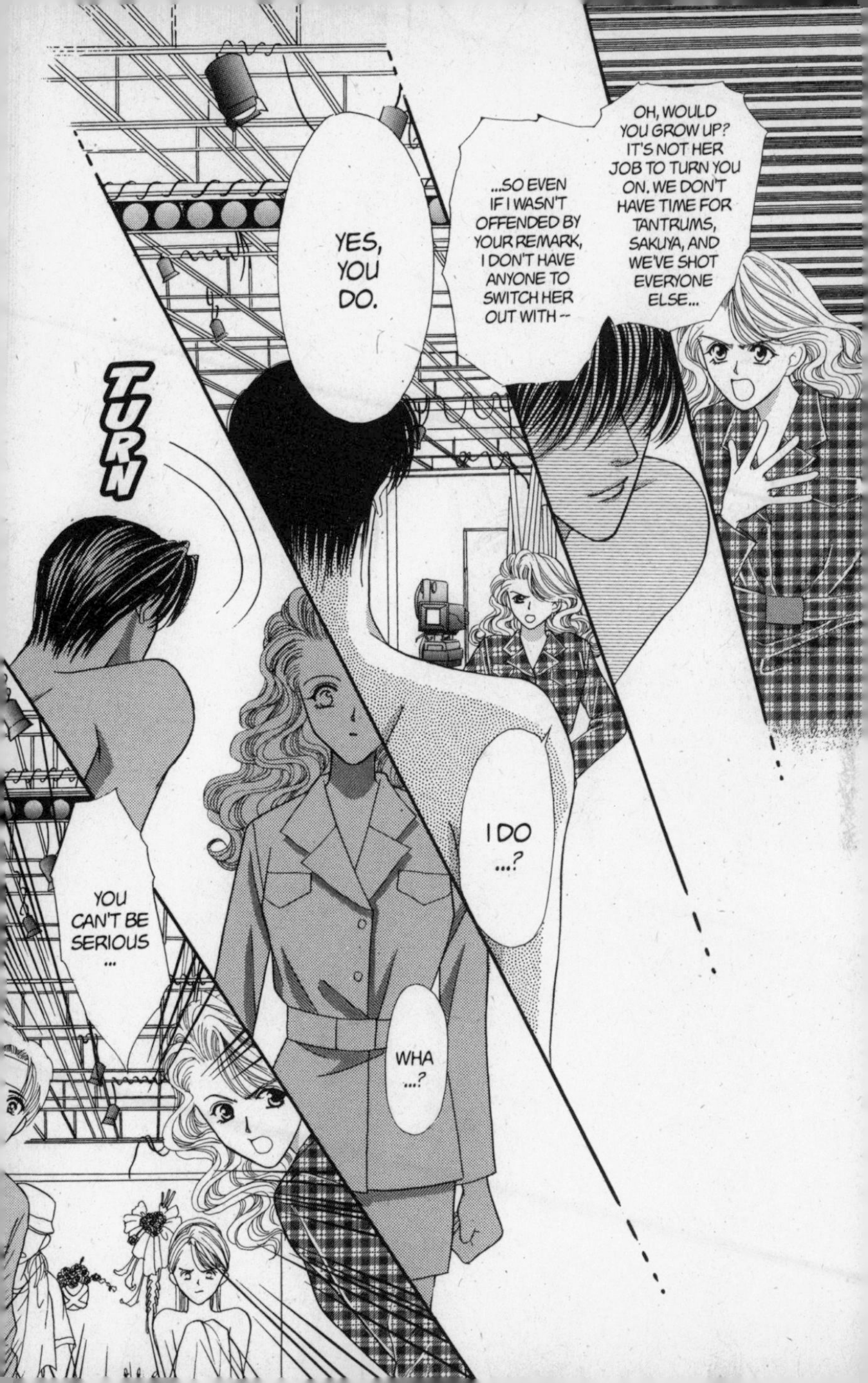
OH, WOULD YOU GROW UP? IT'S NOT HER JOB TO TURN YOU ON. WE DON'T HAVE TIME FOR TANTRUMS, SAKUYA, AND WE'VE SHOT EVERYONE ELSE...
...SO EVEN IF I WASN'T OFFENDED BY YOUR REMARK, I DON'T HAVE ANYONE TO SWITCH HER OUT WITH --
YES, YOU DO.
I DO ...?
TURN
WHA ...?
YOU CAN'T BE SERIOUS ...

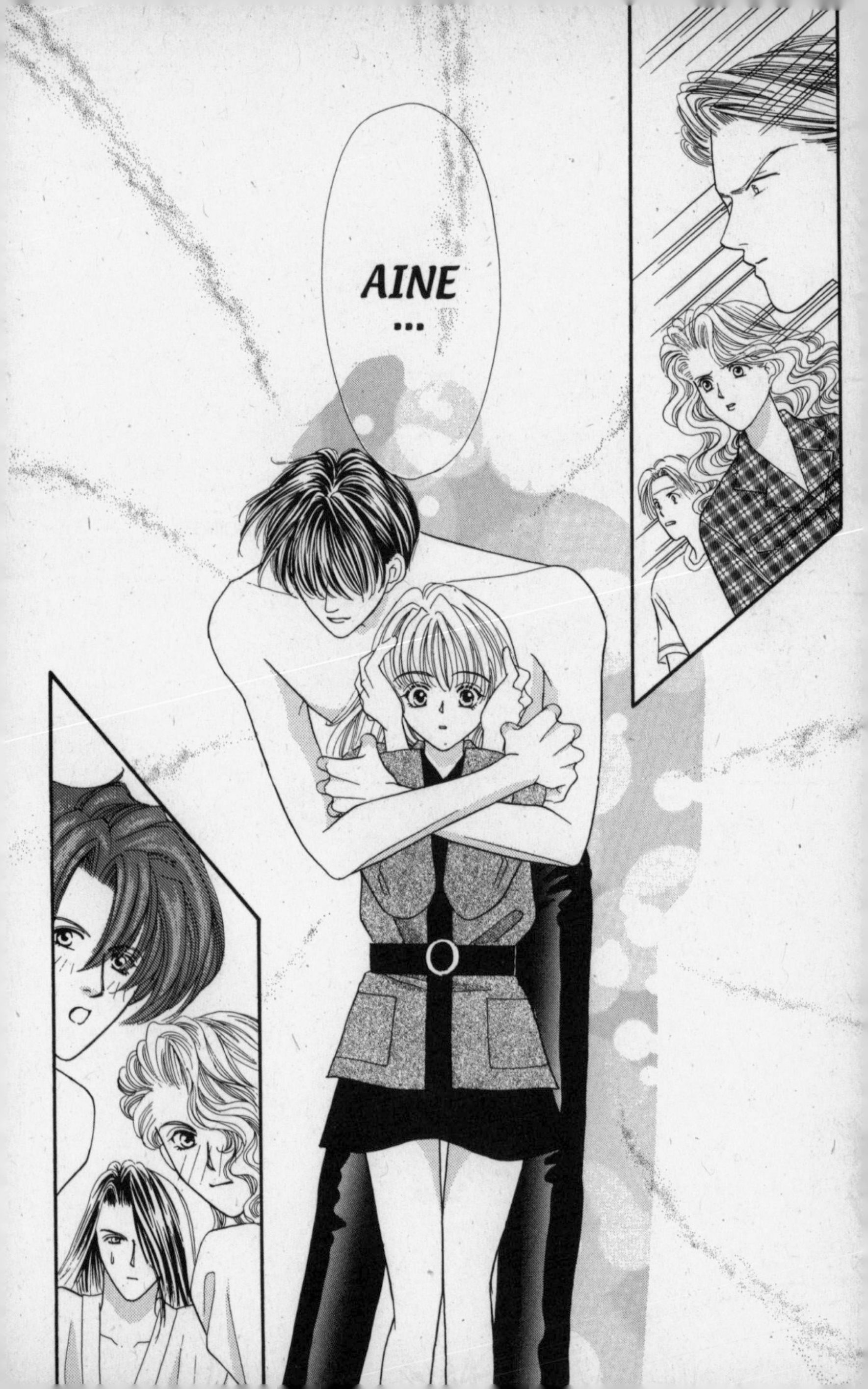
AINE
...

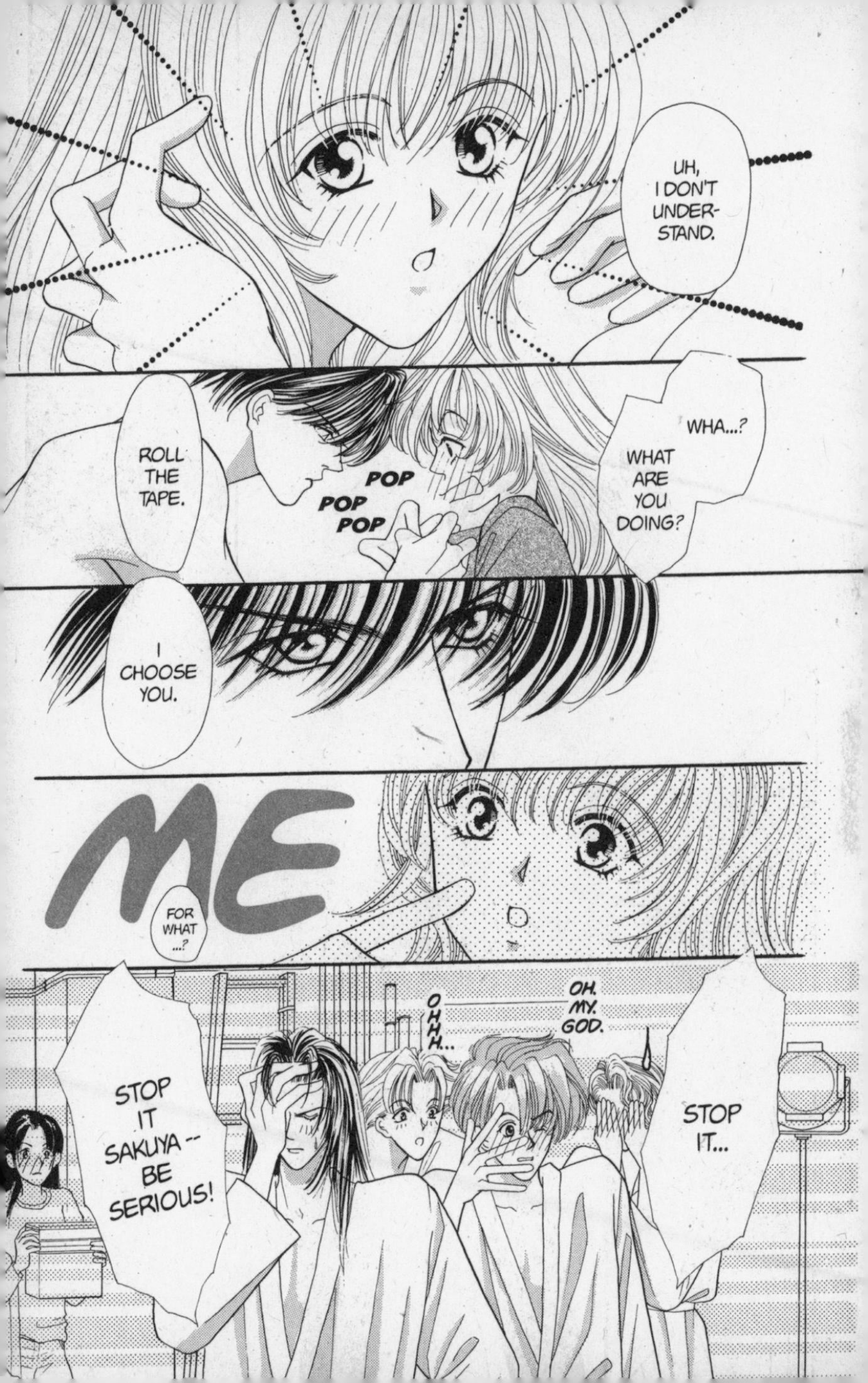
UH, I DON'T UNDER-STAND.
WHA...? WHAT ARE YOU DOING?
POP POP POP
ROLL THE TAPE.
I CHOOSE YOU.
ME
FOR WHAT ...?
STOP IT...
OH. MY. GOD.
OHHH...
STOP IT SAKUYA -- BE SERIOUS!

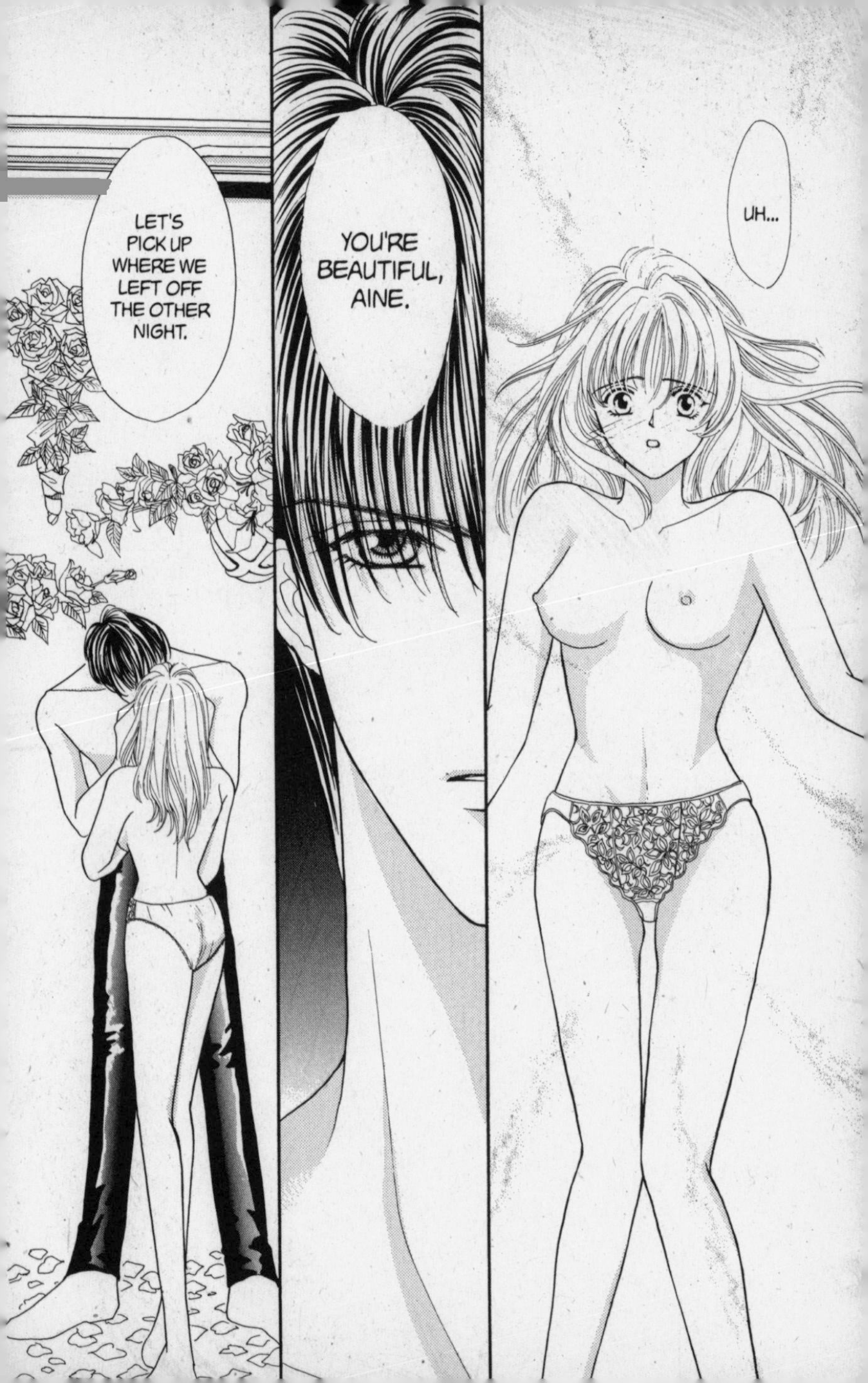
UH...
YOU'RE BEAUTIFUL, AINE.
LET'S PICK UP WHERE WE LEFT OFF THE OTHER NIGHT.

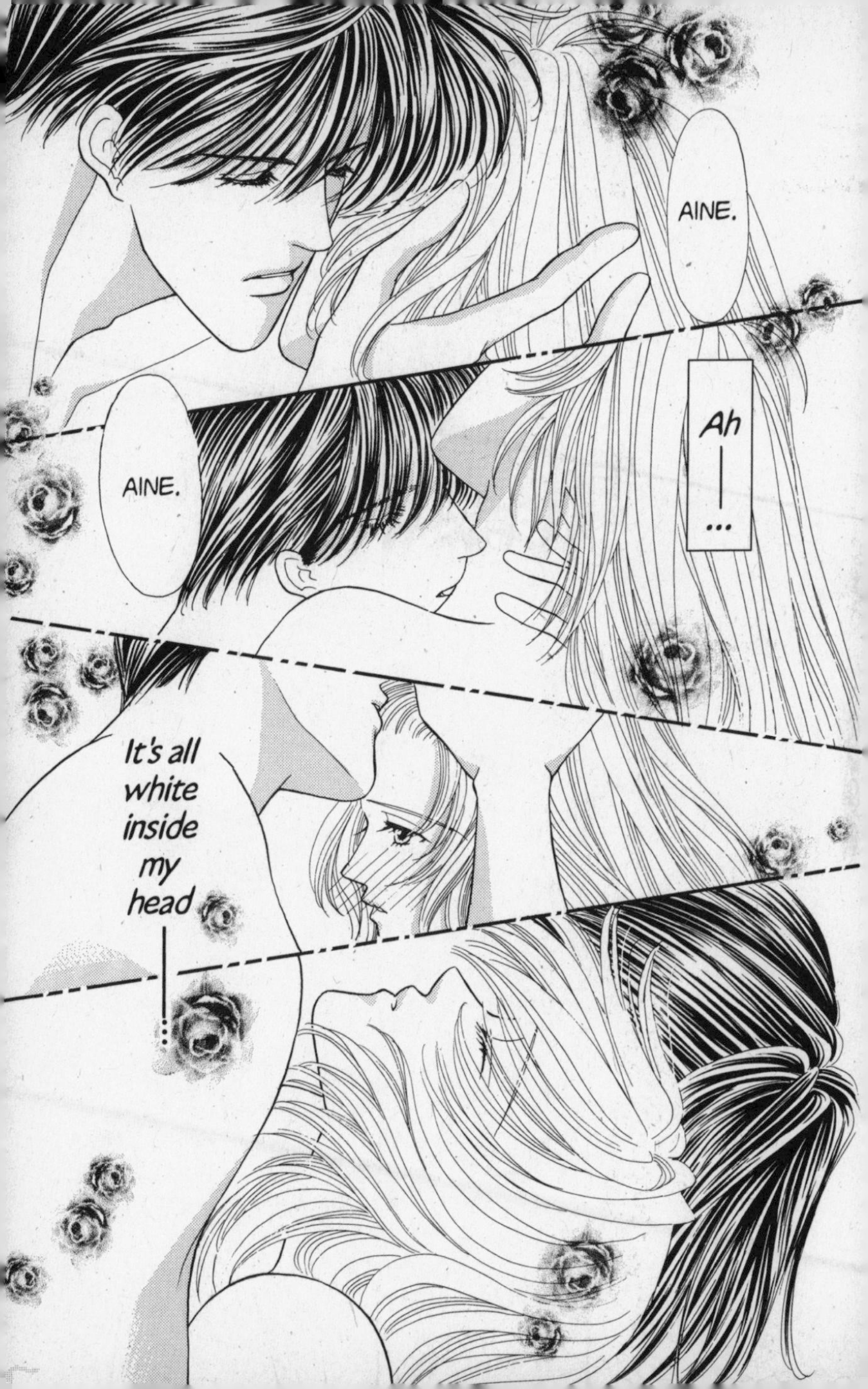
AINE.
Ah —...
AINE.
It's all white inside my head —...

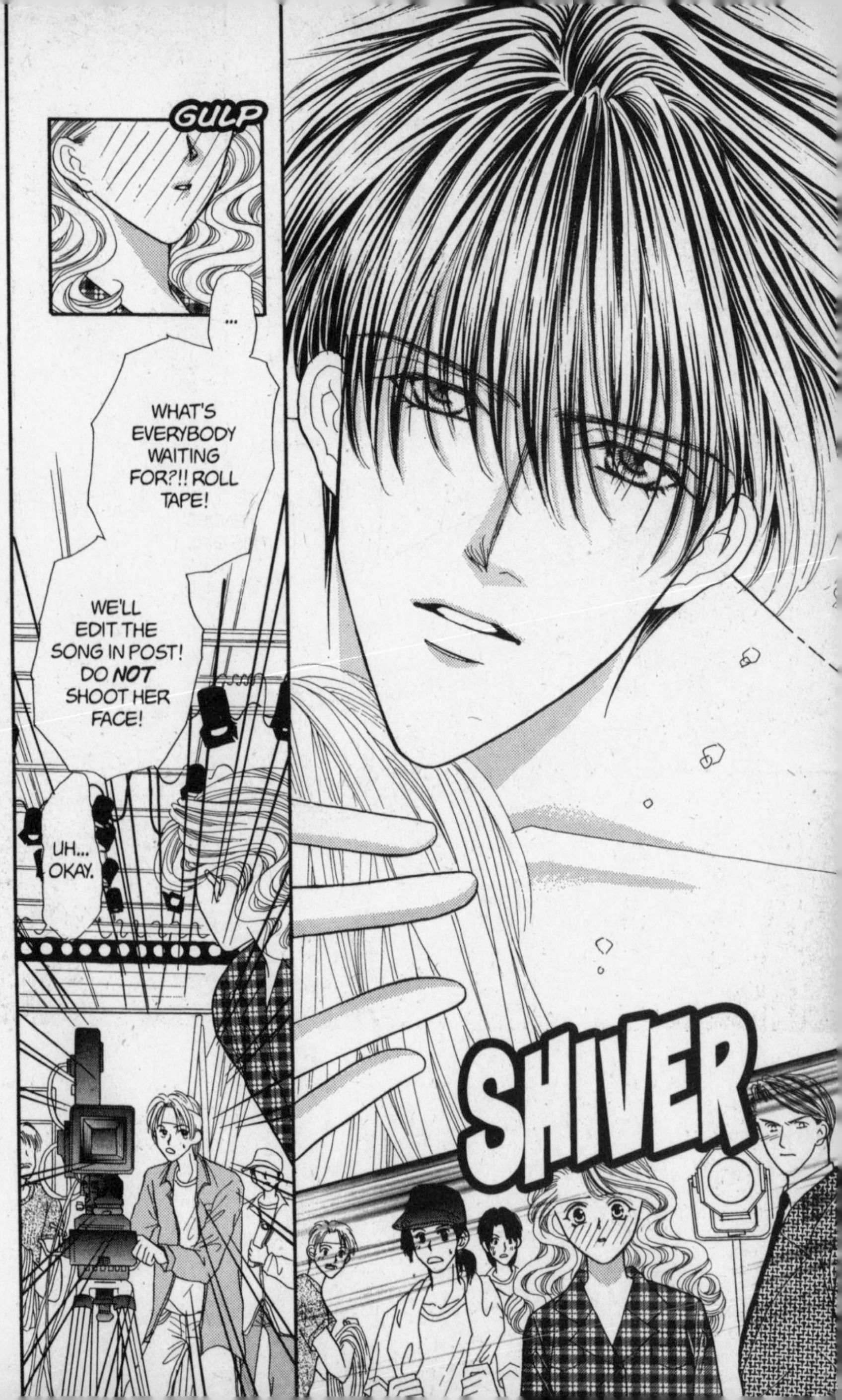
SHIVER
GULP
...
WHAT'S EVERYBODY WAITING FOR?!! ROLL TAPE!
WE'LL EDIT THE SONG IN POST! DO **NOT** SHOOT HER FACE!
UH... OKAY.

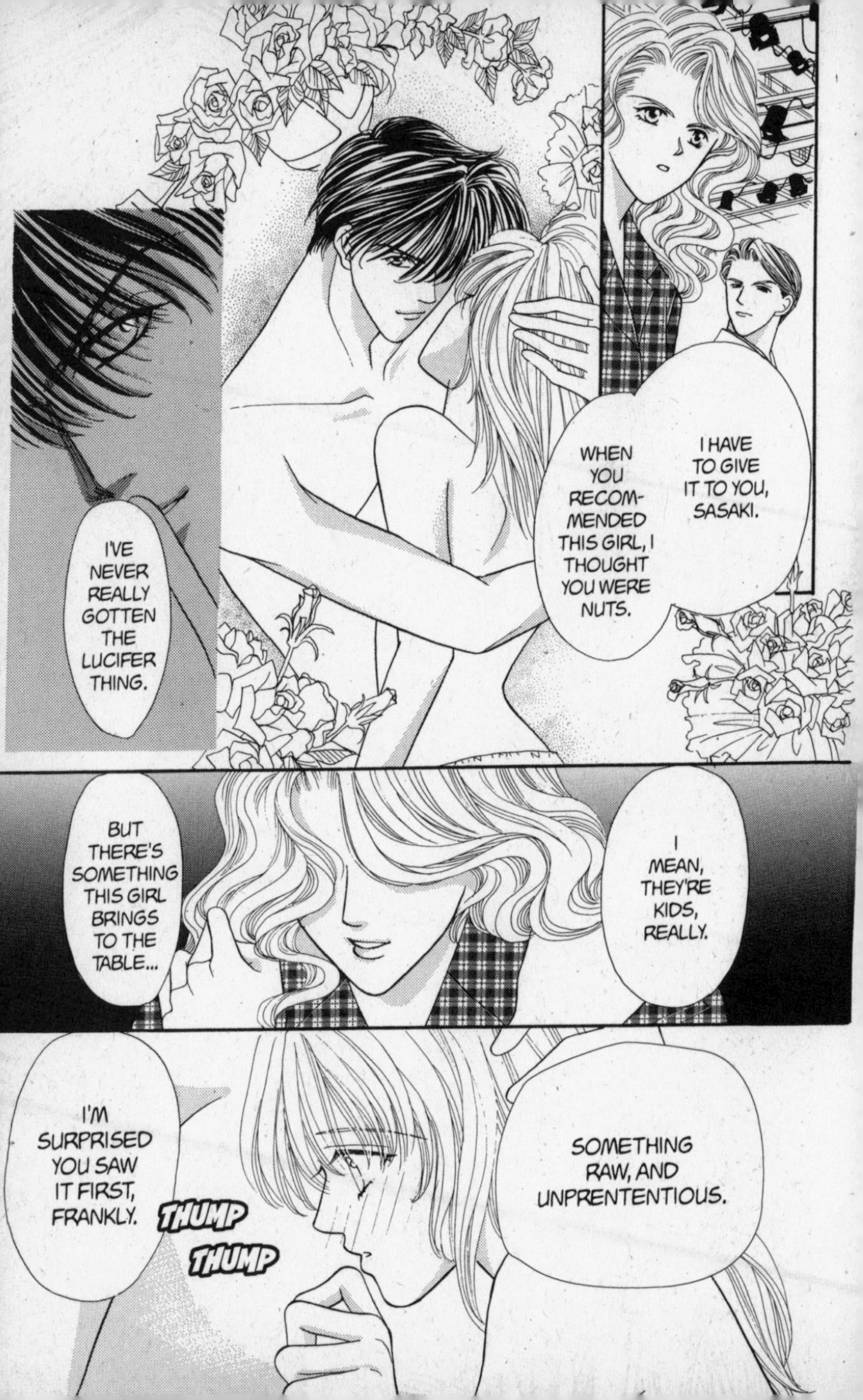
I HAVE TO GIVE IT TO YOU, SASAKI.
WHEN YOU RECOMMENDED THIS GIRL, I THOUGHT YOU WERE NUTS.
I'VE NEVER REALLY GOTTEN THE LUCIFER THING.
I MEAN, THEY'RE KIDS, REALLY.
BUT THERE'S SOMETHING THIS GIRL BRINGS TO THE TABLE...
SOMETHING RAW, AND UNPRENTENTIOUS.
I'M SURPRISED YOU SAW IT FIRST, FRANKLY.
THUMP
THUMP

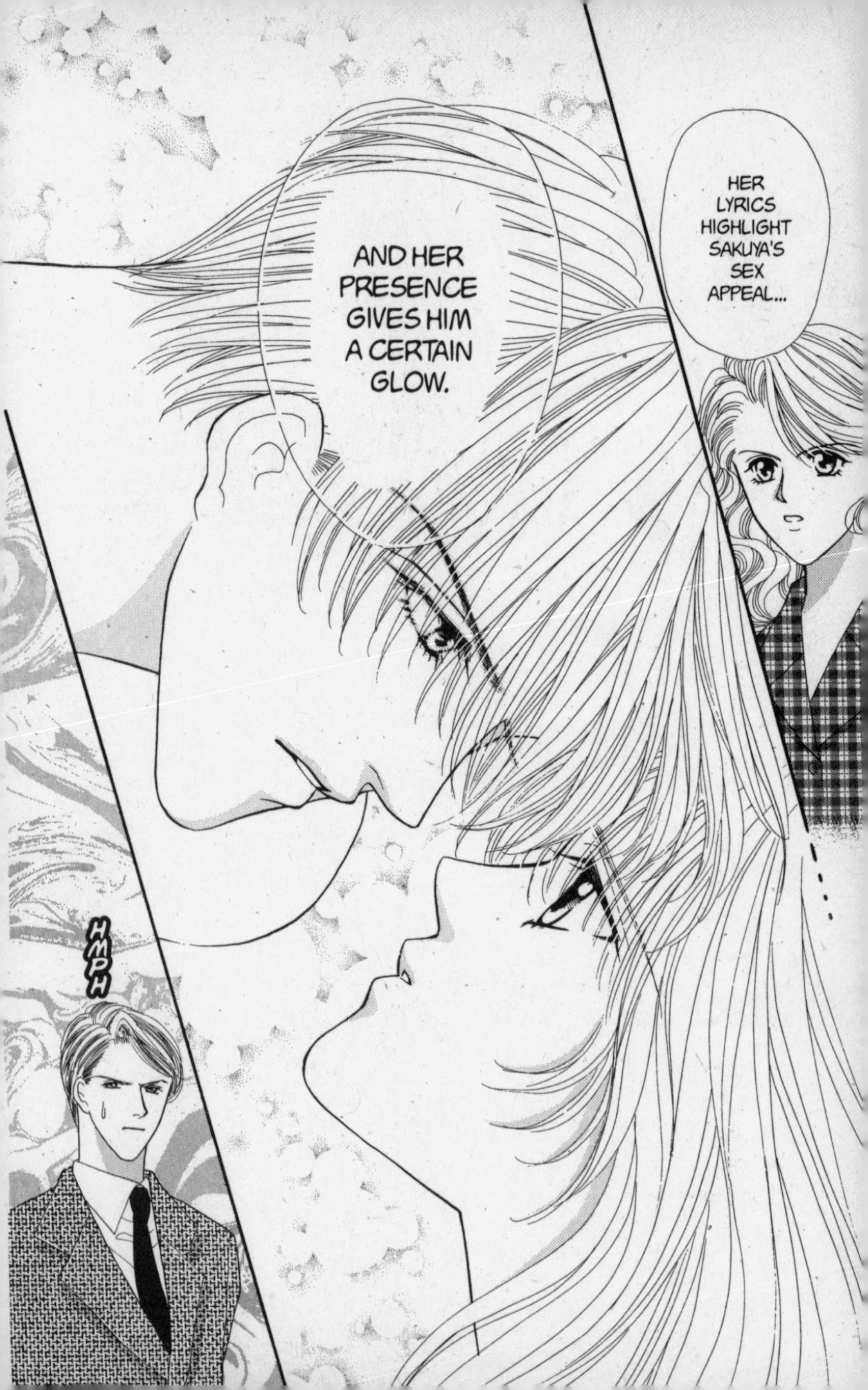
HER LYRICS HIGHLIGHT SAKUYA'S SEX APPEAL...
AND HER PRESENCE GIVES HIM A CERTAIN GLOW.
HMPH

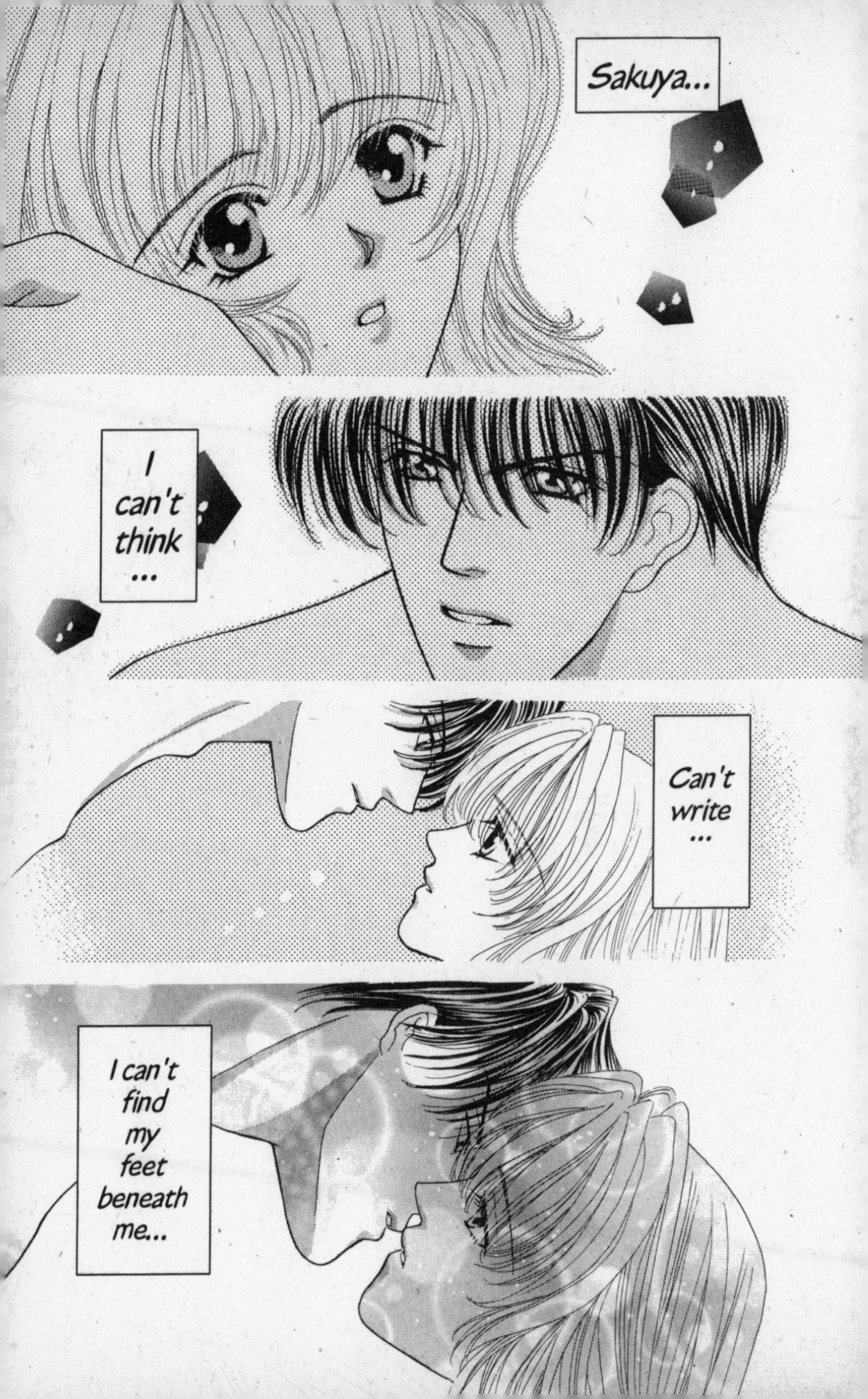
Sakuya...
I can't think ...
Can't write ...
I can't find my feet beneath me...

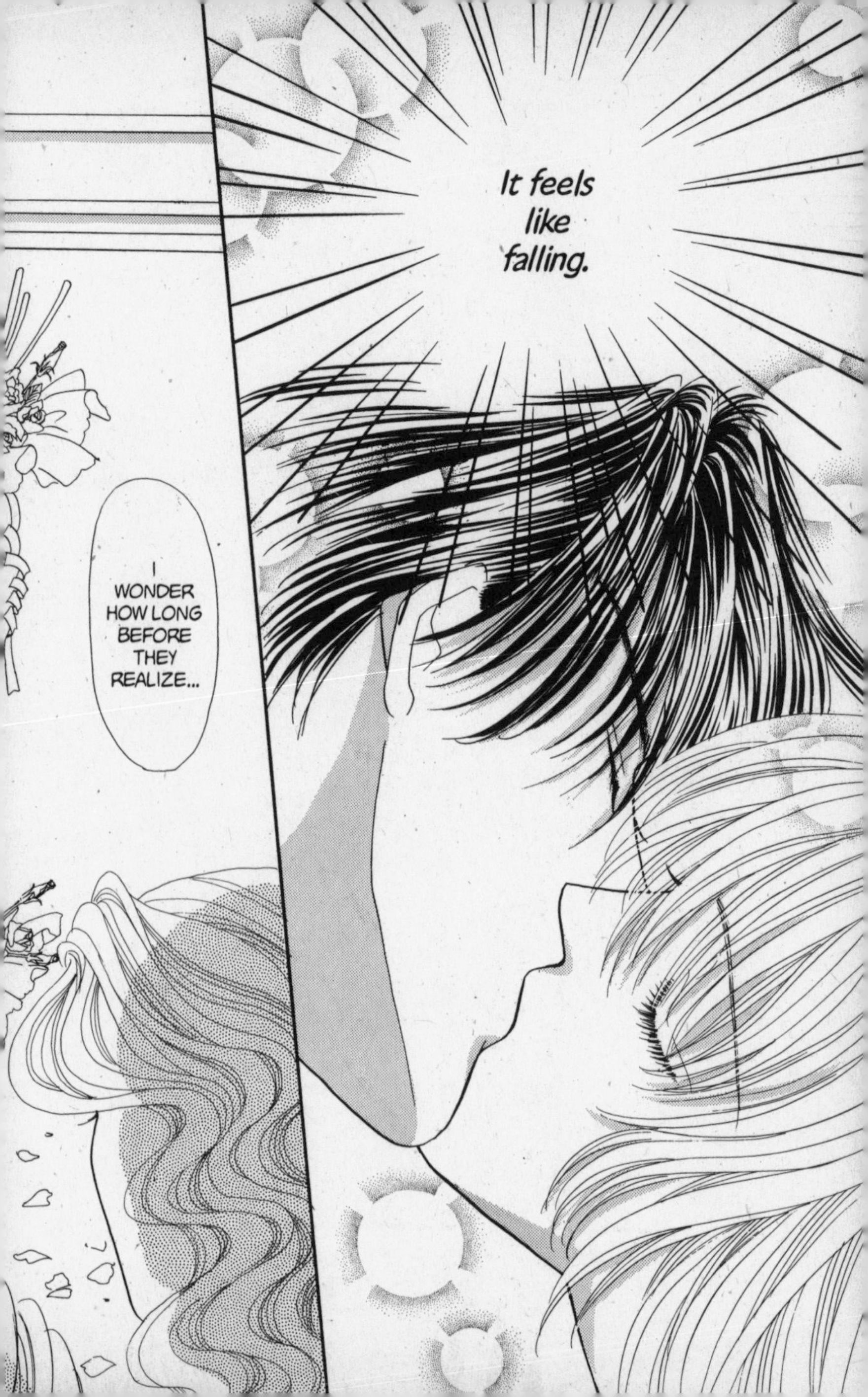
It feels like falling.
I WONDER HOW LONG BEFORE THEY REALIZE...

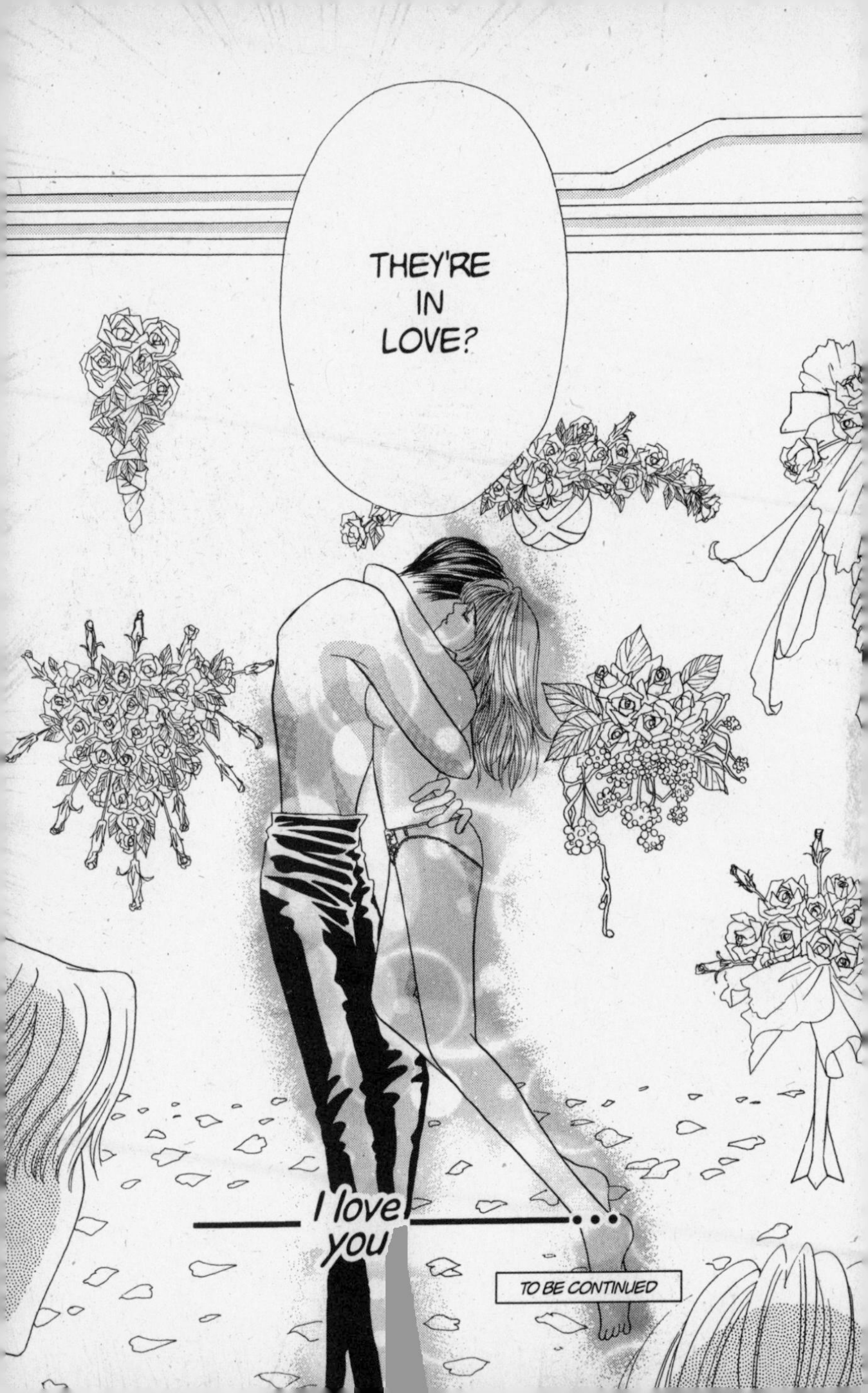
THEY'RE IN LOVE?
I love you...
TO BE CONTINUED

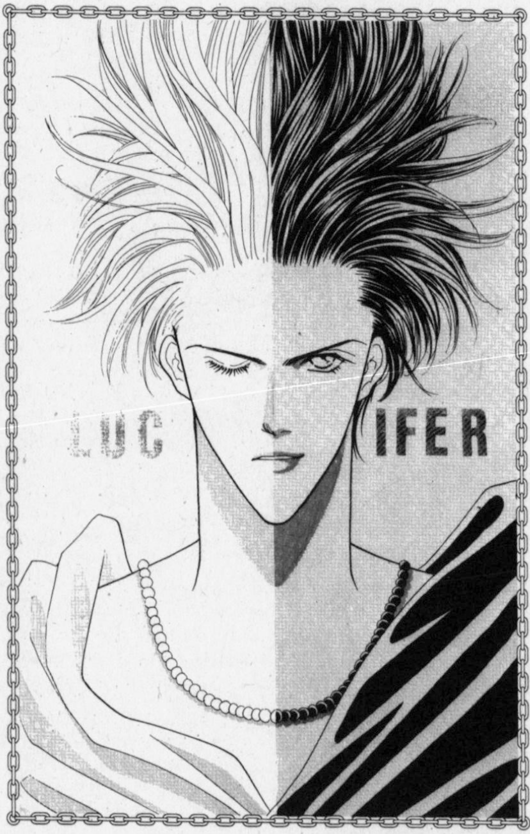
LUC IFER

Lucifer After Dark

by Brandon Niven

Aine never would've dreamed that her lyrics would fall into the hands of Sakuya, the lead singer of Lucifer. And why should she? If da Vinci were alive today, how many aspiring artists do you think would be lucky enough to be almost hit by him in his car? But here's to luck – or destiny (if you will). Aine has become the lyricist she's always dreamed of being.

Now that you've read the first volume of **Kaikan Phrase**, you know that Sakuya intends to school Aine in the ways of eroticism. But besides being Sakuya's object of affection, she also unwittingly becomes an object of abuse. Thousands of Lucifer fans would like nothing more than to see her out of the picture so they could freely fantasize about their idol.

Ever know any sexual teases? Are you one?! I don't think it would be fair to say that women are better teases than guys, or vice versa, rather the one who's more sexually experienced than the other is the one with the advantage. In this case, Sakuya creates a sexual anticipation for Aine, giving her just enough of himself to keep those creative, virgin lyrics of hers flowing. It works. Sexual anticipation is when you can almost feel the other person inside you. Fantasy runs rampant in your mind. Your breath gets heavier and your heart starts beating fast and pounds in your ears. Sound familiar? Since Aine had never even had so much as a first kiss, you can imagine what kind of intoxicating feelings run through that pure body of hers when his body meets hers.

But like any other young woman under the spell of sexual desire, she pays no mind to the warnings of Sakuya's ways with women, and risks herself in his game. It's human nature to want what we can't have. But when the impossible becomes possible, and destiny knocks on your door, think about what you'd do.

Brandon Niven is a freelance journalist who spends a lot of time reading up on Japan's youth culture and entertainment industry while, at the same time, working on his own features.

LOVE SHOJO? LET US KNOW!

☐ Please do NOT send me information about VIZ Media products, news and events, special offers, or other information.

☐ Please do NOT send me information from VIZ' trusted business partners.

Name: _____

Address: _____

City: _____ State: _____ Zip: _____

E-mail: _____

☐ Male ☐ Female   Date of Birth (mm/dd/yyyy): ___ / ___ / _____   (Under 13? Parental consent required)

What race/ethnicity do you consider yourself? (check all that apply)

☐ White/Caucasian   ☐ Black/African American   ☐ Hispanic/Latino

☐ Asian/Pacific Islander   ☐ Native American/Alaskan Native ☐ Other: _____

What VIZ shojo title(s) did you purchase? (indicate title(s) purchased)

_____

What other shojo titles from other publishers do you own? _____

_____

Reason for purchase: (check all that apply)

☐ Special offer   ☐ Favorite title / author / artist / genre

☐ Gift   ☐ Recommendation   ☐ Collection

☐ Read excerpt in VIZ manga sampler   ☐ Other _____

Where did you make your purchase? (please check one)

☐ Comic store   ☐ Bookstore   ☐ Mass/Grocery Store

☐ Newsstand   ☐ Video/Video Game Store

☐ Online (site:_____)   ☐ Other _____

How many shojo titles have you purchased in the last year? How many were VIZ shojo titles?
(please check one from each column)

SHOJO MANGA	VIZ SHOJO MANGA
☐ None	☐ None
☐ 1 – 4	☐ 1 – 4
☐ 5 – 10	☐ 5 – 10
☐ 11+	☐ 11+

What do you like most about shojo graphic novels? (check all that apply)

☐ Romance
☐ Drama / conflict
☐ Fantasy
☐ Comedy
☐ Real-life storylines
☐ Relatable characters
☐ Other ______________________________

Do you purchase every volume of your favorite shojo series?

☐ Yes! Gotta have 'em as my own
☐ No. Please explain: ______________________________

Who are your favorite shojo authors / artists? ______________________________

____

What shojo titles would like you translated and sold in English? ______________________________

____

THANK YOU! Please send the completed form to:

NJW Research
ATTN: VIZ Media Shojo Survey
42 Catharine Street
Poughkeepsie, NY 12601

Your privacy is very important to us. All information provided will be used for internal purposes only and will not be sold or otherwise divulged.